SHINING EYES, CRUEL FORTUNE

SHINING EYES,

The Lives and Loves of Italian

CRUEL FORTUNE

Renaissance Women Poets

Irma B. Jaffe

with Gernando Colombardo

Fordham University Press • New York • 2002

Library of Congress Cataloging-in-Publication Data

Jaffe, Irma B
   Shining eyes, cruel fortune: the lives and loves of Italian Renaissance women poets
/ Irma B. Jaffe with Gernando Colombardo. – 1st ed.
      p. cm.
   Includes bibliographical references and index.
   ISBN 0-8232-2180-6 (hardcover) – ISBN 0-8232-2181-4 (pbk.)
1. Women poets, Italian—16th century—Biography. 2. Poets, Italian—16th century—Biography. 3. Women and literature—Italy—History—16th century. 4. Italian poetry—Women authors—History and criticism. 5. Italian poetry—16th century—History and criticism.   I. Colombardo, Gernando. II. Title.
PQ4063.J34 2002
851.'4099287—do21
[B]

                                                                2001055667

Design: Charles Davey *design* LLC

Printed in the United States of America
02 03 04 05 06 5 4 3 2 1
First Edition

PRECEDING PAGES

Frontispiece. Simon Vouet. *Apollo and the Muses on Mt. Parnassus.* **1635-1640.**
Museum of Fine Arts, Budapest. Photo: Art Resource. (See p. 263, last paragraph.)

For my mother, Yvonne, and Karin

Love, oh love oh careless love,
love, oh love oh careless love,
I used to wear my apron low
Now see what love has done to me.
English folksong

Invisible to each of us in turn,
to love and to receive became twin ropes.
Grasp greedily: you'll end up with a burn.
Let go a bit: it slackens and escapes.
Rachel Hadas

Love spurs me on and reins me in,
reassures and appalls me, burns and freezes me,
gratifies and scorns me, calls me to him and chases me away,
keeps me hoping, and in anguish.
Petrarch

Oh Saki, pour out the wine and let it go 'round,
at first love seems easy but, oh, how hard it turns.
Hafiz

CONTENTS

LIST OF ILLUSTRATIONS

COLOR PLATES

Frontispiece: Simon Vouet. *Apollo and the Muses on Mount Parnassus*. ca. 1635. Museum of Fine Arts, Budapest. Photo, Art Resource.

I   Cristoforo dell'Altissimo. *Portrait of Vittoria Colonna*. 16th century. Galleria degli Uffizi, Florence. Photo, Museum.

II   Alessandro Bonvicino (Moretto da Brescia). *Tullia d'Aragona* (?). 16th century. Pinacoteca Civica Tosio Martinengo, Brescia. Photo, Museum.

III   Alessandro Ardente/Francesco Cellini. *Emperor Augustus and the Sibyl*. ca. 1545?–1576. Villa Guinigi, Lucca. Photo, Museum.

IV   Agnolo Bronzino. *Portrait of Laura Battiferra* [?] ca. 1547–1553. Palazzo Vecchio, Florence. Photo, Art Resource. (See p. 217)

V   Alessandro Allori. *Christ and the Canaanite Woman*. ca. 1585–1590. Church of San Giovannino degli Scolopi, Florence. Photo, Scala/Art Resource.

VI   Giovanni Battista Moroni. *Portrait of Isotta Brembate*. ca. 1550. Accademia Carrara, Bergamo. Photo, Museum.

VII   Anon. (Giovan Paolo Lolmo?). *Portrait of Isotta Brembate, Seated*. ca. 1590? Collection, Counts Moroni, Bergamo. Photo, Count Antonio Moroni.

VIII   Jacopo Tintoretto (School of). *Portrait of Veronica Franca*. ca. 1575. Worcester Art Museum, Worcester, Massachusetts. Photo, Museum.

FIGURES IN TEXT

1   Francesco Bartolozzi (after Titian, ca. 1545). *Portrait of Pietro Bembo*. 18th century. Museo Civico, Padua. Photo, Museum.

2   Giorgio Vasari. *Portrait of Six Tuscan Poets*. 16th century. The Minneapolis Institute of Arts. Photo, Museum.

3   S. Maffeis. *Portrait of Ludovico Ariosto*. n.d. Museo Civico, Padua. Photo, Museum.

4   Map of Italy in the sixteenth century.

5   G. Rossi. *Monuments of sixteenth-century women poets*. Archiginnasio, Department of Drawings and Prints, Bologna. Photo, Archiginnasio.

6   Circle of Palma il Vecchio. *Portrait of the so-called Laura*. ca. 1525. Museo Civico, Padua. Photo, Museum.

FOREWORD

uch labor of love has gone into this captivating collection of many-faceted biographies of twelve Italian sixteenth-century women poets. It is a collaborative work by Irma B. Jaffe and Gernando Colombardo, but, since Jaffe conceived the book and wrote the text, I will refer to her as the author in this introduction.

The subjects vary greatly in personality, social and historical background, and cultural achievement. Some were grand ladies, noblewomen and princesses, others what we would call "middle class," still others prized courtesans, but they all shared a genuine interest in literary achievement, specifically in verse, and they seem to have wished to gain fame above all as poets. Some were conscious of playing a role in raising the status of women in society.

Jaffe aims to convey a sense of the intellectual and emotional atmosphere that shaped the ambitions of these women. In doing so she shows how the liberal spirit of the first half of the century gave way in the second half to a new atmosphere created by the Council of Trent. The author's main concern is to illustrate these lives and to investigate—and, if possible, explain—the historical phenomenon of their rather surprising appearance at that time and in those roles. The matter looms larger than these twelve women, because they were only some of many similar cases. We must therefore ask ourselves why and how this could happen, inasmuch as women in Western and other cultures not expected to be educated in realms reserved for men. It is well known that even as late as the nineteenth century important women writers had to write in hiding, sometimes to the point of concealing their gender when they published or attempted publication; we need only think of the Brontës, Jane Austen, George Eliot, George Sand, and Emily Dickinson.

This is not to say that there was no precedent for these women poets. After all, the earliest of the important lyrical poets in the history of Western literature was a woman, Sappho (born c. 612 B.C.), whom for centuries the Greeks regarded as their foremost lyric poet. Nor was it unprecedented for women of good social standing to write, even to write high literature. The Middle Ages had seen at work Marie de France, Christine de Pisan, and Louise Labé, not to mention religious writers like St. Catherine of Siena in the mid-fourteenth century and bourgeois writers like Alessandra Macinghi Strozzi in the mid-fifteenth. Such grand ladies as Eleanor of Aquitaine and Marie de Champagne patronized and inspired the best writers of their time.

I have already recalled that some of the women here represented were courtesans, and the phenomenon of educated courtesans also was not new. It harked back all the way to the earliest pagan antiquity, and this connection with antiquity was a substantive part of Italian Renaissance Humanism. Indeed, one of the striking features characterizing some of the ladies of the present collection was the ideal connection with the slave or free *hetairai* of ancient Greece, a term that became attached to the fifth-to-third century B.C. phenomenon of cultivated courtesans who, clearly distinct from the common prostitutes or streetwalkers (*pornoi*), operated as entertainers and public hostesses, often becoming mistresses of important men—statesmen, artists, and social leaders. The most famous of the high-class *hetairai*, Aspasia, was the influential mistress of Pericles of Athens and the friend of Socrates. In later, Christian times, courtesans graced or plagued the medieval lay and ecclesiastical courts, including cardinals' courts and papal courts, especially at Rome and Avignon, and the practice continued through the Renaissance.

Despite all these precedents, the Italian courtesan of the sixteenth century was a new woman, a combination of the medieval court prostitute and the medieval lady of court, the lady who "held" court in the presence or in the absence of the lord. These Renaissance women's exalted literary role was also relatively new in the sense that it was a rather widespread phenomenon. They represent a typical Renaissance phenomenon also in the social sense that some of them were social upstarts, in line with the fact that in the Italian Renaissance virtue and merit were no longer tied to social origin, since in that newly open society even once social outcasts such as orphans and illegitimate children could rise to the highest cultural positions; it will suffice to mention the outstanding cases of Leon Battista Alberti and Leonardo da Vinci.

The preceding points should show the rich implications and vast dimensions of the present study, which marks a new and original achievement by combining portrait analysis with poetry and social biography. The following are the women included in this selection.

Veronica Gàmbara, a noblewoman from near Brescia, was one of the few women who held sovereign power. Having been married to the Count of Correggio, after her husband's death she ruled over her domain and successfully managed the difficult position of her small state caught between two powerful adversaries, Charles V, Emperor of the Holy Roman Empire, and Francis I, King of France, competing for hegemony in Italy. She wrote poems and letters, and corresponded with such notables as Pietro Bembo during all her adult life.

Best known in her own time and in ours is Vittoria Colonna, from the noble houses of Colonna of Rome and Montefeltro of Urbino, wife of the Marquis of Pescara, Ferrante of Avalos, and friend and poetic correspondent of Michelangelo. She sympathized for a time with the Reformation. After her husband's death she spent her life in several convents and doing charitable works, and devoted her poetic talent to her husband's memory in poem after poem celebrating his every virtue in praises that he did not entirely deserve. Her poetic style was Petrarchan in a Bembian mood, and in the sixteenth century her fame went far beyond the borders of Italy.

Tullia d'Aragona was a *cortegiana onesta*, that is to say, educated, respectable in manners, selective in her choice of clients, and expensive. She was the daughter of a courtesan from Campania and Cardinal Luigi d'Aragona, a descendant of the Aragonese royal line. Her lovers included some of the most eminent intellectuals of her time, among them Girolamo Muzio, Bernardo Tasso, Girolamo Fracastoro, and possibly even the authoritative Florentine intellectual and critic Benedetto Varchi, known as a homosexual. Tullia d'Aragona authored a poetic dialogue where she ex-

changed opinions about love between herself and Varchi, and she also published poems addressed to other intellectuals, who often reciprocated.

Chiara Matraini was a middle-class, married woman from Lucca, whose family
was involved in a political struggle that Jaffe shows to have strongly influenced her
verse. She wrote and sang Petrarchistic mannerist verse about her love for a married
man who, like Petrarch's Laura, died prematurely. Jaffe offers an original detailed
analysis of a painting representing the Emperor Augustus and the Sibyl, where the
Sibyl is a portrayal of Chiara, apparently commissioned by Chiara herself. ("The Poet
as Sibyl" is this chapter's subtitle.) When Jaffe and Colombardo saw the painting in
Lucca they realized that Chiara was represented in it twice, and this oddity led to the
fascinating iconographical analysis you will read in chapter 4.

The most prolific of these women poets (eight volumes, including a commentary
on the *Orlando Furioso*) was Laura Terracina, who passed from love to love and then
to marriage. She was the most "professional" among the women writers of the Italian Cinquecento. Writing and publishing poetry was for her a true career. She was
forthright and assertive in her protofeminist view of society's injustice to women.

One of the most intriguing chapters deals with the Lucanian Isabella di Morra and
her supposed lover, Diego Sandoval de Castro. Jaffe examines the accepted account of
murder and revenge surrounding the two poets and comes to a surprising conclusion
based on the evidence of a single revealing sonnet.

The relationship between Agnolo Bronzino, one of the great artists of the Cinquecento, and Laura Battiferra, creates the opportunity to know Bronzino as a poet as
well as a painter. However, the crux of this chapter is the painting said to be a portrait
of Laura Battiferra. Jaffe and Colombardo strongly suspect that this extraordinary
profile, generally accepted as representing Laura Battiferra, actually represents someone else, although they do not claim to know who it might be. Laura was an important noblewoman from Urbino who married the Florentine sculptor/architect
Bartolomeo Ammannati. Her poems relate to a number of relationships that typically combined Platonism and Petrarchism. One of these relationships involved Bronzino, who wrote to her and received from her poems of a Platonic/Petrarchist type, in
a typically mannerist predicament of what Jaffe characterizes as "blissful woe."

Gaspara Stampa, born in Padua, lived in Venice, which, like Rome, was generally
a favorable habitat for courtesans, although it is not clear whether she ever was one.
In Venice she held a celebrated literary salon. Her poetry sang her passion for the lord
of Treviso, her lost lover. This chapter's subtitle, "In Love with Love," points to Jaffe's
interpretation of Stampa's important literary production of more than three hundred
poems: rather than a mirror of a true love experience, this poetry would be a mannerist testimony to the search for glory through Petrarchist verse. Jaffe presents Gaspara as a liberal spirit in a conventional world, bohemian in taste and style of life.

Isotta Brembate belonged to a leading Hispanophile family of Bergamo that was
fatally involved in a feud with its fierce rivals, the Albani, partisans of Venice and
France. Several portraits of Isotta and others in these two families attract Jaffe's interest both for their art-historical issues and for their iconographic implications, and it is
precisely Isotta's portrait by G. B. Moroni that prompted Jaffe's attention to this almost
unstudied woman poet. Careful examination of the visual evidence leads Jaffe to a conclusion that differs from what has been accepted by the art world. This chapter includes

poems by two other women who have been completely overlooked in the literature.

Tarquinia Molza of Modena, known as "L'Unica," was the extraordinary recipient of honorary Roman citizenship from the Roman Senate in recognition of her outstanding literary and musical achievements. Surely one of the most brilliant in this group of shining stars, Tarquinia married Paolo Porrini, who allowed and even encouraged her studies. She became encyclopedically learned, and both she and her husband became main characters in Francesco Patrizi's dialogue in four parts, *L'amorosa filosofia*, where Aristotelian and Platonic views of love are discussed and contrasted. Even after her husband's death she held a salon frequented by many intellectuals and prominent personages. She may have been Alfonso d'Este's lover, and it is probably out of jealousy that the Duke banned her from the court of Ferrara, ordered her to break her liaison with the Flemish composer Giaches de Wert, her true passion, and confined her to Modena, where she eventually died. Despite the socio-historical importance of this case, Molza has been largely neglected by literary critics, so that this biography is, like the even more original one of Brembate, one of Jaffe's contributions to our knowledge of the age.

Veronica Franca was a Venetian poet, editor, and "professional" *cortegiana onesta*. Like Tullia d'Aragona, she was the daughter of a courtesan, and like Tullia she was candid about the miseries of a courtesan's life. Her poems and letters show remarkable originality of character. She consorted with important Venetian patricians who provided her with income and protection. In her poetry she rivaled Venetian and other poets and writers. Her approach was generally realistic, perhaps in response to Pietro Aretino's style, even while she contrasted Aretino's unflattering portrait of her profession by protesting that it is a sad and undesirable state, often practiced not by choice. Veronica was a born intellectual who won acceptance and admiration among the literati of Venice, outlived her esteem, and was soon forgotten. She had her moments of happiness, her eyes did shine when her nobleman lover deigned to make love to her, but fortune was as cruel to her, as it was to all the others who lost their lovers, lost their husbands, lost their wealth, and died, most of them, too young.

Moderata Fonte (baptized Modesta da Pozzo) is a fascinating character who, Jaffe aptly points out, made herself a sort of living metaphor, starting with her penname. She was fortunate enough as a child to be encouraged to study, write, and publish by her grandfather and then by her beloved husband. Nevertheless, her main work was an allegorical dialogue, *The Worth of Women*, somewhat a counterpart of Boccaccio's *Corbaccio* as a rather radical poetic indictment of men. The seven women characters who participate in the "trial" of men have a wonderful time exposing the tricks, the shams, and the greed of the accused, and the reader suspects that Moderata had a wonderful time writing her dialogue. Fortune did not continue to smile, however; she died giving birth to her fifth child.

Jaffe's innovative text combines biography and poetic quotation in such a way as to make poetry function as dialogue. Vittoria Colonna "speaks" to her husband: "You do not hesitate to take risks, but we, suffering women, are attacked by doubt and fear!" Veronica Franca scolds the man who attacked her with scurrilous verse: "It is not the deed of a brave knight if, kind sir, you allow me to speak the truth. . . ." Tullia d'Aragona denies her lover's accusations: "If I ever did this, may the sorrow that burdens my heart never come to an end." And so on. Combining biography and poetic text creates a vivid sense of the living presence of women, which is further enhanced by the illustrations. It is rare to find illustrations in a book concerned with poetry, but it is not surprising in this book, both Jaffe and Colombardo being art historians. Several of the chapters are, indeed, art-historical essays offering new interpretations and attributions that will probably stir controversy and possibly clear up a few art-historical quandaries.

Most of the women Professor Jaffe has studied are well known to scholars in the field of Italian literature, although they have never been studied collectively from all relevant angles. Some are less known and deserve more exposure, and a few (the Bergamo group) are practically the author's discovery. Most importantly, the social circumstances that Jaffe brings out point to an aspect of this phenomenon that is of considerable historical interest. This is to say that the fact that so many women managed to escape the prejudice that relegated them to household chores and denied them the right to aspire to literary fame is an aspect of the enthusiasm for knowledge and culture that marked the Italian Renaissance. Similarly, both lay and religious schools of the Cinquecento, especially in Italy, France, the Netherlands, and other regions, attracted legions of devoted students pursuing humanistic/classical studies. This pursuit of studies that were expected to make human beings worthy of the ancient heroes and the sons of burghers and even peasants the rivals of noble souls, was such a far-reaching development that it soon began to worry the authorities. The best example is that of France, where starting with Henry IV and especially under Louis XIII and Louis XIV, the lay colleges were ordered to close their doors unless they turned themselves over to religious orders, such as the Jesuits and the Oratorians. In Cinquecento Italy, not only were all scions of high and low families welcomed to cultural achievements, but women, too, could be, more than allowed, encouraged to pursue them.

For many readers *Shining Eyes, Cruel Fortune* will be a welcome introduction to some remarkably talented women. The topic is timely enough, with our shared concern for female roles and deeds, and because these remarkable women became subjects for other writers' praise as well (the book includes poems by Ariosto, Tasso, and other men) as for artists' portraits and illustrations, this study should be of interest to social historians, literary historians, and art historians, specifically of, but not limited to, the Italian Renaissance. It is thoroughly documented but avoids pedantry, which makes it not only informative but enjoyable reading that should encourage further investigation into the field of women's writing and social roles. Because the poetry is given in English and Italian, an important feature of this book is the CD that is tucked into a back pocket. Scholars of Italian literature Anne Paolucci, Rinaldina Russell, Isabella Bertoletti, Florinda Iannace, and I read selections of the poetry in Italian, thus offering readers wishing to improve their comprehension of spoken Italian the opportunity to hear and read the poems simultaneously, making it particularly useful to students.

General readers will find the story of these women who won esteem in a social climate that was not yet ready to acknowledge "the worth of women" informative and, often enough, surprising. Even more generally, this affirmation of strong convictions in the value of literary and humanistic culture is of vital concern in our age of self-doubt and general skepticism.

Aldo Scaglione
New York University

Author's Note

y interest in Renaissance women poets, triggered years ago when I saw the portrait of Isotta Brembate in the Accademia Carrara in Bergamo, has been fully shared by my colleague of forty years, Gernando Colombardo. Carrying out the research and struggling over the translations for this book side by side has been a joint effort and pleasure, each of us profiting from the special strengths of the other. For the finished book, Colombardo has prepared the bibliography; I am responsible for the conception and the text.

Because this book is about women who have loved and lost, I have chosen the epigraphs as reminders that the naked, blind boy archer has been ever and everywhere gender-careless in letting fly his piercing arrows.

The heading for the preface of this book is a paraphrase from the Greek, "Honor Comes to the Race of Women."

1.
Francesco
Bartolozzi (after
Titian, ca. 1545),
*Portrait of Pietro
Bembo*. 18th
century. Museo
Civico, Padua.
Photo, Museum.

PREFACE
AMBITION COMES TO THE RACE OF WOMEN

This book is about twelve extraordinary Italian women, intelligent, talented, strong-minded, beautiful, and passionate, who, through their poetry, speak to us about their lives and loves and their ambitions across the space of four hundred years. "Sixteenth-century women poets?" My friends always looked so surprised. "Were there any?" Assured that there had been many, my surprised questioners always wanted to know how this came about.

It is a good, important question that merits a volume to itself, but briefly, as I do now, I tried to explain this phenomenon. One can point to several factors that fortuitously combined to create the conditions for this flourishing of women poets. The invention of printing by moveable type in the fifteenth century made possible the production of printed books that were easily reproducible and thus more widely available, which enormously increased the population of readers, including women. As a result, the population of writers, including women, also increased.

The fifteenth-century discovery and revival of classical antiquity created the humanist scholar who wrote his learned prose and poetry in Latin; Italian, the vernacular language, was used for lighter verse and commonplace communication. The humanists believed that Italian did not have the strength and flexibility required for serious writing. Early in the sixteenth century, however, Pietro Bembo (figure 1), who may be called the intellectual hero of the Cinquecento, wrote his *Prose della volgar lingua* (Prose in the vernacular language), which, although not published until 1525, was known in manuscript to many intellectuals some years in advance of publication. Bembo argued that, just as ancient Roman writers had eventually shifted from Greek as they developed their own spoken language, Latin, into a powerful written language, so Italians should shift from Latin to develop their own spoken language, Italian, into a powerful written one. Bembo, an erudite linguist perfectly at ease in Latin, was also a devoted reader of Francesco Petrarch (1304–1374) and held that the fourteenth-century Tuscan Italian of Florence in which Petrarch wrote his *canzoniere* (a body of more or less autobiographical poems) should become the language of written Italian throughout Italy. Almost single-handedly, Bembo created the Petrarchism that governed lyric writing almost to the end of the sixteenth century as Petrarch's *canzoniere* became a model for love poetry. Writers were never without their *petrarchini* (a volume of Petrarch's *canzoniere*) near at hand. Since Dante Alighieri (1265–1321) wrote his *Divine Comedy* and Giovanni Boccaccio (1313–1375) his *Decameron* in the vernacular of Florence, the engraving after Vasari showing them with Petrarch at the

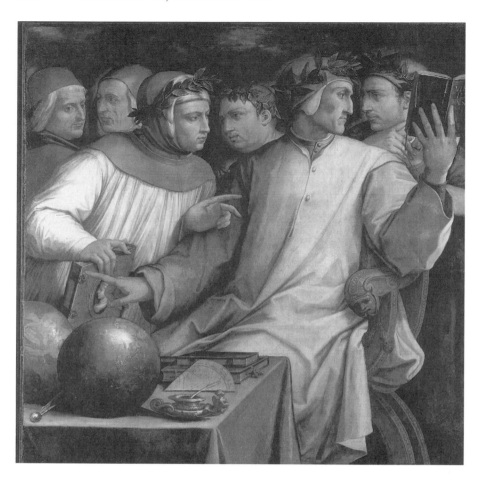

**2.
Giorgio Vasari.
*Portrait of Six
Tuscan Poets.*
16th century.
The Minneapolis
Institute of Arts.
Photo, Museum.**

center of a group of poets and philosophers may be seen as a visual affirmation of the literary argument favoring Tuscan Italian (figure 2).* Our title is meant to suggest Petrarch in two ways: it refers to his characteristic contrasts—*"Pascomi di dolor, piangendo rido"* (I nourish myself on pain, weeping I laugh) †—and to his view of Fortune, which is invariably cruel; our women pursue the misery of love with *occhi lucenti* (shining eyes), fearing, sometimes even knowing, that *fortuna crudele* (cruel fortune) will leave them crying in pain. It is also relevant to observe that "eyes" occurs more frequently in his *canzoniere* than any other noun.

The triumph of Italian over Latin is an important consideration in accounting for the flourishing of women writers in the sixteenth century. In the fifteenth century, the education of young girls began to be taken seriously, and they were taught in classes

---

* According to Jonathan Nelson, "Portraits in Sixteenth Century Florence," *Gazette des Beaux-Arts* (September 1992), the other three figures are Guido Cavalcanti (1255–1300), a poet and friend of Dante; Marsilio Ficino, the classical philosopher who most strongly influenced the development of Neo-Platonism; and Cristoforo Landino, a fifteenth-century humanist. Note that Dante's life slightly overlapped Petrarch's; Boccaccio and Petrarch were friends.

† 134, l.12. For Petrarch's poems we have used Roberto Antonelli, Gianfranco Contini, Daniele Ponchiroli, *Francesco Petrarca Canzoniere* (Torino, 1992), except where noted.

3.
S. Maffeis.
*Portrait of
Ludovico Ariosto.*
n.d. Museo
Civico, Padua.
Photo, Museum.

alongside boys. However, their classical education stopped much earlier than that of the boys. Consequently, few of them learned Latin well enough to become proficient writers, although, as we will see in this book, there were a few exceptions. The acceptance of the printed book written in Italian instead of Latin helped more women enter the population of readers and writers. Because love was the subject that moved most women to write poetry, the respectability as well as the availability of Petrarch's Italian-language *canzoniere*, which celebrate the poet's love for Laura, gave them the opportunity to make their own writing public. (It is a safe guess that women had always written poetry secretly.)

The development of individualism in the Renaissance, the awareness of the person as an individual of independent thought and action probably contributed significantly to a new awareness of women as individuals more than simply wives, mothers, and daughters. Another crucially important book of the early sixteenth century, Ludovico Ariosto's *Orlando Furioso*, brought attention to the unjustifiable inferior status of women throughout history (figure 3). In canto 37, Ariosto writes in praise of women and sharply criticizes men for scorning them:

> *Women, wise and strong and true and chaste*
> *Not only in Greece and Rome*
> *But wherever the sun shines, from the Far East*
> *to the Hesperides, have had their home,*
> *Whose virtues and whose merits are unguessed.*
> *Concerning them historians are dumb:*
> *Contemporary authors, filled with spite,*
> *The truth about such women would not write.*

**4.
Map of Italy in
the sixteenth
century.**

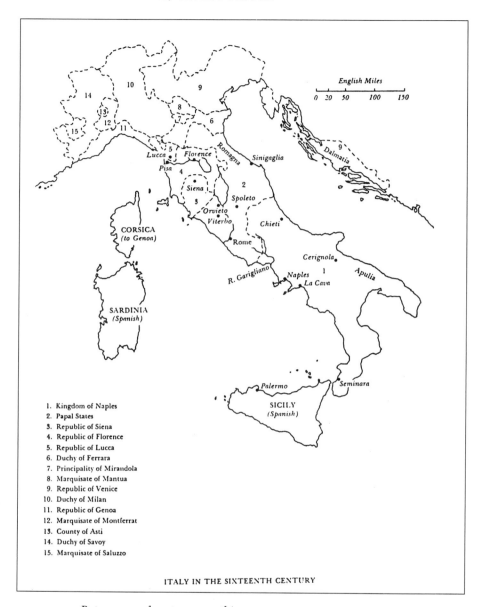

1. Kingdom of Naples
2. Papal States
3. Republic of Siena
4. Republic of Florence
5. Republic of Lucca
6. Duchy of Ferrara
7. Principality of Mirandola
8. Marquisate of Mantua
9. Republic of Venice
10. Duchy of Milan
11. Republic of Genoa
12. Marquisate of Montferrat
13. County of Asti
14. Duchy of Savoy
15. Marquisate of Saluzzo

ITALY IN THE SIXTEENTH CENTURY

> But, women, do not cease on this account
> To persevere in works which you do well.
> Let not discouragement ambition daunt,
> Nor fear that recognition never will
> Be yours. Good no immunity can vaunt
> From change, Evil is not immutable,
> And if in history your page was blurred,
> In modern times your merits will be heard.* (p. 32)

---

* *Orlando Furioso* (Harmondsworth, 1975), trans. Barbara Reynolds. See pp. xxx–xxxi for the original
Italian.

5.
G. Rossi.
*Monuments of
sixteenth-century
women poets.*
Archiginnasio,
Department of
Drawings and
Prints, Bologna.
Photo,
Archiginnasio.

I . *Vittoria Colonna*   II . *Veronica Gambara*
III . *Isabella Andreini*   IV . *Margherita di Valois*
V . *Laura Terracina*   VI . *Tarquinia Molza*
VII . *Laura Battiferri*   VIII . *Tullia d'Aragona*
IX . *Gaspara Stampa*   X . *Costanza d'Avalo*

There can be no doubt that Ariosto's words influenced many writers, and that he contributed importantly to the cultural environment that led many intellectuals to write books in praise of women, and publishers to publish their works. Women took good advantage of this change in their favor.

Our setting is the Italian sixteenth century, the glorious and terrible Cinquecento, which saw the brilliant artistic continuation of the wondrous Quattrocento, the devastation of the land as Spain and France competed for hegemony over Italy, and the radical change in sensibility as the tension and pressure of the Reformation, the Counterreformation, and the revived Inquisition permeated Italian society in the second half of the century. The impact of these events contributed effectively to the shift from High Renaissance classicism to Cinquecento mannerism, a style characterized by a "basic aestheticism which seeks refuge into an aristocratic, hermetically sealed, introspective world of refinement away from a troubled and disappointing external world," as Aldo Scaglione remarks. This was a world ruled by dukes in whose splendid courts entertainment was lavish, where love was the topic of choice in formalized conversations among brilliant, erudite, witty courtiers and ladies, where serious intellectual game-playing at courts and literary academies provided "to some extent, the Petrarcho-Platonic assumption that only a sexually frustrated love could be an inextinguishable and reliable passion." * This was the world of the men and women we present in these pages.

Noblewomen, bourgeois, courtesans from every area of Italy (figure 4) had two things in common, however different from each other these self-aware women were. First, they all shared the heritage of the rich culture that had flourished in the ancient Mediterranean world, and, as if there were a kind of cultural DNA, had persisted through two thousand years and permutations, flourishing again with renewed vigor. Second, they all dreamed of, they all aspired to making their names immortal through their poetry (figure 5); they craved to be remembered on the altar of *carta ed inchiostro* (paper and ink), as Vittoria Colonna promised Veronica Gàmbara she would be (p. 63). Never before had there been such opportunity for women to achieve fame on equal grounds with men, and the possibility whetted their appetite for reward. Such ambition, on such a grand scale, was a new phenomenon in European women's history.

What were they like, and what was life like for them? Fortunately, some of our curiosity about these women can be satisfied, for they have left a record of their thoughts, and we have only to listen to them, to let the poetry speak to us of their hopes, fears, anxieties, and above all, their loves, the blissful woe that was at once the reward and punishment of their generous-spirited feelings for men who, platonically correct, idealized them but in truth hardly appreciated them—even betrayed them. We have few *facts* about these women, and yet, listening to them, we often feel as if we were close friends, hearing their confidential stories, and we call them by their first names; we have been guided in our translations by our desire to make their poems seem to *speak* their thoughts. We will also listen to those men— Ludovico Ariosto, Pietro Bembo, Pietro Aretino, Benedetto Varchi, Torquato Tasso, and many others— lovers and friends, whose poems and dialogues reveal the phenomenal interest in the status of women that emerged in this period which may rightly be called the Women's Renaissance, born later than the *real* Renaissance. Their own awareness of the unjustness of laws and social conventions that gave them inferior status legally and intellectually may surprise us; we will notice the apologetic phrases that appear

---

* Aldo Scaglione, "Cinquecento Mannerism and the Uses of Petrarch", in *Essays on the Arts of Discourse* (New York, 1998), pp. 100–101. For a book-length study of Mannerism as the characteristic style of the sixteenth century, see John Shearman, *Mannerism* (London, 1967).

6.
Circle of Palma il Vecchio. *Portrait of the so-called Laura.* **ca. 1525. Museo Civico, Padua. Photo, Museum.**

repeatedly in their writing, meant to disavow pretensions to talent of which unfriendly male readers might accuse them.

Some of the women in this book had one or more volumes of their poetry published in their lifetime or shortly after; others appeared in contemporary anthologies. There were many more women in this period whose poetry was published—they deserve another volume—and there were some who remain unidentified, known to us only through their portraits, such as the beautiful "Laura" (ca. 1525) (figure 6), so called because she wears a dress embroidered with a laurel motif, symbol of Apollo, god of music and poetry, and the Muses; she displays a book that she holds upright in her left hand: surely a poet, portrayed with such symbols, and probably dead when her portrait was painted, since the book is closed and her head is encircled with a crown of ivy, evergreen symbol of death and undying love. The painting has been thought by some scholars to be an idealized image of Petrarch's Laura, or an allegory, but the way she gazes outward and yet meditatively inward persuades a viewer that she was indeed once a real woman, immortalized not, ironically, as she would have wished, by her poetry, but by the art of someone else, perhaps the painter Palma Vecchio, as has been thought.

In her book *Passionate Minds* (New York, 2000), Claudia Roth Pierpont ends her introduction to eleven twentieth-century women writers with the words, "These are lives in which success is hard won, retreat and even breakdown are common, love is difficult, and children are nearly impossible." Reading our book, it will be evident that for women the twentieth century was not very different from the sixteenth. But there is one overriding difference: the triumph of democracy in the Western world brought the realization that change is effected through economic and political means. Such understanding of the dynamics of social organization was not available to those sixteenth-century women who protested the inequality of their status in society but had no means of changing it. They expressed their anger, indignation, frustration in poems and dialogues, and in letters that offer a penetrating insight into the main stratagem they used to *disarm* the men on whom they depended: they feigned humility and denigrated their abilities, knowing the prejudice against women who had interests beyond their domestic responsibilities—learnedness was not easily forgiven. In this, courtesans had an ironic advantage: the chastity that was demanded of a respectable woman was suspect when she showed intellectual tendencies; for courtesans chastity was irrelevant and they were sought after *because* they were cultivated. In the following pages it will be seen how these exceptional women, most of them knowingly, a few unaware, played out their very special roles.

Irma B. Jaffe
Fordham University (emerita)

E di fedeli e caste e saggie e forti
stato ne son, non pur in Grecia e in Roma,
ma in ogni parte ove fra gl'Indi e gli Orti
de le Esperide il Sol spiega la chioma:
de le quai sono i pregi agli onor morti,
sì ch'a pena di mille una si noma;
e questo, perché avuto hanno ai lor tempi
gli scrittori bugiardi, invidi et empi.

Non restate però, donne, a cui giova
il bene oprar, di seguir vostra via;
né da vostra alta impresa vi rimuova
tema che degno onor non vi si dia:
che, come cosa buona non si trova
che duri sempre, così ancor nè rias.
Se le carte sin qui state e gl'inchiostri
per voi non son, or son a' tempi nostri. * (pp. xxv – xxvi)

---

* Ariosto, *Orlando Furioso*, canto 37, stanzas 6 and 7.

ACKNOWLEDGMENTS

y colleague, Gernando Colombardo, and I wish to thank the directors and staffs of the following libraries for exceptional assistance: Fordham University Libraries, with special thanks to Linda LoSchiavo, Director of the Quinn Library, Charlotte Labbé, and Roger Harris; The New York Public Library Spencer Collection and Rare Books Division; Biblioteca Civica Angelo Mai, Bergamo; Biblioteca Civica Vescovile, Bergamo; Biblioteca Comunale dell'Archiginnasio, Bologna; Biblioteca Universitaria di Bologna; Civico Museo Bibliografico Musicale (G. B. Martini), Bologna; Biblioteca Ambrosiana, Milan; Castello Sforzesco, Milan; Biblioteca Seminario Vescovile, Mondovì; Biblioteca Civica, Padua; Biblioteca Civica A./G. Barrili, Savona; Biblioteca Marciana, Venice.

For his friendship, encouragement, and assistance in a number of ways, Eugenio Viola, Professor of Italian Literature, Libera Università SS. Maria Assunta, Rome, has our infinite thanks. We are grateful to Lillian Golio, secretary of the Art and Music Department, Fordham University, who is constantly ready to answer calls for help. David Hedges's help was indispensable for guidance through some of the mysteries of the computer.

Making the compact disk that is included in this book for readings of some of the poetry has required the cooperation of the Electronic Information Center of Fordham University. We thank in particular Michael Considine and Matthew Schottenfeld for supervising this project, which we believe adds substantial usefulness and enjoyment to our book, and Ralph M. Jennings, general manager of WFUV, for permitting us the use of the sound studio for making the recording. Our great thanks go also to the distinguished professors whose voices are heard on the CD: Isabella Bertoletti, Florinda Iannace, Anne Paolucci, Rinaldina Russell, and Aldo Scaglione.

We thank Mary Beatrice Schulte of Fordham University Press for her editorial expertise.

On a personal note, I want to thank my friends for their very much needed patience with me, especially Farhang Zabeeh, who tried (unsuccessfully) to make me a Stoic. Above all I am grateful to my daughter and her husband, Yvonne Korshak and Robert Ruben, and my granddaughter, Karin Schwartz, for constant enthusiasm that often perked up my flagging spirits. Last, I want to remember my husband, who was unfailingly supportive, and the late Meyer Schapiro, who is always present in my memory and my work.

SHINING EYES, CRUEL FORTUNE

CHAPTER ONE

Veronica Gàmbara

(1485–1550)

 ### *Shining Eyes*

Beautiful, shining eyes,
how can it be that in an instant
so many new moods spring forth in you?
Happy, sad, proud, humble, haughty
they change from moment to moment,
filling me with shy desire
and so many emotions, sweet, fierce, bitter,
crowd together in my ardent heart
at your slightest wish.
Now that you are my life and death,
oh, smiling eyes, blessed and dear,
let them be always serene, joyous, and sparkling.[1] (p. 23) *

eronica Gàmbara (1485–1550) loved the shining surfaces of life. She adorned and surrounded herself with sparkling, precious jewels, clothes of the finest fabrics, gold and silver and crystal, and highly polished furnishings. When she left her palace in Correggio to stay in Bologna for a year or two, she rented a mansion there, which she had furnished in accordance with the splendor becoming to the sister of the governor of the city, writing to her agent, Lodovico Rosso, "I am waiting for all those things without which I would not be able to appear with the elegance that, as you know, is my usual style. Here they don't take high style for ostentation which I have always avoided and is far from my way of doing."[2]

Not only for herself but also for others close to her, she was avid to make an extraordinary impression. In 1549, just a year before her death, she and her daughter-in-law, Chiara, were invited by Margherita, the reigning duchess of Mantua, to attend the wedding of her son, Francesco II, to Caterina, daughter of Ferdinand, King of the Romans. There could hardly be a more magnificent event, and Veronica wrote to Rosso, "My daughter-in-law is very well provided with jewels and gold ornaments, but because at this wedding there will be great doings and the ornaments will be wonderful, I, being rather proud about such things, should like the jewelry of this girl of mine to surpass that of all others. Wherefore I beg you with your usual fidelity and trustworthiness to ask Count Girolamo Pepoli and the Signora his wife if they would do me the favor of lending me a pearl necklace, which I hear is very beautiful, promising them that it shall

---

* Throughout this book, page numbers in parentheses following extracted matter refer to the corresponding text in Italian or English. The Italian text is at the end of each chapter.

1.1.
Franco Savani/
Domenico
Cagnoni.
Veronica Gambara
Writing to Pietro
Bembo.
From *Rime e*
lettere raccolte da
Felice Rizzardi
(Brescia, 1759.)

be kept with such care as is due beautiful things, and that I will return it in a fortnight."
If they had another necklace she would like that, too, "in order to be able to change frequently." In addition to Chiara's neck, Veronica wanted to adorn her hair. "And if in addition," she continues, "they have a garland of pearls or of jewels . . . it would be most acceptable to me." She assured Rosso that she would be glad to give the lenders a receipt.[3]

Even in mourning Veronica managed, in a sense, to shine. When her husband died in 1518 after only ten years of marriage, she reminded visitors to her palace in Correggio of their great love and her great loss by having inscribed over the doorway of their living quarters Dido's lines from Virgil,

Ille meos primus, qui me sibi junxit, amores
Abstulit, ille habeat secum, servetque sepulchro.

He who first linked me to himself has taken away my heart:
may he keep it with him, and guard it in the grave.[4]

She draped their apartments in black, she dressed totally in black, wore a black veil, and wrote to Rossi that she must have a black horse to match the three she already had: "Please beg Signore Conte Alessandro and if begging is not enough, beseech him to do everything possible to get me this horse, promising him that nothing would be dearer to me because then I would have four as black as night, befitting my suffering."[5] Although her biographers write that she wore mourning clothes the rest of her life, we find that in 1520 she wrote her agent to buy for her the most beautiful Flemish cloth he could find ("fra tutti i belli bellissimo"), some kind of preparation for the complexion, and rinses to keep the hair golden.[6]

Shining went much deeper, however, than the superficial gleam of the gems and clothes and the self-dramatizing that Veronica doubtless enjoyed. For this poet surrounded herself with the shining intellectual stars of her time, her peers among whom she shone. Ludovico Ariosto visited her in Correggio as did Francesco Molza, and Pietro Bembo was her literary mentor and admirer from at least 1502, until his death in 1547; she often sent him her poems asking for his suggestions or revisions, as she is shown in figure 1.1.[7] Her mansion in Bologna became a home of the Muses where eminent writers and erudite scholars met and often returned to discuss literature and philosophy as well as the issues of the day, drawn to the palazzo by the intelligence and eloquence of the woman who presided over their conversations,[8] certainly not by her beauty. Her first biographer, Rinaldo Corso, a contemporary writer of some distinction who became a bishop, and who knew her well, writes, "if her face were like her body she would have been perfectly beautiful . . . but although not ugly, it was not at all pretty, which defect was completely compensated for by her eloquence. She spoke in such a lively, witty way that everyone who heard her longed to visit her again. Her healthy complexion was due to not much exercise [!]."[9] A portrait in the sixteenth-century collection of Paolo Giovio identified as Veronica Gàmbara confirms the judgment that she was assuredly not pretty, with features that were "coarse, and masculine" (figure 1.2).[10] The supposed portrait from the Civica Biblioteca di Correggio used as the frontispiece for the first collection of her verse, *Rime e lettere di Veronica Gàmbara* (in 1759) (figure 1.3), cannot be authentic inasmuch as the woman is dressed in a style that came into fashion two decades after her death (apart from the fact that the illustration shows a rather beautiful woman).

Veronica Gàmbara was born of an illustrious noble family at Prat'Alboino in the district of Brescia on 30 November 1485, the eldest of six children of Count Gian-francesco Gàmbara and Alda Pia da Carpi. She was well-educated, was familiar with the

1:2. Anon.
Portrait of
Veronica
Gambara.
16th century.
Unlocated,
formerly Galeria
Giovio, Como.
Photo,
E. Rodocanachi,
La Femme
Italienne
(Paris, 1922).

classical Latin writers, and studied Greek, possibly with Giovanni Britannico or perhaps with her brother Camillo, who translated the comedies of Aristophanes into Italian. She is said to have received a doctorate in philosophy at the University of Brescia.[11]

Talented and accomplished, she began to be much admired among the Este, the Gonzaga, and other noble families, and someone in that circle spoke to a young man about her warmly enough to awaken his interest. He wrote to her, we know, for her pleased, rather unguarded letter in response survives in the ducal archives of Modena. "I am sorry, Messer Barone, that the lot should have fallen to your Lordship to be the first to write the desire you have to know me because, as my desire is by far the greater I should like to have been the first to express it."[12] It is not known who the man was or whether they met, but it seems certain that Veronica did have a serious romance before her marriage that ended unhappily; in a number of love poems she expresses her despair that she has lost the man she loves. Zamboni and other writers believed all of Veronica's love poems referred to the loss of her husband, who died in 1518, but we are not entirely persuaded. In the following poem she writes of a lingering parting, of passionate last words, which surely do not suggest separation because of death:

> *When may I die,*
> *Love, if the sorrow of this cruel parting*
> *does not end my life?*
>
> *Whenever now I think about*
> *what his last look meant to tell me,*
> *and about that slow, lingering parting,*

1:3.
Francesco
Guarisco.
*Veronica
Gàmbara.*
Lithograph,
19th century.
Original image
frontispiece of
*Rime e Lettere di
Veronica Gàmbara*
(1759). Photo,
Museo Civico,
Padua.

with those deep sighs,
how is it that I still have my body and soul?

If when I heard him say
those last words with such fervor
my heart did not break
and I could not die,
when will I ever be able to leave this world?
I will indeed leave it because such suffering
I will not be able to endure; to see myself deprived
and so far away from him, and go on living! (p. 23)

In another poem also held to be on her husband's death she begs (in the present
subjunctive) that his feelings for her be like hers for him, clearly addressing a living
man; moreover, the poem is suffused with the fervor that suggests her response to an
enforced separation from a lover.

Since it was my fixed and fatal destiny
to love you, and live only for you,
may Love inspire your heart with feeling
as great as my profound suffering,

And may your desire be equal
to my ardent yearning;

then never mind the sorrow, the suffering
that makes pain sweeter than any pleasure.

And if I beg such divine favor, dearest beloved,[13]
neither Love nor Fortune ever gave
greater happiness to anyone,

And for all the past pain and misery the
heart has endured, for all it suffered and now sorrows
it will be called sweet, and he forever blessed. (pp. 23 – 24)

However, in a ballad where she writes despairingly that she has lost all hope, the man to whom she refers in the last stanza, her *scorta*, could be her husband or equally possible, the other man, about whom we have speculated above: *scorta* can mean escort, companion, guide, or, occasionally, husband. The ballad "Gone Now Is Hope" (set to music by Bartolomeo Tromboncini),[14] suggests that she had had expectations of future happiness and that circumstances, not death, had deprived her of hope.

Now that hope which once
made me ardent is gone,
it hurts me less because I understand
nothing endures:
          Gone now is hope.

This illusion once kept me
on fire with hope;
now, taking my misfortune as a joke
it has left me weeping,
and loving, and yearning
with fierce, unending passion,
stronger than ever, it leads me
straight and inevitably to death:
          Gone now is hope.

I did hope, and this hope
nursed me with lovely warmth;
now no more hope have I,
and my soul wishes, craves,
only to cry
and prays for death to stop its pain;
for my heart, once its happy dwelling
has lost all hope:
          Gone now is hope.

When he was my guide,
whatever troubles I had seemed trivial;

without him I am lost and dead,
every trifle seems unbearable;
from that time to this I have had
little happiness and great anguish
for having attended to him;
this reward alone keeps me going:

Gone now is hope.

My fond sweet hope
has fled from me, alas!
and leaving me has taken away
my ardent heart, my tired life,
so that frightened
and deprived of all hope,
not living yet I live
entirely without hope.

Gone now is hope. (pp. 24 – 25)

In 1508, by arrangement, Veronica married Giberto X, Count of Correggio, a town most famous today as the birthplace of Antonio Allegri, called Correggio. Her father must have considered Giberto a good match even though he was close to fifty, a widower with a young daughter. His rank was socially acceptable,[15] he had won a good reputation serving under the Neapolitan King Ferdinand I, Popes Sixtus IV, Alexander VI, Innocent VIII, and Julius II, and he was wealthy. Veronica was not beautiful, and she was twenty-three years old—not young to be still unmarried, by the standards of that culture. She joined her husband in Correggio in 1509. They were apparently quite compatible, sharing an interest in decorative art that they expressed by commissioning artists such as Correggio, Antonio Begarelli, Michel Angel delle Crete, and Rinaldo Duro to embellish their palace and gardens with sculpture and other decorations. They took pleasure in the art gallery that had been already established over the years by the lords of Correggio.[16]

According to Zamboni, Veronica had two children, Ippolito and Girolamo, but was unable to have others because of an illness that required a medication that made her sterile.[17] The marriage ended with Giberto's death in 1518. Although it had not been a love match, ten years of presumably happy marriage had created genuine feeling, and Veronica's extravagant mourning was probably quite sincere: her poem on his death, for all of its strong echo of Petrarch, expresses her deep grief.

That bond which heaven ordained
and made everlasting my ties to you
to my great grief has been loosed and undone
by that cruel one that the world calls death.

And so heavy and profound was my sorrow
that all my enjoyment of life was ended,

and if reason had not prevailed
I would have cut my days short.

> *But fearing not to reach that place*
> *so far away from the other one,[18] where his beautiful*
> *face shines more than any resplendent star*

> *My sorrow which neither art nor intellect*
> *could lessen was mitigated by the hope of seeing in Paradise*
> *that soul beautiful beyond all others.* (p. 25)

It is clear that this poem with its reference to the heavenly and everlasting bond is a memorial to her husband as it was always said to be.

On the death of Giberto X, Veronica became ruler of the county of Correggio, one of very few women who held legal authority of any kind. Sometime after he died she went to visit Brescia, her homeland, as it appears from her poem in which she writes of recovering from grief caused by a death.

> *Since I have the good fortune to see you again,*
> *lovely hills, clear, cool waters,**
> *you whom it pleased nature*
> *to make such a charming, colorful place;*

> *I can well say happy the day,*
> *and bless the desire that arose in me*
> *to see you again, while before*
> *death was lying in my grief-captured heart.*

> *Now at last I see you and I feel such delight*
> *that no matter how cruel fortune has hurt me*
> *I put it behind me.*

> *Let the broad and balmy sky above you*
> *oh blessed land, be always serene*
> *since I long for nothing, except for you.* (p. 25)

That Veronica began writing poetry as a young girl and had serious ambitions of becoming known as a poet is evident from a letter that Pietro Bembo wrote her in 1504. He apologizes for the long delay in answering her (two years!) and praises her sonnet, now lost together with her letter, which began "S'a voi da me non pur veduto mai" (although I have never met you).[19] It is clear that she asked him to be a kind of mentor, for he assures her that such would be his great pleasure. It is also clear that Veronica already felt confident of her talent: by that time Bembo had won recognition as an important literary figure, and she must have hoped that given his wide

---

* Petrarch, 126, l.1, *Chiare fresche et dolci acque*. Gàmbara shifts the word *dolci* to modify hills.

acquaintance among the intellectual community he would be of considerable help in advancing her reputation. In the life-long correspondence that began with that first letter, Veronica often included sonnets for which she asked his criticism and suggestions. She was ambitious in everything that concerned herself and her family, even though her letters are full of self-deprecation. "Forgive me for being a woman and ignorant," she wrote Bembo ("my guiding star and friend") in 1531 when she sent him two sonnets, now lost, on the death of Sannazaro. Which one, she asks, did he think best? "They are both beautiful," he assured her, "lovely, full of feeling, and worthy of you. I rejoice over them with you and you have done well to send them to Signor Mussetola. Sanazzaro's dear soul will probably not receive another as beautiful as these."[20] Giovan Antonio Mussetola served Charles V in important political negotiations, and Veronica surely had in mind not only her own advantage but also the future advancement of her young sons in complimenting this highly influential man by sending him a poem that probably included praise of himself and the emperor. Furthermore, she was the widowed ruler of her small state of Correggio, and sharply aware of political necessities.

The most shining years of Veronica's life were those she spent in Bologna, where she decided to move in 1528. Her brother Uberto was governor of the city, and she knew that this alone assured her an almost peerless status in any circle she wished to enter. Her hopes were splendidly fulfilled. Another brother, Brunoro, exiled from Brescia in 1516 because he had fought on the side of Charles V against the (temporarily) victorious Francis I, was living in Bologna, and in 1529 he married Virginia Pallavicini Piacentino, the widowed daughter-in-law of Alessandro Farnese, the future Pope Paul III, who brought him an immense dowry. The marriage was celebrated with great pomp, but one can be sure that even the bride did not outshine Veronica Gàmbara. The following year saw one of the great moments in the life of that splendid city, for it was there in 1530 that Pope Clement VII crowned Charles V (the man whose troops had sacked Rome and made him a virtual prisoner in 1527) emperor of the Holy Roman Empire [21] (figure 1.4). The great and near-great of Europe were in Bologna for the festivities and political possibilities, and with them their courtiers, retainers, poets, and musicians. Parades, pageants, and spectacles of every kind were everyday occurrences. Veronica was in her element with these brilliant entertainments and with the equally brilliant admirers who gathered in her splendid palazzo.

It was likely at this time, after the Peace of Cambrai in 1529 had brought a respite to the wars between France and Spain, and a peace treaty was signed between Charles and the Venetian Republic, that she wrote some of her poems in praise of Charles:

> *That lucky star, unwavering in the heavens,*
> *companion of the great Julius Caesar from his birth,*
> *made him ruler of the world*
> *and gave him divine and immortal life.*

> *Another, even more benign,*
> *was the guiding star of the great Charles,*
> *so great that I expect to see him even greater,*
> *made a god among mortals;*

> *The former, for his conquest of the Indians, the Medes,*
> *the Scythians, Cantabrians, Britons, the brave Gauls*
> *deserved every honor; **

> *The latter, who has already conquered two worlds,*
> *and resolved peacefully so many willful conflicts,*
> *deserves even greater praise and greater glory.* (p. 26)

As sister of the governor she was part of the close circle around the emperor, with whom she was able to establish a cordial relationship. When he left Bologna to go to Germany in 1530, he went by way of Correggio where Veronica, returned to her state for this glorious occasion, welcomed in worthy style this most august personage in all of Europe. She had a broad new avenue constructed to pave the way of the Emperor to her palace, called the Stradone dell'Imperadore. On his return from Germany in 1532 he stopped again at Correggio where he is said to have stayed at her magnificent "casino," a Palazzo delle Delizie that no longer exists. This grand estate of "endless numbers of rooms" included a labyrinth, navigable canals, and fountains that played spectacular water patterns in the spacious gardens. For the occasion of the emperor's second visit Veronica commissioned Antonio Allegri, who had taken the name of his birthplace, Correggio, to decorate two of the rooms of her pleasure palace. The frescoes included a scene of Mary Magdalene, which Veronica described in a letter to Isabella d'Este, inviting her to "come and see" the wonderful work that "Antonio Allegri has just finished, a masterpiece of painting representing Mary Magdalene in the desert, in the shelter of a cave, to do penance; she is kneeling on her right knee, with her hands joined, raised to heaven in the act of begging mercy for her sins. Her beautiful pose, the dignified and intense grief that is expressed in her beautiful face makes everyone who sees it marvel." [22] The fresco was lost with the destruction of the palace.

The emperor surely enjoyed Veronica's wit and famous eloquence, and she won an agreement from him that her state would not be attacked by imperial soldiers and that his generals and commanders would not be allowed to garrison troops in Correggio. Her success with Charles was apparently well known, for Benedetto Varchi addressed a poem to her in which he wrote,

> *your sweet, eloquent speech*
> *appeases the greatest man of our century*
> *indeed the most brilliant genius of all time*
> *far above anyone who would be second.*[23] (p. 26)

Because her brother was appointed papal nuncio to Charles and would no longer be living in Bologna, Veronica decided to remain in Correggio, taking trips occasionally back to Bologna, to Venice, to the shrine at Loreto, and to her native Brescia. At home she was occupied with the literary academy she had founded in 1520[24] and with

---

* The Medes were inhabitants of Media, present-day northwestern Iran; the Scythians inhabited territory that coincides with present-day Crimea; the Cantabrians lived in northern Spain; the Britons in the modern British Isles; and the Gauls lived mainly in what is now France.

1:4.
Giorgio Vasari.
*The Incoronation
of Charles V by
Pope Clement VII.*
Palazzo Vecchio,
Florence. Photo,
Alinari/Art
Resource.

her duties as head of state, which included the welfare of her subjects. When crop fail-ure brought near-starvation to Correggio, she was ready to "pawn herself," she wrote to her agent Rossi, in order to buy grain for her people. "We are so badly off that if God doesn't help us I fear that the majority of people in this land will die of starvation. I am sending this to you deliberately to let you know the dire need. See if it is possible to get grain from Romagna, and let me know the price because I am resolved by duty and by compassion to pawn myself in order to get help for my people." [25] Always acutely aware of the need for good harvests, she invoked the favor of the gods that put bread and wine on the tables of the Correggesi.

> You who showed the primitive world
> how to change hard acorns to beautiful spikes of wheat *

---

* The origin of the word *acorn* pertains to uncultivated field produce.

and how to perform those useful tasks,
you are called a goddess all over the world.

And you, Bacchus, whose virtues are sung worldwide,
first to teach ancient peoples
how to plant the vine along the sunny hillside
and to extract the desirable liquor,

If with sympathetic eye and modest demands
you will continue what so far
thanks to your kindness, you have given us,

You will always see me,
in full-flowering Spring, pure of heart,
honoring your altars with the sap of wine and grain. (p. 26)

She was perforce deeply concerned with the military and political events that had made Italy a battlefield for the contending armies of Spain and France, and it was probably when after a few years of peace war broke out between them again in 1542 that Veronica wrote the poem addressed to the two monarchs whom the Pope was trying to reconcile. She begs them to join their forces against the common enemy, the Ottoman empire.

May your anger and your ancient hatred,
oh, Charles and Francis, be conquered in the holy name of
Christ; and may you be strengthened by his love,
for he, above all others, has been your friend.

Let your arms stand ready
to fight his impious enemy,
and hold not Italy, indeed all Europe,
its shores, its valleys, its hills, in thrall to you.

The Holy Father to whom has been given
the keys of Heaven
turns to you and begs your mercy for his flock;

Let pity rule, rather than wrath,
oh royal majesties, and one sole desire impassion you:
to conquer those who disdain and deny Christ. [26] (pp. 26 – 27)

Veronica's friends included some of the most prominent figures in the literary world with whom she corresponded, often exchanging sonnets, a frequent practice of the time. Ludovico Ariosto mentions her among the crowd of "ladies and cavaliers" that greeted him when he returned from his long voyage.

> *What lovely, wise women and cavaliers are here*
> *on the shore to welcome me!*
> *What friends, to whom I owe eternal thanks*
> *for their delight at my return!*
> *Mamma and Ginevra and other ladies of Correggio*
> *I see at the far end of the jetty:*
> *Veronica da Gàmbara, beloved of Phoebus*
> *and his sacred Aonian Chorus, is among them. **
> (p. 27) (See figure 1.5.)

Pietro Aretino, Iacopo Sannazaro, Benedetto Varchi, Alfonso del Vasto and Vittoria Colonna all wrote poems in her honor. Although there is no evidence that Veronica and Vittoria ever met, they knew of each other and exchanged sonnets. One of the poems Veronica addressed to Vittoria is particularly interesting because it reveals a "feminist" awareness that is one of the cultural phenomena of the sixteenth century.

> *Oh wise and lovely woman*
> *unique in our time, even divine,*
> *to whom those most worthy of fame*
> *bow in reverence,*
>
> *Here on earth your memory will be eternal,*
> *ruinous, ravishing time will never be able to destroy*
> *your name, for your spirit will forever be victorious.*
>
> *Our sex must build a sacred and noble temple*
> *like those of Pallas and of Phoebus †*
> *built of rich marble and pure gold;*
>
> *You are the very model of virtue, oh, Lady,*
> *and I only wish that I could praise you*
> *as much as I revere and love and adore you. ‡* (p. 27)

They also shared a common sympathy for the Reform movement that spread over Italy in the wake of the Lutheran revolt against the Roman Catholic Church and was propagated there with great success by Bernardo Ochino, whose preaching brought thousands to hear him. The Protestants held that God had chosen certain souls for salvation, and that nothing could intervene to prevent the elected from their predestined justification. So we find Veronica writing,

---

* Aonian Chorus: When Phoebus Apollo, god of music, made prophecies, he usually imparted them through women.

† Pallas = Athena; Phoebus = Apollo.

‡ See, in the chapter on Vittoria Colonna, her poem to Gàmbara, "Once again heaven embellishes our age;" especially compare Colonna's l. 10 with Gàmbara's l. 11.

God in His infinite goodness chose his elected
from among all those to come,
predestined to future life
only by the power of his divine will.

He calls and gently enfolds them in his embrace
admonishing them to do good
not by means of prudent and useful works
but by trust in his infinite mercy.

Calling them makes them righteous
and as such He exalts them so that
they are almost the equal of his only Son.

Then what injury or danger can there be
no matter how extreme
that could separate the elected from Christ? (pp. 27 – 28)

Because of the increasingly turbulent religious and intellectual atmosphere in Western Europe in the decade that followed the Lutheran revolt of the 1520s, the death of Pope Clement VII in 1534 was felt to be particularly fateful. Veronica reflects the sense of uncertainty that prevailed while Christendom waited for the election of a new pope.

See, oh Lord, how the tired boat of Peter
tossed in the sea by fierce winds,
goes adrift; she seems to lament
this dangerous, turbulent tempest.

See, Lord, how alone in the vast ocean,
she is wandering, and with desperate cries
is begging for your help. And you allow her
to be guided by a hostile star?

A ship without a helmsman, a flock without a shepherd,
this cannot be: the first attacked by waves,
the second by wolves, both are menaced and will die.

Oh, Lord, help us; may your favor
inspire him whom you will elect
to steer this ship safely into harbor. [27] (p. 28)

The election in 1534 of Alexander Farnese to the papacy as Pope Paul III was greeted with great optimism, for he was known to be a strong supporter of reform. Veronica, however, begs him to save the Church from the Reform with which she had once sympathized.

1:5.
Franco Savani/
Domenico
Cagnoni.
*Veronica Gàmbara
Welcomed into
Parnassus.*
From *Rime e
lettere raccolte da
Felice Rizzardi*
(Brescia, 1759).

> *You who fortunately wear the glorious mantle of Peter*
> *and hold the keys of the heavenly kingdom*
> *thus God's worthy minister*
> *and holy and wise shepherd,*
>
> *Look at the flock entrusted to you*
> *and how the fierce wolf decimates it; then make secure*
> *the former with your sacred knowledge,*
> *and let the others receive their just punishment.*
>
> *Expel without mercy from our rich shelter*
> *the enemies of Christ now that the two monarchs*
> *have given over their ambitions and cares to you.*
>
> *If you succeed, acclaim for your wonderful work*
> *and noble acts will be no less than his*
> *whose great name you have taken.* (pp. 28 – 29)

Veronica was not old when she began to think sadly about the passage of time. Even when she was living splendidly in Bologna she was aware that "Time . . . consumes everything voraciously," as she commented in a letter of 7 April 1529 to Bembo. [28] She saw herself aging, her skin gathering wrinkles, [29] and she meditated on the vanity and brevity of life in a long poem of twenty-seven stanzas, an ambitious and well-sustained work that she sent to Cosimo, Grand Duke of Tuscany, who, she wrote in stanza twenty-six, is the heroic example of greatness crowned by virtue. It was set to music by Nicola Dorati in 1570–71. [30]

Living in the natural setting of Correggio, where she gazed upon its "venerable waters," its "blessed shores," [31] Veronica was acutely aware of nature and the changing seasons, birth and flowering and decay and death. Thus her long poem in eight-line stanzas (*ottave*) begins,

> *When I see the beautiful earth*
> *adorned with myriad scented flowers*
> *like heaven sparkling with stars, and how*
> *earth is resplendent with color,*
> *And every wild beast hungry and alone*
> *moving by instinct*
> *out of the woods and old caves*
> *searching night and day for its mate,*
>
> *And when I see the plants dressed*
> *in beautiful flowers and new leaves*
> *and hear the sweet and happy*
> *songs of so many different kinds of birds,*
> *And the lovely sound of the rivers*
> *as they bathe their blossoming banks,*

so that nature enamored of herself
enjoys seeing her own creation,

   I say, oh how brief
is this poor mortal life!
Just yesterday the bank now so green and blossoming
was covered with snow,
the beauty of the sky was obscured
by heavy clouds,
and these animals yearning and amorous
were alone and hidden in the woods and mountains.

   There were no sweet melodies heard
among plants and charming birds
because the blowing of the angry winds
made the former dry and the latter mute;
the fast flowing rivers and little streams
were frozen still by ice;
all that is now beautiful and gay
was in winter weak and frail.

   Thus time flies, and fleeing,
takes along with it the years, and our lives!
For it is the will of heaven that we cannot hope
to flourish again, as these will do,
certain only of nothing but death
no matter whether high-born or low,
no matter how happy our fortune
time will bring us to merciless death.

   Thus does that cruel one always
deprive of life and honors
the most famous and victorious kings
just when they have the highest hopes,
neither their power can help them
nor their past triumphs and glories;
we are all equals in death's power,
nor can we have any hope to return.

In the next stanzas she turns from time to human folly and vanity.

   And even with all this, miserable and foolish
enemies of our own good and of ourselves,
stubborn and sunk in grave error,
we deliberately search out what is harmful and dangerous;
going to endless trouble and anguish,

with few pleasures and much pain
we look for ways to make life, unfortunately risky
and brief as it is, sad and tedious.

Those who, to win world fame,
follow in the flower of their youth
fierce and dangerous Mars,
and thrust themselves
amid thousands of arrows and swords,
hoping with their skill to make themselves
noble and immortal in some remote land
fall like shattered glass.

Those greedy to acquire treasure
trust themselves to the power of the treacherous seas,
and full of fear and sorrow
wander from one shore to another;
often they cry out for rescue
from the angry roaring waves;
then when success seems most certain,
they lose both hope and life.

Others, spending the best years of their young lives
in the great courts,
seeking accomplishment and honor,
find hatred, envy, insults, and abuse,
thanks to the ungrateful princes
who abandon all principle,
whose hearts are filled with deceit and naked greed
and who bestow dishonor on the world.

Others longing only to be admired
and to be first among the many,
to be clothed in gold
and adorned with precious jewels,
step by step, with fire and sword
they become odious and despicable tyrants;
but at the end of their worthless life,
they die, and with death dies their glory.

How many there are who having fallen in love
with two beautiful eyes and a charming face
feed themselves on doleful complaints
while unsure even of their own feelings!
Neither joy nor pleasure are enough
to draw from their hearts more than a false laugh

and if at times they seem happy
they enjoy for one delight a thousand woes.

One lives without ever feeling at peace
away from the beloved,
one becomes unhappy and annoyed
just because of an unpleasant look or word;
one feels jealous because of a new rival,
almost ready to die from pain and sorrow;
one is consumed by all kinds of trouble
usually no greater than a grain of sand.

And thus without reining in
with reason those vain desires,
swayed by our senses, living the good life,
we create endless torments for ourselves;
how tranquil one would be, how calm and serene,
if one lived modestly and humbly,
without passion and longing,
happily enjoying what heaven has given us.

Now she picks up the perennial literary theme of the golden age.

As in the happy days of long ago
when those happy souls
lived on milk and acorns,
content with such simple food;
and when the great blast of the sounding trumpet
was not heard among soldiers
nor the resounding strikes of the anvil
as the naked Cyclops forged arms.

There was neither hope stirring desire
for fame and honor
nor uncertainty creating anxiety and anguish
for fear of losing them;
nor did they feel joy or pain
desiring to overthrow authorities
or subjugate others
free of those dangerous and malicious human passions.

But with no other cares they were content
to till the hard soil with the plow
and to watch their precious herds
grazing together, in a peaceful contest;
then with happy, sylvan notes

they dispelled the worry that may often frighten one,
singing on the tender grass
with the nymphs and shepherds.

And often at the foot of an elm or near a pine tree
a target was placed
and whoever sent an arrow fastest and closest to it
was crowned with laurel;
then to Ceres the worshippers offered spears of wheat
and wine to Bacchus and in such ways
passing their days they made
miserable and bitter life serene and light-hearted.

This is the life that pleased
father Saturn, and that his children
led for generations,* while ambition
lay dormant in their minds;
but as soon as this plague was born
so was born envy, the two united;
and suddenly the world,
once happy and cheerful,
became miserable.

Because it was much sweeter to sleep
on the grass, under the trees, quiet and secure,
than in golden, purple-hung beds;
and perhaps every dark thought, every bitter pain
was chased away, hearing
with a tranquil, joyous heart
the mooing of the herds at sunrise,
sweeter than the harmony of the most delightful music.

Blessed, then, if mortals may be
called blessed while they live;
and if, living, one can be said to be happy,
it seems to me it must be one who lives in such a state;
but one who wishes to be like the phoenix
and, mortal, to make oneself immortal
must love what makes humankind eternal,
what is sweet at the end but bitter at the beginning:

In the final six stanzas she achieves some of her best poetry as she reaches a more insistent, even visionary tone, moving from contemplation of the world—nature,

---

* Saturn: the Roman god of sowing and harvesting, identified with the golden age in Italy.

time, and human folly—to the immediate perception that true glory can be attained
only with the guidance of virtue.

> *Virtue, I say, flying to the heavens*
> *surrounded by beautiful everlasting light,*
> *although clad in a corporeal veil*
> *leads the soul that follows her,*
> *and carries on her strong wings one who loves her,*
> *nor ever fears the shroud; this invincible power*
> *scorning time and its infinite cares*
> *restores to life one who has been dead a thousand years.*

> *With such noble desire this happy and splendid guide*
> *kindles the soul*
> *which rises to the celestial realm*
> *and carries with it the mind*
> *so that it understands the lofty secret*
> *of heaven and earth; thus aware of*
> *how much less satisfying is every other pleasure,*
> *it follows only that guide and forgets all others.*

> *How many beloved and revered Princes*
> *have lost their names together with their lives!*
> *How many, born poor, live on, gloriously shining*
> *because for their noble and precious gifts*
> *they are happily crowned with the sacred laurel,*
> *and now, like bright stars, blessed, they sparkle above us,*
> *while here in the world they will be forever honored.*

> *I could go on giving examples*
> *of the endless pages that heaven has inspired*
> *throughout history, generously crowning*
> *now this, now that one;*
> *but how many of them have been forgotten*
> *and how many today are neglected?*
> *I speak of one who shines among other lights*
> *as the sun shines among other brilliant stars.*

> *I speak of you, favored branch of that stately tree,*
> *the noble Laurel,*
> *in which one sees at a glance*
> *the virtue that spreads its luster from sea to sea;* *

---

* See the Italian "dal Indo al Mauro": Mauritania, now most of northern Morocco and western Algeria,
bordered on the Atlantic Ocean, which even into the sixteenth century, after Columbus's voyages, was still
thought of as the outer western limit of the world, with the Indian Ocean seen as the eastern limit.

and under its glorious and sacred shadow
one learns to love not gems or gold
but greatness crowned with virtue,
which leaves the whole world speechless.
      Thus following in your footsteps,
I put aside every unworthy thought;
I will follow virtue, always believing that,
if this is not a desirable goal
all others are false; fearing
neither adverse fortune nor cruel destiny,
I will live with her, putting aside all else,
loving her as long as I may live. (pp. 29 – 34)

It may be unkind to remember that virtue was not uppermost in her mind when she wrote to her friend—only a year before she died a few months before her sixty-fifth birthday—that she wanted to borrow those wonderful jewels of the Countess Pepoli. Nevertheless, summarizing her life, Veronica sounds one of the most important notes in the peculiar dichotomy of harmony and dissonance that characterizes the artistic and intellectual spirit of the sixteenth century, the "choice of Hercules" between virtue and carnal pleasure, seen as vice. The theme, often cast in terms of "superior love," which is spiritual and thus virtuous, and "inferior love," which is sensual and thus merely pleasurable, was a mainstay of many dialogues of this period, marked as it was by Plato and most particularly by his *Symposium*. As one would expect, Veronica follows Bembo closely as he appears in Castiglione's *The Courtier*, the defender of spiritual love and of reason as the safeguard against passion. The theme was given visible form in Veronese's *Vice and Virtue*, and other masters including her favorite, Correggio. [32] Impelled by Neo-Platonism, which synthesized ancient philosophy with Christianity, virtue often became identified as sacred love opposed to profane love: in Titian's *Sacred and Profane Love*, the nude female figure of secular love is contrasted with the voluminously clothed figure of sacred love whose hands are even gloved; behind her head two patches of light spread like angelic wings.

In her long poem Veronica frames her self-portrait as a very special woman of her time. Meditative, she does not look out to address a viewer; she looks inward as one who as head of state witnessed the never-ending struggle for power and wealth. She had wanted fame, but in the end it was on the virtue of her poetic gift that she counted for her lasting name. Educated rather than profound, intelligent, serious, and sedate rather than sensitive, Veronica Gàmbara still shines on the altar of paper and ink that she was promised by Vittoria Colonna.

POEMS IN THE ORIGINAL ITALIAN

Occhi lucenti e belli,
Com'esser può che in un medesmo istante
nascan da voi sì nove forme e tante?
Lieti, mesti, superbi, umili, alteri
vi mostrate in un punto; onde di speme
e di timor m'empiete;
e tanti effetti dolci, acerbi, e fieri
nel cor arso per voi vengono insieme
ad ognor che volete.
Or poi che voi mia vita e morte sete,
occhi felici, occhi beati e cari
siate sempre sereni, allegri, e chiari. * (p. 1)

Veronica Gàmbara
◉ **Track 2,**
Reading 1

⁓

Quando sarà ch'io mora,
Amor, se'n questa cruda dipartita
Non può tanto dolor finir mia vita?

Qual or avvien ch'io pensi,
quel che dir mi volea l'ultimo sguardo,
e'l partir lento e tardo,
con quei sospir sì accensi,
come può star in me l'anima e i sensi?
S'allor ch'io gli udio dire
quell'ultime parole in tanto ardore,
non mi s'aperse il core,
e non potei finire.
Quando potrò mai più di vita uscire?
Io n'uscirò, ch'a tant'aspro martire
non potrò mai durar; vedermi priva,
e si lunge da lui, e ch'io sia viva! † (pp. 4–5)

⁓

Poscia che'l mio destin fermo e fatale
vuol ch'io pur v'ami, e che per voi sospiri,
quella pietà nel petto Amor v'inspiri,
che conviene al mio duol grave e mortale:

◉ **Track 3,**
Reading 2

E faccia che'l voler vostro sia eguale
a gli amorosi ardenti miei desiri;

---

* All poems of Gàmbara are from *Rime e lettere raccolte da Felice Rizzardi* (Brescia, 1759), except where noted.
† Francesco Trucchi, *Poesie inedite di 200 autori* (Prato, 1846), p. 47.

poi cresca quanto vuol doglia e martiri,
che più d'ogn' altro ben dolce sia 'l male.

E se tal grazia impetro, almo mio Sole,
nessun più lieto e glorioso stato
diede Amore, o Fortuna al mondo mai.

E quanti per addietro affanni e guai
patito ha 'l cor, ond' ei si dolse e duole,
chiamerà dolci, e lui sempre beato. (pp. 5 – 6)

Or passata è la speranza
che mi tenne un tempo ardendo
men mi duol poichè io comprendo
nulla cosa aver costanza:
　　Or passata è la speranza.

Questa falsa un tempo in foco
ha tenuta pur sperando;
or prendendo il mal mio a gioco
m'ha lassata lagrimando,
ed amando e desiando
mi conduce ogni'ora a morte
con passion tenace e forte
e con più perseveranza:
　　Or passata è la speranza.

Io sperai, e quel sperare
mi nutriva in dolce fiamma;
nè più or spero, e lagrimare
sol quest'alma desìa e brama,
e la morte ognora chiama
per soccorso al suo dolore;
poichè senza speme è 'l core
che già fu sua dolce stanza:
　　Or passata è la speranza.

Mentre ch'ebbi lui per scorta,
ogni mal mi parea lieve;
senza lui smarrita e morta,
ogni poco mi par greve;
lungo affanno e piacer breve
da indi 'n quà sempre ho sentito
per aver con fe servito;
questo premio sol m'avanza:
　　Or passata è la speranza.

Mia soave e dolce speme
da me dunque ahimè! è fuggita;
e al partir ne portò insieme
l'arso cor, mia stanca vita;
tal ch'essendo sbigottita,
e di speme al tutto priva,
non vivendo, resto viva
senza'alfin nulla speranza:
Or passata è la speranza. (pp. 6 – 7)

Quel nodo in cui la mia beata sorte,
per ordine del ciel, legommi e strinse,
con grave mio dolor sciolse e discinse
quella crudel che'l mondo chiama Morte.

E fu l'affanno sì gravoso e forte,
che tutti i miei piaceri a un tratto estinse;
e se non che ragione alfin pur vinse,
fatte avrei mie giornate e brevi e corte.

Ma tema sol di non andare in parte
troppo lontana a quella ove il bel viso
risplende sovra ogni lucente stella,

Mitigato ha'l dolor, che ingegno, od arte
far nol potea, sperando in Paradiso
l'alma vedere oltra le belle bella. (pp. 7 – 8)

Poichè, per mia ventura, a veder torno
voi, dolci colli, e voi, chiare e fresch'acque,
e tu che tanto a la natura piacque
farti, sito gentil, vago ed adorno;

Ben posso dire avventuroso il giorno;
e lodar sempre quel desio che nacque
in me di rivedervi, che pria giacque
morto nel cor di dolor cinto intorno.

Vi veggi'or dunque, e tal dolcezza sento,
che quante mai da la fortuna offese
ricevute ho finor, pongo in oblio.

Così sempre vi sia largo e cortese,
lochi beati, il ciel, come in me spento
e, se non di voi soli, ogni desio. (p. 8)

Quella felice stella, e in cielo fatale,
che fu compagna al nascimento altero
del gran Cesare Augusto, onde l'impero
del mondo tenne, e visse almo e immortale:

Quella, ma più benigna, al bel natale
fu guida del gran Carlo, tal ch'io spero
maggior vederlo, per dir meglio il vero,
e fatto un Dio fra noi d'uomo mortale.

Che se per vincer gl'Indi, i Medi, e i Scithi,
e i Cantabri, e i Britanni, e i Galli audaci,
meritò quello aver tant'alti onori;

Questo, che omai due mondi ha vinto, e uniti
tanti voler discordi in tante paci,
merita maggior lodi, e onor maggiori. (pp. 9 – 10)

～

Benedetto Varchi

. . . 'l vostro dolce dir, facondo
acquete il maggior uom del secolo nostro
anzi di tutti i tempi altero mostro,
a cui lunge sarà chi sia secondo. * (p. 10)

～

Veronica Gàmbara

Tu che mostrasti al rozzo mondo prima
mutar le dure ghiande in belle spiche,
e festi sì co'l utili fatiche,
che Dea ti chiama ogni abitato clima;

E tu, Bacco, del cui valor canta ogni rima,
primo a insegnare a quelle genti antiche
piantar le viti in quelle piagge apriche
per trarne poi liquor di tanta stima;

Se con occhi pietosi e voglia umile
guarderete ambidue quel che finora,
vostra dolce mercè, dato ci avete;

Di sangue eletto al più fiorito aprile
con vino e farro i vostri altari ognora
da me onorar con puro cor vedrete. (pp. 11 – 12)

～

◉ Track 4
Reading 3

Vinca gli sdegni e l'odio vostro antico,
Carlo e Francesco, il nome sacro e santo
di Cristo; e di sua fè vi caglia tanto,
quanto a voi più d'ogni altro è stato amico.

---

* *Opere di Benedetto Varchi* (Trieste, 1859), sonnet CLXII.

L'arme vostre a domar l'empio nemico
di lui sian pronte; e non tenete in pianto
non pur l'Italia, ma l'Europa, e quanto
bagna il mar, cinge valle, o colle aprico.

Il Gran Pastor a cui le chiavi date
furon del Cielo, a Voi si volge, e prega
che de le greggie sue pietà vi prenda.

Possa più de lo sdegno in voi pietate,
coppia reale, e un sol desìo v'accenda
di vendicar chi Cristo sprezza e nega. (p. 12)

Oh di che belle e saggie donne veggio,
oh di che cavallieri il lito adorno!
Oh di ch'amici, a chi in eterno deggio
per la letizia c'han del mio ritorno!
Mamma e Ginevra e l'altre da Correggio
veggo del molo in su l'estreme corno:
Veronica da Gàmbara è con loro,
sì grata a Febo e al santo aonio coro. * (p. 13)

Ludovico Ariosto

O de la nostra etade unica gloria
donna saggia, leggiadra, anzi divina,
a la qual riverente oggi s'inchina
chiunque è degno di famosa istoria;

Ben fia eterna di voi quà giù memoria,
né potrà 'l tempo con la sua ruina
far del bel nome vostro empia rapina,
ma di lui porterete ampia vittoria.

Il sesso nostro un sacro e nobil tempio
dovria, come già a Palla e a Febo, alzarvi
di ricchi marmi e di finissim'oro.

E poichè di virtù siete l'esempio,
vorrei, Donna, poter tanto lodarvi,
quanto io vi riverisco, amo, ed adoro. (pp. 13)

Veronica Gàmbara

Scelse da tutta la futura gente
gli eletti suoi l'alta bontà infinita,
predestinati a la futura vita
sol per voler de la divina mente.

---

* Canto 46, stanza 3.

Questi tale poi chiama, e dolcemente
seco gli unisce, ed a ben far gl'invita,
non per opra di lor saggia o gradita,
ma per voler di lui troppo clemente.

Chiamando li fa giusti, e giusti poi
gli esalta sì che a l'unico suo Figlio
li fa conformi, e poco men ch'eguali.

Qual dunque potrà mai danno, o periglio
ne l'ultimo de gli altri estremi mali
da Cristo separar gli eletti suoi? (p. 14)

Mira, Signor, la stanca navicella
di Pietro, che nel mar, da fieri venti
spinta, va errando; e par che si lamenti
di questa fluttuosa e ria procella.

Mira, che sola in questa parte e in quella
smarrita corre, e con dogliosi accenti
Ti domanda soccorso. E tu consenti
che fin or posi in lei nemica stella?

Nave senza nocchier, senza pastore
non può star gregge, chè dall'onde l'una,
l'altro è da lupi travagliato e morto.

Signor, dunque provvedi; e il tuo favore
spira a chi sappia in la maggior fortuna
questa barca condur felice in porto. *(p. 14)*

Tu che di Pietro il glorioso manto
vesti felice, e del celeste regno
hai le chiavi in governo; onde sei degno
di Dio ministro, e pastor saggio e santo;

Mira la greggia a te commessa, e quanto
la scema il fiero lupo; e poi sostegno
securo l'una dal tuo sacro ingegno
riceva, e l'altro giusta pena e pianto.

Scaccia animoso fuor del ricco nido
i nemici di Cristo or che i duo Regi
ogni lor cura e studio hanno a te volto.

---

* "Un Trentino." *Rime e Lettere di Veronica Gàmbara* (Torino, 1880), p. 77.

Se ciò farai, non fia men chiaro il grido
de l'opre tue leggiadre e fatti egregi,
che sia di quello il cui gran nome hai tolto. (p. 16)

~

Quando miro la terra ornata e bella
di mille vaghi ed odorati fiori;
e che come nel ciel luce ogni stella,
* così splendono in lei varj colori;*
ed ogni fiera solitaria e snella
mossa da natural istinto, fuori
de'boschi uscendo, e de l'antiche grotte,
va cercando il compagno e giorno e notte;

E quando miro le vestite piante
pur di bei fiori e di novelle fronde;
* e de gli augelli le diverse e tante*
odo voci cantar dolci e gioconde;
e con grato rumor ogni sonante
fiume bagnar le sue fiorite sponde,
tal che di sè invaghita la natura
gode in mirar la bella sua fattura;

Dico fra me pensando; Ahi quanto è breve
questa nostra mortal misera vita!
Pur dianzi tutta piena era di neve
questa piaggia or si verde e si fiorita;
e da un aer turbato oscuro e greve
la bellezza del cielo era impedita;
e queste fiere vaghe ed amorose
stavan sole fra monti e boschi ascose.

Né s'udivan cantar dolci concenti
per le tenere piante i vaghi augelli;
che dal soffiar de'più rabbiosi venti
fatt'eran secche queste, e muti quelli;
e si vedean fermati i più correnti
fiumi dal ghiaccio, e i piccioli ruscelli;
e quanto ora si mostra e bello e allegro
era per la stagion languido ed egro.

Così si fugge il tempo, e col fuggire
ne porta gli anni e 'l viver nostro insieme!
Che a noi, voler del ciel, di più fiorire,
come queste faran, manca la speme,

● Track 3

certi non d'altro mai che di morire,
o d'alto sangue nati, o di vil seme;
nè quanto può donar felice sorte
farà verso di noi pietosa morte.

Anzi questa crudele ha per usanza
i più famosi e trionfanti regi,
allor ch'hanno di viver più speranza,
privar di vita e de gli ornati fregi;
nè lor giova la regia alta possanza,
nè gli avuti trofei, nè i fatti egregi;
chè tutti uguali in suo poter n'andiamo,
nè poi di più tornar speranza abbiamo.

E pur con tutto ciò miseri e stolti,
del nostro ben nemici e di noi stessi,
in questo grave error fermi e sepolti
cerchiamo il nostro male e i danni espressi;
e con molte fatiche e affanni molti,
rari avendo i piaceri, i dolor spessi,
procacciamo di far nojosa e greve
la vita che pur troppo è inferma e breve!

Questi per aver fama in ogni parte,
ne la sua più fiorita e verde etade,
seguendo il periglioso e fiero Marte,
or fra mille saette e mille spade
animoso si caccia, e con quest' arte,
mentre spera di farsi a le contrade
più remote da noi alto e immortale,
casca assai più che un fragil vetro, frale.

Quell'altro ingordo d'acquistar tesori
si commette al poter del mare infido,
e di paura pieno, e di dolori
trapassa or questo ed or quell'altro lido;
e spesso de l'irate onde i romori
lo fan mercé chiamar con alto grido;
e quando ha d'arricchir più certa speme,
la vita perde, e la speranza insieme.

Altri ne le gran corti consumando
il più bel fior de' suoi giovenili anni,
mentre che utile, e onor vanno cercando,
odio trovano, invidia, oltraggi, e danni,
mercé d'ingrati Principi che in bando

post'hanno ogni virtute, e sol d'inganni
e di brutt'avarizia han pieno il core,
pubblico danno al mondo, e disonore.

Altri poi, vaghi sol d'esser pregiati,
e di tener fra tutti il primo loco,
e per vestirsi d'oro e andare ornati
de le più care gemme, a poco a poco
tiranni de la patria odiosi e ingrati
si fanno ora col ferro ed or col foco;
ma alfin di vita indegni, e di memoria
son morti, e col morir more la gloria.

Quanti son poi, che divenuti amanti
di duo begli occhi e d'un leggiadro viso,
si pascon sol di dolorosi pianti,
da se stessi tenendo il cor diviso!
Nè gioja, nè piacer sono bastanti
trar lor dal petto se non finto riso;
e, se lieti talor si mostran fuori,
hanno per un piacer mille dolori.

Chi vive senza mai sentir riposo
lontano da la dolce amata vista;
chi a sè stesso divien grave e nojoso
sol per un guardo o una parola trista;
chi da un novo rival fatto geloso,
quasi a par del morir si dole e attrista;
chi si consuma in altre varie pene
più spesse assai de le minute arene.

E così senza mai stringere il freno
con la ragion a questi van desiri,
dietro al senso correndo, il viver pieno
facciamo d'infinit empi martiri;
chè tranquillo saria, puro e sereno,
se senza passion, senza sospiri
lieti godendo quanto il ciel n'ha dato,
si vivesse in modesto ed umil stato.

Come ne la felice antiqua etate,
quando di bianco latte e verdi ghiande
si pascevan quelle anime ben nate
contente sol di povere vivande;
e non s'udiva tra le genti armate
de le sonore trombe il romor grande;

nè per far i Ciclopi l'arme ignudi
battendo risuonar facean l'incudi.

Né lor porgeva la speranza ardire
di poter acquistar fama ed onore,
né di perderli poi grave martire
con dubbiosi pensier dava il timore;
né per mutarsi i regni, o per desire
di soggiogar l'altrui, gioja o dolore
sentivano già mai, sciolte da queste
umane passion gravi e moleste.

Ma senz'altro pensier stavan contenti
con l'aratro a voltar la dura terra,
ed a mirar i suoi più cari armenti
pascendo insieme, far piacevol guerra;
or con allegri e boscarecci accenti
scacciavano il dolor che spesso atterra
chi'n sè l'accoglie, fra l'erbette e i fiori
cantando or con le ninfe, or co'pastori.

E spesso appiè d'un olmo, o ver d'un pino
era una meta, o termine appoggiato;
e chi col dardo al segno più vicino
veloce andava, era di fronde ornato;
a Ceres poi le spiche, e a Bacco il vino
offerivan devoti, e in tale stato
passando i giorni suoi, serena e chiara
questa vita facean misera e amara.

Quest'è la vita che cotanto piacque
al gran padre Saturno, e che seguita
fu da'posteri suoi, mentre che giacque
ne le lor menti l'ambition sopita;
ma come poi questa ria peste nacque,
nacque l'invidia, con lei sempre unita;
e misero divenne a un tratto il mondo
prima così felice e sì giocondo.

Perchè più dolce assai era fra l'erba
sotto l'ombre dormir queto e securo,
che nei dorati letti, e di superba
porpora ornati; e forse più ogni oscuro
pensier discaccia, ed ogni doglia acerba
udir col cor tranquillo allegro e puro,

ne l'apparir del sol, mugghiar gli armenti,
che l'armonia de' più soavi accenti.

Beato dunque (se beato lice
chiamar, mentre che vive, uomo mortale;
e se vivendo si può dir felice)
parmi essere quel che vive in vita tale;
ma chi esser poi desia qual la fenice,
e cerca di mortal farsi immortale,
ami quella che l'uomo eterno serba,
dolce nel fine, e nel principio acerba.

La virtù dico, che volando al cielo
cinto di bella e inestinguibil luce,
se ben vestito è del corporeo velo,
con le forti ali sue porta e conduce
chi l'ama e segue, né di morte il telo
teme già mai; chè questo invitto duce,
sprezzando il tempo e suo' infiniti danni,
fa viver tal ch'è morto già mill'anni.

Di così bel desio l'anima accende
questa felice e gloriosa scorta,
che a le cose celesti spesso ascende,
e l'intelletto nostro seco porta;
tal che del cielo e di natura intende
gli alti secreti; onde poi, fatta accorta
quant'ogn'altro piacer men bello sia,
sol segue quella, e tutti gli altri oblia.

Quanti Principi grandi amati e cari
insieme con la vita han perso il nome,
quanti poi vivon gloriosi e chiari,
poveri nati, sol perchè le chiome
di sacri lauri, alteri doni e rari,
s'adornaro felici, ed ora come
chiare stelle fra noi splendon beati,
mentre 'l mondo sarà, sempre onorati!

Molti esempi potrei venir contando,
de' quali piene son tutte le carte,
che 'l ciel produtti ha in ogni tempo, ornando
non sempre avaro or questa or quella parte;
ma quanti ne fur mai dietro lasciando,
e quanti oggi ne son posti da parte,
un ne dirò, che tal fra gli altri luce,
qual tra ogn'altro splendor del sol la luce.

● Track 5,
Reading 4

Dico di voi, o de l'altera pianta
felice ramo del ben nato Lauro,
in cui mirando sol si vede quanta
virtù risplende dal mar Indo al Mauro;
e sotto l'ombra gloriosa e santa
non s'impara apprezzar le gemme o l'auro
ma le grandezze ornar con la virtute
cosa da far tutte le lingue mute!

Dietro a l'orme di voi dunque venendo,
ogni basso pensier posto in oblio,
seguirò la virtù, sempre credendo
esser, se non quest'un dolce desio,
fallace ogn'altro; e così non temendo
o nemica fortuna, o destin rio,
starò con questa, ogni altro ben lasciando,
l'anima e lei, mentre ch'io viva, amando. (pp. 16 – 22)

NOTES

1 All translations are by Jaffe and Colombardo, except where noted. Veronica's poems in this chapter are drawn from *Rime e lettere raccolte da Felice Rizzardi* (Brescia, 1759), the first collection of her poems. The sonnet "Beautiful shining eyes" was set to music by Aurelio Roccia (1571), Nicola Vicentino (1572), and Luca Marenzio (1582). Marenzio uses a favorite Mannerist trick, a punning relationship between the actual notes as they appear on the music sheet and the accompanying words: here, repeated whole notes (breve) in the soprano part look like pairs of eyes; see Maria R. Maniates, *Mannerism in Italian Music and Culture, 1530–1630* (Chapel Hill, 1979). For the vast number of words and images used by Veronica and all of the other poets in this volume dependent on Petrarch, as in this poem ("Occhi lucenti e belli") which echoes Petrarch's poem 110, l. 13 ("così fu' io de'begli occhi lucenti"), see the *Concordanza delle rime di Francesco Petrarca* compiled by Kenneth McKenzie (Oxford and New Haven, 1912). We will signal a few such borrowings that seem to be of particular interest.

2 "Aspetto tutte quelle robe, senza le quali non potrei comparire con quella grandezza che sapete voi essere di mio costume. Intendete sanamente, che qui non pigliasse grandezza per superbia, la quale fu sempre lontana da me, e da ogni mia operazione." Baldassarre Camillo Zamboni, *Vita di Veronica Gàmbara*, in *Rime e lettere di Veronica Gàmbara raccolte da Felice Rizzardi* (Brescia, 1759), p. lvii. The most recent biography of Gàmbara is Antonia Chimenti, *Veronica Gàmbara: gentildonna del rinascimento: un intreccio di poesia e storia* (Reggio Emilia, 1995), with extensive bibliography.

3 Maud Jerrold, *Vittoria Colonna, with Some Account of Friends and Her Times* (New York, 1906), pp. 164–165.

4 Virgil, *Aeneid* IV, 28–29. Veronica did not mind straining a bit for drama's sake; her husband had not abandoned her, as Aeneas did Dido, nor was she ready to throw herself on her funeral pyre.

5 "Pregate il Sig. Conte Alessandro e non bastando i prieghi, supplicatelo a far ogni opra per farmi aver quel cavallo, promettendogli, s'egli mi donasse uno stato, che non l'averei così caro, perchè avendolo ne avrò poi quattro vieppiù che notte oscuri, conformi proprio a'miei travagli." Zamboni, *Vita di Veronica Gàmbara*, p. xliv.

6 Jerrold, *Vittoria Colonna*, p. 156.

7 See Pia Mestica Chiapetti, *Rime e lettere di Veronica Gàmbara* (Florence, 1879), p. 303: Bembo writes in a letter signed from Padua, 1 April 1504, that he is sorry to have delayed two years in answering her letter.

8 Zamboni, *Vita di Veronica Gàmbara*, p. xliv.

9 "Se il viso di Veronica avesse corrisposto all'altre parti del corpo, ella era perfettamente bella, e piena di grazia infino all'ultima età. Ma'l viso benchè non fosse brutto, non fu però molto dilicato già mai . . . , il qual difetto tuttavia largamente ricompensò l'eloquenza, che dalla sua bocca assai maggiore, che dalla penna usciva sì dolce, e schietta, ch'ogni persona che ragionava seco di qualsivoglia cosa, partivasi con incredibil desiderio di ritornarla a udire. La bontà della sua complessione si conobbe nel poco esercizio." Corso quoted in Zamboni, *Vita di Veronica Gàmbara*, p. lxxxi. Corso goes on to relate that she read and wrote without glasses and lived a healthy life, avoiding fresh air, fresh fruits, and similar food. This last seems almost comical to a modern reader until one realizes that fresh food was in fact dangerous because of the use of manure for cultivation.

10 Jerrold, *Vittoria Colonna*, p. 140, who perhaps was looking at the Giovio portrait when she wrote "coarse" and "masculine."

11 Jerrold, *Vittoria Colonna*, p. 140. In the front of a book written in Greek and published by Aldo Manuzio, discovered in a private library, there is a handwritten notation in Latin, *ad usem Veronica Gàmbara*. For notice of her degree in philosophy see Clementina Courten, *Veronica Gàmbara, una gentildonna del cinquecento* (Milan, 1934), p. 17.

12 Jerrold, *Vittoria Colonna*, p. 147.

13 For "dearest beloved" see the poem in Italian at the end of the chapter: Veronica, like other women Petrarchisti of the sixteenth century, calls the man she loves her "Sun," *Sole*, a metaphor used by Petrarch many times to symbolize his unattainable Laura.

14   Zamboni, *Vita di Veronica Gàmbara*, p. 91, n. xlii, points out that lines 2 and 4 of the first stanza in Italian do not rhyme (the double consonant is sounded). This error leads us to believe the poem is an early one. Zamboni believed he was publishing it for the first time. However, its first publication was as a *frottola* in 1553 by Baldesare Tromboncino (ca. 1470–1535 or later). See Harry B. Lincoln, *The Italian Madrigal and Related Repertories, Indexes to Printed Collections, 1500–1600* (New Haven, Conn., 1988), p. 651. The music was commissioned by Isabella d'Este (Rinaldina Russell, *Italian Women Writers: A Bibliographical Sourcebook* [Westport, Conn., 1994], p. 147). Tromboncino was, with his father, in the service of the Mantuan court off and on, but his career there and elsewhere was a stormy one; he killed his wife for her infidelity in 1499, and although the Marquis, Francesco Gonzaga, forgave him for this crime, he fled from Mantua in 1501 "in a deplorable manner and without our permission," according to a letter of Gonzaga to Marco Lando (*New Grove Dictionary of Music and Musicians*, 2d ed. [New York, 2001], vol. 19, pp. 161–163).

15   The families were even related, in that Veronica's mother Alda and Giberto's mother Agnese were of the Pia family, lords of Carpi. An ecclesiastical dispensation had to be obtained for the marriage.

16   Quirino Bigi, *Notizie di Antonio Allegri, di Antonio Bartolotti suo maestro e di altri pittori ed artisti Correggiesi* (Modena, 1878), p. 8, n. 2.

17   Ceserani Remo, in editing Ariosto's *Orlando Furioso* (Turin, 1969), provides a footnote to canto XLVI, 4, identifying "un'altra Ginevra" as the daughter of Veronica Gàmbara and Giberto X of Correggio. It seems unlikely, however, that Zamboni was mistaken.

18   "The other one": Hell. Cf. Petrarch, 71, ll. 42–45 ("Perchè la vita è breve"): "Ma se maggior paura / non m'affrenasse, via corta e spedita / trarrebbe a fin questa aspra pena e dura / e la colpa è di tal che non à cura" (But if a greater fear did not hold me back, I would take a short and speedy way to end this bitter pain and suffering, and the fault is hers who does not care.)

19   This first line is known from a letter Bembo wrote to Veronica, quoting it, and saying that he had lost the sonnet that began with those words and wondering if she could send him a copy, which he wished to include in the new collection of his poetry. She apparently did not find it. See Zamboni, *Vita di Veronica Gàmbara*, p. xxxvi.

20   "Iscusimi l'esser donna e ignorante. Ho fatto a questi giorni due Sonetti per la morte del Sanazzaro. Li mando a V.S. [Vostro Signoria] come a mio lume e scorta. V.S. si degnerà avvisarmi il parer suo." Bembo's response: "Quanto a'sonetti, essi me sono paruti bellissimi l'uno e l'altro. Sono piri, sono vaghi e affezionati ed onorati infinitamente. Io di loro mi rallegro convoi e ben faceste a mandarli al Signor Mussetola. Peravventura non ne averà la buona anima del Sanazzaro alcuno di veruno altro così belle, come questi sono." Zamboni, *Vita di Veronica Gàmbara*, pp. 111–112.

21   Charles V (also Charles I of Spain) had already been elected emperor in 1519, having defeated contenders Francis I of France and England's Henry VIII.

22   "Venite e vedere! Messer Antonio Allegri ha or ora terminato il capo lavoro di pittura, cioè la "Maddalena nel Deserto," ricoverata in orrido speco, a far penitenza; sta essa genuflessa dal lato destro con le mani giunte alzate al cielo in atto di domandare perdono dei peccati. Il suo bel atteggiamento, il nobile e vivo dolore che esprime, il suo bellissimo viso lo fanno mirabil sì che fa stupore a chi la mira." The letter is quoted in Quirino Bigi, *Della vita e delle opere certe ed incerte di Antonio Allegri detto il Correggio* (Modena, 1880), p. 69. He identifies Veronica's correspondent as Beatrice d'Este, which is incorrect, in that she was long dead; Isabella was a longtime friend of Veronica, and godmother of Veronica's first son, Ippolito.

23   *Opere di Benedetto Varchi*, Biblioteca Classica Italiana, secolo XVI, no. 5, vol. 2 (Trieste, 1859), sonnet CLXII.

24   Viller Masoni, ed. *Correggio: Identità e storia di una città* (Parma, 1991), p. 345.

25   "Noi stiamo tanto male, che se Dio non ci aiuta, dubito che la maggior parte di questa terra morirà di fame. Mando questo mio a posta per dirvi il bisogno appieno. Vedete se fosse possibile il cavar grani di Romagna, ed avvisatemi il prezzo, perchè mi risolve e per debito e per pietà, s'io dovessi impegnar me stessa, di soccorrere questi miei uomini." "Un Trentino," *Rime e lettere di Veronica Gàmbara* (Torino, 1880), pp. 17–18.

26   Alan Bullock has assigned this poem to Vittoria Colonna in two articles, "Un sonetto inedito di Vittoria Colonna" (1971: 229–253) and "Veronica o Vittoria? Problemi di attribuzione per alcuni

sonetti del Cinquecento" (1973: 115–131), both in the journal *Studi e Problemi di Critica Testuale*. His argument is based on a manuscript now in the Este Archives in Modena. We find the evidence unconvincing, however: although we cannot here review the entire argument of the two articles, we will point out that the poems in the Este Archives include some addressed *to* Vittoria, including Veronica's "O della nostra etade unica gloria"; that the poem to Carlo and Francesco was first published as a work by Veronica, by Ludovico Domenichi in 1545, when both Vittoria and Veronica were living; that it was published again by Girolamo Ruscelli in 1553, attributed again to Veronica, which publication was reprinted in 1554. Bullock refers to these publications, but he believes the style is not characteristic of Veronica. On the contrary, we find the style more fitting to her than to Vittoria. Veronica used similar imagery, for example, in her poem, "Tu che di Pietro il glorioso manto," where she writes of the Shepherd that must protect his sheep; in fact, this poem can be seen as a sequel to "Vinca gli sdegni e l'odio vostro antico" inasmuch as she begs Paul III to expel the enemies of Christ, now that the two kings have made peace, suggesting the poem was written after the Treaty of Crépy in 1544.

27   "Un Trentino," *Rime e lettere*, p. 77.

28   ". . . il tempo . . . consuma e divora ogni cosa." Zamboni, *Vita di Veronica Gàmbara*, p. 107.

29   Zamboni, *Vita di Veronica Gàmbara*, p. 126.

30   These stanzas were printed inexplicably in a collection of verse published in 1539 under the name of Vittoria Colonna and again attributed to Vittoria in the *Rime de la diva Vettoria* [sic] *Colonna* (Venice, 1540). There is no doubt, however, that they were written by Veronica and published in 1536: Girolamo Ruscelli, in *Raccolta di Rime di diversi eccellenti Autori Bresciani* (Venice, 1553), p. 236, recounts that Cardinal Ridolfo (probably a member of the family of Pio da Carpi, related to the Gàmbaras, and a friend of Veronica's) gave him a copy of the poem in 1537, telling him that the stanzas were written by the sister of Monsignor [Uberto] Gàmbara and that a number of his (and Veronica's) contemporaries told him the poem was by Gàmbara; Luca Contile told him that Colonna herself had told him it was Veronica's, not hers. Some of the verses appear in a letter from Gàmbara to Lodovico Rosso (see *Dizionario letterario Bompiani*, vol. 6, p. 290). The poem is included in collections of Gàmbara's poetry from the first (Rizzardi, 1759). Nevertheless, in the monumental *New Vogel*, a canonical reference work on music, the error is repeated (vol. I, p. 566), with the stanzas attributed to Colonna. This error is probably due to Nicola Dorati, the composer who set those verses to music published as *Le stanze della sig.ra Vittoria Colonna marchesana di Pescara . . . a quattro voci* (Venice, 1570–1571). Dorati's, however, is not the original error; he followed a publication of Lodovico Dolce, *Stanze di diversi illustri poeti nuovamente raccolte dal Lodovico* (Venice, 1563) (see *Dizionario biografico degli italiani . . . "Dorati,"* p. 244). Because the volume of 1539 entitled *Rime* by Vittoria Colonna is catalogued in the National Union Catalogue under Vittoria's name and Veronica's name is not included, the researcher must be aware that the twenty-seven octave stanzas beginning "Quando miro la terra ornata e bella" are not by Colonna. The last stanza, however, might be problematical: According to the *New Vogel* entry on Dorati, this stanza was written by his son-in-law, Tomaso Burlamacchi. We have found no corroborative evidence for this. "Thus, following in your footsteps," seems to refer to Lorenzo, whose name Veronica invokes in the previous stanza.

31   Her sonnet in praise of Correggio begins, "Venerable waters, and you, blessed shores" ("Onorate acque, e voi, liti beati").

32   Veronese's *Vice and Virtue* is in the Frick Collection, New York. Correggio's *Vice* and *Virtue* are in the Musée Louvre, Paris.

Alla Illustrissima. S.
Donna Dianora
Sanseuerina.

Vittoria Colonna

2:1.
Enea Vico.
*Portrait of
Vittoria Colonna.*
Engraving,
16th century.
Österreichische
Nationalbibliothek,
Vienna. Photo,
Nationalbibliothek.

CHAPTER TWO

VITTORIA COLONNA
(1492–1547)

CRUEL FORTUNE

Vittoria Colonna, Marchesa di Pescara, lived close to the center of the great stage on which the sweeping events of war and peace in sixteenth-century Europe were enacted. Famous herself as a poet, as a woman of extraordinary intelligence, of profound religious piety, she was married to the man recognized as one of the greatest warrior-heroes of his time, and she was the esteemed, almost venerated, friend of the most prominent and influential artists and writers of the first half of the sixteenth century (plate I; figure 2.1).[1]

Vittoria was born at Marino, about twelve miles from Rome, in one of the several Colonna castles, the daughter of Fabrizio Colonna and Agnese di Montefeltro. She was betrothed for political reasons to Ferrante Francesco d'Avalos (figure 2.2) when they were both young children: her father had switched his loyalty from the French to the Spanish in the struggle between the Angevin and Aragon-ese claims to possession of Naples, and he wished to tighten the bonds between his family and the Spanish rulers. In 1501 the French sacked some of the Colonna possessions, and the family fled to the island of Ischia, in the Bay of Naples, where Costanza d'Avalos, her betrothed's aunt, welcomed them. Costanza was already a famous woman, celebrated for her successful defense of Ischia, the key to the Kingdom of Naples, against a fierce French attack,[2] and her court was known for its hospitality to artists and intellectuals.

Vittoria and Ferrante were married with great splendor in Naples in 1509, and for three years the couple lived glamorously amid the wealthy and powerful of the royal court and formed friendships with accomplished artists and writers such as Jacopo Sannazaro, Galeazzo di Tarsia, and Giovanni Angelo Cariteo. They remained childless, however, and in 1515 Vittoria proposed to her husband that they "adopt" his young cousin, Alfonso del Vasto, then thirteen years old. It is said that he had been a difficult child, unruly, refusing to study, interested only in games, until Vittoria took him in hand; under her care he changed so completely that she felt she had in a sense created him, and thus she could no longer be accused of being barren.[3] Alfonso became a leading military and political figure in the service of Charles V.

Ferrante's brilliant military career began in 1512 when he distinguished himself at the Battle of Ravenna, leading a cavalry attack against the artillery of Alfonso d'Este, then allied with France. The French were victorious, and Ferrante was taken prisoner, as was Vittoria's father. The news of this disaster[4] threw Vittoria into a swirling torrent of mixed emotions—love, anger, fear and reproach—that created one of her finest poems. In the form of a letter, it could hardly have cheered her imprisoned husband.

"My dearest lord," she begins, then, immediately revealing the tone and tenor of what he is about to read, she gives the modern reader an intimate glimpse into their relationship:

> *I write*
> *To tell you of my doubts and anxieties,*
> *of the bitter, painful anguish in which I live . . .*

She feels, the poem continues, as if "two raging serpents" are gnawing at her heart. Believing that prayer would protect her husband and her father, she had prayed for their safety, and found—almost blasphemously—that God had not been moved by her extravagant display of love.

> *There was no altar unstained*
> *by my tears, and no statue*
> *that did not receive my devotion.*
>
> *Now I think so much begging must have displeased them,*
> *so much crying, so many prayers,*
> *that even God was not pleased with love beyond measure.*

Ferrante's great bravery at Ravenna compares him with Hector or Achilles, she says bitterly,

> *But what is this to me*
> *Suffering and abandoned!*
> *. . .*
>
> *Some call for war; I only for peace,*
> *saying: it were enough for me if my marquis*
> *remained quietly at home with me.*
>
> *You do not hesitate to take risks,*
> *but we suffering women waiting,*
> *we are attacked by doubt and fear!*
>
> *You, frenzy-driven, thinking only*
> *of honor, unheeding of danger*
> *throw yourself against the enemy with loud shouts;*
>
> *We, timid-hearted, sad of face,*
> *we love you: the sister her brother*
> *the wife her husband, the mother her son.*[5]

Vittoria was living then at Ischia. In the most dramatic passage in this poem (and in her entire oeuvre) she describes to her husband how, as she was lying one day on the rocky shore of the island, nature brought her the first evil portent of his misfortune.

> *One day, while my body was lying somewhere*
> *on our rocky island (my soul is always with you),*
> *I saw a heavy fog rolling over the land*

And the atmosphere became
as black as soot; an evil owl,
dark and blind, sang that day;

The sea, made angry by Tifeo *
oh, horrible monster, boiled up,
and this was on Easter Day, in Spring;

The winds of Aeolus swept on shore,
the dolphins and sirens cried,
and the fish as well; the sea was like ink.

The sea-gods cried,
hearing Ischia say, "Today, Vittoria,
you have reached the limits of misfortune."

Vittoria ran to Costanza, who tried to comfort her, she relates, but she knew her husband's "daring that invites misfortune," his unwillingness to face facts, "never afraid to use his brave right arm." As she spoke,

there was the sad messenger,
with low voice giving us the bad news
which remembering stills burns within me.

Suddenly her mood changes from fear to reproach;

If Vittoria is what you wanted, I was close to you,
but you, leaving me, left her.
Everyone chases after the one that runs away.

Then again her mood changes. Vittoria writes to Ferrante of the husband-and-wife relationship as she thought it should be. At first it seems that she sees the wife's role as ancillary:

One must follow one's husband wherever he goes;
if he suffers, she must feel his pain,
if happy, then so is she. And if he dies, she dies.

But she swiftly corrects that impression, striking the rarely heard—at that time—note of equality between marriage partners:

What one risks, the other must risk,
equals in life, equals in death;
whatever happens to him, happens to her.

---

* Tifeo: Typhoeus, son of Gaea, goddess of the earth, a personification of terrifying natural forces.

She ends her letter not on a note of love, or fear, or sympathy for his plight, but on a note of reproach—this time, angry reproach mixed with sorrow:

> *You live happily and have no sorrow,*
> *thinking always of new successes;*
> *you do not care that you make me starve for your love,*
>
> *But I, indignant and sad,*
> *take care of your abandoned, lonely bed,*
> *mixing my hopes with tears,*
>
> *And with your happiness I temper my pain.* [6] (pp. 58 – 61)

Ferrante and Fabrizio were both released a few months after their capture on their promise never again to fight against the French, a promise immediately broken; in 1513 Ferrante participated in the Lombardy campaign as captain of the Spanish cavalry and took the city of Voghera, which he allowed to be sacked, with six hundred inhabitants massacred. During the next ten years he was almost constantly engaged in warfare and rarely at home with his wife, although he had time for perhaps two love affairs. One particularly distasteful story about his philandering concerns Isabella Cardona, wife of the viceroy of Naples and his comrade in arms. It is said that Ferrante took a string of Vittoria's pearls and presented them as a gift to Isabella. It is also said that Isabella returned them to their owner. Vittoria certainly knew of her husband's romantic wanderings; she told him, perhaps because of the pearl episode, "I could tolerate your giving away our things to satisfy your heart's desire, provided that you do not leave me" ("Sopportar ben potrei che l'haver nostro spargi per sodisfattion del tuo cuore, purchè l'esser tuo non mi furi").[7] She probably wanted to avoid public humiliation, but more than that, she loved her unfaithful husband; her aching pain drives the many love poems she addressed to him, creating a body of work that constitutes the first Petrarchist published *canzoniere* written by a woman. Yet, she was a realist, able to face honestly her problematic marriage; she remembers, Petrarch-like, the day she first saw him:[8]

> *That day when his beloved image entered my heart*
> *where it was to remain peacefully for many years*
> *in loving custody, such did it seem*
> *that I wondered whether it was of a man or god.*
>
> *In that instant, my soul bestowed on me*
> *that sweet freedom that I treasured,*
> *and heedless of itself it flamed with a joy*
> *from which it would never desire to turn away.*
>
> *I saw countless brilliant virtues sparkle all around*
> *and countless splendid rays*
> *adorn his face with a new beauty.*

Oh, how I prayed to heaven, and to love, that
this sweet moment might last forever,
but that wish was far from reality. (p. 61)

and again,

You know, my love, that I never tried to escape
from your gentle prison, nor to free myself
from your tender yoke around my neck; I never took from you
what my soul gave you, that first day.

Time has not changed my feelings
the tie is still as strong as when I tied it,
nor is my heart less loving
because of the bitter fruit that I have gathered;

You have seen that, compared to what your
sharp stabs can do to a loving, faithful heart,
death is nothing.

Although you have loosened that knot,
since I never wanted my liberty
it is now too late to recover it. (pp. 61 – 62)

With Ferrante away most of the time, winning the glory he coveted, rising to a command in the imperial army under Charles V, Vittoria lived mostly at Ischia. Although doubtless lonesome for her husband, her life was far from lonely, with attendance constantly at one or another great festive occasion in Rome or Naples. When the king of Poland married Donna Bona Sforza at the Aragonese court in Naples, she was in the procession to the church, accompanied by six ladies in waiting and six grooms splendidly attired. Vittoria wore a robe of brocaded crimson velvet, decorated with beaten gold, with a belt of the same and a headdress of wrought gold.[9]

The glimpse we get of Vittoria at this time offers a stunning contrast to the austere and pious life she led after Ferrante's death, the defining event that shaped her later years and her poetry. He died in 1525 as a result either of wounds suffered at the Battle of Pavia, or, more probably, of poisoning. As commander of the imperial infantry of the Spanish-Pontifical army at Pavia, he was largely responsible for the brilliant victory that drove the French out of Milan and took Francis I prisoner. He then became treacherously involved in a scheme to rid Italy of Spanish rule also, with the promise of himself becoming king of Naples. Vittoria wrote him to "consider well what you are doing, mindful of your pristine fame and estimation; and in truth, for my part, I care not to be the wife of a king, but rather to be joined to a faithful and loyal man, for it is not riches, titles, and kingdoms which can give true glory, infinite praise, and perpetual renown to noble spirits desirous of eternal fame; but faith, sincerity, and other virtues of the soul; and with these, man may rise higher than the highest kings not only in war, but in peace."[10]

Whether because of her counsel or for other reasons, Ferrante betrayed the schemers to Charles V. It seems likely that they took revenge: he died on 3 December 1525, nine months after Pavia; whatever his wounds, he had been well enough during those months to negotiate with the conspirators, who obviously believed him in condition to be useful to them, and to imagine his own future as king of Naples. In Rome, Vittoria received news that he was ill and hurried to reach him in Milan, but she was informed of his death when she reached Viterbo.

The man for whose love she had desperately, vainly yearned—"you make me starve for your love," she had written—and whom she had been willing to accept as he was in life, faithless, was now dead and finally hers alone. She was free to reinvent him in her art as the flawless hero—no more bitter last lines—but although her language belonged to Petrarch, like so much of sixteenth-century poetry, her poems are not only artful constructions, they are also sincere expressions of her feelings as a woman, faithful in life and death to one whom she helplessly loved.

So, Petrarch-style, for many years Vittoria celebrated and memorialized the inaccessible hero whom she called her "sun," the metaphor Petrarch used often for Laura. There was doubtless an element of self-dramatizing in Vittoria's view of herself as a female Petrarch, and probably also of pride, as the widow of a peerless Italian hero in an Italy overrun by foreign armies[11]: she let realism fade away in the bright glow of her memory.

> *There he was, my beautiful Sun, come back to us*
> *carrying royal spoils and treasure;*
> *oh, with what sadness my eyes remember*
> *those places where he made my days so radiant!*
>
> *Enveloped in palms and laurel*
> *his only prize was honor and glory,*
> *his fearless face and wise words*
> *everywhere inspired confidence.*
>
> *Won over by my entreaties, he showed me*
> *his beautiful wounds, and told me about where and when*
> *and how he won his brilliant victories.*
>
> *How much pain, now, how much joy, then!*
> *Weeping both for the one and the other I am fulfilled*
> *with the few sweet memories and the many bitter tears.* (p. 62)

When Ferrante died, Vittoria at first decided to enter a convent. Her brother, Ascanio, probably realizing the importance to the Colonna family of her growing prestige and influence in the Vatican through her close friendship with Gian Matteo Giberti, head of papal secretaries to Pope Clemente VII, persuaded her to live with him and his wife, Giovanna d'Aragona, in the castle at Marino where she was born. In time, she returned to Ischia, the place she loved most, and to which she returned again and again, and in the following decades she lived in various convents in Rome and elsewhere. She mourned her husband, who becomes godlike as heaven and earth celebrate his advent into the world.

> *Those bright lights that signal*
> *the birth of great intellects were blazing;*
> *sacred souls and chosen spirits*
> *competed to offer their most precious gifts.*
>
> *Nor were the graces and heaven sparing:*
> *the divine planets in their ordered places happily revealed*
> *their benevolent nature*
> *that instills virtue in rare beings.*
>
> *Never a day when the sun shown brighter,*
> *one heard angelic melodies in the air;*
> *such was nature's will and achievement.*
>
> *Earth held lilies and violets at her breast,*
> *the sea and the winds were calm*
> *when my beloved came into the world.* (p. 62)

Vividly, with filtered emotions, she recalled and extolled her "sun" in sonnet after sonnet, as if she had never written, "It were enough for me had my marquis remained quietly at home with me." [12]

After Ferrante's death, Vittoria led a life of almost monastic simplicity, writing, reading, and lending her aid to charitable endeavors. In the months after the hideous sack of Rome by the German, Spanish, and Imperial armies and mercenaries in May 1527, she was tireless in helping to alleviate the misery of the Roman people. [13] However simply she lived, though, she was surrounded by and in correspondence with the most intellectually glamorous figures of the period. Cardinal Pietro Bembo expressed his admiration for her critical acumen in a letter to Paolo Giovio: "She has given a more steady and well-founded judgment, and a more minute criticism, than I have seen on my poetry by the greatest masters. . . . She is certainly that great lady you have honorably described to the world more than once in your prose writings." [14]

As we have seen, Vittoria and Veronica Gàmbara exchanged laudatory verses. [15] In answer to Gàmbara's sonnet to her, Vittoria wrote,

> *Once again heaven embellishes our age* *
> *with ancient glory, and annuls its ruin*
> *since it sends its spirit among us*
> *and beauty thus wins a double victory.*
>
> *I write of you, beautiful woman,*

---

* This sonnet is Colonna's response to Gàmbara's sonnet beginning, "Oh wise and lovely woman" (*O de la nostra etade unica gloria*); see p. 63.

worthy of immortality, to whom all bow,
who transcends beauty and whose soul
will live in every memory.

Radiant spirits will build for you an everlasting altar,
paper will be the marble, ink the gold,
so that truth may command your eternal praise.

With the former or the latter
death and the cruel sting of time cannot take from you
the great rich treasure of immortal fame. (p. 63)

In *Orlando Furioso*, Ariosto, aware of many gifted women among his contemporaries, singles out Vittoria to praise in his stanzas on great women in history:

I will choose one for whom
the others will feel no envy,
they will not be hurt if I omit them
and name only her,
for this woman has not only made herself
immortal with her graceful pen—I hear none better—
but those of whom she speaks or writes
she brings back from the grave to immortality.

As Phoebus adorns his sister
with light brighter then Venus or Maia
or any other star that moves
with the firmament or turns on itself, *
he makes her of whom I speak creative above all others,
and breathes into her such sweetness,
and gives such strength to her high-borne words
that it seems another sun shines above.

Vittoria is her name; as everyone knows,
she was born to victories, and wherever she goes
she bears the trophies and triumphs
won by father and husband.
She is another Artemisia, celebrated
for her loyalty to Mausolus, yet,
how much greater and more beautiful is her work
which does not bury a man but raises him to heaven.
. . .
Women, I declare, in brief, that in every age
many of you earned your way into history

---

* Phoebus = Apollo; his sister is Artemis; Maia is one of the seven sisters of the Pleiades.

but jealous male writers
hid you from history's view:
No longer.
Now you yourselves create your immortality. (pp. 63 – 64)

Vittoria's most famous friend was Michelangelo Buonarroti (figure 2.3). They met during the 1530s and formed a relationship that their letters to each other and his poems to her reveal to have been devoted, perfectly platonic, and, on his side, ardent.[16] Reading Michelangelo's poems, one feels Vittoria had more impact on him than he on her. In the following sonnet he imagines that just as he creates a work of art from rough material, so Vittoria re-creates him from the coarse being he was at birth:

If the spiritual aspect of the face
and gesture of the subject has been well conceived,
it is possible, with great effort, even with a poor sketch,
to give life to stone, for it is not a matter of skill.

Nor is it otherwise, working on plain paper;
before one is ready to take up a brush,
the most highly gifted and keen among artists
verifies and checks, then begins his composition.

So it was that I, a model of little value
at my birth, was reborn, wonderfully improved
because of you, great and worthy lady.

If your kindness increases my powers and files down
my arrogance, what penitence must my fiery nature expect
in order to punish and teach me. (p. 64)

In another sonnet Michelangelo reveals his sympathy with the Italian Reform movement, with which Vittoria also was in sympathy for a number of years, as we shall see: he refers to faith alone as the key to salvation, one of the basic tenets of the Protestant Reform.

There is nothing on earth more base or vile
than I know myself to be, without You.
Wherefore I beg forgiveness
for the exalted ambition of my weak and tired efforts.

Oh my Lord, give me that chain
that links all heavenly gifts,
Faith, I say, toward which I turn and urge myself;
nor, guilty as I am, can I be fully redeemed without it.

2:3.
Frans Floris
(studio). *Portrait
of Michelangelo
Buonarroti.*
ca. 1550.
Kunsthistorisches
Museum,
Vienna. Photo,
Museum.

> This is the great and most rare
> of all gifts, and all the greater for, without it,
> there is no peace or happiness in the world.

> Since You gave fully of Your blood,
> of what use will be the gift of Your mercy
> if heaven is not opened to us with another key? (pp. 64 – 65)

It seems certain that Michelangelo made at least one likeness of Vittoria. References to a carving or a drawing or painting of her are clearly implied in some of his poems, as in the following:

> Although I am quite imperfect, noble lady,
> unworthy of the gift of your great courtesy,
> I tried, at first, with all my heart
> to respond with equal gallantry.

> But seeing that my own virtue could not open
> the path that leads to that goal,
> I have become wiser for my error
> and my arrogant boldness begs pardon.

Now I see very well how mistaken I was to believe
that my frail, weak effort could be compared
with the divine grace that pours down from you like rain.

Skill, and art, and effort surrender;
a heavenly gift, even with countless attempts,
cannot be equaled by mortal powers. (p. 65)

The artist had planned to portray himself and Vittoria together, as implied by the sonnet he wrote after her death that begins, "How can it be, Lady," in which he writes that art triumphs over nature:

Perchance to both of us I may give a long life
in colors or in stone
representing the expression and face of each

so that, for ages after I am gone
it may be seen how beautiful you were,
and how wise I was to love you as I did. (p. 65)

In addition to sonnets addressed to her, Michelangelo courted her with several drawings, including *The Crucifixion* (figure 2.4) in which he conceives Christ as still living, his head up, defiant with the spirit of Michelangelo himself, and a *Pietà* (figure 2.5) with a complex composition in which the triangular cross is echoed by the figural relationships.[17] When Vittoria received *The Crucifixion* she wrote to the artist,

> To the one and only Maestro Michelangelo and my very special friend,
>
> I have received your message and have seen the crucifixion, which surely has destroyed in my memory any others that I have ever seen, nor is it possible to see a better, more alive, more completely achieved image and certainly I could never describe how subtly and marvelously it is done, for which reason I have decided that I do not want one done by some other hand, so please let me know if this is by someone else, in which case, never mind. In any case, if it is yours, I would like to keep it, but if it is not, and you wish to have it copied by one of your assistants, we will talk about that beforehand since knowing the difficulty of making a copy, I would prefer for your assistant to make something else; but if it is yours, please forgive me for not returning it. I have looked at it carefully in the lamplight and with a magnifying glass and in the mirror, and I have never seen a more perfect drawing.
> At your service,
> *La Marchesa di Pescara* [18]

Michelangelo's drawing might have been the inspiration for two of Vittoria's sonnets on the Crucifixion, which were much later set to music by Pietro Vinci.[19]

2:4.
Michelangelo
Buonarroti.
The Crucifixion.
ca. 1540. The
British Museum,
London. Photo,
Museum.

Opening your sacred wounded arms on the cross, Oh Lord
You opened heaven, purgatory, tombs, and monuments,
the veil of the ancient temple,
as well as the shadows and substance of all things.[20]

You illuminate our minds,
once unknowing, and ridding them of dross,
You filled them with the ardent love
that opened Your sacred scriptures.

> *You showed us the sweetness in your authority*
> *and the goodness hidden by our reverent fear*
> *in those precepts of severe and just laws.*
>
> *Oh longed-for peace! Oh blessed*
> *happy days, oh, bountiful mercy*
> *that opened to us grace, light, love!* (pp. 65 – 66)

In the second of the sonnets on the Crucifixion set to music she seems to be looking at the drawing and playing on the word *dissegno* (drawing, design, plan) as she writes:

> *Our mighty Lord hangs from the cruel cross*
> *for our wicked sins, and His sad heart*
> *takes comfort not in worldly values*
> *but only in those virtues that come directly from Him.*
>
> *With divine words He gave us a beautiful design*
> *for living in truth, and colored it*
> *with His own blood; He made works of love*
> *the reason for forfeiting his life.*
>
> *May the soul be kindled and the mind*
> *be fulfilled with light, and may both*
> *strengthen and reinforce our cleansed desires.*
>
> *From His harsh wounds a thousand arrows*
> *pierce me and thus, truly feeling them,*
> *I gain immortal life from His death.*[21] (p. 66)

We do not have poems by Vittoria addressed specifically to Michelangelo, but we know that around 1540 she sent him a collection of her verses. The first edition of her poetry was published in 1538.

In the first half of the sixteenth century, many Italian intellectuals were deeply concerned with what they perceived as abusive practices of the Church, especially with regard to the selling of indulgences, and were accordingly responsive to the Protestant Reform in Germany, though very few were willing to break with the Church entirely. Around 1530, in Naples, Vittoria met Juan de Valdés, a Spaniard who became a leader in the Italian Reform movement. She and her friend Giulia Gonzaga, Duchess of Trajetto, formed a close friendship with Valdés and with his most important follower, Bernardino Ochino, a Capuchin friar who became vicar of his order. Ochino became the most famous religious orator in Italy, attracting thousands to hear him preach his Reform views. In April 1537 Vittoria went to Ferrara, possibly in connection with Ochino's plan to establish a Capuchin convent there.[22]

Ferrara was a center of humanist culture, and Vittoria seems to have relaxed her ascetic ways there, attending the kind of musical and literary events that made the Ferrara court among the most celebrated in the sixteenth century. It was also a center

**2:5.
Michelangelo
Buonarroti.
Pietà. ca. 1540.
Isabella Stewart
Gardner
Museum,
Boston. Photo,
Museum.**

of Reformist thought; Calvin himself had been there the year before. The Duke of
Ferrara at that time, Ercole II, had married a daughter of France's Louis XII, Renée de
Valois, who became a Protestant, and their child, Eleanora, was in Vittoria's arms
when she was baptized. It was at Ferrara that Vittoria met Marguerite d'Angoulême,
Queen of Navarre, and sister of Francis I, with whom she formed an intellectual

friendship.[23] Marguerite addressed a poem to Vittoria that, with its reference to the "elected," a basic Reformist tenet, reveals their Reformist leanings.

> *Happy are you who with an ardent spirit*
> *have returned to the Lord;*
> *you illuminate all those who are gathered in Him*
> *Who turns His intent gaze upon us.*
>
> *Alas for me, who follows*
> *with slow, infirm steps,*
> *I disdained Him in vain, false and silly desires,*
> *and now my soul repents with bitter sighs.*
>
> *Pray for me, you who are one of the elected,*
> *so that the king of Heaven may raise me up with His hand*
> *and welcome me to his bosom.*
>
> *And since you have seen the true light,*
> *help others know that their hopes are not in vain*
> *so that they may feel enlightened and serene.* (p. 66)

When Vittoria sent a bound volume of her poems to Marguerite, it was intercepted by the head of the French police because Marguerite was known to have Reformist views. The agent found expressions in Vittoria's poems that he considered contrary to the true Christian faith and spoke to Francis I about them, but the king merely laughed, "knowing the good name of the Marchesa di Pescara." [24] More important perhaps than her "good name" was the still tolerant attitude of the Church toward the Reform; even Pope Paul III was friendly to the Reformists at the time of his election to the papacy in 1534. In the following years however the divisive forces that threatened the very existence of the Church began to emerge more clearly. Vittoria wrote a sonnet addressed to Paul III expressing her concern:

> *I see your net, Oh Peter,*
> *so full of mud and seaweed*
> *that overwhelmed by waves from without or within,*
> *it could break and endanger the boat*
>
> *Which strangely light and empty,*
> *rides quickly over the choppy sea,*
> *pitching and rolling from stern to bow, from one shore*
> *to another, in grave danger, skirting disaster.*
>
> *Your excellent successor, elected with wisdom,*
> *with his hand and his heart*
> *tries to guide it to port,*

But against his power is opposed
the malice of others: everyone knows that
without your help he will work in vain. (p. 67)

The threat, of course, was very real and it soon became evident that the Church would not continue in its tolerance. Ochino then broke with Catholicism completely, adopting an independent Protestantism and as a result the Capuchin Order—which Vittoria had used her influence to protect—was now denounced for supporting heresy. In 1542 Vittoria severed her relationship with Ochino and his Reform teachings. Under threat of death for heresy Ochino had fled to Zurich, and Vittoria, advised by her new friend, Cardinal Reginald Pole, sent his last letter to her to Cardinal Cervini, together with a letter in which she wrote that she was following Pole's advice that "if a letter or anything else should come to me from Fra Bernardino, I had better send it to your most reverend Lordship, without answering it." In a postscript she adds, "It grieves me exceedingly that the more he thinks to excuse himself, the more he accuses himself, and the more he thinks to save others from the shipwreck, the more he exposes them to the deluge, being himself out of the Ark which secures and saves." [25]

As the years passed, Vittoria turned increasingly to religion, and her poetry became almost entirely spiritual. In some of her most mature verses she still recalls her sadness at the loss of Ferrante, her "sun," but now she transforms her earthly love into spiritual love of the sublime "Sun," as in this poem addressed to the Virgin, one of the sonnets set to music by Vinci.

Oh Virgin most chaste
who lives in the presence of the
true Sun whose eternal light
you saw even here on this vile earth,

As a man you saw Him and also God.
Heavenly spirits full of light surrounded you
and their brilliance illuminated you
as your great gift was bestowed.

Immortal God hidden in a mortal veil
You worshipped and nourished Him as your Son,
you loved Him as a wife, and honored Him as a Father;

Beg His favor then that my sadness
may be turned to happiness, and you, Lady of Heaven,
may you show yourself to me as a Mother. [26]   (p. 67)

In her last poems she is completely concerned with her relationship to God:

When may come the day, Lord, fully and always
centered on You, that I will see you with my mind's eye?

For while it wanders wildly in hazy fog
it may rest in the true light.

Sometimes I see a joyous image,
overshadowed by your presence in my heart;
the vivid colors, although flashing
are yet not bright and fully clear.

Oh, let your wounded hand tear away the veil that
for twenty years has kept me in many ways—
and still keeps me—in this blind error;

May my soul no longer be
reined by darkness or spurred by light, so that
freed, it may see the great Sun in the most blessed heaven. (pp. 67 – 68)

Vittoria's reference to "twenty years . . . in this blind error" seems to refer to the sympathy she had felt for the Reform movement. Now, apparently repentant, she became increasingly austere in her mode of living, starving herself and practicing bodily injury and might have died had not Cardinal Reginald Pole dissuaded her from such rigorous extremes. As her life drew to a close she prayed for death.

Oh, Lord, in that impenetrable light
almost in thick darkness you hide yourself
but you spread your divine grace and radiant shafts
from the eternal light, the source of all good;

Your one gesture creates all things and
leads you to one end, and can make and destroy
the universe; in the profound depths of the earth
and in heaven you are the true monarch.

Look at me again, I beg you, afflicted with grief
in this terrestrial world, and with your everlasting zeal,
attend my torment.

Take my soul now into your realm so that
at least from far it might be warmed by your great light,
and close, I might see again my little one. (p. 68)

Vittoria's last years were filled with sadness with the death of her adopted son, Alfonso del Vasto, and others who were her long-time friends.[27] She died on 25 February 1547.

Vittoria Colonna in her life and poetry exemplified the dominant values of the aristocratic society to which she belonged. Although she writes of equality between husband and wife, this was an ideal, which, like others—courage, honor, loyalty for men, chastity and family devotion for women—it never occurred to her to question. Nevertheless, our reading of her poems leads us to believe that she was a far more passionate woman than previous writers have suggested: physically passionate in her love for her husband; spiritually passionate in her love for Christ.

Alan Bullock has divided her poems into three categories, two of them thematic and one formal: love, spiritual, and epistolary. [28] The thematic poems correspond with three chronological phases: in the first she writes about her suffering at the loss of her husband; in the second the suffering is less apparent in favor of praising him; in the last phase, her most mature work expresses her profound experience of religion. There is an evident self-consciousness in her verse that suggests something of Mannerism in visual art, particularly the deliberate choosing of a model to emulate and the use of strong contrasts: men and women, love and loss, and sudden changes of feeling. Some of her best verse is in the epistolary poem to her husband, in the passage describing the storm, and in the stanza where we see her real longing for her husband as she considers his abandoned bed.

POEMS IN THE ORIGINAL ITALIAN*

Vittoria Colonna

Ecelso mio signor, questa ti scrivo
per te narrar fra quante dubbie voglie,
fra quanti aspri martir dogliosa io vivo.

Non sperava da te tormento e doglie;
ché se 'l favor del Ciel t'era propizio,
perdute non sarian l'opime spoglie.

Non credeva un Marchese ed un Fabrizio,
l'un sposo e l'altro padre, al mio dolore
fosser sì crudo e dispietato inizio;

del padre la pietà, di te l'amore
come doi angui rabidi affamati
rodendo stavan sempre nel mio core.

Credeva più benigni avere i fati,
ché tanti sacrifici e voti tanti
il rettor de l'Inferno avrian placati;

non era tempio alcun che de'miei pianti
non fosse madefatto, né figura
che non avesse de'miei voti alquanti.

Io credo lor dispiacque tanta cura,
tanto mio lacrimar, cotanti voti;
ché spiace a Dio l'amor è fuor di misura,

benchè li fatti tuoi al Ciel sian noti,
e quei del padre mio volan tant'alto
che mai di fama e gloria saran voti.

Ma or in questo periglioso assalto,
in questa pugna orrenda e dispietata
che m'ha fatto la mente e'l cor di smalto,

la vostra gran virtù s'è dimostrata
d'un Ettor, d'un Achille. ma che fia
questo per me, dolente, abbandonata!

---

* Numbers in footnotes at the end of Vittoria Colonna's poems refer to numbering by Alan Bullock, ed., *Rime/Vittoria Colonna* (Bari, 1982).

Sempre dubbiosa fu la mente mia:
chi me vedeva mesta giudicava
che me offendesse absenzia o gelosia,

ma io, misera me! sempre pensava
l'ardito tuo valor, l'animo audace,
con che s'accorda mal fortuna prava.

Altri chiedevan guerra, io sempre pace,
dicendo: assai mi fia se'l mio marchese
meco quieto nel suo stato giace.

Non noce a voi seguir le dubbie imprese;
m'a noi, dogliose afflitte, ch' aspettando
semo da dubbio e da timore offese;

Voi, spinti dal furor, non ripensando
ad altro ch'ad onor, contr' il periglio
solete con gran furia andar gridando.

Noi, timide nel cor, meste nel ciglio
semo per voi; e la sorella il fratre,
la sposa il sposo vuol, la madre il figlio;

ma io, misera! cerco e sposo e patre,
e frate e figlio; sono in questo loco
sposa, figlia, sorella e vecchia matre.

Son figlia per natura, e poi, per gioco
di legge natural, sposa; sorella
e madre son per amoroso foco.

Mai venia peregrin, da cui novella
non cercassi saper, cosa per cosa,
per far la mente mia gioiosa e bella,

quando ad un punto il scoglio, dove posa
il corpo mio chè già lo spirto è teco,
vidi coprir di nebbia tenebrosa,

e l'aria tutta mi pareva un speco
di caligine nera; il mal bubone
cantò in quel giorno tenebroso e cieco.

Il lago a cui Tifeo le membra oppone,
boglieva tutto, oh spaventevol mostro!
il dì di Pasca in la gentil stagione;

era coi venti Eulo al lito nostro,
piangeano le sirene e li delfini,
i pesci ancor; il mar pareva inchiostro;

Piangeano intorno a quel gli dei marini
sentend' ad Ischia dir: "Oggi, Vittoria,
sei stata di disgrazia a li confini,

bench' in salute ed in eterna gloria
sia converso il dolor: ché 'l padre e sposo
salvi son, benché presi con memoria."

Alor con volto mesto e tenebroso,
piangendo, ala magnanima Costanza
narrai l'augurio mesto e spaventoso.

Ella me confortò, com'è sua usanza,
dicendo: "No'l pensar, ch' un caso strano
sarebbe, sendo vinta tal possanza."

"Non può da li sinistri esser lontano,"
diss'io, "un ch'è animoso a li gran fatti,
non temendo menar l'ardita mano.

"Chi d'ambiduo costor trascorre gli atti,
vedrà tanto d'ardir pronto e veloce:
non han con la Fortuna tregua o patti."

Ed ecco il nuncio rio con mesta voce
dandoci chiaro tutto il mal successo,
che la memoria il petto ognor mi coce.

Se vittoria volevi, io t'era apresso,
ma tu, lasciando me, lasciasti lei,
e cerca ognun seguir chi fugge d'esso.

Nocque a Pompeo, come saper tu dèi,
lasciar Cornelia, ed a Catone ancora
nocque lasciando Marzia in pianti rei.

Seguir si deve il sposo dentro e fora,
s'egli pate affanno, ella patisca,
se lieto lieta; e se vi more, mora;

a quel che arrisca l'un, l'altro s'arrisca;
equali in vita, equali siano in morte,
e ciò che avien a lui a lei sortisca.

Felice, Mitridate, e tua consorte,
che faceste equalmente di fortuna
i fausti giorni e le disgrazie torte!

Tu vivi lieto, e non hai doglia alcuna;
ché, pensando di fama il novo acquisto,
non curi farmi del tuo amor digiuna;

ma io, con volto disdegnoso e tristo
serbo il tuo letto abbandonato e solo,
tenendo con la speme il dolor misto,

E col vostro gioir tempr'il mio duolo. * (pp. 41 – 43)

~

Quel giorno che l'amata immagin corse
al cor, come chi in pace star devea
molt' anni in caro albergo, tal parea,
che l'umano e'l divin mi pose in forse.

In un momento alor l'alma le porse
la dolce libertà, che mi godea,
e se stessa obliando lieta ardea
in lei, dal cui voler mai non si torse.

Mille accese virtuti a quella intorno
scintillar vidi, e mille chiari rai
far di nova beltate il volto adorno.

Ahi con che affetto Amore e'l Ciel pregai
che fosse eterno sì dolce soggiorno!
Ma fu la speme al ver lungi d'assai.† (pp. 43 – 44)

~

Amor, tu sai che già mai torsi il piede
dal carcer tuo soave, né disciolsi
dal dolce giogo il collo, né ti tolsi
quanto dal primo dì l'alma ti diede;

⦿ Track 6,
Reading 5

Tempo non cangiò mai l'antica fede;
il nodo è stretto ancor com'io l'avolsi;
nè per il frutto amar ch'ognor ne colsi
l'alta cagion men cara al cor mi riede.

---

* 1.   † 85.

Vist'hai quanto in un petto fido e ardente
può oprar quel caro tuo più acuto dardo
contra del cui poter Morte non valse.

Fa' omai da te che'l nodo si rallente,
ch'a me di libertà già mai non calse;
anzi, di ricovrarla or mi par tardo. * (p. 44)

~

● Track 7,
Reading 6

Qui fece il mio bel Sole a noi ritorno,
di regie spoglie carco e ricche prede:
ahi con quanto dolor l'occhio rivede
quei lochi ove mi fea già chiaro il giorno!

Di mille glorie alor cinto d'intorno
e d'onor vero, in la più alta sede,
facean de l'opreudite intera fede
l'ardito volto, el parlar saggio e adorno.

Vinto dai prieghi miei poi ne mostrava
le belle cicatrici, e'l tempo e'l modo
dele vittorie sue tante e sì chiare.

Quanta pena or mi dà, gioia mi dava,
e'n questo e'n quel pensier piangendo godo
tra poche dolci e assai lacrime amare. † (p. 45)

~

Fiammeggiavano i vivi lumi chiari
ch' accendon di valor gli alti intelletti
l'anime gloriose e i spirti eletti
davan ciascun a prova i don più rari.

Non fur le Grazie parche o i Cieli avari:
gli almi pianeti, in propria sede eretti,
mostravan lieti quei benigni aspetti
ch'instillan la virtù nei cor preclari.

Più chiaro giorno non aperse il sole,
s'udian per l'aere angelici concenti,
quanto volse natura, in l'opre ottenne.

Col sen carco di gigli e di viole
stava la terra, e'l mar tranquillo e i venti
quando il bel lume mio nel mondo venne. ‡ (p. 46)

---

* 45.   † 61   ‡ 16.

Di novo il Cielo de l'antica gloria
orna la nostra etate, e sua ruina
prescrive, poscia che tra noi destina
spirto, c'ha di beltà doppia vittoria.

Di voi, ben degna d'immortal'istoria,
bella donna ragiono, a cui s'inchina,
chi più di bello ottiene, e la divina
interna parte vince ogni memoria.

Faranvi i chiari spirti eterno tempio,
la carta il marmo fia, l'inchiostro l'oro,
ché 'l ver constringe lor sempre a lodarvi.

Morte col primo, or col secondo, ed empio
morso il tempo, non ponno omai levarvi
d'immortal fama il bel ricco tesoro. * (pp. 46– 47)

Sceglieronne una; e sceglierolla tale,   *Ariosto*
che superato avrà l'invidia in modo,
che nessun'altra potrà avere a male,
se l'altre taccio, e se lei sola lodo.
Quest'una ha non pur sé fatta immortale
col dolce stil che il meglior non odo;
ma può qualunque di cui parli o scriva
trar del sepolcro, e far ch'eterno viva.

Come Febo la candida sorella
fa più di luce adorna, e più la mira,
che Venere o che Maia o ch'altra stella
che va col cielo o che da sé si gira:
così facundia, più ch'all'altre, a quella
di ch'io vi parlo, e più dolcezza spira;
e dà tal forza all'alte sue parole,
ch'orna a' dì nostri il ciel d'un altro sole.

Vittoria è 'l nome; e ben conviensi a nata
fra le vittorie, et a chi, o vada o stanzi.
di trofei sempre e di trionfi ornata,
la vittoria abbia seco, o dietro o inanzi.
Questa è un'altra Artemisia, che lodata

---

* 13. This sonnet is Colonna's response to Gàmbara's sonnet beginning *"O de la nostra etade*
unica gloria."

fu di pietà verso il suo Mausolo; anzi
tanto maggior, quanto è più assai bell'opra
che por sotterra un uom, trarlo di sopra.

. . .

    Donne, io conchiudo in somma, ch'ogni etate
molte ha di voi degne d'istoria avute;
ma per invidia di scrittori state
non sète dopo morte conosciute:
il che più non sarà, poi che voi fate
per voi stesse immortal vostra virtute . . . * (pp. 47 – 48)

~

Michelangelo
● **Track 8,**
Reading 7

    Se ben concetto ha la divina parte
il volto e gli atti d'alcun, po' di quello
doppio valor, con breve e vil modello
dà vita a' sassi, e non è forza d'arte.

    Né altrimenti in più rustiche carte,
anz'una pronta man prenda 'l pennello
fra 'dotti ingegni il più accorto e bello
pruova e rivede, e sue storie comparte.

    Simil di me model di poca istima
mie parto fu, per cosa alta e perfetta
da voi rinascer po' donna alta e degna.

    S' el poco accresce, e 'l mie superchio lima
vostra mercé, qual penitenza aspetta
mie fiero ardor, se mi gastiga e 'nsegna. † (p. 48)

~

    Non è più bassa o vil cosa terrena
di quel che, senza te, mi sento e sono;
onde a l'alto desir chiede perdono
la debile mie propria e stanca lena.

    Deh, porgi, Signor, quella catena
che seco annoda ogni celeste dono;
la fede, dico, a che mi stringo e sprono,
né, mie colpe, n' ho grazia intiera e piena.

    Tanto mi fie maggior, quante più raro
il don de' doni, e maggior fia se, senza,
pace e contento il mondo in sé non have.

---

* *Orlando Furioso*, canto XXXVII, stanzas 16–18, 23.
† 236. Poems by Michelangelo are from *Enzo Noé Girardi, ed., Rime di Michelangelo Buonarroti* (Bari, 1967). The numbers follow Girardi's numbering.

Po' che non fusti del tuo sangue avaro,
che sarà di tal don la tua clemenza,
*se 'l ciel non s'apre a noi con altra chiave? * (pp. 48 – 49)*

Per esser manco, alta signora, indegno
del don di vostra immensa cortesia,
prima, all'incontro a quella, usar la mia
con tutto il cor volse 'l mio basso ingegno.

Ma visto poi, c'ascender a quel segno
proprio valor non è c'apra la via,
perdon domanda la mia audace ria,
e del fallir più saggio ognor divegno.

E veggio ben com'erra s'alcun crede
la grazia, che da voi divina piove,
pareggi l'opra mia caduca e frale.

L'ingegno, l'arte, la memoria cede;
c'un don celeste non con mille pruove
pagar del suo può già chi è mortale. † (pp. 49 – 50)

Dunche posso ambo noi dar lunga vita
in qual sil modo o di colore o sasso,
di noi sembrando l'uno e l'altro volto;

⦿ Track 9,
Reading 8

Si che mill'anni dopo la partita,
quante voi bella fusti, e quant'io lasso
si veggia, e com' amarvi i' non fu' stolto. ‡ (p. 50)

Le braccia aprendo in croce, e l'alme e pure
piaghe, largo, Signor, apristi il Cielo,
il Limbo, i sassi, i monumenti, e 'l velo
del tempio antico, e l'ombre, e le figure.

Vittoria Colonna
⦿ Track 10,
Reading 9

Le menti umane infin alora oscure
illuminasti, e dileguando il gielo
le riempiesti d'un ardente zelo
ch'aperse poi le sacre Tue scritture.

Mostrossi il dolce imperio e la bontade
che parve ascosa in quei tanti precetti
de l'aspra e giusta legge del timore;

---

* 289.   † 159.   ‡ 239.

Oh desiata pace! Oh benedetti
giorni felici! Oh liberal pietade
che ne scoperse grazia, lume, amore! * (pp. 51 – 52)

⁓

Pende l'alto Signor sul duro legno
per le nostre empie colpe, e 'l tristo core
non prende tal virtù da quel valore,
che pender sol da Lui diventi degno.

Con divine parole il bel dissegno
fece Ei del viver vero, e poi colore
gli die' col sangue, e che de l'opra amore
fosse cagione ne dà Se stesso in pegno.

Viva di fiamma l'alma, e l'intelletto
di luce appaghi, e con questa e con quella
erga e rinforzi il purgato desire;

Vengano a mille in me calde quadrella
da l'aspre piaghe, ond'io con vero effetto
prenda vita immortal dal Suo morire. † (p. 52)

⁓

Felice voi, che con gli spirti ardenti
avete el core mio Signor rivolto,
ed accendete ognuno a star raccolto
in Lui che verso noi tien gli occhi intenti!

Marguerite
d'Angoulême,
Queen of Navarre

Misera me, che a passi infermi e lenti
seguito ho lui che me sprezzato ha molto;
ond'or del van desio fallace e stolto
l'alma si pente e trae sospir cocenti.

Pregate voi, che degli eletti siete,
per me de'Cielo il Re che la sua mano
mi tenga sopra e mi racolga in seno;

E poichè scorto il vero lume avete,
fate che ancor non sia per gli altri vano;
ma che il provi ciascun chiaro e sereno. ‡ (p. 54)

⁓

---

* 94.   † 6.

‡ From Ludovico Domenichi, *Rime diversi d'alcune nobilissime e virtuosissime donne*
(Lucca, 1559), p. 11.

Veggio d'alga e di fango omai sì carca,
Pietro, la rete tua, che se qualche onda
di fuor l'assale, o intorno la circonda,
potria spezzarsi, e a rischio andar la barca.

La qual non come suol leggera e scarca
sovra'l turbato mar corre a seconda,
ma in poppa e in prora, a l'una e a l'altra sponda
è grave sì ch' a gran periglio varca.

Il tuo buon successor ch'alta cagione
dirittamente elesse, e cor e mano
move sovente per condurla a porto;

Ma contra il voler suo ratto s'oppone
l'altrui malizia, onde ciascun s'è accorto
ch'egli senza 'l tuo aiuto adopra invano. * (pp. 54 – 55)*
⁓

Vergine pura, che dai raggi ardenti
del vero Sol ti godi eterno giorno
il cui bel lume in questo vil soggiorno
tenne i begli occhi tuoi paghi e contenti,

Uomo il vedesti, e Dio, quando i lucenti
suoi spirti fer l'albergo umile adorno
di chiari lumi, e timidi d'intorno
i tuoi ministri al grande officio intenti.

Immortal Dio nascosto in mortal velo
L'adorasti Signor, Figlio Il'nudristi
L'amasti Sposo, e L'onorasti Padre

Prega Lui dunque che i miei giorni tristi
ritorn in lieti, e tu Donna del Cielo
vogli in questo desìo mostrarti Madre. † (p. 55)*
⁓

Quando sia il dì, Signor, che'l mio pensiero
intento e fisso in Voi sempre, Vi veggia?
Ché mentre fra le nebbie erra e vaneggia
mal si puote fermar nel lume vero.

Scorgo sovente un bel dissegno altero
ch'entro'l mio cor lo spirto Vostro ombreggia,

---

* 116. † 100.

ma quel vivo volor, se ben lampeggia
pur non si mostra mai chiaro ed intero.

Deh! squarci omai la man piagata il velo
che'n questo cieco error già quattro lustri *
fra varie tempre ancor mi tiene involta,

Onde non più da rai foschi od illustri
s'affreni o sproni l'alma, ma disciolta
miri il gran Sol nel più beato Cielo! † (pp. 55 – 56)

Signor, che 'n quella inaccessibil luce
quasi in alta caligine T'ascondi,
ma viva grazia e chiari rai diffondi
da l'alto specchio ond' ogni ben traluce;

Genera il tutto ed a fine conduce
un sol cenno Tuo che puri e mondi
far può gli affetti altrui di sozzi immondi
pur che l'uom segue Te, suo vero Duce.

Risguardame, i prego, in questo centro
terrestre afflitta, e come sempre sòle
la Tua pietade al mio scampo proveggia;

Tirann' omai tanto al Tuo regno dentro,
ch' almen lontan mi scaldi il Tuo gran sole,
e poi vicin il picciol mio riveggia. ‡ (p. 56)

---

* A *lustro* is five years.   † 90.   ‡ 88.

NOTES

1   For Vittoria's husband Ferrante Francesco d'Avalos, see the *Dizionario biografico degli italiani* (Rome, 1960–), vol. 4, pp. 623–626. The bibliography on Vittoria is vast. See the comprehensive bibliography published on the Internet, <http://www.iso.gmu.edu/~emoody/vcbiblio.html>, by Ellen Moody.

2   The d'Avalos family held title to the island of Ischia. Costanza's father had been murdered in 1495, her brother killed in the war between Spain and France for control of Naples. She thus became governor (*castellana*). Was she the mysteriously smiling Mona Lisa? According to Benedetto Croce, Costanza was the woman to whom Aeneas Irpino, a contemporary poet, addressed a number of love sonnets, two of which refer to Costanza's portrait having been painted by Leonardo da Vinci; see "Un Canzoniere d'amore per Costanza d'Avalos, Duchessa di Francavilla," *Atti della Accademia Pontoniana* XXXIII, series II, vol. VIII (Naples, 1903), pp. 132–140. Arturo Venturi identified the woman in Irpino's poems as Da Vinci's *Mona Lisa* (*Enciclopedia Italiana*, vol. 20, p. 870).

3   The "adoption" was not formal. As for her "recreating" Alfonso, she is quoted in Pietro Ercole Visconti, *Le rime di Vittoria Colonna* (Rome, 1840), p. lxxviii, and Dennis James McAuliffe, "Vittoria Colonna, the Formative Years, 1492–1525" (Ph.D. dissertation, New York University, 1978), p. 39, "Già sterile non posso esser chiamata, quando ho del mio ingegno generato costui" ("Now I cannot be called sterile since from my own mind I have created him"), rather immodestly albeit inadvertently referring to Athena's creation from the mind of Zeus! Alfonso remained very dear to her; see note 32.

4   The Battle of Ravenna is one of the most famous in Italian military history because of the extraordinary number of men killed: according to the record, twenty thousand men died on the battlefield. In proportion to the size of armies, it can be compared to the Second Battle of the Marne in July 1918.

5   Writing "we," Vittoria refers to women in general, not to her own fears, revealing the awareness of shared concerns among women.

6   Vittoria is greatly indebted in this poem to Latin sources, particularly to Virgil, as shown in detail in Rocco Mazzone, *Vittoria Colonna, Marchesa di Pescara, e il suo canzioniere* (Marsala, 1897), chap. II, and especially pp. 51–52. For all poems by Vittoria in this chapter we have used Alan Bullock, ed., *Rime/Vittoria Colonna* (Bari, 1982), except where noted. We give the entire letter/poem to her husband in the Italian section at the end of this chapter.

7   The incident of the pearls and the quotation are given by Mazzone, *Vittoria Colonna*, p. 73, n. 1.

8   Petrarch, Sonnet III, "Era il giorno ch'al sol si scolorato." For an extended discussion of Vittoria's debt to Petrarch, see Mazzone, *Vittoria Colonna*.

9   The details of this wedding are described in Mrs. Henry Roscoe, *Vittoria Colonna: Her Life and Times* (London, 1868), pp. 47–48.

10   Christopher Hare, *The Most Illustrious Ladies of the Italian Renaissance* (London, 1904). Hare was the pen name of Marion Andrews.

11   Although Italy was not a nation in the political sense, Italians had a strong sense of *italianità*.

12   See her epistolary poem in the Italian section, lines 31, 38, and 39.

13   A number of collections of poems by Veronica Gàmbara attribute to her the poem addressed to Charles V and Francis I, begging them to stop the war against each other. Alan Bullock, the most recent editor of the collected poems of Vittoria Colonna, attributes it to her. See chapter 1, note 26.

14   Roscoe, *Vittoria Colonna*, p. 114.

15   See Gàmbara's poem to Colonna in chapter 1. Note that in Italian epistolary poetic exchanges, the responder must follow the identical rhyme scheme of the original; compare Gàmbara's verse endings in her poem to Vittoria with Vittoria's verse endings in the Italian sections.

16   A vivid glimpse of Vittoria and Michelangelo is given by an artist, Francesca de Hollanda, visiting in Rome. Alfred Reumont, *Vittoria Colonna, Marchesa di Pescara, Vita, Fede e Poesia* (Turin, 1892), p. 169. For Michelangelo's poems we have used Enzo Noè Girardi, ed., *Rime di Michelangelo Buonarroti* (Bari, 1967).

17   See Roger Bainton, "Vittoria Colonna and Michelangelo," *Forum* 4, no. 1 (Spring 1971): 34–41.

18   Unico maestro Michelangelo et mio singularissimo amico,

Ho avuto la vostra et visto il Crucifixo, il quale certamente ha crucifixe nella memoria mia quante altre picture viddi mai. Non se po vedere più ben fatta, più viva et più finita imagine; et certo io potrei mai exsplicar quanto sottilmente et mirabilmente è fatta, per il che son risoluta de non volerlo de man d'altri. Et però chiaritemi: se questo è d'altri, patientia; se è vostro, io in ogni modo vel torrei. Ma caso che non sia vostro et vogliate farlo fare a quel vostro, ci parleremo prima, perché, conoscendo io la difficultà che ce è di imitarlo, più presto mi risolvo che colui faccia un'altra cosa che questa; ma se è il vostro questo, habbiate patientia che non son per tornarlo più. Io l'ho ben visto al lume et col vetro et col specchio, et non viddi mai la più finita cosa.

S[ervitor] al comando vostro
La marchesa de Pescara.

See Sylvia Ferrino-Pagden, *Dichterin und Muse Michelangelos* (Vienna, 1997), p. 399.

19   Pietro Vinci, *Quattordici sonetti spirituali della illustrissima et eccellentissima divina Vittoria Colonna d'Avalos de Aquino Marchesa di Pescara* (Venice, 1580), pp. 6–7, 8–9.

20   "The veil of the ancient temple" refers to the temple of Solomon in Jerusalem, the altar of which was made according to the directions God gave Moses: the ark of the covenant was to be veiled so that the space of the tabernacle was divided between the "the *holy* place and the most holy (Exodus 23:33). The words that we have translated as "shadow and substance," *ombre e figure,* seem inspired by biblical references such as "all my members are as a shadow" (Job 17:7).

21   Vittoria's emphasis here on *feeling* bodily pain is of particular interest because it possibly indicates the influence on her of Ignatius of Loyola, her contemporary, who advocated experience of the senses as a means of understanding spiritual truth.

22   Vittoria wrote to Cardinal Contarini defending the Capuchins from charges of heresy; the letter is quoted in Roger Bainton, "Vittoria Colonna and Michelangelo," pp. 34–41. Note that Vittoria was at Ferrara when Tullia d'Aragona, whom we will meet in the next chapter, was also there. It is doubtful that the courtesan met the great lady, although they were likely aware of each other's presence.

23   Jolanda di Blasi, ed., in *Antologia delle scrittrici italiane dale origini al 1800* (Florence, 1930), confused Marguerite d'Angoulême, Queen of Navarre, born in 1492 (the same year as Vittoria Colonna) with Marguerite de Valois, born in 1523. The Queen of Navarre was herself a gifted poet, esteemed in her day for her writing including the *Heptaméron*, modeled on Boccaccio's *Decamerone.* Her court attracted the leading literary figures of the period.

24   Reumont, *Vittoria Colonna*, p. 169.

25   Maud F. Jerrold, *Victoria Colonna: With Some Account of Her Friends and Times* (New York, 1906), p. 263.

26   Vinci, *Quattordici sonetti*, pp. 16–17.

27   Vittoria's reference to her "little one" in the poem immediately above beginning "Oh Lord in that impenetrable light" must be referring to Alfonso del Vasto, who died in 1546 at the age of forty-four; she apparently still thought of him as her young child.

28   Bullock, *Rime.*

CHAPTER THREE

TULLIA D'ARAGONA
(1505/1510 – 1556)

 *FROM BED TO VERSE*

ith the rebirth of ancient culture in Italy in the fifteenth century there arose a class of female companions called *cortigiane oneste* (virtuous courtesans), who, like their prototypes, the Greek *hetairae*, were talented and educated in literature and the arts. We hear of Lucrezia Porzia, who knew all of Petrarch and Boccaccio by heart; of La Squarcina, who had mastery in Greek; of Nicolosa, who read the Psalms in Hebrew. Women such as these were highly esteemed by their wealthy, often intellectual and artistic patrons, and some managed to live well even beyond the age of sexual desirability. Tullia d'Aragona led a glamorous life, though one that ended sadly. [1]

Tullia is an unusual name, and it seems particularly fortuitous that the daughter of Cardinal Luigi d'Aragona, descendant of the Spanish royal line of Aragon, and Giulia Campana, a well-known courtesan, was given that name at her baptism.[2] She was a precocious child, a new, feminine Marcus Tullius Cicero, it was said, worthy of such a name, and as an adult she continued to be compared with the great master of eloquence.[3] In 1536 when Iacopo Nardi translated into Tuscan an oration of Cicero, he sent a copy to Gian Francesco Stufa asking him to present it to Tullia, who "today is justly considered by all men to be the one and only true heir of Tullian eloquence." [4]

Tullia was born in Rome in the first decade of the sixteenth century. When still a young child, she went with her mother to Florence, as we learn from a verse of one of her lovers, Girolamo Muzio, who also tells us of her noble lineage: "At an early age she lived near the shores of the most beautiful river of Tuscany: Aragona was her family; Tullia her name." A few years later, perhaps after an interval in Siena, mother and daughter were back in Rome, where Giulia must have felt the professional opportunities were better for herself and her child. In Rome Tullia learned the arts of singing and dancing along with lovemaking, and together with her natural gifts of eloquence and charm she became one of the most admired and accomplished women of her time.[5] By 1527, when she was about twenty years old, her home had become a magnet for wealthy, powerful, and, above all, gifted men who formed the intellectual elite of the city. Many professed to love her, some probably did, and Tullia could feel herself surrounded by devoted admirers. The future seemed to promise a life of luxury and love.

But in 1527 Rome fell victim to the ongoing war between Charles V and Francis I. Charles, angered because Pope Clement had made an alliance with Francis, sent his imperial troops—Spanish and German—into the city, and for eight days the inhabitants, wealthy and poor, cardinals, priests, Roman soldiers, men, women, and children, were subjected to every kind of brutality. It is said that three thousand people were killed in the first day of the assault. Treasures of jewels, art, and money were carried away by the invaders. It is not known how this catastrophe affected Tullia, but it was doubtless a harrowing experience; life in Rome as it had been until the sacking must have seemed to come to a stop. As it turned out, however, it was just a pause. Although Rome never completely recovered from the calamitous invasion, most of the survivors managed to pick themselves up and regain their ordinary lives. Sooner than one would have thought possible, Pope Clement VII's court renewed its former splendor, bringing back to Rome the intellectuals who soon filled Tullia's home again, men such as Latino Giovenale, Claudio Tolomei, and Ludovico Martelli,[6] who spent countless evenings discussing the latest cultural and artistic events of the city as well as the poetry and philosophy of their Greek and Roman intellectual forefathers, and inevitably Petrarch, with Tullia at the center of these discussions.[7]

In 1531, however, another calamity struck, this time directly at Tullia. According to the story that circulated through Rome, a certain wealthy German, whom we know only as "Gianni," had begged Tullia to have sex with him, offering her a great deal of money. Although he was wealthy, he was said to be loathsome in bed, and Tullia refused him again and again. Finally he upped the ante, so to speak, going to Giulia to intercede on his behalf and promising to pay Tullia an unheard of one hundred *scudi* per night for each of seven nights. Giulia, according to Rosati, persuaded her daughter to make the deal. Gianni proved to be so disgusting that Tullia threw him out after one night. Nevertheless, one of her young lovers, Paolo Emilio Orsini, was enraged that Tullia had permitted this odious man to sleep with her. His love turned to hate, apparently, and he spread the story around to Tullia's other young adorers, some of whom vowed with him never to see her again.[8]

Humiliated and professionally ruined, Tullia and her mother decided to leave Rome and start life again at Ferrara, where Duke Ercole d'Este and his wife, Renata di Francia, ruled over a court as splendid as a king's. It was a fateful move for Tullia, for there she met Girolamo Muzio, the man who became not only one of the serious loves of her life, but also her greatest and most dependable friend.

Tullia set herself up in Ferrara as she had in Rome, and whatever rumors might have reached there, they seem not to have affected the men; she soon managed to attract the courtiers of the d'Este court, among them Giuglio Camillo, Ercole Bentivoglio, Bernardo Tasso, and Girolamo Muzio. They competed for her favors with poems, and inevitably she gave her preference to Tasso, the most eminent of her new conquests. Hardly had the new relationship begun, however, when Tasso left the service of Ercole d'Este in 1532 for a new patron, Ferrante Sanseverino, Prince of Salerno, who required him to go to Venice. The competition was thus reopened, and Girolamo Muzio won the coveted place as first in Tullia's affections.

Muzio was a prominent intellectual particularly known for his defense of spoken Italian as a legitimate vehicle for serious writing. Born in 1496 into a poor family and without private means, he became a courtier, moving from one to another of the most important courts of the period, including those of Maximilian I; Alfonso I, Duke of Ferrara; Alfonso, Marchese del Vasto; and Cosimo I, Duke of Florence and Grand Duke of Tuscany; he also served Ferrante Gonzaga, Charles V's generalissimo in Italy, France, and Flanders. Except for his period in Ferrara, he was at the service of those nobles who allied themselves with the Emperor Charles V and was thus in sympathy with the Counterreformation.

Muzio fell ardently in love with Tullia, and soon they were exchanging sonnets. Muzio set the Neo-Platonic tone that was to pervade many of their exchanges:

> *While the flames of love, brighter than the shining sun,*
> *blazing within me now as they have since we met,*
> *are strong, oh lovely eyes,*
> *send your ardent rays into my heart.*
>
> *Oh lovely ears, eager and intent,*
> *listen to the sound that came here on earth from heaven*
> *and filled the air,*
> *open your mind to the sacred words.*
>
> *My soul, while you live,*
> *remember that what is eternal glows within you,*
> *open your breast to everlasting love.*
>
> *And remember, too, that the shining light,*
> *the sweet sound, the bright spirit*
> *are for you the stairway to heaven.*[9] (p. 93)

Tullia picked up his image of the flame to begin her response to Muzio.

> *Lovely flame which, from deep knowledge*
> *flashes and descends upon me,*
> *accept my profound feeling happily*
> *as is your revered custom;*
>
> *Now that your noble light illuminates me*
> *and lights up my heart so gently,*
> *may it continue to glow brightly and be protected*
> *against a harsh fire that would destroy it.*
>
> *And with your words help my unrefined talent,*
> *warmed by your warmth, to rise*
> *so that it may sing your virtues everywhere.*
>
> *I hope that I may tell future ages that*
> *you were such a man that deserved a greater pen than mine,*
> *and that it was my glory to love you.* (p. 93)

In another exchange, the Neo-Platonic poets see their souls reflected in each others, but Muzio's love is not blind. Praising her, he nevertheless ends this sonnet with striking candor:

> *My lady, you who are above all others the object*
> *of loving souls and gentle hearts,*

and whose splendid and high esteem
are the fine subject of my pen,

> *In you is reflected the lovely face of your soul*
> *in which shines the beauty of your noble heart,*
> *and in all your passionate endeavors one will see*
> *the flames of celestial love*

> *You will see my soul*
> *reflected in you and made beautiful*
> *looking at you, so that I may glow with your light.*

> *This is how it will be, so the love in my heart*
> *tells me, if bad habits and unworthy thoughts*
> *do not lead you astray.* (pp. 93 – 94)

Tullia begins with an echo of his poem, playing, as he did, on the idea of object and subject. She seeks, humbly, it seems, to reassure him that she will give up her "bad habits" and abandon her life as a courtesan.

> *Dear soul, whose virtue, rare and faithful,*
> *is the object of what my soul most desires,*
> *what makes me yearn to be*
> *the subject of your song.*

> *If the virtues you bestow on me were equal*
> *to my love for you*
> *my pen could honor you; but my unworthy life*
> *has made impossible my desire to honor you.*

> *I will say only that following your destiny*
> *your soul has left you*
> *to enter into me as its true abode,*

> *And my soul, it can truly be said,*
> *united now with yours, as is my star,*
> *is moved by you to change its ways.* (p. 94)

Although her livelihood depended on men, it is notable that among the men who are mentioned by her biographers, few seem to have been wealthy or noble like the fabulously wealthy and powerful banker Agostino Chigi, who kept the famous courtesan Imperia in royal style. There were some, nevertheless, for she lived luxuriously, at least until the last years of her life, and we know of one noble and wealthy lover, Filippo Strozzi, who had to be dissuaded by Francesco Vettori, a courtier who served Giulio de' Medici, from fighting a duel on her behalf.[10] Unlike the descriptions we have of Imperia's palace with furnishings fit for a princess, though, we know of

Tullia's home only that it was a kind of salon where literati mingled and engaged in endless conversations on humanist themes. Tullia clearly preferred to form relationships with men of literary and intellectual accomplishment. Intelligent and gifted as she was, she surely felt the need for intellectual companionship equal to her own, which at that time few women could offer. Moreover, she was ambitious for recognition, and she must have felt that, as a woman, she needed the help of distinguished writers to establish herself as a *poet*. She had often throughout her life to fight off disparagement and actual difficulties, as we shall see, because she was listed as a courtesan in the census of the cities where she lived.

Girolamo Muzio's "virtue" that moved Tullia to believe she could abandon her profession was his intellect. Neo-Platonic poetry aside, however, surely there was also a strong physical bond between them as well. They had beautiful days together, wandering in the countryside and along the banks of the Po, where they lay on the grass and made love. Muzio remembered their joy later, after Tullia left Ferrara ostensibly for Venice, in 1534.

> *Oh, if only by this shady, cool river bank*
> *where now I walk alone,*
> *she of whom my heart always speaks and my heart writes,*
> *were here, and love with her.*
>
> *She would be sitting here near the river,*
> *she would be lying on the grass, and I on her,*
> *and from the forest would appear*
> *the hallowed demigods and sylvan goddesses.*
>
> *Some of them would cut her name into the tree trunks*
> *while I would be looking at her, pouring out words*
> *to express her beauty;*
>
> *Full of pleasure and happy in such love,*
> *she would weave a garland, perhaps of flowers*
> *perhaps of laurel, for my hair.* (pp. 94 – 95)

We must wonder why she left this idyllic scene in 1534.

In 1535, according to Tullia's biographers, Giulia was in Adria, her birthplace, where on 10 March 1535 she gave birth to a baby girl who was named Penelope. The father's name was given as Costanzo Palmieri d'Aragona. Salvatore Rosati writes that the most diligent archival research failed to discover anything beyond the name, adding that it is not known whether Tullia accompanied her mother. There was good reason to keep this event quiet, he points out, because if suspicions were aroused that Giulia had had a baby with an Aragona other than the cardinal, suggesting that this Costanzo had also been the Aragona father of Tullia, gone would be the royal descent. "In all this tangle of confusion," Rosati observes, "one might indeed suppose that Penelope was not Giulia's child but actually Tullia's." He adds, "however, the hypothesis seems unlikely." We, to the contrary, believe that the hypothesis is very likely.[11] There is nothing to show that Tullia and her mother went to Venice when they left Ferrara in 1534; they may have gone straight to Adria so that Tullia's friends would not see her as her condition became evident.

The first we know of Tullia in Venice is in 1536, when we learn that she had taken up again with Bernardo Tasso: Tullia and Bernardo are the principal speakers in the *Dialogo di Amore* by Sperone Speroni, published in 1542. In Speroni's work we get a vivid understanding of one aspect of Tullia that inspired the praise showered on her by so many illustrious writers. She was extraordinarily frank. Accustomed to Neo-Platonic platitudes about the spirituality of love, her listeners must have experienced a frisson of delight hearing of her state: "I know very well that the joy of love cannot be perfect if all the senses are not involved in it." She tells Tasso that he is deluding himself by giving her his love. "I know what I am," she tells him, "and I know what I ought to be, to be worthy of you." She adds that she will change her way of life "and become the kind of woman I would like to be, or die in the attempt." Niccolo Grazia, another speaker in the *Dialogo,* tells her of a published oration by Antonio Brocardo in which courtesans are highly praised: "He proves that the manners and modes of courtesans, if properly understood, are the way that leads upward to the understanding of God." Tullia will have none of it. "Let's leave out the poetry," she says, "if you knew the servility, the vileness, the depths and the inconstancy of such a life, you would blame anyone . . . who said that it was a good one and excused it. And anyone who helps a young girl, foolish enough to be pushed into such a life, to get out of it, is saving her from misery." Brocardo, she surmised correctly, must have been in love with a courtesan because "certainly it was not the truth that made him support so vile a cause."[12] Tasso and Tullia were fated never to have a prolonged affair; he was called to Salerno by his patron in 1536, and Tullia continued holding court for Sperone, Grazia, il Valerio, Francesco Molza, and other poets and intellectuals on the Venetian scene until the following year. She returned to Ferrara in 1537, where for the next four years she spent the happiest period of her life.

Muzio still loved her as ardently as ever, and they resumed their passionate love affair. In a series of five books of eclogues, the first eclogue in Book I, titled "On Lovers," is dedicated to Tullia. Here Muzio introduces the characters of Mopso and Tirrhenia, a shepherd and nymph. The shepherd Mopso (Muzio) is passionately in love with Tirrhenia (Tullia) and begs for her love in verses with sexually explicit images.

> *Let Tirrhenia open the rosy gates . . .*
>
> *Let Tirrhenia pour*
> *Ambrosia and honey from her amorous tongue . . .*
>
> *Open the garden of love*
> *show the sweet apples and the perfumed lilies to the sun . . .*
>
> *Come, and in your soft arms*
> *welcome him who with open arms awaits you*
> *and in your womb happily*
> *receive your lover inflamed with desire.*[13] (p. 95)

Tullia was delighted with the poem, but one day when they were still at Ferrara, she told Muzio that she would like him to change her name, Tirrhenia (which associated her with ancient Rome), to Thalia, the muse of comedy, but in such a way that it would be evident that Tirrhenia and Thalia were one and the same.[14] Accordingly, he titled the fourth eclogue in Book I Thalia and addressed his love with that name. The eclogues were not published until 1550, but their publication at that date suggests that the love he felt for her still glowed.

At Ferrara Tullia outshone all other women, according to Battista Stambellino, who wrote to Isabella d'Este, even Vittoria Colonna, who was there at the same time[15]: "There is a lovely courtesan here from Rome called la Signora Tullia who plans to be here for a few months. She is very charming, reserved, and gifted with an extraordinary manner; she sight-reads every motet and song. . . . Her way of speaking is unique, and there is not a man or woman here that can compare with her, even the most illustrious Signora Marchesa di Pescara who is here, as Your Excellency knows. She is highly knowledgeable and speaks about subjects that are of interest to you. Her house is always filled with brilliant people and is open to everyone, and she has a lot of money, jewels, necklaces, rings, and other beautiful things and in short she is well off in every way." [16]

This same admirer referred in his letter to Isabella to some "strange adventure" that put Tullia, according to Celani, "in a very good light, gaining for her the reputation for respectability that rumor and pasquinades has severely damaged.[17] She has gathered around herself an elite group of poets and gentlemen who adore, court her, overlook her not too reputable past, and recognize in her only the poet, the intellectual, the descendant of royal blood. . . . Muzio and Bentivoglio are profuse in their praises, in poetry and prose."

Because Tullia was so esteemed at Ferrara, it would appear that her politico-religious sympathies at that time might have been with the Italian Reformist movement centered there. Bernardo Ochino, it will be remembered from our chapter on Vittoria Colonna, was in Ferrara in 1537, and Tullia was among the multitude that listened to his preaching. She was, however, characteristically frank and addressed a poem to this leader of the Reform movement in Italy, highly critical of his theology.

> *Bernard, here where the waters of the king of rivers*
> *is most pure, you could have been content,*
> *with your natural gift for speaking, to have lit up*
> *so many hearts with love for holy, eternal works.*

> *Even if you have hidden desires,*
> *and life is like a garment,*
> *you are not of frail and foul flesh and bones,*
> *but a man of the highest order.*

> *Theatre, dance, music,*
> *enjoyed from time immemorial, and of ancient tradition,*
> *why do you forbid them now:*

It would not be sanctity, but arrogance,
to take away free will,
God's greatest gift to us. (p. 95)

The lives of courtiers and courtesans were not entirely their own, however, and in 1541, after four happy years, obligations and needs separated Tullia and Muzio. But the deep attachment they each felt for the other survived the separation, and the following exchange of sonnets reveals their continuing deep affection on meeting again, years later. Muzio writes,

Love lives in my heart and urges me to tell
from what spark comes the new ardor
that has again lighted my soul,
who it may be that sweetly disturbs my mind.

Dear soul, serious, thoughtful friend,
shining eyes, angelic harmony,
all my eager desires are brought back
by the memories of an old flame.

The one of whom I sing was born on the banks
of the sparkling river that has again and again
made green the leaves that crown the eternal laurel;

She lived as a child near the waters
of the beautiful river that is Tuscany's pride,
She is an Aragona; Tullia is her name. (pp. 95 – 96)

Tullia's direct response again echoes his words and thoughts as she refers to their past love and the still-glowing spark that remains between them. Both of them invoke the rivers—the Po, the Tiber, the Arno—that had special meaning for them.

You, the essence of valor and courtesy
to whom fortune is an enemy,
what happy fate brings you today
to see your old flame?

Dear Mutio, a soul ever kind,
ever devoted to my own,
indeed I feel sorrow for your hardships and difficulties,
which you surely did not deserve.

Tho' it was long ago, that time on the Po
when you burned with love for me, I do not believe
that such a bright flame is wholly extinguished,

> *And if one can read the heart in another's face,*
> *I have hope that on the banks of the Arno*
> *you may still hear my name ring clear and bright.* (p. 96)

From Ferrara, Tullia went to Siena, and following her there we find ourselves confronted by another mystery of Tullia's life, apparently as unsolvable now as the birth of Penelope. There is in the State Archives of Siena a signed contract of marriage between one Silvestro Guicciardi of Ferrara and Tullia Palmieri de Aragona dated Tuesday, 8 January 1543, and witnessed by a notary, Sigismondo Manni, who is said to have performed the ceremony in his capacity as a city official. The marriage certificate was found among church papers for that year.[18] There are two mysteries around this surprising document. Nothing is known of this man, and research by Enrico Celani, Rosati, and ourselves has failed to turn up a family name of Palmieri Aragona. This, it will be remembered, was the name of the supposed father of Penelope. Now Tullia is claiming him for her father. And the mystery becomes stranger.

In 1543–44, Siena was under attack by Cosimo I de' Medici, whose forces eventually conquered the city. Life was difficult for the Sienese, and for Tullia there was added suffering. She had made enemies in Rome, probably because she had rejected a man such as Giambattista Giraldi Cinzio; she had found enmity in Venice directed at her by Pietro Aretino and Domenico Venier; and now in Siena again a writer, Agnolo Firenzuola, for some unknown reason—did she reject him?—denounced her in a sonnet that he circulated in the city accusing her of practicing magic and, in a novel, of adultery, "letting her husband die of hunger." This is the only specific reference to a husband we have found.[19]

Early in 1544, one year after the reported marriage, Tullia was accused by persons unknown of living in a zone prohibited to courtesans and of wearing jewels and dressing in a manner that violated statutes of the city regarding courtesans. The revenue office ordered her to appear in court in February. At the trial, she produced her marriage certificate and her lawyer, one Lattanzio Lucarini, persuaded the judge that she was a married woman, winning a judgment that declared that she was not a prostitute but a respectable woman who had the right to dress as she did.[20] Nevertheless, she was denounced again in the same year for wearing a *sbernia*, a luxurious garment made of fur and some elegant fabric, on the holiday of the Holy Spirit when it was the fashion to dress particularly well. Courtesans, however, were forbidden by statute to wear the *sbernia*. Fortunately, the court was again persuaded by her defense, and she was not condemned.

Among the men who signed this denunciation, and perhaps the other, was Ottaviano Tondi. Sometime after this trial, Tondi the accuser became Tullia's lover. It so happens that Tondi was a member of the city council; had she rejected him, and then, faced with a threat, made a deal with him to get her off in exchange for her favor? Apparently a forgiving soul, Tullia mourned his death the following year in a sonnet addressed to his brother, Emilio, which begins,

> *Suffering Siena begs its heroes*
> *to mourn for its great Tondi*
> *whose valor heaven attests*
> *they may well envy.* (p. 96)

Through all of this, we are nagged by the question of where her husband was. At her first trial—and presumably the second—she produced her marriage certificate as proof of her respectability. Why did she not produce the husband? Why was there no husband on the scene to defend his wife? After the second trial she took Tondi as her lover, which we believe Tullia would not have done had she been married. Furthermore, with poems of praise to quite a few other men, why is there no poem or letter to Silvestro Guicciardi? Nor any poem or even letter *from* him? Perhaps our readers will arrive at the same suspicion that we ourselves have reached: that the marriage certificate was a spurious document, manufactured with foresight for exactly the purpose to which it was put. This Silvestro Guicciardi was conveniently "from Ferrara," which would explain why no one in Siena knew anything about him, if anyone were to ask. And possibly Tullia had had some previous experience manufacturing documents when Penelope was born. Against this suspicion, however, one must consider the *Trattato del Matrimonio* (Treatise on Marriage) by Muzio, published in 1550 with a dedication to Tullia in which he wrote, "There was already seen in you that charisma of the woman whose modesty, as one reads in Ecclesiasticus [VII:21] is more precious than gold. . . . That quality that you were able to make evident to the world so as to show that your past life was the result of necessity, but this [you chose] of your own free will: that, in the past, destiny governed you but now your virtue governs you." [21] Rosati and Celani both take Muzio's "this" to refer to Tullia's marriage, certainly a possible interpretation, but there is some ambiguity in what Muzio wrote, and no specific reference to marriage: Muzio might have meant that she chose of her own free will the change in her mode of living in 1550, when she was living alone in Rome. The *Treatise on Marriage* could well have been inspired by his own marriage around 1550 to a lady-in-waiting of Vittoria Farnese, Duchess of Urbino. There is also to consider with regard to the mystery of her supposed marriage a poem Tullia wrote to Francesco Maria Molza: she consoles him because "Perduto hai meco la più fida scrota" (you have lost, like me, your most faithful companion). Her "most faithful companion"? Until 1541 her most faithful companion was Girolamo Muzio, but because the context of the poem is about losing someone through death, "most faithful companion" cannot mean Muzio. If it refers to her supposed husband, Silvestro, how long had she known him? In any case he must have died soon after the marriage in 1543, for Molza himself died in 1544. [22]

In 1545 Tullia decided to leave Siena, an uneasy city, constantly under threat and occupied by foreign troops, a pawn between the French and Spanish—"forced to suck the poison of brutal rage," she wrote in a sonnet to Francesco Crasso. She moved to Florence where she hoped, vainly, as it turned out, to escape finally from the harassment that had plagued her in Siena. At thirty-five Tullia was still captivating, although she did not have the features of a conventional beauty. Vettori, in the letter to Strozzi mentioned earlier, comments that he knows Strozzi loves her for her wit, for it couldn't be for her beauty. Giovanni Battista Giraldi writes scurrilously in his *Ecatommiti* that her face was neither beautiful nor pleasing, that she had a large mouth and thin lips, and that her nose was long, lumpy, and thick at the end. Giraldi's mean-spirited description aside, we may notice that although the encomiastic poems and letters addressed to her pay more or less conventional compliments to her beauty, they praise her again and again for her qualities of mind and spirit, for her extraordinary charm, and for her lovely voice, both singing and speaking. Francisco Maria del Molza writes of her brilliant intellect, "the best part of you"; Ercole Bentivoglia writes how every unworthy thought was extinguished when a sweet glow, a celestial desire was born from the first moment he saw her, and how her voice is inspired by Euterpe, muse of music and lyric poetry; Cardinal Hippolito de' Medici, whose desperate love Tullia rejected, writes in a begging sonnet of her beautiful soul which shines in her eyes, and the unearthly sound of her voice. Giulio Camillo, an esteemed writer on religious themes, praises her, as did many others, for her critical acumen and for her voice that he said echoes those of the muses on Mount Helicon.[23] And often we hear of her splendid eyes; "beautiful eyes, charming eyes, amorous and loving eyes, more beautiful than the stars and the sun," Muzio wrote in his eclogue dedicated to her. And even Giraldi admitted that it was her eyes that "lit fire in the heart." Niccolò Martelli, founder of Florence's literary academy, L'Accademia degli Umidi, expressed in a letter to Tullia what many of her friends must have written, or said, to her.

> To Signora Tullia d'Aragona,
>   Grace and virtue, lady, since they are gifts and riches of the soul and partake more of the divine than of the human, are not subject to the violence of years. Thus you remain young and beautiful, perhaps even more so, and your delicate face has the same angelic look that it had and will have to the end. Because the beauty that the heavens bestowed upon you was for infinity, time, which comes to an end, cannot hurt you. Your skin, whiter than alabaster or the purest snow, is still fresh, because you are moderate and restrained in everything you do. And so you still appear to the eyes of others as the symbol of Love. But this is the least of the beauty one perceives in you, compared to that virtue that dignifies you and is most evident in you, that quality that amazes those that hear you sing and play whatever instrument with your white, beautiful hands. Your charming conversation makes everyone sigh with chaste desire. I do not even speak of your eloquence in public or in private, because if there were once a TULLIO d'Arpino, there is now in this world a TULLIA D'ARAGONA through whom, by your pen, the soul of Poetry and Philosophy creates a celestial composition which makes the paper on which you write marvel and rejoice.[24] (p. 103)

How she really looked we cannot know for certain, except that she was blonde, probably not naturally, since blonde hair was considered a requirement for female beauty. Given her celebrity, it seems likely that more than one artist painted her portrait, but there is no surviving likeness that can be identified positively as Tullia d'Aragona. A portrait of a young woman by Alessandro Bonvicino, called Moretto da Brescia, was for many years identified as Tullia, and although there is no hard evidence to support the identification, there are clues that leave open the possibility that the subject really is Tullia d'Aragona (plate II). The woman is shown a little more than half-length, standing against a background of laurel leaves, and leaning against the upper part of a thin slab of marble on which she rests her left forearm. Her head is tilted toward her left side, her left arm rests on a marble stand inscribed with the lettering inscription *Quae Sacro IOANNIS/CAPUT SALTANDO/OBTINIT* (She who dancing obtained the head of St. John). This is curious, for in the New Testament story (Mat thew 14:3–12) the dancer was Salome; the image, however, shows the sitter repre-sented as a woman holding a gold scepter in her left hand, suggesting that it represents not Salome but her mother, Herodias, King Herod's wife, who told her daughter to request John's head when Herod, delighted with Salome's dancing, offered to give her anything she asked for. The subject wears her hair braided around her head and or-namented with pearls and leaves, suggesting a wreath. Her dress is green velvet and a transparent shawl partly visible under her outer garments is held by a knot on her right shoulder. A fur garment is wrapped around her so that it is draped over her left shoulder and bodice, while it has fallen from her right shoulder and only a small bit of it can be seen hugging her upper right arm. Over this fur is a red velvet mantle that has also fallen from her shoulders, so as to expose the fur.

The portrait was acquired early in the nineteenth century by Count Paolo Tosio of Brescia from an ex-nun who apparently saved it when her religious order was sup-pressed during the Napoleonic era and the convent demolished. The painting had been in the convent for many years, and when it first came to attention in 1814 it was called "Herodias with a Fur and a Scepter in her Hand." Now in the Tosio collection in the Pinacoteca Tosio-Martinengo in Brescia, it has been identified as Tullia d'Aragona since 1823, when Caterina Piotti made an engraving of it printed with Tullia's name under the image and a verse presumably written by Piotti, which reads, "Qual fu la culla mia / Mostra lo scettro d'oro; / l'ingegno mio qual sia / Mostra il cresente alloro" (The scepter shows my birth, the growing laurel shows my talent, such as it is). Although the Piotti engraving does not show the Latin inscription on the stone, suggesting that the inscription was painted in after 1823 and was therefore not a part of the original iconography, the curator of the museum, Dr. Elena Lucchesi Ragni, informs us in a let-ter of 7 July 2000 that during the restoration of the painting it was established that the painted Latin words were contemporary with the rest of the painting.[25]

Thus the portrait's modern career as "Tullia d'Aragona" was begun, although it is not known how or why Piotti identified it as representing the poet. It is true that Tul-lia always vaunted her high birth, and insisted on being known as a poet, but the scepter and the laurel leaves are not in themselves proof that the painting represents Tullia. Dr. Ragni's entry in the exhibition catalogue, *Dichterin und Muse Michelangelos,* speculates that the identification of Tullia with Salome is based on both women's hav-ing been corrupted by their mothers. Although we believe the identification remains doubtful, taken together with two further clues, it may be somewhat strengthened. First, that wonderful fur and velvet wrap. Is this what fashion called a *sbernia*? Could this really be Tullia flaunting her right to wear that luxurious garment? Second, to see Tullia in the person of Herodias/Salome: was there a "John" (Gianni) who lost his head over Tullia, who had her portrait painted perhaps hoping to awaken her sympa-thy for him? Yes, there was the loathsome, wealthy German.

With the evidence so far available, we cannot know with any degree of satisfaction who is represented in the portrait. It seems more likely that the beautiful sitter was an actress who played the role of Herodias or Salome in a sixteenth-century entertain-ment. Perhaps further clues will emerge in still unlooked-for places. For now, we must leave the question without a satisfying answer.

In Florence Tullia set about finding patrons and creating a circle of intellectuals

3.1.
Titian.
*Portrait of
Benedetto Varchi.*
**ca. 1540.
Kunsthistorisches
Museum, Vienna.
Photo: Erich
Lessing / Art
Resource.**

around herself that included the famous doctor Girolamo Francastoro[26] and some members of L'Accademia degli Umidi, among whom was the celebrated Benedetto Varchi; once again she fell in love (figure 3.1). Varchi, a homosexual, did not fully return this love but became one of her staunchest admirers. Though most of his writing is seen today as superficial, he was greatly admired in his own day for his lectures at the Academy of Florence, especially those that dealt with the ongoing debate on language, and for his scholarly history of Florence from 1527 to 1530, commissioned by his patron Cosimo de' Medici, in whose court he served with a large stipend. She hoped that Varchi would make her his muse as Muzio had:

> *Oh, Varchi, whose rare and precious gifts*
> *inspire all who know you,*

why cannot I, as I would wish,
fill my heart with your wisdom?

With such guidance, I know that I would escape
the hands of a fate that deprives me
of my former pleasures, and all my laments
I would change to joyous songs, and become cheerful.

Alas, I see very well that my destiny
is hostile to such virtuous and happy hopes
because I am overwhelmed under heavy burdens;

But if this is what I deserve,
let your pen rescue my name, at least,
from the claws of inevitable Death. (pp. 96 – 97)

Varchi and Tullia herself are cast as the principal speakers in Tullia's most important work, her *Dialogue on the Infinity of Love*, her contribution to the literature of sixteenth-century conversations on love which were stimulated by Plato's *Symposium*, made accessible by Marsilio Ficino's translation in 1474. The discussion supposedly takes place in her home, and centers on the two natures of love, carnal, and spiritual/intellectual, with ideal love seen as combining both. We may take the views expressed by the characters as truly reflecting those of their counterparts in real life. Tullia's ideas, evident, as may be expected, also in her poems, if not original are clearly expressed, and she shows herself in her character of "Tullia" cleverly replying to "Varchi's" views, which she renders with undoubted accuracy in his subtle, analytic style of argument. Of love, she says, "Honorable love, the quality that is felt by noble people, rich or poor, who are cultured and virtuous, is not born of desire like the other kind, but of reason; it has as its aim the transformation of the lover into the beloved with the desire of the beloved to be transformed into the lover . . . and since this transformation can only exist on the spiritual plane one experiences only spiritual feelings, those engendered by sight and sound and even more, by imagination. It is quite true that the lover, desiring the beloved, in addition to spiritual union wishes also for corporeal union so that they become one, and since it is not possible for two bodies to interpenetrate, the lovers can never fully consummate their desires, and since they can never reach their goal, it is not possible to love to the limit." Furthermore, she says, "I am well aware that neither we nor plants and animals can be blamed or praised for what nature gives us. This kind of love creates the most noble of nature's offspring, and thus is not lascivious or disreputable but actually admirable, provided it is kept under control and not allowed to be excessive, which happens among humans, who have been given free will." [27]

Although several men are present in the scene of the *Dialogue*, including a medical doctor, Latanzio Benucci, who speaks only near the end, the argument is a witty intellectual duel that the author sets up between "Varchi" and "Tullia," in which she shows the latter the equal of the man who at the time was the most admired intellectual in Florence. She has them spar, thrust, and dodge adroitly as they turn their subject, love, round and round, viewing it in countless ways. A particularly interesting exchange centers on homosexuality, which "Tullia" has "Varchi" defend as the most real and true and virtuous love because it is completely spiritual, "as much more worthy than the other as the body is less worthy than the soul." In her own character she points out that carnal love is praiseworthy because it generates offspring, permitting the species to survive, and so gives Varchi the opportunity to claim that the spiritual love between men is more virtuous because generating a beautiful soul is far more praiseworthy than generating a beautiful body.[28]

The *Dialogue* was written in 1546, apparently, for she wrote to Varchi about it in August of that year. Muzio wrote a preface for it and took it to Venice, where it was published in 1547. In his preface Muzio refers to his having the *Dialogue* published without Tullia's consent, and also to his having restored the name Tullia to the character that she named Sabrina. But the *Dialogue* includes her dedication of it to Cosimo de' Medici, so it is obvious that she planned to have it published, with "Sabrina" substituting for herself, a subterfuge for the sake of modesty inasmuch as she makes the woman of the dialogue so witty and clever in argument, and so much admired.

In light of the real relationship of Tullia and Varchi, the *Dialogue* is both piquant and poignant. In it they are friends on an equal intellectual basis. An exchange of poems between them, however, shows that she was more in love with Varchi than he with her. She is suffering because he is not giving her the love she wants although he protests, not without some ambiguity, that he does indeed love her. The literary conceit in which they address each other as Damon and Phyllis is drawn from the third eclogue of Virgil:

> If the heavens are always serene and the meadows green
> for your beautiful flocks, sweet shepherd,
> pride of Arcadia and Tuscany
> most brilliant of the brilliant and esteemed,
>
> If the wise and blessed fates which all men cheer
> turn so much in your favor
> that Phyllis can never take back
> the heart she has given, nor you your pledged love:
>
> Tell me, dear Damon, if there can be a soul
> so mean and cruel that being loved,
> offers torment and death instead of love?
>
> How I would tremble, alas, if your learned pen
> did not relieve my fear of being paid
> with such a reward; hard indeed is my fate. (p. 97)

To which Varchi replied,

> Nymph, more beautiful than any shepherd has ever seen
> in the woods, or streams or meadows,

or more honored by the graces and the muses
always more loved by the most loved and esteemed:

So may the fates be less savage to Damon
nor may Phyllis ever return his surrendered heart,
and may her love for him be stronger than for others
who were never so happy and blessed.

How can there be a soul so mean and cruel
which, being truly loved, would not love unto death
a soul so noble?

Thus, if you believe not in my learned,
but my faithful pen, love and do not doubt,
for your happy fate will be well rewarded with honors. (pp. 97–98)

In the meantime, on 19 October 1546, about a year after Tullia's move to Florence, Cosimo promulgated a sumptuary law that specified that prostitutes were not allowed to wear dresses made of wool or silk, but required to wear a yellow veil to distinguish themselves from "respectable" women. Tullia ignored the law, and the following April she was called before a magistrate demanding that she comply. She sought help from Varchi, who had a good relationship with the duke, asking him to write a letter for her that she could send in her own name to the duchess, begging her to persuade her husband to exempt her from this law. He did so "gladly," and Eleonora did come to her aid. Cosimo signed a memorandum: "grant her pardon as a poet" ("Fasseli gratia per poetessa"), and an official of the duke sent her a copy of the decision on 1 May 1547, which stated that in recognition of "the extraordinary command of poetry and philosophy of this esteemed writer, Tullia Aragona is exempted from all obligations with regard to her clothes and activities." [29]

In gratitude, Tullia addressed a sonnet to Eleonora.

How should I address you, Woman or Goddess?
For such beauty and virtue
shines in you that your divine splendor
is more brilliant than the brightest flame.

I have the happy thought of writing about you
to express my thanks and esteem,
but neither pen nor human voice can reach
to where my aspiring heart rises.

I know that all my good fortune comes from you,
like the light at dawn of that star
that rises in the east before the sun,

> *But in the end my humble verse*
> *can never attain such nobility;*
> *let my heart requite you, rather than my words.* (p. 98)

To Cosimo, too, she sent a sonnet in appreciation of his generosity:

> *If the ancient shepherds scattered*
> *roses and blossoms in the temples*
> *and perfumed with incense the altars to Pan,*
> *it was to make the nymphs sweet and loving to their lovers.*
>
> *Oh, my lord, what kind of flowers,*
> *what lovely aromas can I offer, worthy of your name*
> *and the many great gifts and favors*
> *that you constantly shower upon me.*
>
> *Surely there is no temple, or altar or gift*
> *of such great value that might*
> *equal the value of your generosity.*
>
> *Thus, may your breast, where your virtue lies,*
> *be the temple, your wise heart the altar,*
> *my soul your sacrifice, if you will accept it.* (p. 98)

Sometime during 1546–47 Tullia met Piero Manelli, the last great love of her life. Tullia was now about forty; Manelli, born in 1522, was twelve years younger, and their affair was another disaster for her, pathetically evident in her poems. Time and again she writes of her anguish, thinking she had been freed from the turmoil of her former love, only to find herself captured once more. In one of her loveliest poems she writes,

> *The lovely Philomela,* escaped*
> *from the hated cage, looks splendid*
> *as she darts among the trees and greenery,*
> *returned to liberty and a happy life.*
>
> *I, too, from amorous ties*
> *was freed, scoffing at the torment and bitter pain*
> *of the unbelievable grief that is reserved for one*
> *who has, for loving too much, lost her soul.*
>
> *Alas, oh willful star! I would have done well*
> *to take my treasure from the Temple of Cyprus †*
> *and walked proudly away;*

---

* Philomela is associated with the nightingale.
† The Temple of Cyprus refers to the Temple of Venus, goddess of love, on the island of Cyprus.

> When love said to me: "I will end
> your feeling of freedom," and made me prisoner
> of your power, to reawaken my pain. (pp. 98 – 99)

and again,

> Love once burned within me
> with a slow fire, and my anguished heart
> was so filled with longing that, whatever else it might be,
> my martyrdom was for him a delight and a joke.

> Then slowly anger and piety
> put out the flame, and I, no longer bound,
> free from the long, ferocious longing,
> was happily singing wherever I went.

> But, alas, heaven was not satisfied,
> nor tired of hurting me; despite my sighs
> I am led again into my former ways,

> And with such a sharp, stinging spur to my side
> that I fear I will fall under the first attacks,
> but I would rather die. (p. 99)

He was accusatory and proud, Tullia was abject.

> If I ever did this, may the sorrow that
> burdens my heart never come to an end;
> if I did this, let my lost hopes live
> in the eternal enmity of our eyes.

> If I did this, let every day
> be empty of the happiness whence flows my well-being;
> if I did this, let no one offer me
> the olive branch to soothe my pain;

> If I did this, then may you feel no pity
> and may my sadness increase,
> grief and suffering destroying me, as always.

> But if I did not, let your harsh pride
> be transformed to love and may I enjoy forever
> the sweet fruit of my desire.
> transformed to love. (pp. 99 – 100)

Sometimes, apparently, she was able to feel that he loved her—but then she worried that she would lose him.

> If a loving mother loses her only child
> and a profound grief
> presses on her wretched and longing heart,
> she can at least hope for comfort, for help;
>
> If a skillful captain confronts a great danger
> with gallant bravery,
> but is overwhelmed, he hopes in the end
> to prevail and show himself dauntless;
>
> If a helmsman in a tempestuous sea bewails himself,
> almost frightened to death,
> he still has hopes of reaching a harbor;
>
> But I, if it should happen that I lose my love,
> either by my own fault or by ill fortune,
> I would have no hope, or desire, for comfort. (p. 100)

Her anxiety was not without cause. He did of course leave her for another woman.

> Perhaps, little bird, out of pity for my anguish,
> hearing my sad lament,
> you come to me, who, full of fire and flame,
> is burning and consumed with desir.
>
> Lovely little bird; you share my torment,
> which turns all past pleasure into pain,
> singing in a doleful, broken voice,
> seeing me ready to perish with grief.
>
> I beg you, with a fervor equal to my agony,
> fly to that pleasant countryside
> where lives the one who gives me both life and death,
>
> And singing, tell him he must give up his present love,
> turning his face toward Rome, his back to her,
> if he wishes to find me, my soul united with my body. (p. 100)

He did not come back.

In 1548 Tullia decided to move to Rome, possibly because of some business affair pertaining to property; the reason for her departure from Florence is not known.[30] She wrote Varchi a "goodbye forever" letter, sent him some small farewell gifts including her pair of doves that would soon have eggs (but not the magpie that had often amused him: Giulia, she explained, did not want to give up the little bird), and begged not to be forgotten. She left Florence with Giulia and Penelope on 15 October 1548.

On her return to Rome Tullia lived in the Palazzo Carpi (now destroyed) in the Campo Marzo, a high-rent section of the city. She was still entered as a courtesan in the city tax records, where she is reported to have been taxed as such to pay for the repair of a bridge.[31] We know nothing of her life except that she sustained a terrible blow when Penelope died suddenly on 1 February 1549. Her mother died soon after. Perhaps a year or two later Tullia, alone and seemingly in reduced financial circumstances, moved to the Trastevere quarter, where she lived in an inn. One hears of no friends remaining except the ever-loyal Muzio, who visited the city briefly when he was sent there by his patron at the time, Ferrante Gonzaga, to observe the election of the new pope succeeding Paul III, who died on 10 November 1549. The last she saw of Muzio was sometime in February 1550, when Giulio III was elected and his mission was completed.

Rome seems to us the most likely place where Tullia wrote her epic poem, *Il Meschino, detto Il Guerrino*. It was published in 1560, four years after her death, meeting with considerable success, it appears, because the same publishing house brought out a second and third printing in 1575 and 1594. The publication carried a dedication by the editor, Claudio Riniero, to Giulio della Valle, Gentiluomo di Mantua, dated 3 August 1560, and a highly interesting preface by Tullia. In his dedication, Riniero says that the manuscript was handwritten by the author herself and that he had had it in his possession for several years. According to Rosati and Celani, Tullia composed this epic poem in Florence during her few years there (1545–48); Gloria Allaire believes it dates to 1536–47.[32] However, the poem, a work of thirty-six cantos with 3,558 eight-line stanzas plus the summary stanzas heading each canto, is never mentioned by Tullia or any of the intellectuals with whom she corresponded; Muzio took her *Rime* and her *Dialogo* to Venice and oversaw their publication. Why not *Il Meschino* if it existed? She habitually sent her work to Varchi for his help in revising and correcting it; for this reason some writers think that Tullia had little ability and that her poems are more the work of Varchi than herself; we, on the other hand, think that her performance in *Il Meschino* shows considerable talent and intelligence, while there is not the slightest indication that she ever sent any of it to her friend. It is not credible to think that Tullia from time to time would not have sent parts of such a work to Varchi, asking his help with this long and difficult project.

We believe that Tullia undertook this epic when she found herself alone in Rome with no distractions and time, too much time, on her hands with nothing to do. This major work, far longer than anything she had ever attempted, was to be her last testament in proof that although she had become a courtesan by necessity, she had always been first and foremost a poet; it was to be her legacy to posterity that would immortalize her name. It is most plausible to believe that the poem came into Riniero's hands when her belongings were dispersed here and there after her death.

The circumstances surrounding this publication raise some suspicion that Tullia was not in fact the author of *Il Meschino*, but the tone and content of the preface are familiar to us from what we have learned about her and persuade us to accept it as hers; in her preface, Tullia explains that she wrote the poem because the indecency in the works of even the most important writers, from Boccaccio to Ariosto, made them inappropriate to be read by young girls, nuns, respectable women, and even those who, forced by unfortunate circumstances in their early years, fell into error, as had happened to her. She had learned too soon, she writes, about the sensual world, and she knew from her own experience the injury that results from exposure to salacious words and knowledge. Trying to find a work free of such flaws, she came upon the chivalric romance of *Guarino Mezquino* by Alonso Hernández Alemani, published in Seville in 1512, 1527, and 1548. This was actually a translation from an original fifteenth-century Italian romance by Andrea da Barberino, *Guerino il Meschino*. Tullia should certainly have known the Italian work, for it had had six editions in the fifteenth century and others in the sixteenth, including one in 1553, but she claims in her preface that it was the Spanish work that she used, as if it were the only version she knew. Its only fault was that it was written in prose, and so, for her pleasure and practice, she says, she undertook to make a translation in Italian verse. Most likely she had both the Italian and Spanish before her as she worked.

Typical of its genre, and more or less faithful to its models, *Il Meschino* recounts the adventures of Guerrino, who, taken by the Turks as a baby from his princely parents in Albania, was sold in Constantinople and thus came into the hands of a wealthy merchant whose wife was unable to have a child. She had him baptized, naming him Meschino (poor little thing). He grew into a handsome young man. Somehow entering the tournaments of the emperor, he showed his prowess in jousting and was bought from the merchant by the emperor's son. Passing through various triumphs and disasters in search of his parents, imprisoned and many times near death, he defeats his enemies, sometimes overcoming whole armies as well as giants and monsters of all kinds. Meschino has a number of amorous encounters and plights his troth to the daughter of the king of Solta because she rescued him from prison, but because she is a Muslim he does not consider his vow binding and he abandons her. Finally he falls in love with Queen Antinisca, and after further horrendous adventures, including a stay in the underworld, he marries her. In the meanwhile, he has found his parents, put his father on his rightful throne of Albania, and returns to Antinisca. They have three sons; he survives her after twelve years of marriage and retires to the wilderness, where he lives as a hermit until he dies at the age of fifty-seven.

Although Tullia in her preface attacks what she considered "lascivious and wicked things" in Boccaccio, Dolce, Ruscelli and Bembo, and assures her readers that *Il Meschino* is fit for the most innocent eyes and ears, there are a number of sexy scenes. In canto eight, for example, she describes how the innkeeper's daughter came to the hero at midnight, slipped off her clothes, and lay beside him nude; Meschino politely took off his clothes, and after they made love he turned her over to his traveling companion. They all enjoyed "a friendly night"—and that's not all.

We may admire *Il Meschino* for its sheer bulk, but as a work of art it cannot compare with her *Dialogue on the Infinity of Love*, in which she sustains at length and with lively wit her psychological and intellectual gifts. In some of her sonnets, especially those to Manelli, she shows herself capable of expressing deep despair, and in her encomiastic verses, although sometimes marred by a zealous effort to please, we hear some of the graciousness that drew people to her. She lived the ambiguous life of a woman both liberated and hobbled, vaunting free will and dependent on the favor of others. Her *Dialogue* is studded here and there with references to women's disadvantaged position in society: "If it had been up to Madonna Laura to write about him," she answers Varchi's reference to Petrarch, "you would have seen matters go rather differently," [33] but in her time and in her position, with all her daring frankness, her pen could only occasionally hint at what she perceived. The weakness of *Il Meschino* is probably due to her failing health.

Tullia died on 12 or 13 March 1556. She made her will on 2 March, and thus left the legacy of another mystery: After specifying minor gifts of her clothes and furniture to the wife of the innkeeper and to her maid, with a little money, various sums to nuns and orphans and to the friars of the Church of Sant'Agostino to light candles on her tomb and say a mass for her each year on the anniversary of her death, plus another required of all courtesans to give to the Monastery of the Converted, the will designated "Celio" as the heir to her entire estate. Still a minor, Tullia says in her will, this boy is to stay in the care of Pietro Chiocca, who was in the service of Cardinal Cornaro, and receive the interest on the estate to study literature and other subjects until the age of twenty-five, at which time he is to receive the capital.[34] Although the boy Celio is not further identified in the will, several deeds were attached to it for special gifts: in one of these deeds she refers to Celio as her son. There is no clue as to the father nor when the boy was born.

There is one more unhappy surprise to relate: In her will we discover that at the time she died Tullia was severely disabled, unable to write: "Being disabled, I have had this [will] written by a person faithful to me and I have signed it with my own hand." [35]

Tullia was buried in the Church of Sant'Agostino, laid in the tomb with her mother and Penelope. The funeral was to be simple, without ceremony, attended by the friars of Sant'Agostino and the Company of the Crucifixion of which she was a member, and no one else, according to her instructions. But there was really no one else to attend, anyway.

POEMS IN THE ORIGINAL ITALIAN*

Mentre le fiamme più che'l sol lucenti,
onde amor m'arde e già gran tempo m'arse,
vaghi occhi miei non vi si mostan scarse,
mandate nel mio core i raggi ardenti;

Orecchi miei, mentre bramosi e intenti
notate 'l suon, che di su in terra apparse,
e ne van le sue voci all'aura sparse,
inviate a la mente i sacri accenti;

Anima mia, mentre in mortale oggetto
scorgi ch'eterno è quel che dentro avampa,
allarga il seno al sempiterno zelo;

E vi rimembri che sì chiara lampa,
sì soave tenor, spirto sì chiaro,
sono a voi scala da salire al cielo. (p. 73)

Girolamo Muzio
◉ Track 11,
Reading 12

~

Fiamma gentil che da gl' interni lumi
con dolce folgorar in me discendi.
mio intenso affetto lietamente prendi,
com' è usanza a tuoi costumi;

Poi che con l'alta tue luce m'allumi
e sì soavemente il cor m'accendi,
ch'ardendo lieto vive e lo difendi,
che forza di vil foco nol consumi.

E con la lingua fai che'l rozo ingegno,
caldo dal caldo tuo, cerchi inalzarsi
per cantar tue virtuti in mille parti;

Io spero ancor a l'età tarda farsi
noto che fosti tal, che stil più degno
uopo era, e che mi fu gloria l'amarti. ‡ *(p. 73)*

Tullia d'Aragona
◉ Track 12,
Reading 11

~

Donna che sete in terra il primo oggetto
a l'anime amorose e ai gentil cori,

Girolamo Muzio
◉ Track 13,
Reading 12

---

* All poems, except where noted, are from Enrico Celani, *Le Rime di Tullia d'Aragona* (Bologna, 1968), who gives Roman numerals to Tullia's poems and Arabic numerals to poems by others to Tullia.   † 5.   ‡ XXXII

e i cui gloriosi e alteri onori
sono al mio stile altissimo soggetto;

In voi stessa si volga il chiaro aspetto
de l'alma vostra, in cui degli alti cori
risplende il bel, e 'n tutti i vostri ardori
fiammeggiar si vedrà celeste affetto.

Vedrete in voi mirando l'alma mia,
ch'in voi sempre si specchia e si fa bella,
per infiammarvi in me del vostro lume.

E 'l farà sì, per quel che mi favella
nel petto amor, se rio mortal costume
*dietro a bassi pensier non vi disvia.** (pp. 73 – 74)

⁓

Tullia d'Aragona
◉ Track 14,
Reading 13

Spirto gentil, che vero e raro oggetto
se' di quel bel, che più l'alma disìa,
e di cui brama ognor la mente mia
essere al tuo cantar suggetto;

Se di pari n'andasse in me l'affetto
con le tue lode, onor render potria
mia penna a te; ma poi mia sorte rìa
m'ha sì bramato onor tutto interdetto.

Sol dirò, che seguendo la sua stella,
l'anima tua da te fece partita,
venendo in me, com' in sua propria cella;

E la mia, ch'ora è teco insieme unita,
ten può far chiara fede, come quella,
che con la tua si mosse a cangiar vita.† (p. 74)

⁓

Girolamo Muzio
◉ Track 15,
Reading 14

O se tra queste ombrose e fresche rive
ch'or cercan solitari i passi miei,
meco ne fosse, e con Amor colei,
di cui'l cor sempre parla, e la man scrive;

Ella a seder quì presso a l'acque vive
si porria in grembo a l'erba, io in grembo a lei,
e da i boschi trarriano i semidei
il sacro aspetto, e le silvestri Dive.

---

* 2.   † XXXIV

Io lei mirando, a dir del suo valore
snoderei la mia lingua; alcun di loro
segneria per li tronchi il chiaro nome.

Ella placida, e lieta in tanto onore,
forse di vari fior, forse d'alloro
tesseria una ghirlanda a le mie chiome.[36] (p. 75)

⁓

Apri Tirrhenia le rosate porte:
. . .

Spargi Tirrhenia . . .
L'ambrosia e'l mel de l'amorosa lingua

. . .

Apri 'l giardin d'Amor, dimostra al Sole
I dolci pomi, e gli odorati gigli.

. . .

Vien Nimpha bella, e fra le molli braccia
Raccogli quel, che con le braccia aperte
Disioso t'aspetta; e nel tuo grembo
Ricevi lieta l'infocata amante.[37] (p. 76)

⁓

Bernardo, ben potea bastarvi haverne   *Tullia d'Aragona*
co'l dolce dir, ch'a voi natura infonde,
quì dove'l Re de fiumi ha più chiare onde,
acceso i cuori a le sante opre eterne.

Che se pur sono in voi pure l'interne
voglie, e la vita al vestir corrisponde,
non huom di frale carne, e d'ossa immonde,
ma sete un voi de le schiere superne.

Hor le finte apparenze, e'l ballo, e'l suono,
chiesti dal tempo, e da l'antica usanza
a che così da voi vietati sono?

Non fora santità, fora arroganza
torre il libero arbitrio, il maggior dono
*che Dio ne die ne la primiera stanza.** (pp. 77– 78)

⁓

Amor nel cor mi siede e vuol ch'io dica   *Girolamo Muzio*
di qual esca racceso a l'alma mia
sia 'l novo ardor, qual il suggetto sia
ch'è de l'animo mio dolce fatica.

---

* XXXV.

Alma gentil d'alti pensieri amica,
lumi amorosi, angelica armonia,
fan ch'ogni mio disir lieto s'invia
per le vestigia de la fiamma antica.

Colei ch'io canto nacque in su le sponde
del chiaro fiume che d'eterni allori
ben mille volte ornò le verdi chiome;

Visse in tenera etate presso a l'onde
del più bel fonte che Toscana onori:
la sua stirpe è Aragon: Tullia il suo nome.* (p. 78)

Tullia d'Aragona

Voi ch'avete fortuna sì nimica,
com'animo, valor e cortesia,
qual benigno destino oggi v'invia
a riveder la vostra fiamma antica?

Muzio gentile, un'alma così amica
è soave valore a l'alma mia,
ben duolmi de la dura e alpestra via
con tanta non di voi degna fatica.

Visse gran tempo l'honorato amore
ch'al Po già per me v'arse, et non cred'io
che sia si chiara fiamma in tutto spenta,

Et se nel volto altrui si legge il core,
spero ch'in riva d'Arno il nome mio
alto sonar ancor per voi si senta. † (pp. 78 – 79)

Siena dolente i suoi migliori invita
a lagrimar intorno al suo gran Tondi,
al cui valor ben furo i cieli secondi,
poscia invidiaro l'onorata vita. ‡ (p. 79)

Varchi, il cui raro ed immortal valore
ogni anima gentil subito invoglia,
deh! perchè non poss'io, com' ho la voglia,
del vostro alto saver colmarmi il core?

Che con tal guida so ch'uscirei fore
de le man di fortuna che mi spoglia

---

* 1.   † XXXII.   ‡ XXXVI:1–4.

d'ogni usato conforto: e ogni mia doglia
cangerei in dolce canto, e'n miglior ore.

Ahi, lassa! Io veggio ben che la mia sorte
contrasta a così onesto e bel desire,
sol perchè manch'io sotto l'aspre some.

Ma, s'a me pur così convien finire,
la penna vostra almen, levi il mio nome
fuor de gli artigli d'importuna Morte. (pp. 83 – 84)

~

Se'l ciel sempre sereno e verdi i prati,   *Tullia d'Aragona*
sieno al bel gregge tuo, dolce pastore
vero d'Arcadia e di Toscana onore,
più chiaro fra i più chiari e più pregiati;

Se tanto in tuo favor girino i fati,
che mai tor non ti possa il dato core
Filli, nè tu a lei tuo santo amore,
onde vi gridi ogni uom saggi e beati;

Dinne, caro Damon, s'alma sì vile
e sì cruda esser può. Ch'essendo amata
renda invece d'amor tormenti e morte.

Ch'io temo (lassa) se'l tuo dotto stile
non mi leva il dubbiar, d'esser pagata
di tal mercede, sì dura è mia sorte. † (p. 85)

~

Ninfa, di cui per boschi o fonti o prati,   *Benedetto Varchi*
non vide mai più bella alcun pastore,
o delle grazie e delle muse onore,
più cara sempre a'più cari e pregiati:

Così siano a Damon men feri i fati,
nè gli renda mai Filli il dato core,
ed ella arda per lui di saldo amore,
più ch' altri fosse mai lieti e beati.

Come alma esser non può si cruda e vile,
la quale essendo veramente amata,
non ami un cor gentil già presso a morte?

---

* XXVIII.   † XXX.

Dunque, s'a dotto no ma fido stile
credi, ama e non dubbiar; chè ben pagata
*sarà d'alta mercè tua dolce sorte.** (pp. 85 – 86)

Tullia d'Aragona

O qual vi debb'io dire o Donna o Diva,
poi che tanta beltà, tanto valore
riluce in voi, che'l vostro almo splendore
abbaglia qual fu mai fiamma più viva?

Mi dice un bel pensier, che di voi scriva,
et renda grazie e qual si deve honore,
ma dove s'erge l'animoso core
non giunge penna, o voce humana arriva.

So ch'ogni favor da voi mi viene,
come la luce al dì da quella stella
che surge in Oriente innanzi al Sole.

Ma poi che pur al fin mai si conviene
a tanta altezza l'humil mia favella;
v'appaghi il core in vece di parole.† (pp. 86 – 87)

Se gli antichi pastor di rose e fiori
sparsero i tempii, e vaporar gl' altari
d'incenso a Pan, sol perchè dolci e cari
avea fatto a le Ninfe i loro amori,

Quai fior degg'io, Signor, quai deggio odori
sparger al nome vostro che sian pari
a i merti vostri, e tante e così rari
ch'ognor spargete in me grazie e favori?

Nessun per certo tempio, altare, o dono
trovar si può di così gran valore,
ch'a vostra alta bontà sia pregio eguale.

Sia dunque il petto vostro, u'tutte sono
le virtù, tempio; altare il saggio core;
vittima l'alma mia, se tanto vale. ‡ (p. 87)

Qual vaga Filomela che fuggita
è da l'odiata gabbia, ed in superba

---

* Opere di Benedetto Varchi.   † XI.   ‡ I.

vista sen va tra gli arboscelli e l'erba
tornata in libertade e in lieta vita;

Er'io da gli amorosi lacci uscita,
schernendo ogni martìre e pena acerba
de l'incredibil duol ch'in sè riserba
qual ha per troppo amar l'alma smarrita.

Ben avev'io ritolte—ahi, stella fera!—
dal tempio di Ciprigna le mie spoglie,
e di lor pregio me n'andava altera;

Quand'a me Amor: "Le tue ritrose voglie
muterò" disse; e femmi prigionera
di tua virtù, per rinovar mie doglie. (pp. 87 – 88)

⌣

Amore un tempo in così lento foco
arse mia vita, e sì colmo di doglia
struggeasi 'l cor, che quale altro si voglia
martir, fora ver lui dolcezza e gioco.

Poscia sdegno e pietade a poco a poco
spenser la fiamma, ond'io, più ch'altra soglia,
libera da sì lunga e fera voglia,
giva lieta cantando in ciascuno loco.

Ma'l ciel nè sazio ancor, lassa! nè stanco
de' danni miei, perchè sempre sospiri,
mi riconduce a la mia antica sorte;

E con sì acuto spron mi punge il fianco,
ch'io temo sotto i primi empii martìri
cader, e per me mal bramar la morte. † (p. 88)

⌣

S'io 'l feci unqua che mai non giunga a riva
l'interno duol, che 'l cuor lasso sostiene;
s'io 'l feci, che perduta ogni mia spene
in guerra eterna de vostr'occhi viva;

S'io 'l feci, ch'ogni dì resti più priva
de la grazia, onde nasce ogni mio bene;
s'io 'l feci, che di tante e cotal pene,
non m'apporti alcun mai tranquilla oliva;

---

* XL.   † XXXIX.

S'io 'l feci, ch'in voi manchi ogni pietade,
e cresca doglia in me, pianto e martìre
distruggendomi pur come far soglio;

Ma s'io no'l feci, il duro vostro orgoglio
in amor si converta: e lunga etade
sia dolce il frutto del mio bel disire. (p. 88)

~

Se ben pietosa madre unico figlio
perde talora, e nuovo alto dolore
le preme il tristo e suspiroso core,
spera conforto almen, spera consiglio;

Se scaltro capitano in gran periglio
mostrando alteramente il suo valore
resta vinto e prigion, spera uscir fuore
quando che sia con baldanzoso ciglio;

S' in tempestoso mar giunto si duole
spaventato nocchier già presso a morte,
ha speme ancor di rivedersi in porto;

Ma io, s'avvien che perda il mio bel sole
o per mia colpa, o per malvagia sorte,
non spero aver, nè voglio, alcun conforto.† (p. 89)

~

Se forse per pietà del mio languire
al suon del tristo pianto in questo loco
ten vieni a me, che, tutta fiamma e foco,
ardomi, e struggo colma di disire,

Vago augellino, e meco il mio martire
ch'in pena volge ogni passato gioco,
piangi cantando in suon dolente e roco,
veggendomi dal duol quasi perire;

Prègoti per l'ardor che sì m'addoglia
ne voli in quella amena e cruda valle
ov'è chi sol può darmi e morte e vita:

E cantando gli di' che cangi voglia,
volgendo a Roma 'l viso, e a lei le spalle,
se vuol l'alma trovar col corpo unita. ‡ (p. 89)

---

* XLII.   † XLIII.   ‡ XLIV.

NOTES

1 Even so, Tullia fared better than most courtesans: she did not become destitute. While some courtesans were able to save the wealth they accumulated and died comfortably in bed, others lost their clients as they aged, and, either because their lovers took back their jewels and other gifts or they were less prudent than they should have been, died miserably, reduced to begging on the streets; many were destroyed by syphilis, known as pox. The good times and the horrible ending are recorded in two poems, "Il Vanto e Il Lamento della Cortigiana Ferrarese" (The Boast and the Lament of the Courtesan of Ferrara), reprinted in Arturo Graf, *Attraverso il cinquecento* (Turin, 1888), Appendix A, pp. 355–366.

2 The fullest account of Tullia's life is by Salvatore Rosati, *Tullia d'Aragona* (Milan, 1936). A more recent account, closely following the factual details given by Rosati, much briefer but with some details added, is found in Enrico Celani, *Le rime di Tullia d'Aragona* (Bologna, 1968), which also includes the poems of Tullia that appeared in her book *Rime della Signora Tullia d'Aragona, et di diversi a lei* (Venice, 1547). Our account of her life depends on both of these sources; we have translated all the poems in this chapter from Celani, except where noted.

3 Alessandro Zilioli, quoted by Celani, *Rime di Tullia d'Aragona*, pp. xxii–xxiii, wrote that intellectuals were amazed when they heard her as a young girl speak and write in Latin on philosophical and literary subjects.

4 Celani, *Le Rime di Tullia d'Aragona*, p. xlix.

5 Celani claims (*Le Rime di Tullia d'Aragona*, p. xxii) that the cardinal left her a comfortable fortune, which allowed her to be well educated; Rosati, on the other hand, believed that the cardinal did not believe Tullia was his child and left no legacy to Giulia or her child, so that Tullia was obliged to take up her mother's profession out of necessity; Tullia, in her preface to her epic poem *Il Meschino detto il Guerrino*, laments her early introduction to sex, and elsewhere she makes clear that she considered a courtesan's life undesirable and would not have chosen it if she had been able to do otherwise. This is probably why Tullia considered free will as God's greatest gift, as she wrote in her poem to Bernardo Ochino (see pp. 77 – 78; p. 95).

6 Claudio Tolomei (1492–1555 / 57) published, in 1514 at the age of twenty-two, a long poem, "In Praise of the Women of Bologna." He had a distinguished career as a writer and diplomat. Ludovico Martelli (1503–ca.1531) escaped from Florence after killing a *landsknecht* and went to Rome. He wrote sonnets, madrigals, *canzoni*, music for carnivals, and, most interesting in our context, a tragedy in imitation of *Electra* that he titled *Tullia*. Benedetto Varchi (*Storia Fiorentina*) wrote of him, "If his mind were equal to his talent and had he had good judgment, he would have been one of the most unusual and most praised men of our century" (*Dizionario enciclopedia della letteratura italiana* [Laterza, 1967], vol. 3, p. 527).

7 According to Rosati (*Tullia d'Aragona*, pp. 52–53), Tullia went to Bologna in 1529 when Pope Clement, who had been in effect a prisoner of Charles V at the time of the sack, crowned him emperor of the Holy Roman Empire. As we have seen, Veronica Gàmbara also went to Bologna for this event, and, given its immense importance, we can easily imagine that Vittoria Colonna might also have been there.

8 We follow Rosati's account (*Tullia d'Aragona*, pp. 59–60), which gives this as the reason for Tullia's departure from Rome; it differs somewhat from Celani's account in details. According to Celani, pp. xxvii–xxviii, note 1, some of Tullia's devoted young men had published a *cartello di sfida* (a public poster) declaring themselves the champions and protectors of the illustrious Tullia d'Aragona, "for the infinite virtue that shines in her more splendidly than in all other women, past, present, and future" ("*per le infinite virtù quail in lei risplendono è quella che più merita che tutta le alter donne de la preterita, presente e futura etate*"); Rosati also refers to the poster, which included Paolo Emili Orsini among the signers. Giovanni Battista Giraldi conceived a vicious enmity against Tullia, and he recounted the story of the filthy German in his book *Gli Ecatommiti*.

9 This and all poems in this chapter are from Celani, *Le Rime di Tullia d'Aragona*, except where noted.

10 Rosati, *Tullia d'Aragona*, pp. 57–58.

11   Although we do not know when Giulia Campana was born, we can speculate reasonably that she was probably at least seventeen years old when Tullia was born. If Tullia was born in the first decade of the sixteenth century and had become a well-known courtesan by the second half of the 1520s, we suppose that she was born around 1507; this would make Giulia about forty-five years old in 1535, give or take a year or two. Though not impossible, it is unlikely that she would have had a baby at that age.

12   Georgina Masson, *Courtesans of the Italian Renaissance* (New York, 1976), pp. 100–101. See also Janet L. Smarr, "A Dialogue of Dialogues," *MLN* 113, no. 1 (January 1998): 204–212.

13   *Egloghe del Muzio Justinopolitano* (Venice, 1550), "*Le Amorose,*" *Libro Primo . . . alla Signora Tullia d'Aragona*, pp. 5–6.

14   According to one version of the story of the founding of Rome, Tirrhenia was the wife of Aeneas and the mother of Romulus, whose daughter, Alba, became the mother of Rome. Muzio thus identifies Tullia as "Rome." Tullia did not know the word "comedy" in the modern sense of "funny"; she identified herself as the muse of comedy who inspired poems that ended happily instead of tragically.

15   The letter to Isabella d'Este from Battista Stambellino is dated 13 June 1537. See Rinaldino Russell and Bruce Merry, eds., *Tullia d'Aragona, Dialogue on the Infinity of Love* (Chicago, 1997), p. 22, n. 3. This book provides an English translation of Tullia's dialogue; for the original Italian see Giuseppe Zonta, ed., *Trattati d'amore del cinquecento* (Bari, 1912), pp. 185–248.

16   Celani, *Le Rime di Tullia d'Aragona*, pp. xxix–xxx, note 1. (*V. Ecc. Intenderà come è sorta in questa terra una gentil cortegiana di Roma, nominata la S.ra Tullia la quale è venuta per istare qui qualche mese. . . . Questa è molto gentile, discreta, accorta et di ottimi et divini costumi dotata; sa cantare al libro ogni motetto et canzone . . . si porta che non c'è homo nè donna in questa terra che la paregi, anchora che la ill.ma S.ra Marchesa di Pescara sia ecc.ma, la quale è qui come sa V. Ecc. Mostra costei sapere de ogni cosa, et parla pur sieco di che materia te aggrada. Sempre ha piena la casa di virtuosi et sempre si può visitarla, et è ricca de denari, zoie, colanne, anella et altre cose notabile, et in fine è ben accomodata in ogni cosa. . . .*).

17   Battista Stambellino refers to the story of a young man, desperately in love with Tullia, who stabbed himself in her presence when she repeatedly refused to marry him. Her mother, her maids, and her bodyguard, hearing her scream, came running into the room. They tried to get the would-be lover out of the house but afraid to lift him because of the wound, they finally left him in the room, locking the door from the outside. Tullia sent for a soldier friend of hers whom she knew could handle emergencies; he arrived with two companions, and all three remained with her through the night. In the morning they found the young man unconscious, lying in a pool of blood, and carried him away to where he could be helped. While the young man lay for weeks hovering between life and death (apparently he survived), all of Ferrara heard the story of the virtuous Tullia, who refused a treasure of gifts the young man had offered to marry him (see Rosati, *Tullia d'Aragona*, pp. 116–124).

18   Celani, *Le rime di Tullia d'Aragona*, p. xxxi. See also Rosati, *Tullia d'Aragona*, p. 133, and Salvatore Bongi, "Documenti senesi su Tullia d'Aragona," *Rivista Critica della Letteratura Italiana* 4 (1886): 187.

19   Masson, *Courtesans*, p. 110.

20   Celani, *Le Rime di Tullia d'Aragona*, pp. xxx–xxxv.

21   Celani, *Le Rime di Tullia d'Aragona*, pp. xlix–l; Rosati, *Tullia d'Aragona*, p. 134.

22   The poem to Molza is in Pierantonio Serassi, *Poesie di Francesco Maria Molza* (Milan, 1808). Molza's wife survived him by many years; therefore, his "most faithful companion" was not his wife. Not to leave any stone unturned, we further present the following: Tullia had a pet that lost an offspring and was evidently mourning. She wrote a poem in which she addresses her pet: "Because maternal love afflicts your heart / making you search everywhere / for your son, Lilla my darling / you cry, and your suffering increases with your tears: / You, an animal that cannot reason / you cannot understand, alas, how wicked and hostile / destiny has been to both of us / taking from you your little one and from me my love." Was love taken away from Tullia through death? Was this love Silvestro who might have died, or Manelli who abandoned her, or Bernardo Tasso who left her because he had to return to his patron in Salerno, or someone else? We still hope to find the answer to the mystery of Tullia's supposed marriage.

23   *Rime della Signora Tullia d'Aragona*, pp. 35–37.

24 Salvatore Bongi, "Il Velo Giallo di Tullia d'Aragona," *Rivista Critica della Letteratura Italiana* III, no. 3 (March 1886): 85–86.

> La grazia et la virtù, generosa signora, per esser doti et ricchezze del animo et parte-cipare più del divino che del humano, non sogghiacciono alla violenza degli anni. Dato che anchora et giovane et belle sete, anzi bella tanto, che, 'l disgeno del viso delicato ha quelle medesime sembianze che prima d'Angelo s'havea, et haverà per insino a l'ultima hora; perchè essendo quella bellezza che i cieli sì largamente vi diedero infinita, non può il tempo, che ha a finire, usare in lei per nuocerle, così in un tratto, tutte le ragioni sue. La bianchezza delle carni similmente, che vinceven l'alabastro et la purissima neve, si sono mantenute freschissime, per esser voi, non pur nel cibarse, ma in tutte le altre vostre ationi moderata et continentissima; tal che anchora vi rappresentate agli occhi d'altrui con l'in-segne nel viso gratiose d'Amore. E questo è il men bello che si scorga in voi, rispetto a quella virtù che vi esalta et così sopprema vi mostra, la quale empie di stupore le genti a udirve si dolcemente cantare, et con la man bianca et bella qual si voglia stromento leg-giadramente sonare. It ragionamento piacevole poi, adorno di honesti costumi, et le maniere gentili fanno sospirare altrui con castissime voglie. Della eloquenza in privato e in pubblico non parlo; perchè se allora fu un TULLIO d'Arpino, hoggi è nel mondo una TULLIA d'ARAGONA, che veramente si può dire honor secondo, a cui l'alma Poesia et la nobil Filosofia fanno un componimento celeste; che difuso pel mezzo della penna vos-tra, con meraviglia si rallegrono le carte a esser vergate da così dotta mano. . . . (p. 81)

25 We wish to thank Dr. Ragni for her letter. Her interpretation of the portrait, together with her colleague Ida Gianfranceschi, is discussed in *Dichterin und Muse Michelangelos* (Vienna, 1997), pp. 209–212.

26 Girolamo Francastoro belongs to the history of literature and medicine for his poem *Syphilis sive de morbo gallico* (Verona, 1530). The poem recounts the events in which a shepherd named Sifilo was stricken with the disease by Apollo as a punishment for some infidelity; hence the name. In his poem Francastoro writes that the disease had been treated with a remedy made from the *lignum vi-tae*, but when Ilceo, a woodsman, was punished with the disease for killing a deer, a nymph took him underground, dipped him in a silver river, and cured him; thus was mercury discovered as a remedy. In the sixteenth century it was not known how the disease was communicated.

27 Zonta, *Trattati d'amore*, pp. 222–223, 226; Russell and Merry, *Dialogue*, pp. 91, 94.

28 Zonta, *Trattati d'amore*, pp. 227–229; Russell and Merry, *Dialogue*, pp. 96–97.

29 The fullest account of the story of the yellow veil is found in Salvatore Bongi, "Il velo giallo."

30 Rosati thought half-heartedly that Giulia may have persuaded Tullia to start Penelope on her career as a courtesan. It is fruitless to try to guess why they moved.

31 It was the practice to tax women who lived by sex to pay for city repairs and improvements. Celani (*Le Rime di Tullia d'Aragona*, p. xix, n. 4) relates that Pope Leo X opened a new street in Rome paid for by taxing prostitutes. Giulia, walking one day on this street, accidentally bumped into a lady who began to insult and scold her. Giulia replied, "Lady, excuse me, but I know you have more right on this street than I have."

32 Neither Rosati or Celani gives any reason for assuming that *Il Meschino* was composed in Flo-rence; Gloria Allaire offers a number of arguments in support of her dates of 1536–47, but after a very careful reading we do not find them persuasive; see Allaire, "Tullia d'Aragona's *Il Meschino al-tramente detto il Guerrino* as Key to a Reappraisal of Her Work," *Quadrini d'Italianistica* XVI, no. 1 (1995): 33–50.

33 Russell and Merry, *Dialogue*, p. 69; Zonta, *Trattati d'amore*, p. 201.

34 In the event of Celio's death before the age of twenty-five, Tullia made other provisions, in-cluding ten *scudi* each year to an orphan girl to help her get married (Celani, *Le Rime di Tullia d'Arag-ona*, p. xliii).

35 Celani, *Le Rime di Tullia d'Aragona*, pp. xli–xliii.

36 Not in Celani. From Pietro da Trois, *Scelta di sonetti e canzone de' più eccellent rimatori di ogni se-colo*, Part II (Bologna, 1709).

37 "Le Amorose," pp. 6–7.

38 *Opere di Benedetto Varchi* (Trieste, 1859), vol. II, p. 971.

4.1. Anon. *Portrait of Chiara Matraini*. 1555. Thomas Fisher Rare Books Library, University of Toronto Library, Toronto. Photo, Library.

CHAPTER FOUR

Chiara Matraini
(1515–1604)

❧ THE POET AS SIBYL

Born into a large, respectable, affluent family, but not of the nobility, Chiara Matraini was a year old when her father died and her uncle, Ridolfo Matraini, became her guardian. He arranged her marriage in 1530 to one Vincenzo Cantarini, of whom nothing more is known except that he died in 1542.[1] Shortly after the marriage Lucca was shaken by the turbulence of a rebellion of the city's working class protesting restrictive policies of the city government, run largely by the nobility, that had brought financial hardship to the city's silk workers. Ridolfo and other members of the Matraini family, although wealthy, became leaders among the rebels in this "Uprising of the Ragged" *(sollevazione degli straccioni)*, as the rebellion was called, and when peace was restored with most of the power still in the hands of the nobility, the family suffered punishment, with some members exiled, others imprisoned, and one beheaded.[2] Chiara chose to remain identified with the Matraini family even after her marriage, and she thus suffered from the family's disrepute as aggressive commoners as well as from the general lack of respect she endured because one in her social class was generally considered to have no right to intellectual pretensions. Her resentment on this account, as well as the enduring effect on her of the rebellion, is clear in a letter to an unknown correspondent, M. L. "Why do you feel it necessary to show me how inappropriate it is for a woman born not of noble blood, not brought up in great palaces, not surrounded by immense wealth to go about continually spending her time studying and writing, unlike the customs of our city? . . . I must tell you that although I may not be born of noble or royal blood . . . my family is not unworthy, or poor, or low-class but of good blood and possessed of means won in a free city, and are good-spirited people. If we looked at things honestly we would certainly see . . . that it is not ancient blood, not the gold or the purple, which commands the subservience of the common people, but the shining spirit of virtue that makes a man truly noble."[3] The rebellion may also be reflected, as we shall see, in the painting she commissioned.

It was the animating desire of Chiara's life not only to transcend actually the limitations she felt were imposed on her by her social class and gender, but also to be *acknowledged* as a woman beyond class and gender. Rather than negative revenge, as Rabitti sees it, it was her positive determination to prove her right to be appreciated for her intelligence, talent, and refined feelings that motivated her.[4] The ordinary chores and obligations that were laid on respectable women, she wrote to Cesar Coccapani, her advisor in her middle age and possibly her lover,[5] had prevented her from fully realizing her natural gifts. "It is very true that if I had had the freedom that my nature required, I might have done things worthy of memory."[6]

She was superior to most people, she felt, even in her way of loving. It is interesting that she addresses women specifically as she portrays herself in the Neo-Platonic role of the chaste, spiritual lover. In her first volume of poems, which carries her profile portrait (figure 4.1), she writes,

> *Spurring reason, and reining in my senses,*
> *I began, women, to love, with utmost love,*
> *divine beauty, so that among the inspired*
> *my spirit may live nobly and triumphant;*
> *may its glorious light in my ardent soul*
> *bring forth wonderful fruit from humble roots;*
> *such is the quality of its light that leads the soul*
> *to create the most beautiful works.* (p. 126)

The majority of the poems in this 1555 volume, which carried her profile portrait (figure 4.1), reflect her unhappy love affair with a man who had died probably the previous year. It is particularly in the role of a Petrarchan lover that she expressed the rare joy and the almost constant suffering that her affair brought her. In common with her *petrarchisti* contemporaries, she frequently used oxymora such as "icy fire" and "sweet pain" and antitheses such as hope/fear and noble/base. Like Petrarch, who, on a certain day, he tells us, was "assaulted" by love at first sight of Laura, Chiara,[7] specifies the day when she too was "assaulted" by Amor:

> *It was at that very moment*
> *when the sun entered the second equinox,[8]*
> *when light and dark were in perfect balance*
> *ready to welcome the coming of the new day.*
>
> *That Love took hold of me*
> *and awakened me to a shining dawn*
> *that brought glory and virtue*
> *and everlasting daylight to my soul.*
>
> *Then, singing together with my living Sun*
> *how lovely was the sweet harmony, the looks and words*
> *that delight the Soul,*
>
> *May they be blessed, those first lovely melodies*
> *that sounded to me like those heard only by the soul*
> *in heaven among the happy angels.* (p. 126)

In imitation of Petrarch's Laura-inspired lyric poetry as it was presented in the sixteenth century, she arranged her poems to follow the design of his *canzoniere*.[9] The arrangement made her easily recognizable to Cinquecento readers as the Petrarchan lover, gender-reversed to make the additional point that women, or *this* woman, can love as men do. Inspired by his love for the doubly inaccessible Laura, Petrarch's story is divided into two parts, the first concerned with Laura living, the embodiment of perfect beauty and virtue, and married; the second with Laura dead. The man with whom Chiara fell in love was married and Chiara presented herself in the Petrarchan role of the lover whose beautiful and virtuous beloved, was, alas, also inaccessible (although in truth, it seems, not entirely) and also died.

Bartolomeo Graziani had married Elisabetta Sergiusti in 1542. About five years later "he fell in love with a woman of low repute, Donna de' Matraini, a poet."[10] Graziani seemed eccentric to some who knew him—he was nicknamed "il fantastico" and was said to be high-tempered. He was apparently unconventional: he turned his house into some kind of an "academy," according to Gherardo Sergiusti, a relative of Elizabeth, where, to please "the wicked widow," he welcomed a crowd of young students from Pisa who "spent the day and night laughing, cavorting around, telling dirty jokes, and doing all kinds of disgraceful things."[11] A few lines in Chiara's poetry suggest that he may have been a painter or poet and that he may have made a portrait of her, either painted or in words: my poetry, she tells him, is unworthy of praising sufficiently

> *your divine gift*
> *in which I sweetly and proudly see myself reflected.* (p. 126)

Elsewhere she refers to his writings. He must have been an artist of some kind, for, mourning his death, she associates him with Parnassus and the muses. All song has ended,

> *everyone was sad and silently grieving*
> *with sobs and deep loud sighs*
> *that could make stones break with pity,*
> *and bring rain from Heaven on the clearest day.*
> *Parnassus is forever darkened by a dark cloud . . .*(pp. 126 – 27)

and she writes of the laurel and myrtle that must crown his tomb,

> *and the woodland gods*
> *of elm and cypress trees that make a thousand trophies*
> *for your wonderful, glorious works.* (p. 127)

Graziani was blinded by his infatuation, Sergiusti asserts, bewitched by the poet's "sorcery" (a familiar accusation, we may note, made against women whose "bewitching" beauty and charm enthrall their hapless males). It seems that Chiara encouraged the belief that she had some extraordinary powers: when she was apparently thrown out of the apartments where Graziani was living she let herself be heard to murmur, "I am leaving this place but I will contrive that those who stay here will have little pleasure in it."[12] When, ironically, her lover Graziani died—a murder victim—she lamented his death in a long *canzone* in which she wrote of having foreseen the tragedy, "the homicidal crime that God would avenge."

> *Bright, eternal, happy soul*
> *whose life was cut short in its mid-years,*

now you have risen to the blessed;
turn now to that high place the face
shining and divine that you used to show me:
but look back at the suffering your noble compassion
has caused me, and you will see
those eyes you loved full of bitter tears
bathing my faithful, grieving breast.

A more profound wound, or horrible event
(What misery!) Heaven could not show me than this,
alas, that my heart foresaw—
you know that I told you so. (p. 127)

Further on, she continues,

I saw your deadly distress
in a horrible, atrocious, fatal vision,
I saw you give your mortal veil
to the ugly, angry Serpent,
intent only on your destruction,
your heart eaten away, your life spent. (p. 127)

Her reputation for possessing prophetic gifts was apparently well known and was remembered after her death. Francesco Agostino della Chiesa wrote in 1620 that "Chiara Matraini, a most distinguished Lady, had the quick intelligence not only to see, but to foresee events."[13]

Sergiusti himself prophesied that she would suffer even more than those she was said to have abused, and deserving or not, suffer Chiara certainly did, not only after Graziani's death, but before, during a period of separation. For some unknown reason, her beloved left Lucca, possibly forced to leave because of their scandalous relationship, possibly because he went off to fight in the ongoing war between Spain and France over the hegemony of Italy; in one sonnet she tells him that she hopes "to see you decorated with the greatest honors" (p. 127). It is possible, of course, that the honors she hoped he might win would be for his art, but is also possible that this sonnet was addressed not to Graziani but to an earlier lover, possibly even her husband, for we have learned from Sergiusti's account that Chiara was already known as a poet in 1547, when her affair with Graziani apparently began. She seems to have included in her 1555 collection some poems that she might have written before she knew Graziani. In an early poem it seems evident that she had loved more than once, for she writes of thinking she had escaped the bonds of love forever, but finds herself now "swept away":

Although my heart thought itself
freed from amorous bonds
and I had frozen insistent desire,
firmly shutting it inside of me,

> *How sweet that fire was when your kindness*
> *finally caught me in its net of love*
> *and entirely swept away every defense*
> *so that from pain came pleasure.*

> *May the net of love be always*
> *filled with wise talk and sweet song,*
> *and divine virtue:*

> *Such angel-like beauty has never been seen*
> *in another soul in this world,*
> *I will follow it wherever heaven's destiny leads.* (pp. 127 – 28)

We gather that she might have had an unhappy affair with a man who apparently did not return her love, or perhaps it was Graziani who made her suffer.

> *I am a wild animal, fleeing through the forest*
> *with an arrow in my heart,*
> *I run away from what would end my suffering*
> *and seek the one who is destroying me bit by bit.* (p. 128)

Whether or not there were others before Graziani, for the purpose of her *canzoniere* and for the sake of the self-image she created, she had only one true love of her life, ideal because it was not only physical but spiritual and therefore chaste. She adored her beloved, the perfection of all human virtues, she tells the reader in a *canzone*:

> *I tell you that whatever desire you have*
> *to know what there is in the world of beauty and honor*
> *worthy of eternal, immortal glory,*
> *look at my beautiful angel who,*
> *however much others may be loved*
> *and worthy of true and immortal memory,*
> *is the greatest of all;*
> *for it is the will of God, Nature, and Love*
> *as if they were his temple*
> *to reveal in him its gifts*
> *of all good things, of every beauty gathered in him.* (p. 128)

When she was separated from her beloved she was distraught, and, dramatically, she wanted to die. She chose the madrigal form in which to sing of her anguish:

> *My heart stopped, my blood froze*
> *when I looked at the devoted face of my dearest love,*
> *and heard his sweet, resigned voice saying,*
> *with a long, deep sigh, Oh, my life,*

sadly I must go, but my heart I leave in pledge;
then bitter grief flashed in his eyes
and his handsome face turned pale.
What I felt in that moment only Love knows
and every stricken heart knows it, too;
almost dead, with feeble and broken voice,
and with great effort, I managed to say, "Goodbye, my lord,"
I could say no more.
I wanted to die. (p. 128)

In a particularly vivid sonnet following their separation, one sees Chiara walking alone in a countryside, comparing her misery with the happiness she sees in nature. It is springtime, and all is renewed; the meadows are brightened by new blossoms blown over them by a gentle breeze, birds sing with their happy lovers, and everything joyful now returns, but, she writes,

mournful winter never leaves me, alas;
far from my beautiful Sun
I feel constantly its hellish love;
  Nor can I find escape from my aching loneliness,
for so fierce is the suffering in my heart
that neither time nor words can end it. (p. 129)

Nevertheless, she did find words, and there are more than twenty poems in which she laments his being away from her. Promising to love him forever, she turned as she did time and again, to Petrarch (135, l. 30), perceiving her lover as a magnet:

Oh my sweet, beautiful, living magnet
who, leaving me, almost like magic
held my soul so tightly that
to you alone it will remain forever united. (p. 129)

How long they were separated we do not know. Nor when he was murdered. Nor how he was killed. Nor why he was killed. It seems most likely that his murder was in revenge for his adultery—Matraini writes of betrayal by a friend to whom he gave some confidence:

Why, so brave and so good,
did you bare your trusting breast to so vile a hand? (p. 129)

—and of envy:

Just when I was enjoying the sweet peace
and happiness in the first hopes of
gathering fruit, and flowers from the top
of the highest laurel, that hideous Serpent appeared.

> *To cruel Fortune, graceless Fortune*
> *you raised me with those sublime thoughts*
> *so that (falling) I would eat my heart out*
> *and scratch the painful wound that you have poisoned.*
>
> *Now you have done your worst,*
> *malicious envy: now my sweet, dear joy*
> *is hardened with the most bitter venom.*
>
> *You have torn all goodness out of my life:*
> *now I will never again see a bright, clear light*
> *until once more I see my shining Sun.* (p. 129)

However it happened or why, or when, he was dead. By 1555 she had put her life together in what turned out to be the first part of her canzoniere. Of the 104 poems in this collection, most of them were inspired by love, happy or miserable. Toward the end of the volume, however, a new note of religiosity is sounded. Although spirituality had been an important aspect of her relationship with her beloved, her imagination was fired by his physical as well as his spiritual beauty; it was not imbued with religion as such. Putting aside the final five poems of the volume, which are encomiums, the last nine are specifically religious, prayerful in tone. She begs God for forgiveness for having "taken the wrong road."

> *Father in Heaven, after many, many years*
> *in which I wandered away from your light*
> *and went astray in this mortal shade,*
> *I pray that you will put my soul on the good path;*
>
> *And let the foolish and false thoughts*
> *that made me stray from your right way*
> *be turned always with your help*
> *toward more worthy tasks and a better life.*
>
> *Steer the sails of my tired boat*
> *away from the rocks to a safer place,*
> *O Lord, that I may stay far from Charybdis and Scylla.*
>
> *Gather into yourself my lost high hopes*
> *and turn my studies and my talent*
> *to a more praiseworthy and more tranquil life.* (pp. 129 – 30)

She begs the Virgin to intercede for her, to turn away the wrath of God which she incurred:

> *Virgin in whom lived the eternal Sun,*
> *wholly filled with his divinity*

like an enlarged image of real things
is contained in a small sphere,

Wholly without stain, in you is enclosed
the radiance of the sun almost as if enclosed in glass;
with pure love, chaste and sincere,
you bowed humbly to your great destiny.

From you only is reflected his love
that is aflame in both, and his divine fire
which desires to be your son and father:

Oh pray that he does not turn his wrath
against us who caused it, step by step,
thou elected bride, daughter, and mother of God. (p. 130)

The shock of Graziani's death might well have turned her thoughts to heaven. It is also true that the Council of Trent had sharply altered the cultural atmosphere of Italy in the second half of the Cinquecento. Where an unconventional, scandalous way of life had previously brought on the wrath of society, it now brought on the terrible danger of being charged as a heretic by the Inquisition, for such behavior was seen as clearly irreligious and enemies could report "suspicious," unconforming conduct. Not only unconventional behavior could become suspect: sympathy with the Italian Reform movement, influenced by Protestantism, which was widespread among the cultural community throughout Italy, was also risky in the extreme; although they were loyal to the Church and wanted to reform it from within, former sympathizers with the Reform cooled or kept their views to themselves. As we have seen, even such a one as Vittoria Colonna, whom Chiara revered and to whom she addressed at least one or two poems,[14] broke her friendship with Bernardino Ochino, leader of the Italian Reform movement, when he came under attack by the Church and was forced to flee to Zurich. Whether through fear or newly stimulated faith, Italians of the second half of the Cinquecento became far more pious than they had been earlier. So with Chiara, who might well have felt it necessary to prove her piety. Although in her 1555 volume she constantly insists on the spiritual quality of her relationship with Graziani, she clearly was fascinated with his physical beauty; their affair was grounded in life. It is true that some of the poems inspired by a beloved are repeated in the 1597 volume, but the result of deletions and changes in it is to shift the emphasis from the love story to her spiritual narrative, as Elaine MacLachlan points out. Furthermore, whereas in the first volume she calls upon her dead Beloved, now among the blessed in heaven, to bring her to him, in the 1597 work "the concept of an angelic, salvific man is largely cast out and replaced by a direct involvement of the poet with her own salvation through an individual relationship of the poet to God, mediated, if at all, by the Virgin Mary and not by her dead lover."[15]

That religion had come to play a crucial role in Chiara's life by 1576 is evident in the commission by which she ordered the erection of an altar next to the sacristy in her parish Church of Sta. Maria Forisportam, near where she was born, and where

4.2.
Inscription in marble plaque near the altar commissioned by Chiara Matraini, Church of Sta. Maria Forisportam, Lucca. Photo, Colombardo.

she was eventually buried. The commission is recorded in the inscription carved into the marble plaque on the wall to the left of the altar (figure 4.2).

D.O.M.
CLARA MATRAINIA LUCENSIS
QUAE CUM. ALIQUOD PIETATIS
A.C. RELIGIONIS OPUS CONFI
CERE CUPERET
HANC ARAM VI
VENS IN DEI HONOREM ERIGEN
DAM CURAVIT A.D. MDLXXVI

(Chiara Matraini of Lucca wishing to accomplish a work of piety took care to order this religious work in honor of God while she still lived A.D. 1576)

To the right of the altar, another inscription reads

CONSPICIT ALBUNEA CAESAR MONSTRATE SIBYLLA
COELESTEM PUERUM VIRGINIS IN GREMBO
PROSTERNIT SE SUBITO ET SUBMISSUS ADORAT
QUEM REGUM DNVM NOSCERET ATQUE DEUM

(The Heavenly Child in the Lap of the Virgin is revealed by the Albunean sybil to Caesar who bows and humbly adores Him whom he acknowledges as the Lord of Kings and God.)

Near the floor of the altar there is the notice

SEPULTURA
DI M. CHIARA MATRAINI

(This is the grave of M. Chiara Matraini.)

Possibly ill and anticipating her death and her burial in this church, Chiara made her first will that year, stipulating, among other requests, that a painting she had earlier commissioned from Alessandro Ardenti in which she wished to be represented as a sibyl, be finished by Francesco Cellini: "To the painter Francesco Cellini di Lucca, a bequest of 660 *scudi* gold for the purpose of finishing the painting for the altar she [Matraini] has decided to have made in the church of Sta. Maria Forisportam where her tomb is . . . [and furthermore] to incise the epitaph which is between the altar and the door of the sacristy."[16] Upon completion the painting was hung over her altar, where it remained until the twentieth century, when it was moved to its present location in Lucca's Museo Nazionale di Villa Guinigi (plate III). It is not known when Cellini finished the painting but it is likely that it was ready shortly after the altar was erected in 1576.[17]

The subject of the painting is the story of the Emperor Augustus and the Tiburtine sibyl. *The Golden Legend* recounts that when the Roman Senate wished to deify Augustus as a supreme peacemaker, the emperor, aware of his mortality, consulted the sibyl to ask if there would ever be a man greater than he. The sibyl's answer came at noon on the day of Christ's nativity, when the Virgin appeared in the sky at the center of a golden ring that formed around the sun. A voice said, "The Woman is the Altar of Heaven," and the sibyl then prophesied, "The Child will be greater than you." Augustus thereupon dedicated an altar to the Virgin on the supposed site in Rome of the Church of Santa Maria d'Aracoeli.[18]

The painting was obviously of great importance to Chiara, as evident in the provisions of her will, and yet it has received no extended scholarly attention. There has thus been no attempt to deal with what we see as a number of intriguing problems that it poses: When did she commission the painting? Why did she wish to be portrayed as a sibyl? What role, if any, did she play in choosing the subject and its composition? We will undertake now to take up these issues which may lead us to a plausible iconographical interpretation of the painting and to a further understanding of the woman and poet.

Chiara would have been in her sixties when Cellini carried out his commission according to her will of 1576, while the image of the sibyl is of a much younger woman in face and figure—a slightly "mythologized" Chiara, Giovanna Rabitti thought, obviously worried about the discrepancy. Although Rabitti gives 1576 as the date of the commission to Ardenti,[19] we feel this must be ruled out: if she gave the commission to Ardenti in 1576, why did she commission Cellini to finish it that same year? In fact, Ardenti was no longer living in Lucca. He left Lucca in 1572 to take up residence in Turin as the *scultore ordinario* to Emanuele Filiberto, Duke of Savoy. In 1576 when Chiara requested in her will that Cellini, a Lucchese artist, finish the painting, Ardenti was no longer available.[20] He is documented in the vicinity of Lucca from 1539, when he painted a *Nativity* for a small church in the suburb of Antraccoli until the 1560s when he executed a number of paintings for churches in Lucca. Thus, Chiara surely could have ordered the painting from him around 1545 when she actually was still young, although already known locally as a poet. He could have begun Chiara's painting anytime within that span of years from ca. 1539 to the 1560s, and therefore, judging her age from her appearance to have been between thirty and thirty-five when she was painted as the sibyl, it would appear that Ardenti worked on the painting ca. 1545.

We do not know why he did not finish it but we may hazard a guess. Around 1547 Chiara was hounded out of the city because of the scandalous affair with Graziani. The exact years in which she was absent from the city are not known; she may have left and returned more than once. She was apparently reluctant to live there, but by 1576 she was again settled in Lucca where she remained for the rest of her life.[21]

It should be noticed that in addition to the sibyl, there is another woman prominently represented in *Emperor Augustus and the Sibyl*. Near the center of the painting this woman stands side-by-side and almost cheek-to-cheek with a man next to her. In front of her and the man beside her, at their feet, is a nude *putto*, who looks out at the viewer as he raises his left arm, pointing upward with his finger toward the couple. This, of course, is *Amore*, drawing the viewer's attention to them as lovers. Below Cupid is a small dog, a traditional symbol of fidelity. Floating directly above the couple, in the vision, another nude *putto* holds an open scroll with the words *HIC PUER MAIOR EST TE IPSUM/ ADORA* (Adore this Child who is greater than you), the oracle attributed to the Tiburtine sibyl. Above this *putto* is the Christ child holding a globe, and held by the Virgin on one knee (see page 120). The dog, the two *putti* and the Child are visually connected rising on a vertical line that includes at its center the woman and the lover. Given the prominence of this woman in the composition, and highlighted as she is, we must recognize that she represents someone of importance. Comparing her face with Chiara's portrait as a sibyl, we recognize the same woman in both plump, round faces and deep-lidded eyes. The profile drawing of Chiara reproduced in her volume of poems published in 1555 is not informative enough as a portrait to use as a comparison, but in the almost full-face engraving of the poet that appeared in her volume of commentary on the seven penitential psalms of David published in 1586, showing her as a much older woman, we still find a resemblance to this deep-lidded, highlighted woman (figures 4.3, 4.4; plate III). We therefore believe that the elderly woman in bright light represents Chiara (*chiara*, light) and that, odd as it seems, she is figured twice in her painting. But this oddity raises the question "why?" which we will take up later.

In a sense, all creative writers are role-players, for writing and speaking are enactments of thought and feeling. Publishing one's writing is exhibiting one's words on a stage where they can interact with themselves and move readers or listeners. Most writers, especially when they are writing directly or indirectly about themselves, want to present themselves in a favorable or at least interesting light, or to move others to sympathy. Role-playing helps the writer to project private yearnings that reflect the true self, and it is in this light that we see the choices Chiara Matraini made in the roles she played: poet, scholar, faithful lover, and devout Christian. The "Chiaras" of the poems are, like all art, recreations of life, creations not of nature but of imagination.

4.3.
Alessandro
Ardente/
Francesco
Cellini.
*Augustus and the
Sibyl*, detail,
plate III.
*Chiara Matraini
and Her Lover.*

We recognize her presence in her poetry, in which she is to be found often, quite literally: the word *chiara* (light, bright), with gender or number changes, appears with its myriad shades of meaning, literal and metaphorical, with extraordinary frequency in her *canzoniere*. Our view of Chiara, our conviction that she is represented twice in the painting she commissioned, and our interpretation of the painting is derived from our reading of her poetry, together with what we know of her life.[22]

Turning to *Emperor Augustus and the Sibyl,* first let us try to sort out the two hands. Because Chiara as the sibyl is the star of the drama, with Augustus as the costar, they were most probably painted first and thus by the first painter, Ardenti. Chiara's figure is well modeled and convincingly set in the pictorial space. The same strengths and large scale can be seen in the treatment of the emperor, the nude boy holding the scepter, and the three male figures in the foreground at the far right. The Madonna, too, is well situated in the illusionistic three-dimensional pictorial space, although her hands are not skillfully drawn, and the head of the Child is firmly modeled. These figures exhibit the skill of the artist in giving them substance, and we would argue that they were executed by Ardenti. The *putti,* the angels—note particularly the bent left leg of the angel carrying the banner—and the body of the Child are not well proportioned, but the group of five figures that includes the elderly Chiara is more problematic: Chiara, the man next to her and the coiffed woman seem squeezed into the composition, as if not present in the original concept. The pose of the man beside Chiara is unreadable and points to a repainting that we will take up. The two male figures on her other side, one kneeling, the other standing, are rather well painted, except for the thin arm that crosses over the chest of the standing man, and his hand (compare the other male arms and hands); we will comment on this arm and hand later. The boy standing behind the emperor at the far left is convincingly three-dimensional, while the man next to him is barely realized. Attributing the sibyl and emperor (earthly power) and the prophet group and the heavenly vision (spiritual power) to the original artist, we must assume that Ardenti also executed the original balanced composition, about which we will also have more to say.

**4.4.
Anon.
*Portrait of
Chiara Matraini*,
1586.
Pinacoteca di
Brera, Milan.
Photo, Museum.**

But we must consider now why Chiara chose the role of a sibyl for her portrayal. It is evident that she identified with the legendary women because they wrote in verse, as she did, and because they had prophetic power as she felt herself to have. And beyond that, they were not associated with any class: indeed they were in a class by themselves, as Chiara herself wanted to be, figures of *authority,* of world-encompassing knowledge, who were seen as peers of the male prophets of the Old Testament. But why the Tiburtine? Chiara and her family had been made to suffer profoundly by the authorities of Lucca, all of them men. Why the Tiburtine indeed: that was the sibyl who was able to tell the most powerful man on earth that his power was limited and only mortal: this was Chiara's message—her warning—to the men of Lucca. What did she contribute in creating the actual image? Although one must consider the possibility that Chiara's choice for her own representation as a sibyl was sparked by having read the story, it appears much more likely that she had been inspired from having actually seen one or more paintings on the subject of *Emperor Augustus and the Sibyl* in which the focus is on the moment when the sibyl gestures upward as she draws the emperor's attention to the heavenly vision.

There is, in fact, one painting in particular whose close resemblance to the Ardenti/Cellini painting appears almost certainly to have been the stimulus for the commission.

In *Emperor Augustus and the Sibyl* (ca. 1540) by Benvenuto Tisio di Garofalo (1481–1559) (figure 4.5), as in Ardenti/Cellini, the emperor kneels and the sibyl stands beside him with her left arm raised and her index finger pointing to the vision. A small dog is also included in both compositions.

We may in fact gain insight into how far the Ardenti/Cellini work goes in expressing Chiara's ideas and personal wishes by comparing it with Garofalo's, noting especially what changes were made. Whereas the space itself in Garofalo's composition seems to have no special meaning, the spaces of the Ardenti/Cellini composition are iconographically determined. The area bounded by the bottom margin, the two sides, and an imaginary line drawn across the painting at the level that crosses the tip of the sibyl's extended index finger form a square. In Christian symbolism, the square when contrasted with a circle symbolizes the earth while the circle expresses heaven or eternal existence.[23] In Chiara's painting, indeed, the earthly figures are within the square, the heavenly figures within the circle; the sibyl's prophetic power, signified by her upraised arm, earns her a small space in heaven, at least up to her elbow. The composition itself is thus intellectual and establishes the Neoplatonic theme of the painting, the duality of matter (inferior in quality and lower in position) and spirit (superior and higher). Because this theme pervades Chiara's poetry and, as we have seen in her letter quoted earlier, she was concerned to be acknowledged as an intellectual, we believe Ardenti worked out the composition according to her concept.

Turning to the figures, on the right is a group of prophets, traditional counterparts of the sibyls, representing the Old Testament, not present in Garofalo's work. (The importance of the prophets to Chiara will lead to her book of 1586, *Considerationi Sopra i Sette Salmi Penitentiali del Gran Re e Profeta David.*) The prophet Isaiah, the Tiburtine sibyl's complement in prophecy, is in the foreground, and behind him are King Solomon and the Psalmist, usually identified as King David. As truth-tellers of the *Old* Testament, they point the way to the *higher* truth according to Christian belief. Because they fit the overall Neo-Platonic theme of the lower leading to the higher, we believe that Chiara chose to include them, and, intent on their being identified and sensitive to the importance of words, she had the artist include inscriptions on the tablets as traditionally ascribed to them. Each holds a tablet. That of Isaiah foretells the birth of the Virgin: *ECCE VIRGO CONCIPIET ET PARIET FILLIUM* (Behold a virgin shall conceive and bear a son [Isaiah 7:14]); that of King Solomon reads *TOTA PULCRA ES ET MACULA NON EST IN TE* (You are entirely beautiful, without a stain [Song of Solomon 4:7]); that of David, *ET ERIT DOMINUS REX SUPER OMNEM TERRAM* (And the Lord will be King over all the earth [Psalm 47:7]).

At the left is the emperor kneeling, with his arms crossed to emphasize his submissive position, but, most important for the fundamental meaning of the scene is the position of his foot extended so that his heel is on the ground but the ball and toes are stepping on the sibyl's foot. This pose signifies the emperor's supreme authority on earth. The sibyl, however, with her right arm extended, holds her book of prophecy *over* the ruler's head, and with the index finger of her raised left hand, she points to the vision, the Virgin and Child in a golden nimbus surrounded by angels, one of which carries the scroll with the inscription, *HIC PUER MAIOR TE ET IDEO ISSUM ADORA* (Adore this child who is greater than you). Thus the image is a visual statement of the transfer of ultimate authority; like the vertical alignment of the dog,

4.5.
**Benvenuto Tisio
di Garofolo.**
*Augustus and the
Sibyl.* ca. 1540.
**Photo,
Alinari/Art
Resource.**

4.6.
Rogier van der
Weyden.
*The Bladelin
Altarpiece*
(detail),
*Augustus and
the Sibyl.*
ca. 1452-1455.
Staatliche
Museum.
Photo, Foto
Marburg / Art
Resource.

putti, the loving couple, and Christ child to which we have called attention, like the upward-pointing fingers of the prophets, it moves visually upward in harmony with the rising level of spirituality of the figures. But as we have suggested, it may also very well have been as a warning to Lucca's nobility, which had put its foot down so heavily on the people of the city because of the uprising and had remained in power; indeed, this may have been the original reason for the commission. Chiara's resentment was steady.

It seems not to have been noticed previously that the pose of the emperor's foot on that of the sibyl is peculiar to the Italian treatment of the subject.[24] It does not occur in Northern painting, where the relationship between the sibyl and the emperor is always shown in the traditional pose of a saint introducing a donor to Christ or the Virgin in an altarpiece for which the donor paid, the pose seen, for example, in Roger Van der Weyden's *The Bladelin Altarpiece* (figure 4.6). In Italy the motif appears in this subject as early as the fourteenth century, in a partially surviving wall painting in the Santuario Casa Sta. Caterina in Siena (figure 4.7). Here the two actors in the drama stand facing each other. The sibyl points upward to where the now-lost vision was painted. Her scroll reads *HIC PUER MAIOR TE ET IDEO ISSUM ADORA*. The Emperor has raised both hands, palms upward in a gesture of amazement. His right foot steps on the sibyl's left foot at exactly that point on the ground under the area to which the sibyl is pointing, where the vision has been painted in the sky, thus emphasizing the relationship—although he is the greatest power *on earth* and can symbolically step on her, she symbolically holds the upper hand because she has the power to foresee the advent of the Greater One. Michele da Verona, active between 1515 and 1531, painted the scene, now in the Museo Civico, Verona (figure 4.8), with the emperor standing to the side and slightly behind the sibyl, his left foot extended, stepping on the sibyl's extended left foot. The fresco by the Sienese painter Balthazar Peruzzi (1481–1536) in the Chiesa di Sta. Maria in Fontegiusta, in Siena (figure 4.9), shows the sibyl and the emperor facing each other as in the earlier wall painting in Siena, their feet extended toward each other, the emperor's left foot stepping on hers. At the left two women, one directly under the vision, may represent Anne, the mother of Mary, the other possibly Elizabeth, the mother of John the Baptist whose voice crying in the wilderness called out the coming of Jesus. As we have mentioned, this foot motif also appears in the painting by Garofalo that we believe to have sparked Chiara's interest in the subject, given her belief in her own prophetic powers.

4.7.
Anon.
Augustus and the Sibyl.
ca. 1520.
Santuario Casa
Sta. Caterina,
Siena.
Photo, Frick
Art Reference
Library, New
York.

It is probable that the difference between the Italian and Northern iconography with regard to the feet goes back to the Byzantine tradition where power relationships are underlined symbolically with the more powerful foot stepping on a subordinate one, as seen in Italy, in the Emperor Justinian mosaic in the Church of S. Vitale in Ravenna (figure 4.10).

Returning now to the Ardenti/Cellini painting, we notice that the Old Testament group at the right fills the space occupied in Peruzzi's painting by the Romans. We believe that Ardenti, who could well have seen the Peruzzi work as well as Garofalo's, might have designed his composition to include the Romans but that it was Chiara's intervention that changed the identity of this group: including the Old Testament in the drama gave her an opportunity to identify herself in the company of the Biblical figures, Solomon and the Psalmist, David, poets, and Isaiah the prophet whose

4.8.
Michele da
Verona.
*Augustus and
the Sibyl.*
ca. 1520.
Museo Civico,
Verona. Photo,
Alinari/Art
Resource.

prophecy "The Lord himself will give you a sign. It is this: the maiden is with child and will soon give birth to a son whom she will call Immanuel" (Isaiah 7:14) is seen in the Christian tradition as foretelling the birth of Christ. She is placed close to the horizontal and vertical center of the painting. Because of the prominent position of *Amore*, in front of both her and the man beside her, we take the man to be her lover, and their placement on the vertical that rises from the dog to the Christ child— halfway between earth and heaven—to symbolize both the earthly and spiritual nature of love: "Love is midway between the human and the divine" she wrote in her letter to M. L.[25]

This brings us to the knotty problem of trying to identify who the other contemporary figures represent. While they cannot be surely identified, we will offer the following possibilities, assuming that they represent persons important in Chiara's life.

4.9.
Balthazar
Peruzzi.
*Augustus and
the Sibyl.*
ca. 1505.
Chiesa di
Fontegiusta,
Siena. Photo,
Art Resource.

The boy at the far left may represent her son, Federico, born in 1533, painted by Ardenti in 1545. Still a child, he would not yet have begun the litigation against his mother; if he had been painted in the later phase of 1576 he would have been forty-three years old, with bitter years of litigation between him and his mother. Why did she not have Cellini obliterate him? Perhaps it would have seemed to her as if she had killed him—it is very hard to destroy a likeness and one is apt to save even a poor, unflattering photograph rather than tear it up. The man next to the boy, whose head is just above the sibyl's extended right arm, is not well painted and looks squeezed in, like an addition not originally intended and is hardly there. We speculate this figure may represent her husband who had died in 1543, and further suggest that her husband had been included in the earlier composition of ca. 1545 before the beginning of her affair with Graziani, where he had been in the position now occupied by the unidentified "lover." When the painting was taken up by Cellini in 1576, Chiara may then have wanted to preserve the memory of Graziani whom she had loved so passionately, and to express her fidelity to him so many years after his death.[26] She therefore moved her husband, squeezing him into the space next to her son. This would explain why the head of the figure now occupying the space formerly occupied by her husband does not appear to belong to the body; some poor repainting was done apparently to change the pose of the figure originally depicted as well as to change the face, and to squeeze in the elderly Chiara and the group around her which includes a coiffed woman directly under the vision of the Virgin and Child, probably representing Anne, the mother of the Virgin, and the two male figures next to Chiara. They are dressed in togas, Roman style, identifying them as belonging to the early Christian period. We have pointed out above some difficulty in rendering the arm and hand in an otherwise well painted figure: this may be, in fact, not a difficulty of rendering but possibly a reference to the man with the withered hand in Mark 3:1–6. We have been curious about the dog, usually a symbol of marital fidelity when seen at the feet of a *married* couple; here Chiara might have defiantly, as was her wont, wish to state her fidelity even to a man to whom she was not married, believing that sincere spirituality transcended earthly matters.[27]

By 1576 Chiara was well along into the piety reflected in her writings after 1555 in four specifically religious books. The painting taken as a whole is thus slightly more religious than we believe the original composition to have been.[28] It is a portrayal of Chiara as she had come to see herself and wanted others to see her, and visualizes what we have come to know of her and her development: poet, lover, learned intellectual, a woman who has submitted to the power of men but has won the authority to make them kneel by her prophetic gifts; a woman whose life journey has taken her from the perception of earthly love and beauty to the understanding of spiritual love and beauty; a devout believer in her Christian faith; in her life and in her art, the interpreter of Truth: Neo-Platonist to the core. Why did Chiara wish to commission a portrait of herself? Because at the time of the original commission, ca. 1545, as we have argued, she wished to be celebrated as a prophetess-poet and chose the image of the sibyl, easily recognized in the sixteenth century, to identify herself in a public statement; later, in the revised portrait, she wished to be identified for her spirituality as well. Quite simply, she commissioned the painting because she considered that art is eternal, and she yearned for undying fame.

> *Sweet-smelling laurel which heaven*
> *imbues with such rare and lovely attributes*
> *that your green and honor-giving leaves*
> *need never fear summer's heat or winter's cold.*

> *If the great Lord of Delos * and the opulent river banks*
> *where the clear water bathes your roots*
> *be forever adorned with your branches*
> *that cover you with verdant hue*
>
> *Then bow your lofty crown to me,*
> *that I may scent your leaves*
> *and with happy thoughts rise to heaven,*
>
> *Let your undying verdancy flow into me*
> *so that, singing sweetly in my verse,*
> *I may change myself into a swan.* (p. 130)

**4.10.
Anon.
*Emperor
Justinian and
His Attendants.*
Church of S.
Vitale, Ravenna.
ca. 1547.
Photo, Scala/
Art Resource.**

Chiara Matraini wished to be remembered. *Emperor Augustus and the Sibyl* sums up *how* she wished to be remembered.

---

* Apollo was born on the island of Delos.

POEMS IN THE ORIGINAL ITALIAN

We have followed the numbering order for the poems as in Rabitti's critical edition of Matraini's poems, *Rime e lettere* (Bologna, 1989), repeated by MacLachlan. A numeral preceded by the letter "A" refers to the poem in Chiara's 1555 volume as numbered by Rabitti and MacLachlan; preceded by "C" it refers to her 1597 volume. For the texts of the poems we have used first editions of both the 1555 and 1597 volumes in the collections of the Biblioteca Statale (Public Library), Lucca, retaining the spelling.

Chiara Matraini

Con sproni alla ragion, col freno a sensi
presi donne ad amar, quant'amar lice
la divina beltà, che fra gli accensi
miei spirti vive altera, e vincitrice
fammi i bè lumi suoi ne l'alma intensi
gran frutto eterno trar d'humil radice;
ch'è tal la virtù loro alta, e gradita,
ch'a bellissimo oprar l'anima invita.
(A:79, ll. 1–8) [29] (p. 106)

~

Con giusta meta il Sol librava intorno
dal secondo Equinotio, e'l tempo e l'hora
già de l'ugual bilancie uscivon fuora
per far al nuovo dì lieto ritorno.

Quand'Amor diemmi assalto, e à bel soggiorno
destomi, a contemplar l'ardente Aurora
ch'in me gloria, e virtute adhora adhora
crea dentro à l'alma; et un perpetuo giorno.

Poscia cantando col mio vivo Sole
fu tanta l'armonia dolce, e gl'accenti
che si bearon l'Alme, e le parole.

Sian benedetti i primi alti concenti
che mi feron sentir, quel che la suole
l'alma fu in ciel fra gli angeli contenti.
(A:6) (p. 106)

~

Vostro divino ingegno,
in cui mi specchio dolcemente, et ergo:
(A:9, ll. 11–12) (p. 107)

~

ne mai più viso, ò canto
s'udio, ma ciscun tristo, e mesto tacque

con pianti, che potean rompere i sassi
della pietade; e gravi alti sospiri,
ne più sereno giorno il Cielo aperse.
Parnaso un nembo eterno ricoverse;
(A:82, ll. 110–115) (p. 107)

~

e boscarecci Dei
d'olmi, e cipressi poi mille trofei
far per l'opre tue altere, e gloriose:
(A:82, ll. 153–155) (p. 107)

~

Chiara, eterna, felice, e gentil'alma,
che fornito il tuo corso à mezzo gl'anni
volata sei fra l'anime beate;
volgi la vista hor da superni scanni,
che mostrar mi solei si chiara & alma:
e mira in quanto duol l'alta pietate
di tè m'ha posto; e quelle luci amate
da tè, colme vedrai di pianto amaro
bagnare il fido, mio dolente petto.
. . .
Più grave doglia, o fiero horribil caso
(misera) non poteva il Ciel mostrarme
di questo, ohime, che tanto il cor previde
tu l'sai, s'io il dissi . . .
(A:82, ll. 1–8, 41–44) (pp. 107 – 8)
. . .
io sentendo il tuo mortale affanno
in'horribil visione, atra, e funesta
vidi farti lasciar la mortal vesta
à cruda Serpe irata, e nel tuo danno
intenta solo, ond'il cor morse e spenta
fu la tua vita
(A:82, ll. 93–98) (p. 108)

~

vedervi ornato de più cari fregi:
(A:18, l. 11) (p. 108)

~

Mentre che'l cor da gli amorosi nodi
pensava di tener sempre disciolto,
e, d' ostinata voglia un gelo accolto
l'havea d'intorno con più saldi chiodi,

⦿ Track 16,
Reading 15

Dolce mio foco, con si cari modi
ne l'amorose vostre reti involto

fu, ch'ogni schermo finalmente tolto
gli havete, e par che del suo mal si godi.

Fur le reti amorose il dolce canto
di celeste armonia sempre mai pieno,
e'l parlar saggio, e la virtù divina:

L'angelica beltà, ch'in si bel manto,
d'altra anima nel mondo huom vide a pena
così si segue quanto il ciel destina.
(A:5) (pp. 108 – 9)

~

Fera son'io di quest'ombroso loco,
che vò con la saetta in mezzo il core
fuggendo (lassa) il fin del mio dolore;
e cerco chi mi strugge à poco à poco;
(A:35, ll. 1–4) (p. 109)

~

Dico, che qual'huom brama
saper quant'hà di belle & honorate
virtù, degne d'eterne immortal gloria
il mondo in questa etate,
miri il bell'angelo mio, che quanto s'ama
degna di vera & immortal memoria
di tutte ei sol trionfa, & hà vittoria,
però che Dio, Natura & Amor volse,
mostrar de le sue gratie un vero essempio
in lui, com'in suo tempio,
dov'ogni bene, ogni bellezza accolse.
(A:9, ll. 27–37) (p. 109)

~

● Track 17,
Reading 16

Smarrissi il cor; ghiacciossi il sangue, quando
dipinto di pietà, l'almo mio Sole
vadii con'un sospiro, ò mio sostegno
dirmi con dolci & humili parole
mesto me'n vò, ma 'l cor ti lascio in pegno.
In questo, l'aspro suo dolore accolto
sfogò per gli occhi, e impallidi il bel volto.
Quel ch'io divenni all'hor sasselo Amore,
e, sallo anchora ogn' invescato core,
chè, quasi morta, in voce rotta e frale
a gran pena formai: Signor mio, vale.
E più non potei dire,
chè mi sentì morire.
(A:34) (pp. 109 – 10)

~

Ma da me, lassa, un lagrimoso verno
non parte mai, che lunge al mio bel sole
lo provo ogn'hor ne l'amoroso inferno;

Ne trovo scampo a le mie doglie sole,
che si fero è 'l martir nel core interno,
che tempo ne ragion frenar lo puole.
(A:37, ll. 9–14) (p. 110)

~

Viva mia bella e dolce calamita,
che partendo con sì mirabil modo
stringeste l'alma in quel tenace nodo,
ch'a voi sol la terrà più sempre unita.
(A:40, ll. 1–4) (p.110)

Perchè à tanto valor, tanta bontade
per man si vili il fido seno apristi?
(A:82, ll. 166–167) (p. 110)

~

Hor che mia dolce pace e desiata
lieta godea ne le speranze prime
di coglier frutti e fior da l'alte cime
de rami santi, in quei ria Serp'è entrata.

◉ Track 18,
Reading 17

O Fortuna crudel, Fortuna ingrata,
tu mi levasti in quel pensier sublime,
perchè (cadendo) il cor mi roda, e lime
il duol ch'hà l'alta piaga avelenata.

Hor' hai fatto l'estremo di tua possa,
maligna invidia; hor la mia dolce e cara
gioia hai temprato del più amaro tosco.

Hor d'ogni bene hai la mia vita scossa:
hor non più luce havrò serena e chiara
fin che chiaro il mio Sol non riconosco.
(A:77) (pp. 110 – 11)

~

Padre del Ciel doppo molt'anni, e molti
che senza il lume tuo da tè son ita
per quest'ombra mortal chiusa e smarrita
prego ch'à buon sentier l'anima volti;

E fà si che i pensier fallaci e stolti,
che m'han dal dritto tuo sentier partita
à più honorate imprese a miglior vita
stian sempre col tuo aiuto ogn'hor rivolti.

Trai da gli scogli a più secura parte,
Signor, la vela del mio stanco legno,
tal ch'io stia lunge da Cariddi e Scilla.

Raccogli in tè l'alte speranze sparte
e, volgi questi studi, e quest'ingegno
à più lodata vita, e più tranquilla.
(A:92) (p. 111)

⁓

Vergine in cui l'eterno Sol si pose
con la sua gran divinitade intera
come talhor contiensi in poca sp[h]era
la grand'imagin de le vere cose,

Senza macula integro in te s'ascose
quasi raggio di Sol ch'in vetro fera;
e, col suo puro ardor casta, e sincera
humil'al gran disegno ti dispose;

Da tè sol si reflesse in lui l'amore,
ch'ambe n'accese, e'l suo divino foco,
ond' esser volse di tè figlio, e padre:

Deh prega gir non lasci il suo furore
sopra di noi concetto à poco à poco,
sposa eletta di Dio figliuola, e madre.
(A:93) (pp. 111 – 12)

⁓

● Track 19,
Reading 18

Odorifero lauro ove dal Cielo
tanta gratia, e virtù rara s'infonde,
che le tue verdi & honorate fronde
più non ponno temer l'estate o il gelo.

Se de' tuoi rami il gran Signor di Delo
s'adorni sempre, e quelle ricche sponde
dov'hai radici sovra alle chiar'onde,
verdeggin di lor bel nativo stelo:

Piega alquanto ver mè l'altera cima
sì ch'io possa odorar delle tue foglie,
e con vaghi pensier volarne in cima,

Che se la tua virtute indi m'accoglie,
spero, cantando dolcemente in rima,
mutare in cigno le primiere spoglie.
(C:18) (pp. 124 – 25)

APPENDIX

In a letter to a friend, Batina Centurione, Chiara describes a day's outing in the countryside that constitutes a verbal painting of *secular* figures in a landscape.[30] This is art-historically interesting in that it expresses a sensibility in the sixteenth century that, along with religious, allegorical, and mythological paintings of figures in landscapes, contributed to the actual entering of the secularized subject in Western art. A parallel development can be perceived in literature. The poet tells of her visit to a villa of a friend where in company with a group of young friends she spent a day in a country garden, perfumed with flowers, she writes, the soft air filled with the singing of birds. Among the company there were musicians, one of whom, in love with one of the women, sang this madrigal, apparently composed on the spot:

> *Mentre scherzando vola*
> *zeffiro intorno al crespo oro lucente*
> *della mia donna, e dolci baci invola*
> *fra le rose e rubin soavemente,*
> *cantin le gratie a prova*
> *e vaghi e lieti Amori*
> *sparghin le rose e fiori*
> *sovra'l suo grembo e dolcemente mova*
> *dal suo bel seno Amore il freddo ghiaccio*
> *sì ch'io l'accoglia alle mie fiamme imbraccio.*

> *While zephyr playfully flutters through*
> *the shining golden curls of my lady*
> *and gently plants sweet kisses*
> *between the roses and the rubies,*
> *may the graces rehearse their song*
> *and charming, gay cupids*
> *scatter roses and flowers*
> *over her lap, and let Love*
> *gently take from her heart the icy cold*
> *so that I may hold her in my ardent arms.*

Chiara included in her letter two other poems that were sung in the course of that day in the country. However, while she writes of "Mentre scherzando vola" that "uno de sopradetti musici . . . cominciò questo mio madrigale per lui fatto a cantare" (one of the above-mentioned musicians . . . began *my* madrigal which he put to song), she does not use the possessive in connection with the other two, and it remains unclear as to whether they were her own compositions with which her friends were familiar or simply popular songs generally known to the neighborhood. She writes of "Zeffiro spira" that they were sitting at tables that had been set up for a "delicious" lunch when one of the musicians among them began to sing "la canzonetta sotto scritta" (the little song written below):

> *Zeffiro spira e tremolar d'intorno*
> *fà sopra le fiorite e verdi sponde*
> *i fior, l'herbe, e le fronde*
> *d'ogni bel chiaro e limpido ruscella*
> *e sopra ogn'arboscello, ogn'augeletto*
> *di questo in quel boschetto*
> *lieto sen và cantando d'ogni intorno,*
> *il Ciel vago & adorno*
> *d'insolito splendore hoggi si mostra*

e con lieto soggiorno
di fior l'herbe e le piante ingemma e in ostra.

 Zephyr breathes lightly over the
flowering green banks of the sparkling clear stream
and makes the flowers and the grass and the leaves flutter;
the gentle wind
blows over the young trees and bushes
whence from all around
comes the singing of the birds,
and the southern sky, wondrously adorned
with lovely white puffs
in the brilliant day
bejewels the grass and plants.

After the song Chiara and her friends played some games, and the hours passed "delightfully" until it was time for the evening repast. They left the garden, she writes, and in a shady valley ran into some local folk returning from a festival carrying their rustic musical instruments. These were prevailed upon to sing and dance, which they did to the great enjoyment of the sophisticated urbanites. Meanwhile, servants prepared another fine feast spread on a white, flower-decorated tablecloth laid on the grass. They dined under shady trees beside a murmuring brook as evening came on. Finally it was time to go and they returned to the villa "cantando la sotto scritta canzone si come in lieto tempo e luogo si richieda" (singing the song written below, just as may be recalled in a happy time and place):

 Venite, almi pastori,
ad onorare il Maggio,
e su l'erbette e i fiori
seguite lieti il vostro bel viaggio.
 Ben venga Maggio.[31]

 Ninfe leggiadre e belle
sovra le verdi rive
scalze, succinte e snelle
coronate d'olive,
seguite liete il gonfalon selvaggio.
 Ben venga Maggio.

 Ciascun s'allegri e canti
dei suoi felici amori,
l' amate con gl' amanti
a l'ombra degl' allori
fin chè 'l Sol mostri il suo bel chiaro raggio.
 Ben venga Maggio.

 Lieti sempr' ogni giorno
vengan gli vaghi amori
scherzando a fonti intorno
con ghirlandette e fiori,
mentre che dolce spira il fresco oraggio.
 Ben venga Maggio.

Cantin le bianche ninfe
per vaghi monti e piani,
corrin le chiare linfe
saltin Fauni e Silvani
sott' ogni quercia e verde ombroso faggio.
    Ben venga Maggio.

Come divine shepherds
to celebrate May,
step lightly over the grass and flowers
as you begin your yearly migration
    Welcome May.

Beautiful, graceful nymphs
barefoot on the grassy riverbank
and slender in your tucked-up skirts,
crowned with garlands of olive branches
gaily follow nature's banner.
    Welcome May.

Let everyone rejoice
and sing of their happy loves,
the girls with their lovers
in the shadows of the laurel,
until the sun brings out his bright beams.
    Welcome May.

Happy every day
let the joyful lovers
garlanded with flowers
skip playfully around the spring
while gently blows a cooling breeze.
    Welcome May.

Let the white-veiled maidens sing
over mountains and plains,
let the vital juices course,
let the fauns and forest spirits leap
under every green and shady oak and beech.
    Welcome May.

The song ended as they reached the villa. Promising to meet again to enjoy another such day together, they went to their separate rooms and slept until dawn on soft white beds.

NOTES

1   See Giovanna Rabitti, "Linee per il ritratto di Chiara Matraini (Lines for the Portrait of Chiara Matraini)," *Studi e Problemi di Critica Testuale* 22 (April 1981): 141–165. Her account of Matraini's life is drawn from manuscript sources that she lists in an unnumbered note (p. 141). The "Portrait" (il ritratto) is a written interpretation of Chiara's life and work, not a visual image. Modern scholarship on Matraini begins with Luigi Baldacci, "Chiara Matraini, poetessa lucchese del XVI secolo," *Paragone* 4 (June 1953): 53–67. A detailed analysis of Chiara's poetry is found in Elaine MacLachlan, "The Poetry of Chiara Matraini: Narrative Strategies in the *Rime*" (Ph. D. dissertation, University of Connecticut, 1992). For a modern edition of Chiara's poetry see Chiara Matraini, *Rime e lettere*, Giovanna Rabitti, ed. (Bologna, 1989). The first volume of Matraini's poems appeared in *Rime e prose di Madonna Chiara Matraini, Gentildonna Lucchese* (Lucca, 1555). Chiara Matraini, *Lettere di Madonna Chiara Matraini, gentildonna lucchese con la prima e seconda parte delle sue rime* (Venice, 1597), repeats with corrections, revisions, and additions a volume brought out in 1595 under the same title. MacLachlan stresses the differences between the volumes of 1555, 1595, and 1597. For titles and descriptions of all of Matraini's original editions, see Alan Bullock and Gabriella Palange, "Per una edizione critica delle opere di Chiara Matraini," *Studi in onore di Raffaele Spongano* (Bologna, 1980). We are not here concerned with Matraini's volumes of religious poetry.

2   Pietro Giordani, *Prose scelte* (Livorno, 1849), "Degli annali lucchesi," p. 433, an account of the uprising. On 1 May 1531 about two hundred workers marched through Lucca, helmeted and carrying weapons and waving "torn black flags," whence the name of the uprising that ignited the whole city for two years.

3   "Ma perchè vi siete primieramente sforzato dimostrarmi quanto disdicevole sia à donna non di più alti sangui nata, ne dentro i più superbi palagi, fra copiose e abbondantissime ricchezze nodrita, andar continovamente il tempo consumando negli studi e nello scivere fuori in tutto dell'uso della nostra città. . . . La onde . . . vi dico, che quantunque io d'alto e real sangue nata non sia . . . non però di ignobile famiglia ne di poveri, e bassi progenitori . . . ma di chiaro sangue, e di honesti beni di Fortuna dotata in città libera, e di gran d'animo generata sono. Benchè se con dritto occhio riguardar vorremo . . . vedremo certamente che non l'antiquità de sangui, nel soggiogar de popli non l'oro ne la porpora, ma l'animo di virtù splendido far l'huomo veramente nobile." Matraini, *Rime e prose,* pp.105–106.

4   Giovanna Rabitti, "Linee per il ritratto," p. 147, considers revenge the central motive of the poet's life. We disagree on this point, and we also perceive duality in the poet's personality where Rabitti sees ambiguity. See also Rabitti's "La Metafora e l'esistenza nella poesia di Chiara Matraini," *Studi e Problemi di Critica Testuale* 27 (October 1983): 109–145.

5   The question of Coccopani's relationship with Chiara is unresolved. We will return to this problem further on in connection with our discussion of her portrait as a sibyl.

6   "E ben vero che s'io avessi . . . alquanta di libertà che a tale mia inclinazione si richiedeva . . . avrei forse fatte cose degne di memoria." Rabitti, "Linee per il ritratto," p. 155.

7   For the presence of Petrarch's *Canzoniere* in Matraini's oeuvre, see MacLachlan, "The Poetry of Chiara Matraini," especially pp. 55–65.

8   The second equinox falls about September 21.

9   The issue here is not just that Chiara was a *petrarchista*; Petrarch was indeed the prevalent model for the large majority of Cinquecento poets. Chiara, however, appropriated not only his imagery and vocabulary but also the form of the autobiographical narrative that had been constructed and reinforced by Pietro Bembo, who owned the original Petrarch manuscript that is now in the Vatican Library. Through Bembo's influence, this plan was also imitated by others in this period.

10   "Si incominciò a innamorare di una disonesta Donna de'Matraini che faceva poetessa." Rabitti, "Linee per il ritratto," pp. 141–142.

11   "Una Accademia che per satisfare alla scelerata vedova, haveva missa in Casa sua, dove stando la notte, non che il giorno da tutte l'hore a ridere Burlare, dir mille Sporcitie, e fare infinite cose dishoneste, (perchè vi andavano molti giovani secolari, che di Pisa erano venuti a Luccha nelle va-

cantie." The story of the scandal involving Chiara and Bartolomeo Graziani was recounted by a relative of Graziani's wife, Gherardo Sergiusti, in writing his autobiography; the source and the main outlines of the account are given by Rabitti, "Linee per il ritratto," p. 141; the quotation here cited is from p. 142.

12   "Io mi parto di questa Casa, ma farò tanto, che quelli, che vi restano, La goderanno assai poco." Rabitti, "Linee per il ritratto," p. 143. Graziani lived in a residence that was associated with the Convent of Sta. Maria Corteorlandini. The building now houses the State Library of Lucca, on the top floor of which is the sixteenth-century library that remains untouched since the time when Graziani lived there; it contains thirty thousand uncatalogued books, including incunabula.

13   "*Chiara Matraini . . . essendo nobilissima Sig.a con prontezza d'ingegno . . . non solo vedeva ma prevedeva le cose.*" Quoted in Giorgio Giorgi, *Le chiese di Lucca,* "S. Maria Forisportam" (Lucca, 1974), p. 120.

14   For the importance of Vittoria Colonna as a model for other women poets of the period, see Rinaldina Russell, "Chiara Matraini nella tradizione lirica femmenile," *Forum Italicum* 34, no. 2 (Fall 2000): 415–427. One of Matraini's sonnets to Vittoria Colonna was probably written in 1547, marking Vittoria's death:

> *Quanto l'alta Colonna il suo Sole*
> *avanzò in Ciel mentre ella i santi carmi*
> *cantava in terra, e ne' più saldi marmi*
> *l'opre di lui intagliava eterne e sole,*

> *Tanto l'alto suo stile avanzar suole*
> *mio ingegno, onde non posso a tanto alzarmi,*
> *però conviensi e la vettoria e l'armi*
> *rendere a lei che 'l mondo onora e cole.*

> *Ella qui morta, e in Ciel bella e viva,*
> *merita sol la gloriosa palma*
> *e corona di lauro, edera, oliva;*

> *Ma voi di ricca e preziosa salma*
> *meritate e di fiamma ardente e viva*
> *ornata aver di me sempre mai l'alma.*

> *High as the noble Colonna, her great love,*
> *rose to heaven, while she here on earth*
> *celebrated his eternally great deeds,*
> *with sacred odes cut into hardest marble,*

> *So far does her pen inspire my mind*
> *beyond where I am used to raise myself;*
> *but the arms and the victory should be*
> *rendered to her whom the whole honors and reveres.*

> *Here on earth dead, she is alive and beautiful in heaven,*
> *and alone deserves the glorious palm*
> *and crown of laurel, ivy, and olive.*

> *But both deserve that the precious earthly remains*
> *be celebrated by the ardent,*
> *living flame of my soul.*

From Giovanna Rabitti, "Inediti Vaticani di Chiara Matraini," in L. Salerno, ed., *Studi di filologia e critica offerti dagli allievi a Lanfranco Caretti* (Rome, 1985), pp. 225, 250.

15   MacLachlan, "The Poetry of Chiara Matraini," pp. 151, 153.

16   We wish to thank Signore Giorgi Tori, director of the State Archives of Lucca, for sending us a photocopy of Chiara's will. Almost nothing is known of Francesco Cellini. He is mentioned in Thieme-Becker, *Allgemeines Lexikon der Bilden den Künstler von der Antike bis zur Gegenwart* (Munich, 1992), for a painting, not identified, dated 1576. He is not listed in Jane Turner, ed., *Grove History of Art* (New York, 1996). An early written reference to Chiara's burial place goes back to a few years after she died; Francesco Agostino della Chiesa, in *Theatro delle donne letterate* (Mondovì, 1620), published the wall inscription and refers to the altar painting with her portrait "said to represent the sibyl" *("Il suo ritratto dicesi che sia nella Chiesa di S. Maria Forisportam . . . rappresentante la Sibilla").* Quoted in Giorgio Giorgi, *Le chiese di Lucca,* p. 121.

17   The painting is oil on canvas, 335 x 240 cm, catalogued in the *Museo Nazionale Villa Guinigi* (Lucca, 1968), pp. 191–192, as *La Sibilla Cumana predice ad Augusto la venuta del Salvatore.* Writers on Ardenti in major art dictionaries—including, among others, *Thieme-Becker, Saur,* and the *Dizionario biografico degli Italiani*—all follow the title given by the Museum. Rabitti, "Linee per il ritratto," p. 148, also refers to the sibyl in this painting as the Cumana, as does MacLachlan, "The Poetry of Chiara Matraini," p. vii. St. Augustine in *The City of God* and Lucius Lactantius in his *Divine Institutes* of 1465 do not attribute specific oracles to the sibyls, though, since the publication in 1481 of the *Discordantiae Sanctorum* by Filippo Barberii, a general accord following Barberii's identification of the sibyls with specific oracles developed in which the sibyl who prophesied the birth of Christ to Augustus was the Tiburtine, also called the Albunea. The majority of paintings we have seen on this subject name the Tiburtine as the sibyl represented in the scene; some leave her unnamed, as in *Augustus and the Sibyl.* Because Tiburtine is the most generally accepted name given to the sibyl who figured in the legend and is the alternate name for the Albunea sibyl named in the altar inscription, we have so chosen to refer to the sibyl in the Villa Guinigi painting. For a substantial account of the sibyls, see G. Pozzoli, F. Romani, and A. Peracchi, eds., *Dizionario d'ogni mitologia* (Milan, 1824), vol. 5, pp. 612–622.

18   Jacobus de Voragine (William Caxton, trans.), *The Golden Legend* (London, 1922), vol. 1, p. 27. The respectability of the sibyls in Christian art derives largely from St. Augustine, *City of God,* Book 18.

19   Rabitti, "Linee per il ritratto," p. 148; Matraini, *Rime e lettere,* p. 34.

20   Despite his obligations as *scultore ordinario,* however, Ardenti continued to paint in Turin where a number of his religious works survive. Scholarship on Ardenti is concerned with the problem of the possibility that there were two artists of the same name, one from Faenza, the other from Lucca. The evidence seems to us to point to only one. Although bibliographical references to Ardenti refer only to religious paintings, an engraving after a portrait by Ardenti of a man holding a book shows him to have been a portraitist of impressive powers. Dr. Colombardo and I are currently doing research on this portrait, about which nothing is now known.

21   Rabitti, "Linee per il ritratto," p. 150, n. 22.

22   MacLachlan stresses the differences between the volumes of 1555, 1595, and 1597, seeing among them *two* stories rather than one, the first telling an earthly love story, the second and third a spiritual one. We, on the other hand, see both the earthly and spiritual stories as comprising one *canzoniere,* reflecting the interior life of the poet as it developed over time.

23   George Ferguson, *Signs and Symbols in Christian Art* (Oxford, 1975), p. 153.

24   This does not mean that all Italian artists followed this iconography of Augustus and the sibyl. Tintoretto, for example, did not.

25   "Amore è mezzo tra le cose humane e le divine." Matraini, *Rime e lettere,* p. 107.

26   Some writers whom we have cited here have taken up the question of whether Coccapani was Chiara's lover, with varying opinions. The letters exchanged between Coccapani and Chiara do not indicate a romantic relationship.

27   There is also a dog near the bottom margin of Garofalo's *Augustus and the Sibyl,* but there it obviously does not represent fidelity; the dog is sleeping, and we believe it symbolizes the natural world "asleep," unaware of the momentous event that was occurring.

28   MacLachlan emphasizes the increased spirituality of Chiara's poetry as reflected in her 1595 and 1597 volumes, compared to her 1555 book.

29   These lines, revised, appear in C:14, ll. 57–64. The word *donne* (women) is deleted, and *la divina beltà* (divine beauty) is changed to *l'alma vostra beltà* (your divine beauty). We have chosen the original version in the 1555 volume because it reveals her concern to justify her love affair as spiritual, especially to women, who may have been more offended by it than men.

30   Matraini, *Rime e lettere,* pp. 22–25.

31   Lines 24–25. The verses sung on this occasion recall the more famous fifteenth-century *canzone a ballo* (song and dance) by Angelo Poliziano that begins, "Ben venga Maggio." His second line, "E'l gonfalon selvaggio," occurs in the tenth line in the verses in Matraini's letter and refers to a Tuscan custom: on the first day of May young men would place a branch at the door or window of their beloveds; Poliziano calls this branch "a banner of the woodlands" *(un gonfalon selvaggio)*. It is unclear if Matraini wrote this *canzone* or if it was a popular spring song; the latter seems more likely because she writes that they all sang together as they returned to the villa. The fourth line of the first stanza, "il vostro bel viaggio" (your nice trip, which we translate, "your yearly migration"), refers to the annual trek to the pastures.

5.1.
Anon.
View of the
Castle of
Favale.
n.d. Photo,
Basilicata.

CHAPTER FIVE

Isabella di Morra
(1515/20–1548?)

& Diego Sandoval de Castro
(CA. 1505–1546)

🌰 The Scene of the Crime – Revisited

lhe tragic story of two poets, Isabella di Morra and Diego Sandoval de Castro, was narrated first by a nephew of Isabella, Marcantonio di Morra, who published his account in 1629.[1] Angelo de Gubernatis repeated the story as a preface to the ten sonnets and three *canzoni* of Isabella that have survived. He was unsure of Isabella's birth year, which he calculated to have been around 1520, but put her death at 1548. Benedetto Croce repeated the nephew's account with added information from the Archivo General de Simancas, Spain. He put the date of her death in 1546; his account has become the accepted version by other writers who have related the story. But Croce himself raised a number of questions about "this secret drama about which we know nothing": "Did Sandoval court her? Did he make her the object of his Petrarchist fantasies? Did he really love her? Did Isabella, forlorn and hoping to find freedom, reciprocate his feelings? Was she at least happy about [his] amorous correspondence?"[2] We, too, have questions in addition that we will raise as we recount this puzzling affair, questions that have led us to consider a surprising and heretofore overlooked possibility wrapped in this "secret drama."

Giovan Michele di Morra, Isabella's father, an educated man who belonged to the Neapolitan circle of humanists, was lord of the fief of Favale (present day Valsinni), in the southern area of Italy called Basilicata (figures 5.1, 5.2). He had been feuding with the Prince of Salerno, Ferrante Sanseverino, who possessed the neighboring estate of Rotondella and who had lodged a complaint with the Spanish authorities who governed the Kingdom of Naples, accusing Giovan Michele of mistreating some of the men in his princely retinue. Not coincidentally, the prince had his eye on the Favale estate. The great events of 1527–28 played into his hands—temporarily. They also shaped the life of Isabella di Morra.

In the ongoing war between Francis I, King of France, and Charles V, Emperor of the Holy Roman Empire (and King of Spain, as Charles I) the French forces were defeated at Pavia in 1525 by Spanish and Imperial troops led by Vittoria Colonna's husband, Ferrante d'Avalos. Francis I was taken prisoner. "All is lost save life and honor,"

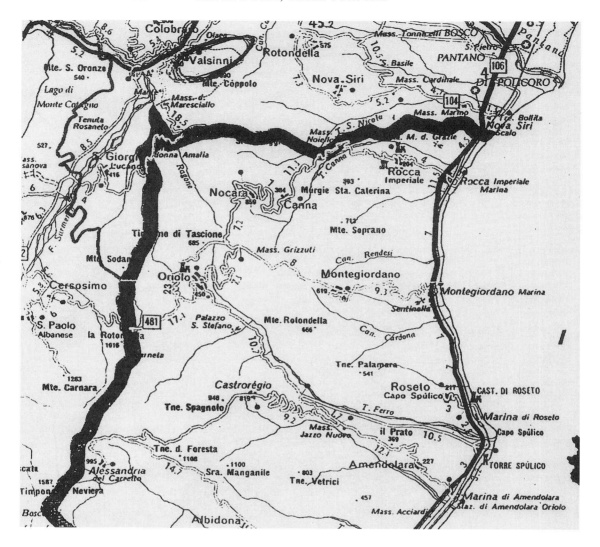

**5.2.
Map of
southeastern
Italy, showing
location of
Valsinni,
formerly Favale.**

he famously shouted, as he was led away to the enemy camp. Ferrante, however, did not get to keep his great prisoner; the king was taken to Spain.[3] His sister Margaret, Queen of Navarre and Vittoria Colonna's friend, went there to plead with Charles for her brother's freedom. Francis was liberated when he agreed to the Treaty of Madrid in 1526, but he immediately repudiated it, forming the League of Cognac with Pope Clement VII, England's Henry VIII, and the city-states of Venice and Florence. To punish the pope, Charles V sent his army against Rome, which sacked the city horribly for a week in May 1527.[4] Meanwhile, the French had conquered Genoa and, led by Andrea Doria, were on their way to rescue Clement in Rome when the pope surrendered. The French then continued south instead, to try once again to oust the Spanish and take over Naples.

Giovan Michele di Morra miscalculated and joined the French forces. When they were forced to abandon their attempt, he became persona non grata in the Neapolitan realm, was declared a rebel, and was deprived of his fief, which he held at the pleasure of the Spanish King of Naples. He fled to France in 1528. He left behind his wife, Luisa Brancaccio, his daughters Isabella and Portia, and four of his sons: Decio, Fabio, Cesare, and Marcantonio, the eldest; the last boy, Camillo, was born after he left.[5] He took with him Isabella's brother Scipione, the only son who had cultural interests. Naming his children, except for Isabella, after Roman emperors and heroes (and the noble wife of Brutus, Portia) did not have the desired effect on his sons. Isabella grew up in the Morra castle with the usual small army of servants, including the children's schoolmaster (alas for him!), her helpless mother, her sister, about whom we hear nothing, and her brothers, who were uncouth, unruly, barbarous brutes.

The brothers were at home in the craggy wilderness inhabited by deer, rabbits, and birds. Isabella, sensitive and refined by nature, was a stranger in the harsh environment. Young and isolated from people like herself, confined to the precincts of the Morra castle perched on a high-rising cliff above the Ionian Sea, she nevertheless realized that she had been born with a special gift that deserved to be recognized, and she yearned for such recognition.

> I write of the fierce assaults of cruel fortune,
> crying over my young life
> as it passes away in this vile, miserable countryside,
> with no one to praise me.
>
> Though my cradle was humble, I dream of a fine tomb,
> for I follow the beloved muses,
> and I hope to find sympathy somewhere,
> despite blind and bitter fortune,
>
> With the favor of those sacred goddesses,
> and to find myself perhaps on a happier shore
> in spirit, at least, if not in person;
>
> And perhaps there lives a noble king
> who may bury in marble
> this body in which I am enveloped.[6] (p. 154)

It appears that she had only the schoolmaster to talk with about poetry and her literary interests; we hear nothing about her relationship with Portia.

Isabella idealized her father, who evidently gave her very little thought. His escape to France was highly successful, for he was living very comfortably with an annual pension as a courtier among the retainers of Francis I. He could have returned to Favale, in fact, in 1533, for his sons and his brother successfully petitioned to have the paternal estate returned to the family with their promise to pay a large fine over the following ten years, and Giovan Michele's crime against the state was pardoned. He, however, along with other refugees from Naples and Florence, achieved distinction in France, serving in the army and as a councilor to Francis, who surrounded himself with some of the most brilliant artists and writers of the period. He stayed in France, and his daughter waited in vain for a ship that he would send to rescue her.[7]

On the heights from which I can gaze over the sea,
I, your daughter Isabella, often stand, watching
for a shining ship to appear
which will give me some news of you, my father.

But my contrary and cruel Fortune
admits no comfort to relieve my sad heart
but rather does that rebel to all pity
turn my dearest hopes to tears;

For I see no oar cleaving the waves
nor sail billowing in the wind
so empty is this unhappy shore.

So I inveigh against Fortune
and embrace my hatred for this ugly place,
the sole cause of my torment. (p. 154)

But even in the remoteness of Favale life had its surprises. And for Isabel, hope:

If to my looming hope you bring
no new impediment, cruel Fortune, or pitiless Death,
as you often have done, I will have shattered this prison
and shaken loose its chains.

But thinking of that day I burn and freeze
for fear and desire are my companions,
to them I open or close the door
and in doubt I destroy myself and crumble with grief.

Hope, I think, reveals its wings,
and to its door my happy thoughts fly
to rid my soul of its constant anguish.

But Fortune leads fear
along the steep, narrow, deceptive path
so that, even as I hope, I despair. (pp. 154 – 55)

What was this hope? Had someone promised to help her escape? Or was it the appearance in her life of a suitor, indeed a betrothed, who came into her life? We hear of him in one of the very few happy poems she wrote (at least among the thirteen that have survived), full of hope rather than despair, a poem to Juno, the goddess of marriage.

Sacred Juno, if carnal love
is an enemy of your noble heart,

grant to me with your sacred and fulsome love,
days and years of bright happiness.

To you I consecrate my virginal purity,
to you, oh goddess, and your kindness.
Oh, let only what is blessed and beautiful
fill the sky with sweet fragrance.

Encircle with a golden chain,
the neck of your most loving and humble servant
for I seek to serve only you.

Guide Hymen, with his courtly tenderness,
and make the marriage knot in which I am enlaced
so precious that one soul reigns in our hearts. (p. 155)

Surely she was looking forward to marriage. Whom did she expect to marry? There is no clue that might identify the man. Certainly it was not Diego Sandoval, the only man with whom history has associated her, for he was already married. What happened? Did her fiancé die? Did he abandon her? We shall probably never know. Whoever and whatever, the affair ended, and Isabella was left devastated. Now she sees stark loneliness is to be her destiny unless her father, with the help of King Francis, can rescue her from the physical and emotional wilderness in which she is condemned to live and she poured her grief into a long *canzone* in which she addresses Fortune, the source of all her misery. The poem gives the reader vivid metaphors of her emotional state, beginning with the wing metaphor of her poem of hope, which reappears, the wings now broken:

Since, cruel Fortune,
you have broken the wings
of that lovely hope that rose in my heart
so that I live starved of every pleasure,
I will relate with my untaught and weak pen
some part of the suffering
of which only you have been the cause,
amid the thorns, among the crude manners
of unreasoning people, devoid of understanding,
where, with no support,
I am obliged to live in oblivion.

You, cruel one, in those few years of childhood
have deprived me of my dear father.

The momentary joy, "that lovely hope that rose," has been crushed, and she is once again living in lonely isolation. If only her father could come to her rescue. But fortune was not so disposed.

> *Caesar* * *prevents him from helping me*
> *—oh unheard of cruelty, preventing a father*
> *from helping his daughter* (pp. 155 – 56)

The goddess was as pitiless to her as she claimed, and in the worst way, for once again she had held out hope. Somehow, despite being kept in seclusion, Isabella came to know a woman—identified by Croce as Giulia Orsini, princess of Bisignano—who in 1537 and 1538 was living not far away in Senise, the region watered by the Siri (or Sinni) River. She was married to Pietro Sanseverino, who had led a punitive expedition against the rebellious barons of Basilicata, among whom was Giovan Michele di Morra.[8] Despite the family hostility, Isabella formed some kind of friendship with Giulia, who apparently was going to help her to escape from Favale.

> *Oh, Siri, my beloved river,*
> *how proud you can be of your rich and happy banks*
> *and of the land that is named for you,*
> *the name so dear now to my heart.*
>
> *Here lives the woman who can soothe the angry sky*
> *and keep my hope alive*
> *despite the bitter, harsh goddess*
> *who ceaselessly exults in my misery.*
>
> *The fragrance of the vermillion rose*
> *on the gentle breeze that nourishes the soul is*
> *no less sweet than the perfume of the sacred golden lily.* [9]
>
> *Because of her my life will be joyous,*
> *unburdened by anxieties*
> *and my head will be encircled with laurel.* (p. 156)

But years passed. The promise of escape was never fulfilled. She rails against Fortune:

> *These years, said to be the flower of one's life*
> *I have spent wilting and forgotten, deserted and alone,*
> *as if I were a blind, sick hermit,*
> *without knowing the pleasure of beauty.*
> *You have had no pity for me,*
> *and you have stifled it in others*
> *who might have helped me*
> *to put aside and free from its harsh prison*
> *my veiled, tired spirit which, like snow in sunlight,*
> *will now slowly seep away under your relentless glare,*
> *as long as I live.* (p. 156)

---

* Caesar = Charles V.

The "others" who might have helped her failed her. Fortune was against her. Again Isabella is in despair. The Siri River with its once "rich and happy banks" has become "muddy." Perhaps she is contemplating suicide. She does indeed throw herself symbolically into the river.

> Muddy Siri, now that I feel approaching
> the bitter end of my suffering,
> tell my dear father of my pain
> if ever his cruel destiny permits him to return.

> Tell him, dying, I scorn
> bitter Fortune and my wretched fate,
> and as a pitiful, solitary act
> I consign my unhappy name to your waves;

> When it reaches your stony bank
> (what thoughts you give me, oh alien star)
> then of everything will I be totally deprived.

> With a raging storm stir up the waves
> and say, "while she lived, they, not her eyes,
> were flooded with the tears of Isabel." (pp. 156 – 57)

Miserable fate! Through no fault of her own she must watch herself disappear like melting snow, without ever knowing the happiness of being entirely what she is—a woman.

> Here I cannot feel like a real woman
> because of you who has set me in such a solitary state
> that death would be sweeter than life.

She still clings to the image of the only man whom she can still idealize.

> The dear tokens of my beloved father
> surround me with tears. [8]

But her sense of the injustice she has suffered at the hands of Fortune is uppermost in her mind.

> Oh, miserable fate
> to eat the bitter fruit that others gathered
> I who have never wronged anyone,
> whose spotless innocence would soothe
> a tiger or serpent,
> but not you, more beastly and cruel to us
> than Procne to her son or Medea to her brother . . .

Her brothers are brutes, her mother is old and feeble,

> *Bastions of support for their mother*
> *her sons should have been*
> *but because of your tempests, iniquitous and furious,*
> *they are today in a weak and pitiful condition*
> *and the legacy of our ancestors' nobility*
> *down to this day will be exhausted in them*
> *if from his high estate*
> *pity does not move the heart of the King of France,*
> *. . .*
> *Ah, Fortune (why at least can you not do this?)*
> *Let my sighs reach that mighty monarch.* (p. 157)

Isabella's desire for glory as a poet must have been nourished by contacts, at least in writing, with the world beyond Basilicata. She must have dreamed that with her escape from Favale would come the opportunity to associate with other poets. She wrote, in fact, to the poet Luigi Alamanni (1495–1556), who had conspired against Cardinal Giulio de' Medici (later Pope Clement VII, elected in 1523) and had fled to France. She addresses him as *"caro Luigi,"* and very likely asked him, naively, how one achieves fame as a poet. Perhaps it was in response to her question that he addressed a *canzone* that ends,

> *He who desires a long life,*
> *who hopes for a divine name,*
> *who yearns for eternal honor,*
> *to those who aspire*
> *to the laurel crown*
> *let their steps and their hearts be so directed.*
> *that their poetic ardor may have the vigor and strength*
> *to defy time.*[10] (pp. 157 – 58)

Finding no help on this earth, Isabel tried to turn her thoughts and her poetry to heaven, and with resignation came a new insight:

> *There was a time, as you know, when I wrote*
> *bitterly and harshly, lamenting against Fortune*
> *as if no one else in the world*
> *suffered so from her fierce power.*
>
> *Now my soul repents its blind error*
> *for in such writing there is no glory*
> *and although it lives meagerly*
> *it hopes to become rich in the shining light of God.*

> *Neither Time nor Death nor vicious, violent hand*
> *can steal the eternal joyous treasure*
> *from the King of Heaven.*
>
> *There you know no summer or winter,*
> *neither burning heat nor freezing cold.*
> *Thus, Brother, any other hope is vain.* (p. 158)

Now she realizes that raging against Fortune will not bring her the coveted laurel: "in such writing there is no glory." Praise will better woo the Muse. Naively, it seems—for who is there to praise?—she addresses the Virgin in a long *canzone* with "no other care in [her] fervent heart than to follow Her."

> *What in days past,*
> *pained my weary body,*
> *forced to live in this lonely, dark wilderness,*
> *now delights my soul,*
> *for I begged God in his mercy*
> *to let me see the sure path to Him.*
> *Now with my mind turned to the Queen of Heaven,*
> *with the most sincere humility*
> *my soul goes along the lonely road toward its resting place,*
> *so that, fleeing from these sad and difficult times,*
> *my thoughts do not wander elsewhere*
> *light-hearted and happy in this shady woods . . .*

She had complained bitterly that she was a prisoner in the wilderness of Favale, but now it seems to her that

> *Only in the wilderness can one find tranquility. . . .*

And the "shady woods" had prepared her for "everlasting life."

> *Because of you, my lovely caves,*
> *dense woods and worn stones,*
> *swift Sinno, clear springs and rivulets,*
> *green countryside tread by others,*
> *forbidden to me,*
> *I am the companion of those divine spirits*
> *now up above in everlasting life;*
> *and in the sun-filled and glorious folds*
> *of our Mother, our Father, and God*
> *I hope to see myself*
> *free of the dark clouds of earthly life*
> *and to place my sunny thoughts in those folds,*

among the blessed,
or in the distant happy path
of our Savior's mercy.

However much the bright sun warms and reveals,
Oh my song, to one who sees with pious eyes it is nothing
compared to the Queen of Heaven, Mother of God. (pp. 158 – 59)

There are very few dates around which to structure Isabella's life. The French attempt to take Naples in 1528 brought about the flight of her father to France. He went
first to Rome, taking his second son, Scipione, who remained there to continue his
studies and eventually joined his father in France. According to the memoirist, Isabella's brother (perhaps her twin) was "highly intelligent, with a tenacious memory, educated in fine literature, and especially knowledgeable in Latin and Greek."[11] Even
allowing for much exaggeration, the fact seems to be that Scipione had had some
more than rudimentary education so that he was not a very young child when Giovan
Michele left him in Rome.[12] He and Isabella might have been young teenagers in 1528.
However, in her long *canzone* beginning "Since, cruel Fortune" she accuses Fortune of
having deprived her of her father since *infanzia,* which can mean infancy or childhood
or even simply a very young person, so we cannot guess the exact year in which she
was born; a spread of 1515–1520 seems appropriate.[13]

The next date we have is crucial. However, because the heart of the story as related by Isabella's nephew and others is the relationship between Isabella and Diego Sandoval, we must first review what has been written about it by the nephew, by Croce,
and by others, before we can take up this crucial date.

Diego Sandoval was of a noble Spanish family on which Charles V had bestowed
two estates, one in Cosenza in the province of Calabria, the other in what is called today Nova Siri, but then known as Bollita, in Basilicata, quite close to Valsinni (Favale),
the estate of the Morra family, also overlooking the Ionian Sea. Sandoval was handsome, quick-tempered, a brave soldier, and a poet who belonged to the prestigious
Florence academy, but he probably would not have made it into history had it not
been for his neighbor, Isabella di Morra. Born in the first decade of the Cinquecento,
he passed his youth as a wealthy Spanish nobleman, much of the time fighting against
the French in one battle after another. He seems not to have stayed long anywhere.
He lived now and then on his estate in Cosenza and sometimes in Bollita, where his
wife, Antonia Caracciolo, made her home. Because Bollita is not far from Favale,
somehow, the narrators say, Isabella and Diego came into contact—when and how no
one claims to know. Two scholars have recently pointed out that the poetry of both
Isabella and Diego contains phrases, images, and structural similarities that echo each
other's. F. Vitelli writes, "Sandoval breathes in the verses of Morra in a subtle and
tricky way," assuming that Morra's verse was inspired by him.[14] Tobia Toscano points
out several specific resemblances such as those between the first line of Isabella's *canzone* "Alla Fortuna," "*Poscia che al bel desir troncate hai l'ale,*" and two sonnets of Diego,
one whose first line is "*Poscia ch'al bel desir Sebeto udir non lice*" and the other whose
fourth line is "*ch'al desir tronca l'ale, ond'io tutt'ardo,*" but such similarities could spring
from no more than a general source of imagery from which they (and other southern

poets) drew. Diego's poems, including those in which mutual echoes appear, were published in 1542.

None of the poems in the surviving work of either of the two poets can be identified as having been specifically directed from one to the other; those of Isabella include no love poem addressed to a man,[15] while Diego's poems are the conventional Petrarchist laments of a lover praising his beloved and "suffering" because of his longing, possibly referring to a specific woman, but, equally possible, referring to one or another of the women "beloved" by the poet—or even to a "fantasy instead of a person," as Yolanda de Blasi describes the artificial outpourings of Cinquecento passion.[16] Characteristic are these two poems:

> These are the flashing eyes that send
> a thousand messages of love armed with cupid's darts,
> when desire first enters the heart
> making pain sweet and crying a mere game.

> These are the tresses which
> I am hoarse with praising,
> this is the lovely face which gives me respite
> from my cares,

> These are the beauties that I love so much,
> that day and night I long for
> and that give me few hours of serenity,

> This is the lovely face that I desire
> the face I call for with my sighs;
> it alone can soften my suffering. (p. 159)

> When love opens her beautiful eyes
> that make the sun marvel and pale
> and brings a new day
> full of soft breezes that gently blow,

> I cannot look into them
> and I close my eyes only to wish them open;
> I blush and turn pallid,
> embarrassed that one should see me so.

> My soul melts with affection
> and my sad heart feels a sharp pain,
> happy and hopeless at the same time.

> The pleasure of seeing such beauty
> and the pain of hopelessness fills my mind
> thus am I both blessed and miserable. (pp. 159 – 60)

Around 1542 Don Diego was accused and sentenced in absentia by the (Spanish) Neapolitan authorities for some undetermined offense. He went to live in Benevento, an area under papal control that offered him refuge. His estate in Bollita, where his wife lived, however, was in the Neapolitan Realm, and he apparently traveled there secretly. Did he also manage to travel secretly to nearby Favale? Did this wealthy, handsome, quick-tempered, brave soldier and poet become Isabel's lover? What is reported by the nephew is that her brothers Marcantonio, Decio, Cesare, and Fabio had somehow learned that Diego had sent their sister a letter in the name of his wife with some poems enclosed; others have surmised that she might have answered him, and Croce and those after him refer to letters and poems.[17] The brothers were informed that the message was carried by the schoolmaster, the nephew continues, and although, according to de Gubernatis, "Isabella had received it from the schoolmaster in the name of donna Antonia, the brothers, who had become barbarous and cruel in this harsh place, ferociously killed the schoolmaster and stabbed [to death] their innocent sister, believing . . . that Don Diego, learning of the intercepted letter, would petition the governor of the Province to take Isabella out of the hands of her brothers."[18] The youngest brother, Camillo, was not living in Favale and did not participate in the murders.

The brothers evaded capture, and two of them escaped to France; they were judged guilty *in absentia*. Soon, however, the two escapees returned to Favale with the evident intention of concluding their revenge for the insult to their honor. Together with two uncles, Cesare, Fabio, and Decio conspired to kill don Diego, who had fled to his refuge in Benevento. They managed to place a spy among Diego's bodyguard and, informed by him of Diego's movements and the road he traveled between his refuge in Benevento and his furtive visits to his castle in Bollita, they ambushed Sandoval and his well-armed troop, killing him and dispersing his men, as we learn from the testimony of Antonio Baratuccio, a fiscal lawyer sent to investigate Diego's murder. In his written report he described the ambush and mentioned the bitter hostility between Diego and the Morra brothers, "who had earlier killed a sister of theirs and a teacher."[19]

In a letter of 15 October 1546 from the Viceroy of Naples, Pietro di Toledo, to the emperor, Charles V, the viceroy proposed that Diego's estate in Cosenza be given to Geronimo Fonseca, who had been in charge of it when Sandoval had been sentenced *in absentia*. The emperor replied in a letter of 8 November, asking how Diego, who had probably fought with him in Algeria in 1541,[20] had been killed. On 4 December the viceroy sent the emperor the following report, which he got from Alonso Basurto, governor of the province of Basilicata: "I rode immediately [on your orders] to golita [Bollita] where I found Signora antonia caracciolo, wife of don diego de castro . . . and this said Signora placed charges against the baron of favale and his brothers because she suspected that they had killed him or had him killed because the said don diego had flirted with a sister of the said baron and they had found certain letters and sonnets in her possession that the said don diego sent her and furthermore she had answered and shown interest and for this reason she [Antonia] had publicly proclaimed that the brothers had killed him." An imperial secretary summarized this report with a note: "He was killed because of some foolishness with the sister of a baron."[21]

Thus the period of Diego's murder is firmly established as sometime in the fall of 1546. According to the story, Isabella and the schoolmaster were killed probably not much earlier. Now let us look at that crucial date to which we referred earlier.

Francis I, the king whom her father served and on whom she thus depended for her eventual escape from Favale, died on 31 March 1547. Isabella, as de Gubernatis writes, "had rested all her hopes on King Francis I, and learning of his death, wrote a new sonnet against Fortune."[22]

> *Fortune, who raises to high estate*
> *the most contemptible villain, the vilest heart,*
> *now you put my heart to grief and me to tears*
> *more afflicted and disconsolate than any other.*
>
> *I see my king conquered by you, and laid low*
> *under your horrible wheel,*
> *he who since the time of Caesar, among other great Heroes*
> *was the greatest hero who ever lived.*
>
> *I am a woman and I say that*
> *you, Fortune, feminine as you are called ★*
> *have for enemy every decent heart,*
>
> *And I scream again and again in my crude verse*
> *that whoever wishes to be your friend*
> *is a most malignant and uncommon monster.* (p. 160)

From the context, and because Isabella writes that Francis *was* the greatest hero since Caesar, it is clear that he had died, and because he died in 1547 we know that Isabella was still alive in that year, a fact that de Gubernatis took into account in fixing the date of her death in 1548 but that Croce and those that followed him overlooked; Croce put the year of Isabella's death in 1545 or 1546. [23] Her poem about Francis written in 1547 was among those published by Ludovico Domenichi in *Rime Diverse d'Alcune Nobilissime, et Virtuosissime Donne* (1559), which contains all thirteen of her surviving poems: ten sonnets and three *canzoni*. The poem is authentic. She cannot have died in 1546.

Now, we must ask, how reliable is nephew Marcantonio's account, which Croce accepts as far as it goes? We find that he was born in 1561, so that even if he heard the story as a very young child, perhaps five years old, at least twenty years had passed since the tragedy. His father, Camillo, who told him the story, was Isabella's youngest brother, born in 1528. He was raised in the court of the prince of Salerno, and at the age of sixteen he was sent to fight first against the French in Lombardy, then against France's allies of the moment, the Turks. Returning to Naples after peace was restored with the treaty of Crépy in 1544, he went into the service of the Spanish army and finally settled in Naples permanently in 1558, when he married a Giulia dei Morra, apparently a distant relative.

Croce comments, "[Marcantonio] thus heard the story [of the tragedy] from his father, who certainly could not have been substantially mistaken as to the facts, even if

---

★ Fortune, in Italian *Fortuna*, is in the feminine gender.

in some details he was not well informed or his memory was imperfect."[24] But Camillo most certainly could have been "substantially mistaken," considering that, except for a few of his earliest childhood years, he had lived in Salerno at the court of the prince until 1544, when he was sent north to fight in Lombardy and then served at some undisclosed places against the Turks before returning to Naples.[25] During the years 1545–46 he was clearly not in or even near Favale. His testimony is thus hearsay and surely not to be taken as completely reliable. He died, moreover, in 1603, so Marcantonio must have heard the story not less than twenty-six years before he published it.

We know, however, that the schoolmaster and "a sister of the barons," as both Baratuccio and Basurto refer to the murdered woman in the documents held in the Spanish archives, which include the testimony of Antonia Caracciolo, were murdered in 1546. We believe that the crimes really were committed by the Morra brothers because it is unlikely that Camillo would have invented such a story to tell his son Marcantonio about the family. Marcantonio says Isabella was the murdered sister. This we now see is impossible, because Isabella's poem lamenting the death of Francis I had to be written after 31 March 1547, the day Francis died. Then who was the murdered woman?

It is extremely curious that the only notice of Portia di Morra occurs in connection with her birth, "the youngest daughter" of Giovan Michele Morra and his wife, Louisa Brancaccio. In the early seventeenth century, when Marcantonio di Morra wrote his family's story, Isabella was known as a poet; Portia had disappeared from memory. It was therefore inevitable that Isabella, with her name still relatively famous—her poetry was included in *Rime de cinquanta illustri poetesse* brought out even years later by the publisher Bulifon in 1692—would become the tragic heroine of the Morra family. The sister who was murdered, however, could be no other than Portia. The romantic story of two poets is crushed under the slim weight of a sonnet. It was Isabella's sister Portia to whom Diego sent poems.

When did Isabella die? Ludovico Dolce published eight of her sonnets and one *canzone* in 1552 in his *Rime di diversi illustri signori napolitani*, the first time Isabella's poetry appeared in print. How did he happen to have them? Did she send them to him, yearning, as she always had, for fame? In 1555 the book was reprinted, with her poems included, and in 1556 a new edition was brought out with two more of Isabella's sonnets and two more of her *canzone* added, which Dolce had gotten from Marcantonio Passero, the book dealer and poet-patron whom we will meet as Laura Terracina's mentor and friend. Because Passero had some of her poems, they may have been circulating in academic circles in Naples, suggesting that Isabella sent her poems to various poets in Naples, as she had sent one to Luigi Alamanni in France. Inasmuch as the second printing in 1555 contained no poems that were not in the 1552 book, but the third edition of 1556 included those somehow acquired by Passero, we have entertained the possibility that Isabella might have lived until 1552 and died before 1555. However, Laura Terracina, who wrote sonnet after sonnet in praise of one woman or another, did not address a poem to Isabella. It can hardly be doubted that she had read Isabella's poems, at least by 1552, when they were published within her own circle of poets and patrons, and because Passero had acquired some of them it is all but certain that she read them in manuscript as they circulated in Naples. This leads us to believe that Isabella died much before 1552, so that Laura did not consider it worthwhile to address a poem of praise to a dead woman, and Dolce would have gotten the eight sonnets and one *canzone* from here and there as they circulated around Naples.

All things considered, we have come to believe that Isabella died in 1547 or 1548. We may imagine that she was surely despondent over the terrible murders; she was alone, her sister and the schoolmaster gone. Perhaps these events are behind her poem "Oh miserable fate / to eat the bitter fruit that others gathered." There is no grave, no marker, the local church where she might have been buried no longer exists, no clue as to where she might have been buried. It is plausible to believe that Isabella was despondent enough to throw herself in the Siri River, into which she had once symbolically thrown her name, although for a Catholic this was a sin for which she could go to hell for eternity (see "Muddy Siri").

A further question arises from the tragedy of Favale: Who tipped off the Morra brothers about that fatal letter? The most likely informer was she who gave an account of the events to Basurto when he interviewed her: Antonia Caracciolo. It was she who put the blame on the brothers. Was she a jealous wife who wanted nothing less than complete revenge and devised a simple plot to achieve it? So we believe.[26]

POEMS IN THE ORIGINAL ITALIAN

Isabella di Morra
◉ Track 20,
Reading 19

I fieri assalti di crudel fortuna
scrivo piangendo la mia verde etate
me che 'n sì vili ed orride contrate
spendo il mio tempo senza loda alcuna.

Degno il sepolcro, se fu vil la cuna,
vo procacciando con le Muse amate,
e spero ritrovar qualche pietate,
malgrado de la cieca aspra importuna;

e, col favor de le sacrate Dive
se non col corpo, almen con l'alma sciolta,
essere in pregio a più felici rive.

Questa spoglia, dov'or mi trovo involta,
forse tale alto Re nel mondo vive,
che 'n saldi marmi la terrà sepolta. * (p. 141)

~

D'un alto monte, onde si scorge il mare,
miro sovente io, tua figlia Isabella,
s'alcun legno spalmato in quello appare,
che di te, padre, a me doni novella.

Ma la mia avversa e dispietata stella
non vuol ch'alcun conforto possa entrare
nel tristo cor, ma di pietà rubella
la salda speme in pianto fa mutare:

Ch'io non veggo nel mar remo nè vela
(così deserto è l'infelice lito)
che l'onde fenda, o che la gonfi il vento.

Contra Fortuna allor spargo querela,
ed ho in odio il denigrato sito,
come sola cagione del mio tormento.† (p. 142)

~

Se a la propinqua speme nuovo impaccio,
oh, Fortuna crudele o l'empia Morte,

---

* All poems by Morra are from Gubernatis, *Le Rime* (Rome, 1907), III.
† V.

com' han soluto, ahi lassa, non m'apporte,
rotta avrò la prigione e sciolto il laccio.

Ma pensando a quel dì, ardo ed agghiaccio,
chè 'l timore e 'l desio son le mie scorte;
a questo or chiudo, or apro a quel le porte,
e, in forse, di dolor mi struggo e sfaccio.

Con ragione, il desìo dispiega i vanni,
ed al suo porto appressa il bel pensiero,
per trar quest'alma da perpetui affanni;

Ma Fortuna al timor mostra il sentiero
erto ed angusto e pien di tanti inganni,
che, nel più bel sperar, poi mi dispero. (p. 142)

~

Sacra Giunone, se i volgari amori
son de l'alto tuo cor tanto nemici,
i giorni e gli anni miei chiari, felici,
fà con tuoi santi e ben concessi ardori.

A voi consacro i miei verginei fiori,
a te, o Dea, e ài tuoi pensieri amici;
o de le cose sola alme beatrici,
che colmi il ciel de'suoi soavi odori.

Cingimi al collo un bello aurato laccio
de' tuoi più cari ed umili soggetti,
che di servir a Te sola procaccio;

Guida Himeneo con sì cortesi affetti,
e fà sì caro il nodo, ond'io m'allaccio,
ch'una sola alma regga i nostri petti. (pp. 142 – 43)

~

Poscia ch' al bel desir troncate hai l'ale,
che nel mio cor sorgea, crudel Fortuna,
sì che d'ogni tuo ben vivo digiuna;
dirò, con questo stil ruvido e frale,
alcuna parte de l'interno male
causato sol da te, fra questi dumi,
fra questi aspri costumi
di gente irrazional, priva d'ingegno,
ove, senza sostegno,

● Track 21,
Reading 20

---
* I.   † IV.

son costretta a menare il viver mio,
qui posta da ciascuno in cieco oblio.

. . .

   Tu, crudel, de l'infanzia in quei pochi anni,
del caro genitor mi fésti priva,

. . .

   Cesar gli vieta il poter darmi aìta.
O cosa non più udita,
privar il padre di giovar la figlia! * (pp. 143 – 44)

⁓

Isabella di Morra
⦿ Track 22,
Reading 21

   Quanto pregiar ti puoi, Siri mio amato,
de la tua ricca e fortunata riva,
e de la terra che da te deriva
il nome ch'al mio cor oggi è sì grato,

   S'ivi alberga colei che 'l cielo irato
può far tranquillo, e la mia speme viva
mal grado de l'acerba e cruda Diva
ch'ogn'or s'esalta del mio basso stato.

   Non men l'odor de la vermiglia rosa
di dolce aura vital nodrisce l'alma,
che soglian farsi i sacri gigli d'oro.

   Sarà per lei la vita mia gioiosa,
de' gravi affanni deporrò la salma,
e queste chiome cingerò d'alloro. † (p. 144)

⁓

   Quella ch'è detta la fiorita etade,
secca ed oscura, solitaria ed erma,
tutta ho passato qui cieca ed inferma,
senza saper mai pregio di beltade.
È stata per me morta, in te, pietade,
e spenta l'hai in altrui, che potea sciorre
e in altra parte porre
dal carcer duro il vel de l'alma stanca,
che, come neve bianca,
dal Sol, così, da te, si strugge ogni ora,
e struggerassi, infin che qui dimora. ‡ (p. 144)

⁓

   Torbido Siri, del mio mal superbo,
or ch'io sento da presso il fin amaro,

---

* Canzone, ll. 1–13, 17–19.   † VI.
‡ Canzone, ll. 23–33.

fà tu noto il mio duolo al padre caro,
se mai qui 'l torna il suo destino acerbo.

Dilli come, morendo, disacerbo
l'aspra fortuna e lo mio fato avaro
e, con esempio miserando e raro,
nome infelice a le tue onde io serbo.

Tosto ch'ei giunga a la sassosa riva
(a che pensar m'adduci, o fiera stella!)
come d'ogni mio ben son cassa e priva,

Inqueta l'onde con crudel procella,
e dì: me accrebber sì, mentre fu viva,
non gli occhi no, ma i fiumi d'Isabella. * (p. 145)

~

Qui non provo io di donna il proprio stato,
per te, che posta m'hai in sì ria sorte,
che dolce vita mi sarìa la morte.

I cari pegni del mio padre amato
piangon d'intorno. Ai! Ai! misero fato,
mangiare il frutto, ch'altri colse, amaro
quei che mai non peccaro,
la cui semplicità farìa clemente
una tigre, un serpente,
ma non già te, ver noi più fiera e rea
ch'al figlio Progne ed al fratel Medea.

. . .

Bastone i figli de la fral vecchiezza
esser dovean di mia misera madre;
ma per le tue procelle inique ed adre,
sono in estrema ed orrida fiacchezza;
e spenta in lor sarà la gentilezza
da gli antichi lasciata a questi giorni,
se da gli alti soggiorni
pietà non giunge al cor del Re di Francia.

. . .

Ai! Ai! Fortuna (e perchè far no 'l dèi?)
che giungan al gran Re gli sospir miei.† (pp. 145 – 46)

~

Chi desìa lunga vita,
chi vuol divino nome,

Luigi Alamanni

---

* X.   † Canzone, ll. 34–36, 37–44, 56–63, 70–72.

chi brama eterno onore
a quegli, a cui gradita
fronde adornò le chiome,
rivolga i passi, e'l core,
che'l poetico ardore
tanto ha vigore, e forza
che il tempo non l'ammorza. * (p. 146)

Isabella di Morra

Scrissi con stile amaro, aspro e dolente,
un tempo, come sai, contro Fortuna;
sì che niun'altra mai sotto la luna
di lei si dolse con voler più ardente.

Or, del suo cieco error l'alma si pente,
chè in tai doti non scorge gloria alcuna;
e se de' beni suoi vive digiuna,
spera arricchirsi in Dio, chiara e lucente.

Nè Tempo o Morte il bel tesoro eterno,
nè predatrice o violenta mano
ce lo torrà davanti al Re del Cielo.

Ivi non nuoce già state nè verno,
chè non si sente mai caldo nè gielo;
dunque ogni altro sperar, Fratello, è vano. † (pp. 146 – 47)

~

Quel che gli giorni a dietro
noiava questa mia gravosa salma,
di star fra queste selve erme ed oscure,
or sol diletta l'alma;
chè da Dio, sua mercè tal grazia impetro,
che scorger ben mi fa le vie secure
di gire a lui, fuor de le inique cure.
Or rivolta la mente a la Reina
del Ciel, con vera altissima umilitate,
per le solinghe strade,
senza intrico mortal, l'alma cammina
già verso il suo riposo,
chè ad altra parte 'l pensier non inchina,
fuggendo il triste secol sì noioso,
lieta e contenta in questo bosco ombroso.

. . .

---

* Agostino Gabbi, *Scelta di sonetti e canzoni* (Venice, 1727–39), p. 432.
† II.

Sol de l'Erémo la tranquilla vita.
　　Per voi, grotta felice,
boschi intricati e rovinati sassi,
Sinno veloce, chiare fonti e rivi,
erbe, che d'altrui passi
segnate a me vedere unqua non lice,
compagna son di quelli spirti divi,
ch'or là su stanno in sempiterno vivi;
e nel solare e glorioso Lembo
de la Madre, del Padre e del suo Dio
spero vedermi anch'io,
sgombrata tutta del terrestre nembo,
e, fra l'alme beate,
ogni mio bel pensier riporle in grembo,
O mie rimote e fortunate strade
donde adopra'il Signor la sua pietade.

　　Quanto discovre e scalda il chiaro sole,
Canzon, è nulla, ad un guardo sì pio,
ch'è Regina del Ciel, Madre di Dio.* (pp. 147 – 48)

⁓

　　Questi son gli occhi, onde di strali, e foco
mille messi d'Amor armati usciro,
quando nel cor giunse'l primier sospiro,
che'l penar mi fa dolce, e'l pianger gioco.

　　Queste son quelle chiome, a cui son roco
gridar ch'allentin l'aspro mio martiro.
questo è quel chiaro volto in cui respiro,
che del mio male e d'altro gli cal poco.

　　Queste son le bellezze ch'io tant'amo
che dì e notte di me lor voglia fanno
e mi dan poche dolci ore serene.

　　Questa è quella sì vaga del mio danno,
la qual io sempre ne' sospir miei chiamo,
che potria sola rallentar mie pene. † (p. 149)

⁓

　　Quando Amor i begli occhi intorno gira,
che fanno al sole meraviglia e scorno
et apportano al giorno un nuovo giorno
d'un'aura pieno che soave spira.

⦿ Track 23,
Reading 22

---

* *Canzone*, ll. 1–15, 90–108.
† Tobia R. Toscano, ed., *Diego Sandoval di Castro, Rime* (Rome, 1997).

Non ponno in lor i miei far lunga mira,
ond'io li chiudo e desioso torno
spesso ad aprirli, e arroscio e 'mbianco e scorno,
per la vergogna ch'ho di chi mi mira.

~

L'anima ancora langue di dolcezza
e 'l cor doglioso acerba pena sente,
allegrezza provando e noia estreme.

Il piacer dal mirar tanta bellezza
e 'l duol dal disperar nasce a la mente:
così beato e son misero insieme.* (p. 149)

Isabella di Morra

Fortuna, che sollevi in alto stato
ogni depresso ingegno, ogni vil core,
or fai che 'l mio in lagrime e 'n dolore
viva più che altro afflitto e sconsolato.

Veggio il mio Re, da te vinto e prostrato
sotto la rota tua, piena d'orrore
lo qual, fra gli altri Heroi, era maggiore
che da Cesare in quà fosse mai stato.

Son Donna, e contra de le donne dico
che tu, Fortuna, avendo il nome nostro,
ogni ben nato cor hai per nemico.

E spesso grido, col mio rozzo inchiostro,
che chi vuole esser tuo più caro amico
sia degli uomini orrendo e raro mostro. † (p. 151)

---

* Toscano, *Rime*.   † VIII.

NOTES

1   The basic source for the account of Isabella di Morra's life is the memoir by her nephew, Marcantonio di Morra, son of her youngest brother, Camillo. This was published in Naples in 1629 under the title of *Familiae nobilissimae de Morra historia.* The section pertaining to the Morra family was translated from Latin into Italian by Brunella Carriero under the title "Dolce vita mi saria la morte," *Isabella Morra nella cronaca di famiglia* (Valsinni, n.d.). Following Marcantonio, Angelo de Gubernatis recounted the story as a preface to his edition of her poetry, *Isabella Morra, le rime* (Rome, 1907). Bianca Molari, *Isabella di Morra* (Naples, 1907), gives a fancied-up account based on the nephew's narrative. Benedetto Croce incorporated Marcantonio's story and added substantially to it through archival research in his publication *Isabella di Morra e Diego Sandoval de Castro con le edizione delle "Rime" della Morra* (Bari, 1929; rpt., Palermo, 1983). Other writers, among many, include Aldo Zaccone, *Itinerario poetico di Isabella Morra,* http://www.siris.it/morra/html/aldo-zaccone.html (1989); Franco Vitelli, "Sul testo delle 'Rime' di Isabella di Morra," in A. Granese et al., eds., *I Gaurico e il Rinascimento meridionale: Atti del Convegno di Studi* (Salerno, 1992), pp. 445–464; Juliana Schiesari, "Isabella di Morra (c. 1520–1545)" in Rinaldina Russell, ed., *Italian Women Writers* (Westport, Conn., 1994), pp. 279–285; Tobia R. Toscano, ed., *Diego Sandoval de Castro: Rime* (Salerno, 1997); and Irene Musillo Mitchell, *Isabella Morra, Canzoniere* (West Lafayette, 1998), a bilingual edition of Morra's thirteen surviving poems. The order of Isabella's poems together with their place in her life, is the conjecture of the present authors, who are also responsible for the translations.

2   Croce, *Isabella di Morra e Diego Sandoval de Castro,* p. 32.

3   See chapter 2.

4   We have touched on this history in chapter 3.

5   We read that Giovan Michele left Favale in August 1528 (di Morra, *Familiae nobilissimae,* p. 10; Carriero, "Dolce vita," p. 20); Camillo was born on 30 September, 1528 (di Morra, *Familiae nobilissimae,* p. 16; Carriero, "Dolce vita," p. 28), after the father's departure, so there could not have been any more children. However, we read that Portia was the last born (di Morra, *Familiae nobilissimae,* p. 11; Carriero, "Dolce vita," p. 22). Because Latin and Italian have gender endings, we are meant to understand that Portia was the last-born girl, Camillo the last-born boy.

6   Our source for Isabella's poems is de Gubernatis, *Le Rime,* which repeats the ten sonnets and two of the *canzoni* originally published in Lodovico Domenichi, ed., *Rime diverse d'alcune nobilissime et virtuosissime donne* (Lucca, 1559). De Gubernatis found the third *canzone.*

7   Croce, *Isabella di Morra e Diego Sandoval de Castro,* pp. 15–16.

8   Croce, *Isabella di Morra e Diego Sandoval de Castro,* pp. 30–31.

9   Croce, *Isabella di Morra e Diego Sandoval de Castro,* p. 30, identified Giulia Orsini, the woman to whom Isabella alludes, by means of the vermillion rose, part of the devise of the Orsini family. The sacred golden lily refers to the Lily of France. De Gubernatis believed Isabella's friend was Antonia Caracciolo, Diego's wife (*Rime,* pp. 24–25), but Croce proves otherwise.

10   De Gubernatis, *Le Rime,* p. 24, says that she wrote a sonnet to Alamanni but gives no further information about this. For Alamanni's poem, see Agostino Gabbi, *Scelta di Sonetti e Canzoni* (Venice, 1727–39), p. 432.

11   Di Morra, *Familiae nobilissimae,* p. 10 (Latin), Carriero, "Dolce vita," p. 21 (Italian).

12   Di Morra, *Familiae nobilissimae,* p. 10; Carriero, "Dolce vita," p. 21. Scipione came to the attention of the French ambassador to the Holy See, who, impressed with his intelligence and learning, sent him to join his father at the French court. He eventually became an official there, perhaps secretary to Catherine de' Medici.

13   Giovanni Caserta, writing in *Isabella Morra e la società meridionale del cinquecento* (Matera, 1976), considered it likely that Isabella was born between 1516 and 1518.

14   Vitelli, "Sul testo delle *Rime,*" p. 445.

15   It must be emphasized that, with only thirteen poems surviving, the full range of her writing is surely not known; we can guess that there might well have been nature poems, encomiastic poems to writers she would have wanted to know, like the one to Luigi Alamanni, and even perhaps political poems. And perhaps there actually *were* love poems.

16   Yolanda di Blasi, ed., *Antologia delle scrittrici italiane dalle origini al 1800* (Florence, 1930), p. 82.

17   Croce claims that it was rumored in the neighborhood that there was an ongoing correspondence between Isabella and Diego, but he gives no evidence for this. There is no way, moreover, that he could have known about rumors 350 years after the tragedy.

18   De Gubernatis, *Le Rime*, p. 13: "*dicendo Isabella che'l'avea ricevuta, in nome di Donna Antonia, i fratelli che il luogo agreste avea reso ferini e barbari, senza indugio, ferocemente uccisero il pedagogo e pugnalarono la sorella, quando si persuasero che Don Diego fatto consapevole della lettera intercetta, sollecitava il governatore della provincia (della Basilicata), perchè sottraesse Isabella dalle mani dei fratelli.*" De Gubernatis's version relates that there was in fact a plan to help Isabella escape from Favale, one devised by Diego Sandoval and his wife Antonia, whom de Gubernatis believed was the woman Isabella referred to in "Oh, Siri, my beloved river. . . . Here lives the woman who can soothe the angry sky and keep my hope alive. . . . Because of her my life will be joyous." The letter, in this version, contained details about this escape plan. Bianca Molari embroidered this version in *Isabella di Morra*.

19   Croce, *Isabella di Morra e Diego Sandoval de Castro*, p. 13, relates that "*Marcantonio che solo era stato imprigionato come complice dell'eccidio, dopo lungo carcere fu . . . graziato.*" ("Only Marcantonio was imprisoned as an accomplice and after serving a long term was . . . pardoned.") But on p. 33, he writes, "*Non pare per altro che all'eccidio partecipasse o che di esso fosse accusato il primogenito [Marcantonio], il quale rimase in casa e nel giugno del 1546 strinse perfino nozze con una Vardella Galeota di Napoli.*" ("It does not appear, however, that the first-born [Marcantonio] participated in the murder [for] he remained at home and in June, 1546, he even married. . . .") The murders obviously occurred later that year, after the June marriage: Croce was right the first time. The lapse is interesting, however, for it reveals a lack of attention that led Croce astray, as we will see below. Archivo General de Simancas, E 1036–104, "Copy of a report [made by] the fiscal lawyer Antonio "Baratucho" [Baratuccio] on the cause and death of don Diego de Sandoval." We wish to thank Doctor Francisco Javier Alvarez Piñedo, subdirector general of the State Archives in Simancas, for kindly sending us photocopies of the record relevant to the murder of Diego Sandoval.

20   Croce, *Isabella di Morra e Diego Sandoval de Castro*, p. 21.

21   Archivo General de Simancas, "Copy."

22   De Gubernatis, *Le Rime*, p. 45.

23   Croce, *Isabella di Morra e Diego Sandoval de Castro*, p. 33.

24   Croce, *Isabella di Morra e Diego Sandoval de Castro*, p. 9.

25   Croce, *Isabella di Morra e Diego Sandoval de Castro*, p. 9.

26   The Morra brothers escaped to France again after the murder of Sandoval. Decio became a priest and abbot of an Augustinian abbey in Limoges; Cesare married a French woman with an estate in the same region. In Favale Marcantonio went to prison, and, after serving a long term, was finally freed. Croce, *Isabella di Morra e Diego Sandoval de Castro*, pp. 12–13.

CHAPTER SIX

LAURA TERRACINA
(1519 – CA. 1577)

 *FEMINIST*

aura Terracina was the most prolific of the Italian women poets of the sixteenth century.[1] Eight volumes of her poetry were published in her lifetime, a ninth collection was not published, and there remains a codex in the National Library of Florence with more than two hundred of her uncollected poems.[2] Of the published works, the most important is her third book, *Il Discorso Sopra il Principio di Tutti i Canti di Orlando Furioso* (Commentary on the Beginning of All the Cantos of Orlando Furioso), published in 1549, which we will discuss in detail at the end of this chapter.[3]

Laura's poetry is pervaded by her generally dark view of the society in which she lived. Besides attacking injustice to women, the single most important subject of her poems, she inveighs against every kind of human frailty and the reader hears her shouting futilely against the wind in poems addressed to traitors, hypocrites, liars, faithless friends, usurers, and the greedy and lustful: "Whom shall I attack first," she writes, "since all are equally sinful?"[4] Is she perhaps overly self-righteous when she describes herself, however, in a poem she wrote at the age of about forty as wondrously free of those faults of which she is so aware in others?

> *I was born into an old noble family;*
> *I am neither homely nor very beautiful;*
> *I have always been a foe of meanness*
> *and snobbery, but a friend to humility.*
>
> *I have fled from laziness and have loved work*
> *as anyone can see and say of me*
> *and I love to praise women, now this one, now that one*
> *with sincere love and honesty.*
>
> *I do not value praise nor flatterers,*
> *nor elegant clothes nor female adornments*
> *as I clearly show;*
>
> *Honesty and decorum are the flowers*
> *with which I adorn my head and my body,*
> *for which I thank heaven and our wonderful century.* (p. 187)

How clearly she saw herself we shall see for ourselves as we confront her life, her loves, and her poetry.

Laura was born in the family villa at Chiaia, a suburb of Naples, overlooking the Tyrrhenian Sea.[5] The Terracina family had won its name in the thirteenth century when Laura's ancestors were rewarded with the territory of that name near Naples for aiding the Colonna family in its struggle with the papacy. In the fourteenth century Musa da Terra- cina was rewarded with the territory of Bacio for his military service to the French rulers of Naples. However, in the next century when the Spanish under Alfonso V seized Naples (1443), the family switched its loyalty to the new rulers. In 1507 Paolo Bacio Terracina, Laura's father, obtained a baronetcy from Ferdinand V (Ferdinand the Catholic), King of Naples, for services rendered. The support of the Terracinas for the Spanish rulers put them at risk, especially in 1547 during a popular uprising, when her uncle Domenico, who had been elected as a representative of the people, betrayed their trust by supporting the Spanish viceroy, Pietro Toledo, in his effort to promote the government's attempt to establish the Spanish Inquisition in Naples. Laura, with her family, remained loyal to the viceroy, but she was far from blind to the intrigues and betrayals not only in the political life of Naples but in society-at-large.

> *I see the world askew, I see it senseless;*
> *I see every virtue abandoned*
> *and the Arts held in disrespect:*
> *my talent might just as well be buried.*
>
> *I see that hate and envy have taken hold*
> *of friends, and I see that faithlessly*
> *goodness has been betrayed to Evil*
> *and Heaven is intent on our destruction.*
>
> *No one stands up firmly for the common good,*
> *all speak out for themselves*
> *while every heart is filled with trivia,*
>
> *I see this, and seeing it, I even hate myself,*
> *so that, disgusted, I would like to see either myself*
> *or the whole world blind.* (p. 187)

For an author whose first volume, published in 1548, was a best-seller, reprinted five times in her lifetime,[6] she seems unduly despairing, but despair is the leitmotif that tones much of her vast production. There is not one happy poem in all her work. Characteristic is her sonnet,

> *When I watch the flight of a bird*
> *and hear it greet the dawn with its song*
> *all the more does sadness rise up in me, all the more*
> *my weak yet fierce will wrings my blazing heart.*
>
> *Because I know well that*
> *I am doomed to suffer endlessly,*

I feel I would like to abandon
this hostile world.

Thus miserable, in terrible pain,
I spend my days in agony,
moaning wretchedly and shamefully with jealousy.

I would like to steal
the chariot of the sun, there on the horizon,
and were I to fall, like Phaeton, I would not care. (pp. 187 – 88)

Throughout her life she was tantalized with successes that never brought full satisfaction, with hopes of love that were frustrated again and again.

Laura was quite young when she began to feel the ambition that became the crucial motivation of her life—to be famous as a poet:

That ancient laurel whose leaves
forever blaze with the golden light of dawn
is not yet ready for me, my talent unpolished,
to be placed among the famous scholars and artists:

If that talent struggles desperately
to create poems, plain and simple as they are,
it is not for praise, not to have them admired,
but to gain time whose ceaseless passing breaks my heart.

But if even a small spark of talent
reveals itself in me, or some sign that
a benign heaven has instilled some gift in my heart,

Do not call it mine, woman as I am
of little talent, but a spark of love
that the goodness of God has placed there as a pledge. (p. 188)

Having, at first, no connections among the literary establishment, she was fortunate to engage the interest of Marc Antonio Passero, at one time a professor at the University of Padua, who enjoyed a wide acquaintance among the literati in Naples whom he was pleased to help in one way or another. Laura credited Passero in her first volume for his guidance in her early years. In her poem addressed "To Marc Antonio Passero" she writes,

My friend, I know that you have given me my voice
and it is only right for me to put you foremost
and as much as I can with my feeble voice
praise you to the skies with my poem.
And when my harsh voice cannot

say enough about how much I esteem you,
I will show you with my heart, and with my eagerness
that I love you as much as one can love. (p. 188)

It was probably he who set her about cultivating the most celebrated writers and poets among her contemporaries with encomiastic verses that, included in that first published collection, doubtless contributed to its extraordinary success. Recognition came before that first volume, however, since she was admitted to one of the Neapolitan academies, the Accademia degli Incogniti, in 1545.[7] It was possibly Vittoria Colonna, with her singular prestige, who indirectly helped her achieve this first important victory. Passero sent Vittoria some of Laura's poems, which Vittoria acknowledged with a poem that, however brief, might well have provided the support Laura needed to win the favorable attention of the academy.

Since, lovely lady, I, too, am a woman,
when I read your poems,
graceful and concise as they are,
and expressed in whitest paper and clearest ink,
poems that gild our iron century, *
I am amazed. (p. 189)

As a member of the Academy Laura took the academic name of Febea and came into association with the leading figures in Neapolitan cultural life, whom she cultivated with laudatory verses such as the sonnet she addressed to Angelo Di Costanzo, in which she plays on his name [8]:

The sweet sound of the famous lyre
given to you by the great shepherd of Delos
inflames my heart with such fervent zeal
that I am spurred on, compelled to sing.

But such is fear that
my voice is muffled when I desire to praise you,
and my warm desire is frozen
fearing that you will explode to Heaven in anger.

For you are heaven's divine ANGEL
and the most CONSTANT † among all the others
and my plain language cannot rise to such heights.

Thus do I sing only the melody
and leave to you the words,
wrapping myself in your gracious mantle. (p. 189)

---

* "In whitest paper and clearest ink": that is, frankly and honestly.

† Laura pushes the word *costanza* beyond its usual meaning (constant, firm, steadfast) in order to make her pun, implying that his fame will endure longer.

Although her style lacked the more characteristic marks of literary Mannerism
with its artificial "distortions, exaggerations and rhetorical stylizations,"[9] Laura was
fond of literary devices such as this pun on Angelo's name. She brought this taste to
fulfillment in her masterpiece, the *Commentary.*

Laura's serious career as a poet got its start when she was admitted into L'Accademia degli Incogniti. Her extraordinary success for about ten years began in 1548 with
the first publication of her poems, *Rime,* edited by Ludovico Domenichi for the publisher Giolito in Venice. There were several reasons for the volume's exceptionally favorable reception, despite Laura's often prosaic poetry. The unadorned language of
her poems gives them an unmistakable energy that introduced a compellingly plain-
speaking voice into Italian Cinquecento poetry. But her success doubtless owed in
part to the praise she tirelessly lavished in poem after poem addressed to important
men and women. Her own social standing as a member of a noble family put her on
a familiar footing with the great Neapolitan families, and she was welcomed in the
princely palaces of Salerno and Bisignano. She wrote of their proprietors with fulsome praise of their many virtues; she was on terms of friendship with such women
as Lady Maria and Lady Giovanna di Aragona, with Clarice Orsino, Princess of
Stigliano, with Lady Isabella Colonna and others, in all of whom she found great
beauty of face and spirit. They doubtless read Laura's books, at least the poems addressed to themselves, and Lady Maria Colonna addressed a poem to Laura that indicates she had read Laura's third book, the *Commentary:*

> *You with your talent make more worthy*
> *the nobility of your blood;*
> *the needle and cloth put aside,*
> *you turn your hand to pen and ink, scorning common work,*
> *indeed you yourself adorn with jewels and majesty*
> *this ignoble age . . .* (p. 189)

In stanza three, Canto 37, of the *Commentary,* Laura hoped women would give up
"needle and cloth," and begin to study and write.

Laura wrote more than one hundred laudatory poems to women, mostly of noble
families, and because praise of women was fashionable among male writers and welcomed by many women, surely this, too, swelled Laura's readership.

The success of her first volume gave her dubious satisfaction, however, for she herself knew it was due partly to the praise she offered to those she addressed, rather
than to her poetic power. Although she disdained praise—"I do not value praise or
flatterers," she wrote in her self-portrayal—she well knew that it was valued by others, and praise was the key Laura used to open the door to the recognition that she
craved,[10] bowing to her own recognition of necessity: did not men writers, many of
them courtiers, live by praising their patrons and their families? Praise was in fact the
poetic coin of the day. Although her laudatory verses were usually reciprocated in
more or less extravagant expressions of admiration, occasionally she was disappointed. When, with several volumes already published, she sent a sonnet to Laura Battiferra, the latter was reluctant to answer her, as we know from a letter of Battiferra to
Benedetto Varchi. "I received . . . a sonnet from Signora Laura Terracina, to which I

wrote a response; but I did not send it. Now, since she has been begging for my answer, I am sending it to you [for your opinion]." The response seems not to have been sent.[11]

Varchi himself had received one of Laura Terracina's laudatory poems years earlier, apparently, because she refers to herself in the poem as a young woman and he in his response addresses her as "dear girl."

> *Varchi, in whom blond Apollo*
> *has instilled the virtues of the sacred laurel,*
> *so that he has no desire to hear any others*
> *but to your song only does he listen with pleasure.*

> *A great desire is hidden in my heart*
> *where your art has enclosed it,*
> *urging me to speak out, and I blame you*
> *for my boldness, which is greater than my knowledge.*

> *This poem reveals the crass ignorance*
> *of a young woman who with unsure steps*
> *is searching in the blank sky for guidance.*

> *So she abandons to you the task that she herself began,*
> *and leaves it to you, as a wise and trusted man,*
> *to express what she wanted to say.* (pp. 189 – 90)

Laura could hardly have been satisfied with Varchi's corresponding response with its evasive flattery, its ambiguous reminder that only the most aggressive writers make it into the heaven of literary critics, and its final refusal to be taken in by her pretense of humility.

> *Laura, dear girl, in whom heaven encloses*
> *graces and virtues like the other one of old,*
> *rarely is one other than Phoebe*
> *so crowned with laurels.*[*]

> *With your sweet song*
> *the grassy, flowering, leafy banks*
> *of the beautiful Sebeto*
> *subdue the singing fountains of the Tuscan muses.*

> *And you, who in our day,*
> *wisely show that you realize*
> *Minerva sends the most fierce and savage to heaven,*

---

* The other Laura refers to Petrarch's Laura. Phoebe, as goddess of the moon, is related to Apollo, the sun-god, to whom Laura has referred in her poem as having inspired Varchi. Phoebe (Febea) is the academic name Laura chose for herself.

> Why do you present yourself to me so humbly
> To me, unqualified as I am
> to praise the noble ambition that is yours, not mine? (p. 190)

In truth, Laura was not really humble. Although she knew her gift was not as great as she wished, she correctly judged her talent well worth serious respect and she claimed humility as a writer and as a woman—often she wrote that she was "only a woman"—to disarm possible antagonistic readers. Even to Passero, at the very beginning of her career, she had sounded this theme,

> Here are the poems, my dear Marc Antonio
> which you have requested me to do,
> I have done them, as a woman, which I am.
> Do not blame them if I fail in my verse;
> my talent is not equal to my desire,
> nor to my obedience, much as I might want to do well.
> Therefore, accept my love if not my poems
> which are not graceful and polished, as I would wish (p. 190)

and in her *Commentary* she addressed a foreword in form of a verse to Ludovico Dolce.

> Here is my discorso, dear Dolce.
> I have looked it over hurriedly, and no one else has seen it,
> and if my language seems quite masculine
> I beg your pardon; and if I seem arrogant
> it is because I did not know if feminine poetry
> might be worthy enough to offer you.
> However, I am satisfied that it is finished and
> with my sweat I have honestly fulfilled my promise to you. (p. 190)

Although Laura realized that her poetic power fell short of her aspirations, it is clear that her self-disparagement as a writer and a woman was not completely sincere. Had it been, she would not have complained as she often did that she was unappreciated, that all she earned with her hard work was "blame, shame, anxiety, hate and torment," as she wrote, in one poem, while in another, to Camilla Pellegrino, like herself a poet, she asks,

> Why do I keep on cultivating the green laurel
> to crown other heads unworthy of honor;
> why do I consume my mind and heart
> if the world cares only for silver and gold?

> Since I expect nothing from my work
> but scorn, jealousy and insult
> why do I spend everyday, every hour
> bothering Apollo and the chorus of the muses

if those who are embellished and honored
praise me to my face and then fiercely tear me down,
together with my work, my writing.

Let the crazy world be, let me keep hoping
that my beautiful laurel that often flowers
be ever green and proud of its fame. (p. 191)

We must see her humility more as a disarming ploy than a straightforward confession of inadequacy. That it did not always work we can only infer from the poem to Pellegrina, for we have no poems by any of her contemporaries in which she is attacked with "scorn and insult."

One further consideration must be factored into accounting for Laura's success: her poems were revised and edited by established male writers. While it is true that her spectacular success began with the recognition of her talent by Ludovico Domenichi, whom she had never met, she enjoyed close and helpful friendships with highly cultivated men in Neapolitan intellectual circles and beyond, despite the fact that she herself was poorly educated. We doubt that her male friends were motivated to help her solely because of their admiration for her poetic gift. Although Laura lacked the kind of beautiful features that make women obviously attractive to men, she is said to have been pursued by many men, including the literati among her colleagues in the Academy: according to one source, she was once assaulted in her writing studio by one them, from whom she ran screaming for help.[12] Angelo Borzelli observed from her engraved portraits that she had an "esuberanza di forme che destavan desideri," literally, "an exuberance of form that awakened desire"; in other words, Laura looked voluptuous (figure 6.1).[13] This was not entirely to her advantage, inasmuch as general opinion associated intellectual activity in a woman with loose morals. Knowing this, she took care to dress sedately, to present herself without feminine adornments, and to insist publicly on her virgin state and her intention to remain so until she married.[14]

There will be only one who will make me change
from my present state and have all of me for himself:
when heaven wishes to give me a husband
he shall have this flower that I keep untouched within me.
If one should want to behave otherwise
his bold thought would be useless:
sooner would the troubled, resounding river
run backward to the foothills of the Alps.[15] (p. 191)

But she seems to have been irresistibly attractive. Would-be lovers pined in vain, as did the smitten priest Don Desiderio Cavalcabò. She was, he wrote, a "nest of love, a fountain of virtue, modesty's home and perfection's example." Who could ever describe, he asks,

The various beauties of her ample bosom
where with great delight

**6.1.
Enea Vico.
*Portrait of Laura
Terracina.* ca.
1550. From
*Le medaglie del
Doni* (Antonio
Francesco Doni).
Achille
Bertarelli Print
Collection,
Castello
Sforzesco, Milan.
Photo,
Bertarelli
Collection.**

one could nestle in those fair and sweet apples?
But the Reverend was never to enjoy that delight.

> *In vain have I cast my words to the winds,*
> *in vain have I sighed and cried,*
> *whether by speaking or by writing,*
> *I have had no answer to my prayers.* (p. 191)

Laura's rejection of Cavalcabò is clear. Her relationship with another cleric,

Diomede Carafa, bishop of Aviano (and later a cardinal), has been considered problematic and has inspired two different interpretations: according to Maroi, Laura fell madly in love with him and Carafa struggled mightily to resist her temptation; according to Borzelli, however, Carafa fell in love with Laura, who reproved him for his "indecent thoughts." Both writers relate the story of a painting by Leonardo da Pistoia (Leonardo Grazia) in Sta. Maria del Parto in Mergellina, on the outskirts of Naples. Commissioned by Carafa, the painting represents St. Michael slaying the dragon, symbolizing the triumph of Christ over the Antichrist, good over evil (figure 6.2).[16] What is most striking about the painting is the face of the dragon, a woman's face, which Maroi and others identify as that of Laura Terracina. She thus believes that the "pious" bishop, tempted by the *"formosissima"* ("plump," i.e., voluptuous) poet, commissioned the work to exorcize her, the incarnation of his passionate desires. Borzelli, on the other hand, does not see in the dragon the face of Laura but probably that of another woman with whom the painter himself was in love and who rejected him. There is possibly a clue in a poem by Laura addressed to Leonardo, from which we infer that the artist asked Laura to write on his behalf an insulting poem to a woman who had "insulted" him, which, strangely, she did, against her own judgment, but not without scolding him.

> *I have often heard you proclaim,*
> *inflaming the air with your heated breath,*
> *that for a woman to speak against women is very unpleasant,*
> *whether for good reason or bad,*
> *but to gratify your expressed wish,*
> *I have written, although I should not have.*
> *I am certain that the woman did insult you*
> *but you yourself are to blame for it.* (pp. 191–92)

We tend to agree with Borzelli's view, for in Canto 31 of the *Commentary*, addressed to Carafa, she writes,

> *For several days, Monsignor, I have been aware*
> *of your feelings, even more of your intention,*
> *but since it is not obvious, and does not matter*
> *I have not felt, nor do I feel now any fear,*
> *I care little for your thoughts about me,*
> *indeed, think whatever makes you happy;*
> *there is no anxiety in my heart about this,*
> *for my part, I am going to sleep, so go to sleep yourself.* (p. 192)

The comical last line would seem to finish any speculation about Laura's feelings for Carafa.

But did any of the Academy men with whom Laura mingled so freely touch her heart? Luigi Tansillo, one of the preeminent poets of the Academy, pursued her. At first the relationship seemed only one of mutual admiration. They exchanged encomiastic poems, Laura modestly, as usual, disclaiming her own ability:

6.2.
Leonardo Grazia
da Pistoia.
*St. Michael
Slaying the
Dragon.*
ca. 1545.
The Church of
Sta. Maria del
Parto a
Mergellina,
Naples.
Photo, Luciano
Pedicini/
Umberto
Santacroce.

> *Whoever thinks, much less says*
> *that my muse can be compared*
> *to the elegance of your beautiful poems*
> *is both dull and foolish,*
> *oh, Signor Tansillo, honor of our times;*
> *but only out of great ignorance*
> *I have finally taken up paper and ink.*
> *I am a woman, and not ashamed of it;*
> *you may make what you want of this.* (p. 192)

In his response, Tansillo is unrestrained in his praise of her talent, comparing her to the great women poets of ancient Greece and the two great moderns, meaning surely Vittoria Colonna and Veronica Gàmbara, although he does not name them.

> *If Sappho, if Corinne, if Centona,*
> *if whoever of the ancient world might be mentioned,*
> *if the two moderns whose names resound*
> *so that they cede nothing to masculine fame,*
> *if on the hills of Parnassus and Helicon*
> *none of these had put her foot,*
> *you alone would suffice to show*
> *how high a woman of talent can rise.* (p. 192)

But soon it became evident that Tansillo's feelings did not stop with admiration:

> *The sun has turned eight days*
> *in its coursing from east to west*
> *and I, to avoid the blazing light of your face,*
> *which is my orient, do not look up from my balcony.*
> *Why have you tied my heart in such a knot*
> *that it will remain eternally tied?*
> *Regal soul, worthy of an empire,*
> *look, now and then, at your prisoner.* (p. 192)

Laura had apparently given him some encouragement, for he wrote,

> *oh my shining star, do not make*
> *my sweet hope die at birth*
> *and make night begin at the dawn of day* (p. 192)

but she apparently became distant as he became more urgent. However ardently he wooed her, Laura remained unresponsive, and nothing came of this affair. Eventually in 1550 Tansillo married someone else. What Laura might have expected, or wanted, of this relationship we cannot know, but the affair left her with a bitterness that she never forgot. Years later, lamenting the death of friends, she adds,

> *I do not care about Tansillo,*
> *I do not mourn his death because*
> *he believed he held the wheel of Fortune in his hands.* (p. 193)

In about 1547 Laura did fall in love with Giovan Vincenzo Belprato, Count of An-
versa, the man to whom Domenichi, at the suggestion of Passero, addressed the dedication of Laura's first volume in 1547, shortly before its publication in 1548.[17] Belprato
was an intellectual, a poet, and a wealthy man who, for a while, seemed also to be in
love with her. He visited Laura in Chiaia, he called her his muse, of course, and wrote
that he hoped to spend the rest of his life with her. She believed him, although perhaps
cautiously, for she wrote him that she thought it would be wonderful to love without
suspicions and jealousy, which, she added with naive guile, she knew was the experience of *other* people. She was incredulous when his ardor obviously cooled,

> *How could it ever happen that a kind heart*
> *might be revealed in the end as arrogant and harsh?*
> *and cover up truth with lies so well*
> *that they would boom from Bactria to Thule?*
> . . .
> *How could it happen that this love*
> *and trust, and these love letters*
> *can lose, in a moment, their fruit and their flower?* (p. 193)

and deeply hurt when she discovered that he was courting another woman, Vittoria Capana, who lived nearby and was also a poet.

> *I feel such great anguish when I see my count*
> *visiting in my small village;*
> *with all his noble and lordly virtues*
> *he doesn't understand why my face is wet with tears,*
> *nor do I dare to raise my lowered head*
> *if my eyes do not meet that beautiful face;*
> *no longer able to offer him my regard,*
> *I take and accept one-half of his heart.* (p. 193)

Eventually her hurt changed to anger, which she recorded with a flash of that wit
that underlies her *Commentary*:

> *I certainly regret and lament*
> *having put a jackass, even though made of gold,*
> *among spirited and beautiful war horses.* (p. 193)

Then there was Giovan Alfonso Mantegna di Maida, a doctor and occasional poet
and one of the men who helped Laura by revising and correcting her poems; she dedicated her *Quarte rime* to him and thanked him again for his help in *Quinte rime*. It is
clear that Mantegna's help was not unrelated to his feelings for her. He evidently

perceived that she wanted to be loved for her mind, not her body and he courted her with poems that seem meant to reassure her that although he was not unaware of her physical beauty, it was her spiritual beauty that he loved.

> *Laura, spiritual as you are, you have also received*
> *from nature her every gift*
> *and heaven laments that*
> *she has reposed every blessing in your earthly veil;*
> *your beauty is a Sun*
> *more lovely than the world is perfect,*
> *while I am your shadow*
> *on which you soulfully and playfully gaze;*
> *with your smile*
> *you reveal the glory of paradise*
> *and all who see you hope*
> *never to see the last evening.* (p. 193)

In her corresponding poem she answers,

> *Kind gentleman that you are*
> *you give me infinite virtue*
> *and such a vivid sense of heaven*
> *that it frees me from my earthly desire for life.*
> *And constantly contemplating all the loveliness*
> *of the beauty you write about*
> *I cheerfully scorn this world*
> *and with utter, careless boldness,*
> *I turn away from it, looking toward*
> *the blazing realms and the souls in Paradise*
> *where my spirit is completely nourished*
> *and hopes never to see the last evening.* (p. 194)

Her response evades the personal tone of Mantegna's poem and ignores the worldly aspects of his praise and, echoing his last line, deliberately alters its meaning, moving it from the earthly realm to that of the spirit as if she wants to distance herself from him physically. This we infer also from a sonnet to her in which he stresses her intellect, but acknowledges his disappointment that she has refused his desire to make love to her.

> *Laura dear, whose divine mind*
> *has always been the abode of the fairest thoughts*
> *in order to govern the world*
> *by the authority of your supreme talent.*
>
> *For a long time now my pure and sincere heart*
> *yearns to adore you so that*

looking at you as I would a celestial goddess,
I am freed of every harsh and bitter pain.

   But because I cannot be
so divine, so brilliant, I do not try to dazzle
the mortal eye, but the intellect.

   One who hopes to be eternally happy
cannot expect success when the passage to virtue
that the road reveals, is forbidden him. (p. 194)

Again she turns away his real desire, addressing his intellect.

   Your kind pen is one with your beautiful thought
that the sacred Idea must govern not only me
but the Tuscan scholars and writers;
let him fear who cares least about authority.

   *Now if you make the goddesses tremble,** *
where will I find thoughts clear enough,
what mind free of all thick fog
will have a pen so noble as to be worthy of you,

   What divine mind, what brilliant talent
will I ever see again unless, I'm afraid,
your great intellect remains after you?

   From now on I yield to the great Mantegna,
I wish to learn more about his Idea, since
honor forbids to me the passage that the road reveals. (pp. 194 – 95)

But finally, it appears from her poem addressed to him and entitled "Enigma," that she did yield her honor to the great Mantegna.[18]

   Once upon a time I was free
from amorous and vain desires
saving the beautiful flower of my green years
for sacred love.

   Now I find myself, though desiring
to take the right way, on a path so wicked
that I am in anguish and feel my heart leaving my body
I have forgotten my early resolve.

---

* The Muses.

But do not think that my desire
is a sign of lust
for I nourish myself with virtue and I relish honor

So much that being thirty-two years old
in the year fifteen fifty-one
I have tied into one knot two desires. (p. 195)

So we infer here that she has finally at the age of thirty-two given up her chastity and is suffering pangs of remorse. One would reasonably conclude that she loved him so fervently that she was unable to keep her resolve to remain chaste until marriage. But although they had a happy time together, for a while, suddenly it was over, this time leaving not Laura but her lover in despair. We find a hint of the trouble between them in the quatrains of one of his sonnets where he writes,

The burning desire, the aura * that is born
in my soul when I see your beauty
and the majesty of your bearing
to which every other beautiful woman must defer,

This, which hardly pleases you,
is often what makes me fall
into the turbulent waters of harsh cruelty
and sometimes makes me walk on air. (p. 195)

But Laura was wary of love. Her distrust is evident in a number of poems where she blames the god of love, Amore, as the cause of the kind of torment she herself had suffered over Belprato and perhaps others of whom we have no record. Although some of those poems may well have been written on request, her own attitude is perfectly clear in a poem to Diomede Carafa. If love ruled the world justly, she says, and stopped his trickery and evil-doing, life would be free from malice, but because Amore is "naked, blind, seductive and quarrelsome, it is no wonder that he makes everyone miserable; if he was a god, he was the god of Hell." Her rejection of Mantegna was gentle but unmistakable.

The kindness that you show
to this modest bosom, and your sincerity
assures me of such love
that I feel finally forced to become frank.

Since you have offered your honesty
to a heart that is pure and tender

---

* *L'aura* is a pun on Laura's name, probably used by every Italian poet from Petrarch on whose beloved was a Laura. See, for example, chapter 7, on Laura Battiferra.

you must put your admired pen
to a noble and difficult task.

    Sing, then, your infinite praises
even though you do not use your talents
for Laura, who rejects your fervent desire.

    Your work, your virtue, your way of life
will make Heaven eternally serene;
you need never fear oblivion. (pp. 195 – 96)

She apparently recoiled from his passion, his "burning desire," and she brought to an end a relationship that Mantegna had thought made even Apollo jealous.

    If it is anger because of jealousy that moves
your wrathful thought, oh sacred Apollo,
to deprive me of the sight of that proud face
from which flows every grace,

    I hope somehow to find pardon,
because dear Laura, worthy of an empire,
for whom I yearn, I blaze, I perish,
holds my heart, nor can it go elsewhere.

    And Love who through her is master of the world
wishes that I burn in the snare of her blond hair.
and shiver in the sun of her bright eyes.

    Thus does heaven also wish that I consume myself
between fire and ice, alas, for I know not
how I might live without sleep's welcome. (p. 196)

Except for "Enigma," which appeared in her sixth volume of 1558 but which internal evidence proves had been written seven years before, Mantegna disappears from Laura's poems after 1552, the year in which she published her fifth volume, *Quinte rime.* Whether because of the breakup or simply by coincidence, she brought out no new work for the next six years.

In the meantime, another man enters into Laura's life. Polidoro Terracina appears in the second, fourth, fifth, and sixth of Laura's volumes, in which she writes love poems "at his request" to a woman with whom he was apparently in love,[19] but it is not until we read the unpublished poems in the codex that we find he has become her husband: a series of three poems to Polidoro begins with a sonnet, "On the Illness of Signore Polidoro Terracina, My Husband," in which she expresses the anxiety she felt and her relief at his recovery from an "unknown sickness."

There is no record of their marriage, which must have occurred in 1560 or 1561, when Laura was in her early forties. Sadly, we find not a trace of happiness in her poems to her husband, although she apparently loved him. Addressing the god of love, she asks,

> *Why, why did you pierce my side*
> *and wound my heart with your golden arrow,*
> *you cruel tyrant, you perfidious lord*
> *because I now enjoy the name of Polidoro?*
> *You could have left me with my treasure*
> *with my private life and with my chastity*
> *and not have given me tears and sorrow*
> *if you had not tied both of us to one laurel tree.* (p. 196)

Looking back to her poem "Enigma," addressed to Mantegna, where we learned that she had not "saved the beautiful flower of her green years but had tied into one knot two desires," we find that Laura's claim here to have been a virgin when she married Polidoro was surely untrue. Did Polidoro know this? He was tormented with jealousy, as we know from Laura's poems.

> *Since I have never, nor will ever belong to another*
> *why do you give yourself so much misery?*
> *If, as you know, from the moment I was born heaven gave me*
> *to you alone, forever, why do you torment your heart?*
> *You know that I am and always have been,*
> *on my honor, your faithful servant,*
> *why do you give yourself, with nothing to fear,*
> *such distress that you want to die?* (p. 196)

She had constantly to reassure him, probably without success.

> *It is true that love consuming and destroying me*
> *and fleeing from me when I call*
> *believes he can take from me the sacred pledge.*
> *Let him think that I am a woman of little sense*
> *and that like a mouse he can nibble at my heart,*
> *and will gnaw without leaving a mark,*
> *there is no need because of this to pay a penalty,*
> *because as much as it is possible to love, I love you.* (pp. 196–97)

We have no evidence of Polidoro's feeling for Laura, other than his jealousy, for he was not a writer. That he played a role in her career, however, is evident from the fact that Giovanni Andrea Valvassori, the Venetian publisher who had brought out her fourth and fifth books, asked him to persuade Laura to write a second book on the *Orlando Furioso*. She accordingly obliged her husband and in 1567 brought out her eighth volume, *The Second Part of the Commentaries on the Second Stanzas of the Songs of Orlando Furioso*, based like the first *Commentary* on Ludovico Ariosto's masterpiece.[20] To make clear what might well be called Laura's virtuoso performance we will take up for discussion only one, the first.

This extraordinary work incorporates a singular idea: it is composed, like the *Orlando Furioso* of Ariosto, of forty-six cantos; each of Laura's cantos has seven stanzas, not counting a dedicatory or introductory stanza that precedes each canto proper; the final line of each stanza, except the seventh, with two final lines, repeats in sequence the eight lines of Ariosto's first stanza of each canto.[21] If you read the last lines of Laura's stanzas in any of her cantos, you will duplicate Ariosto's first stanza in the corresponding canto. In these final lines, while repeating those of Ariosto, Laura cleverly and wittily inflects their meaning, sometimes making minute changes in order to make her point. That this was her intention is clear in a poem from her first volume of poems, addressed to Diomede Carafa, bishop of Ariano, in which we also learn that she was working on her *Commentary*, published in 1549, since the first volume was published in 1548.

> *You will read as a curiosity*
> *these verses of mine full of ignorance:*
> *do not believe that I am*
> *matching my verses or my opinion to Furioso:*
> *I have done them to escape boring idleness*
> *which exerts too much influence on our thoughts.*
> *However, I have companioned them in a woman's voice*
> *to make them more pleasing and playful. (p. 197)*

To examine in detail the relationship between Ariosto's *Orlando* and Laura's *Commentary* we will choose as an example the first stanza of Ariosto's canto 37 and from Laura's matching canto 37, five of her seven stanzas, the first four and the seventh, each stanza ending matching one of Ariosto's eight lines. Let us first summarize Ariosto's first seven stanzas:

Stanza 1: Our gifts from Nature must be cultivated by hard work. Women have indeed shown they can work expend great effort night and day, and produce admirable work, but if they had applied themselves to those studies that make mortal efforts immortal.

Stanza 2: If they had been able to make their merits famous without asking help from writers whose hearts are so eaten with envy that they cannot praise others, their names would rise perhaps higher than that of any man.

Stanza 3: Men not only praise each other but also put women down as "impure"; they do not want to see women rise, and do what they can to keep them down, afraid the honor of women would obscure their own "like clouds cover the sun."

Stanza 4: But neither speech nor writing has had the power to extinguish the fame of all women.

Stanzas 5 and 6: These stanzas mention women who deserve eternal fame for their military victories, and comment that of a thousand worthy

women hardly one is named because the writers of their times were envious, wicked liars.

Stanza 7: (the last on which Laura provides "commentary"): Ariosto
enjoins women to follow their own course without fear that their noble
efforts will be ignored as they have been in the past because nothing lasts
forever, neither good nor bad, "so even though until now paper and ink
were not for you, now they are."

Now, turning to the substance of what we have been describing, we will look first
at Ariosto's first stanza of his canto 37, whose eight lines (set in boldface in the following extracts) provided the final line for each of Laura's seven stanzas in her canto 37.
In order for the reader to understand Laura's linguistic tricks, we provide here Ariosto's original Italian together with our translations.

> ***Since, like acquiring some other gift***
> ***that Nature cannot bestow without great effort,***
> ***tirelessly night and day***
> ***with great diligence and persistence,***
> ***there are courageous women and with good***
> ***success they have created not inconsequential work***
> ***So had they done, putting themselves to those studies***
> ***that make mortal efforts immortal.***

> *Se come in acquistar qualch'altro dono*
> *che senza industria non può dar Natura,*
> *affaticate notte e dì si sono*
> *con somma diligenza e lunga cura*
> *le valorose donne, e se con buono*
> *successo n'è uscit'opra non oscura*
> *così si fosson poste a quelli studi*
> *ch'immortal fanno le mortalvirtudi*

Before starting the *Commentary* proper, Laura begins with an introductory stanza
in praise of a woman, Veronica Gàmbara, a poet like herself, who did take up paper
and ink, as the canto will plead that more women should do.

> *Oh were there many in the world like you,*
> *women who would put a brake on men*
> *writing at full speed against us*
> *cruel writings, full of venom,*
> *then, perhaps, to the far shores of Aeolia*
> *would go our name and great shouts of honor;*
> *but because nothing is said against them*
> *they vilify our reputation.*

The first stanza of Laura's canto 37 then begins:

> *I do not think that writers who have written*
> *blamefully against us, or in faint praise,*
> *have accomplished so much in the world, and in art,*
> *that they might not be challenged for their deceit*
> *since they have dismissed our talents*
> *and spoken as unjustly as possible for all to hear,*
> *oh, if they but gave themselves to something worthwhile*
> **like acquiring some other gift.**

> *Non credo non, che gli scrittor, che carte*
> *han scritto in biasmo nostro, e in poco lode*
> *c'habbian si ben compito il mondo, e l'arte*
> *che non si possa oprar contra lor frode*
> *poi c'hanno posto il ben nostro da parte,*
> *e in mal quanto si può per tutto s'ode.*
> *Deh fossero almen dati a un'atto buono,*
> **se come in acquistar qualch'altro dono.**

Laura's witty teasing is this: Ariosto referred to women who might have done something worthwhile had they studied; Laura changes the gender of the word *poste* in Ariosto, ending in *e*, which is feminine plural, to *dati*, which has the same meaning as *poste*, but she puts it in the masculine plural, ending with *i*, thus twitting the male writers who might have done better "acquiring some other gift." This is the kind of twist that Laura gives to her *Commentary*: it is not just an echoing of words, but a true comment, mostly gently acerbic. Following are the second, third, and fourth stanzas of her canto 37:

> *If women by themselves*
> *had been able to write a great deal,*
> *the men perhaps would not have silenced*
> *those that, now keeping quiet, have hidden more than*
> *infamy. But because it is necessary to depend on*
> *male writers for our absurd living,*
> *they must indeed work hard in their writing*
> **that Nature cannot bestow without great effort.**

> *Che se da lor medessime potuto*
> *havessero le Donne scriver molto*
> *li Scrittor forse non havrian taciuto*
> *quel c'hor tacendo, han più che infamia occolto,*
> *ma, perchè è vuopo mendicare aiuto*
> *a gli scrittor, per nostro viver stolto*
> *però si fan si caldi in lor scrittura,*
> **che senza industria non pùo dar natura.**

Oh, if only women would give up the needle,
the thread and cloth, and take on the burden of study
I think they would give you writers great difficulties,
even worse than the Carthaginians inflicted on Rome.
But because they are few who do this,
not much fame crowns our heads, not many
courageous women are there who write, as I say
tirelessly night and day.

Deh, se lasciasser l'ago, il filo, il panno,
e dello studio togliesser la soma,
credo c'ha voi Scrittor farebbon danno
anzi più mal che non fer gli Afri a Roma,
ma perchè poche son,che questo fanno
poca fama circonda nostra chioma,
non molte Donne al scriver, qual ragiono,
affaticate notte, e dì si sono.

Oh talented ladies, do not let that keep you
from putting the ship of virtue at risk
drop your needles, be ambitious
to take up pen and paper
so that you will be not less celebrated
than those of whom I am complaining,
now pay attention to your reading
with great diligence and persistence.

Non restate per ciò Donne ingegniose
Di por la barca di virtude al scoglio
lasciate l'ago , fatevi bramose
sovente in operar la penna e il foglio
che non men vi farete gloriose
di questi tal di cui molto mi doglio
hor state dunque attente in la lettura,
con somma diligentia e lunga cura.

Note that Ariosto gives credit to women for their diligence and persistence in doing their *customary* work, Laura asks them to apply diligence and persistence to their reading.

In her fifth stanza Laura points out that men grandly give themselves praise but in the end they will be fooled, for women will wear the crown of laurel and all the world will hear that

there are courageous women, and rightly so

le valorose donne e se con buono.[*]

In the sixth stanza Laura accuses men of pretending to praise them, but although they delight in giving each other the greatest

> **success, they create works that are not not inconsequential.**

> **Successo ne uscito opra non scura** †

In the seventh, the last stanza, she begs women with renewed urgency to occupy themselves with literature.

> *Now let us give ourselves totally to serious*
> *occupations, let these neglected voices be heard,*
> *let our women not be so quiet*
> *that they fail to be heard above the voices of men.*
> *Let us escape from this subjection*
> *by pursuing blessed, soul-enhancing literature.*
> *Thus did men put themselves to those studies*
> **that make mortal talents immortal.**

> *Hor diamoci talmente alla virtute,*
> *e diasi luoco a queste lingue osure,*
> *che non saran le nostre cosi mute*
> *che non bastino a vincer lor scritture*
> *uscemo homai da questa servitute*
> *in seguitar le sante, alme Letture.*
> *Così si fosser posti a quelli studi*
> **ch'immortal fanno le mortai virtudi.**

With a final grammatical trick, changing the feminine ending of *poste* to the masculine *posti*, Laura changes "women" to "men."

The *Commentary* reveals the heart and soul of a woman for whom intellectual work was life itself, and canto 37 is central to her thought as it takes up the theme of the gender war that Laura fights in poem after poem. Why is the human male hostile to the female, she asks in canto 5, when in the animal world "the male does not make war against the female . . . the female bear wanders through the forest without fear of the male . . . the lioness lies beside the lion . . . nor does the cow fear the bull?"[22] Women *did* have much to lament, with no control over their dowries and totally dependent on their husbands or other male members of their families, and much to fear, with women beaten and murdered by their husbands or lovers a commonplace not only in the lower classes but among the nobility in the Neapolitan area, some of whom Laura knew: Giulia Orsini was killed by a prince of Bisignano, Eleonora

---

* This is a particularly broad example of how Laura changes the meaning of Ariosto's words. In Italian the words are identical, but Laura has changed the meaning of "and if with good" to an idiomatic phrase, "and rightly so."

† Here Laura changes Ariosto's adverbial "of it" (*n'*) to the negative "not" (*ne*) to create a double negative that changes Ariosto's meaning to its opposite.

Piccolomini was poisoned by her husband Bernardino Sanseverino who paid off thirty thousand *scudi* to Pietro Toledo to "resolve his problem with the law." We must read Laura's poems keeping in mind the social milieu which she observed with acute perception. Like her first *Orlando*, her second, too, was a moralizing reflection on the villains of human society and the flaws of her century.

It seems gratuitous to observe that this talented but unhappy woman found only more cause for unhappiness as she grew older. In her seventh volume, *On All the Widows of this Our City of Naples Titled and Not Titled*, she writes of one of the widows but doubtless she was thinking of herself, not necessarily as a widow—we do not know when Polidoro died—but as aging:

> *This morning she was a young girl and now is old,*
> *time destroys every mortal thing*
> *and is pleased at our misfortunes*
> *which he calls forth, and then keeps moving on,*
> *and when we start to enjoy life*
> *just at that moment Death sucks our blood,*
> *so the fruit is lost with the flower*
> *for everything is thwarted by Death.* (p. 197)

In her fifties she began to see old friends disappear.

> *I, too, wish to die: why am I living?*
> *Why do I still pursue Apollo?*
> . . .
> *Who will listen to me now, as before*
> *since time has taken away*
> *Ottinello, Terminio, and Tarcagnota?* (p. 197)

In 1572 Laura went to Rome, hoping perhaps to make new contacts. There she cultivated the leading churchmen, and remembered them in a collection of poems to Pope Gregory XIII and many cardinals that remained unpublished. There is no mention of whether Polidoro accompanied her or when she returned to Naples.

The last we know of Laura is the collection to the cardinals which she put together in November 1577. Even the date of her death is unrecorded.

Unlike the other women poets of her time Laura was a *career poet;* probably more than any of the others she was obsessed with writing and wrote because she was driven, like all artists, by the mysterious energy of creativity. Not the greatest of the women poets of the Renaissance, Laura's poetry is nevertheless "indispensable," as Angelo Borzelli wrote, "for anyone who wishes to know who was who in sixteenth-century Neapolitan life." [22] Far beyond the limits of Naples, however, her contribution to making her century aware of the unjust treatment of women throughout history gives her an honored place in the entire history of women in society, and her skill and imagination in creating her masterpiece, her *Commentary . . . on Orlando Furioso* assures her a secure place in the history of Italian literature.

POEMS IN THE ORIGINAL ITALIAN*

Fu già di nobilità mia stirpe antica
nè brutta fui, nè pur cotanto bella;
di vizi stata son sempre rubella
d'alteri odiosa e d'umiltade amica.

Laura Terracina

Fuggito ho l'ozio, amata ho la fatica,
si come ogniun di me vede favella;
e lodar son forzata or questa or quella
con amor puro e con la mente aprica.

Nè lode prezzo mai, nè adulatori
nè veste adorne e nè domeschi effetti,
come oggi al general chiaro dimostro;

Ma sol d'onesti ed onorati fiori
me vo fregiando il capo e gli alri oggetti,
mercè del cielo e del bel secol nostro. † (p. 163)

Veggio il Mondo fallir, veggiolo stolto,
e veggio la virtute in abbandono;
e che le Muse a vil tenute sono,
talche l'ingegno mio quasi è sepolto.

Veggio in odio, ed invidia tutto volto
il pensier degl'amici, e in falso tuono,
veggio tradito il Malvagio dal buono,
e tutto a' nostri danni il Ciel rivolto

Nessuno al ben comun tien fermo segno;
anzi al suo proprio ogniun discorre seco,
mentre hà di vari affetti il petto pregno.

Io veggio, e nel veder tengo odio meco;
talche vorrei vedermi per disdegno
o me senz'occhi, o tutto il Mondo cieco. ‡ (p. 164)

Quando sento destar, più d'un' Augello,
e col suo cantar salutar l' Aurora

---

* See publication data for Laura's poems in note 1. We have not changed spelling or
accent marks (or the lack of accent marks) from the original publications.
† *Seste rime.*   ‡ *Rime*, p. 31.

tanto più cresce il duol, più fiamma accorsa
l'ingordo mio desio, caduco, e fello.

Perchè conosco ben, che il gran flagello
più m'invita a dolermi, ora per ora:
e per la meglio vorrei esser fuora
e questo Mondo tanto a me rubello.

Così dolente i sì gran pena mia
trapasso il giorno con angoscie, ed onte
in molesti sospir di gelosia:

Vorrei allor, ch'è il Sol sull'Orizonte
rubargli il carro, e non m'incresceria
cader con quel, come cadeo Fetonte. (pp. 164 – 65)

~

Quel primo lauro, che ha perpetua aurora
con gli aurei crini splendidi e infiammati,
non vuol tra i dotti e spiriti lodati
il rozzo ingegno mio si ponga ancòra:

Chè, s'ei ben s'affatica e suda ognora
a formar versi incolti e poco ornati,
no 'l fo per lode, nè per farli amati;
ma per dar tempo a tempo, che m'accora.

Ma se pur di virtù breve scintilla
in me si mostra, o di valor un segno
grazia del Ciel benigno in cor mi stilla,

Come donna ch'io son di poco ingegno,
non chiami mio, ma de l'amor favilla
che la bontà di Dio ne dà per pegno. † (p. 165)

~

Amico lo sò, che tu m'hai posta in voce
et a me, mi convien ponesti in cima,
et quanto posso con la debil voce
alzarvi infino al ciel, con la mia rima,
e quando non potrà la roca voce
dir tanto quanto la mia mente stima
vi mostrerò col core, e col desir
che quanto amor si può tanto v'amo io. ‡ (pp. 165 – 66)

~

---

* *Rime*, p. 34.   † *Rime*, p. 8.

‡ *Commentary*, canto 46, p. 74.

Per esser donna anch'io, donna gentile,
s'io leggo i vostri versi
così leggiadri e tersi
spiegati in vive carte e in puro inchiostro
con che indorate il ferreo secol nostro,
tanto stupore io piglio. * (p. 166)

                                                           Vittoria Colonna

~

Il dolce suon della famosa lira
che vi donò quel gran pastor di Delo,
m'imfiamma il cor d'un sì vivace zelo,
ch'a cantar mi costringe, sprona, e gira.

    Pur il timor è tal, che il tutto mira,
che la mia voce nel più bel dir celo:
anzi il caldo desio diventa un gelo
temendo assai ch'al Ciel non caschi in ira.

    Perchè, essendo di lui ANGEL che tra gli altri sono,
e'l più COSTANTE che tra gli altri sono,
non può la bassa lingua alzarsi tanto.

    Ond'io cantando, a l'armonia m'inchino,
e cedo a voi della mia voce il suono,
e col vostro valor lieta m' ammanto. † (p. 166)

Laura Terracina

~

Voi che la nobiltà del sangue vostro
con la vostra virtù più degna,
l'ago e il panno lasciato, e penna e inchiostro
la man porgete, che vil opere sdegna
e d'altro pure che di gemme e d'ostro
voi stessa ornate e questa etade indegna. ‡ (p. 167)

Maria Colonna

~

Varchi, in cui dalle sacre amate fronde,
il biondo Apollo ogni eccellenza infuse,
tal che le voglie di tutt'altri escluse,
solo al canto di voi gode o risponde;

    Un bel disìo, che nel mio cor s'asconde,
dove l'alta virtù vostra lo chiuse
vuol ch'io mi scuopra, e me stessa v'accuse
del mio ardir, ch'al saver non corrisponde.

Laura Terracina
◉ Track 24,
Reading 23

* The Interdata Network, Casoria, Italy, <http://www.idn.it/orgoglio/napoleta/storia/laura/13htm>. This poem is not in Alan Bullock, ed., *Rime/Vittoria Colonna* (see Chapter 2).   † *Rime di Angelo di Costanza* (Venice, n.d.), p. 111.
‡ Angelo Borzelli, *Laura Terracina, poetessa del cinquecento* (Naples, 1924), pp. 13–14, n. 1.

Questo vi mostra una ignorante spressa
di giovin donna, che con passo errante
va cercando del ciel la dritta via;

Perchè lascia l'impresa, in ch'era messa,
e cede a voi com'uomo saggio e costante
quel che pensava di dover dir pria. * (p. 168)

Benedetto Varchi

● Track 25,
Reading 24

Laura novella, in cui chiude ed ascondi
quante già nell'antica ascose e chiuse
grazie e virtuti il ciel, rade volte use
di pari ornar, se non la Febea fronde:

Al vostro dolce suono ambe le sponde,
u' più fiate le toscane muse
vinser cantando i Menci e l'Aretuse,
inerbi e 'n fiori il bel Sebeto, e 'n fronde.

E voi, ch'a nostri di Minerva stessa
col senno ne rendete e col sembiante,
che i più feri e selvaggi al cielo invia,

Perchè mostrarvi a me tanto dimessa
a me, che di lodar non son bastante
vostra alta impresa, non che farla mia? † (pp. 168 – 69)

⌣

Laura Terracina

Ecco le rime, O Marco Antonio mio
le quai mi commandasse, ch'io facessi,
l'ho fatto, come donne, che son io,
non le biasmate, se in rima io cadessi
l'ingegno in me non pareggia il desìo,
et l'ubidir, più che fai bene elessi,
dunque de l'amor pigliate, & non i versi
che non so, qual vorrei, leggiadri e versi. ‡ (p. 169)

⌣

Ecco il discorso pur Dolce gentile
in fretta da me visto, & non d'altrui
e se la lingua mia fu si virile,
perdon vi chieggio, e s'arrogante fui
ch'io non sapea se'l verso feminile
fosse degno apparir dinanzi a vui,
pur sodisfatto ho al fin col mio sudore
alle vostre promesse & al mio honore. § (p. 169)

---

* *Lettere à Benedetto Varchi* (Bologna, 1859), p. 963.
† *Lettere à Benedetto Varchi*, p. 964.   ‡ *Rime*, p. 22.
§ *Commentary*, p. 3.

A che vo' coltivando il verde alloro
per fare a l'altrui chiome indigno onore
a che struggo ad ogn'or la mente e 'l core
se 'l mondo istima solo argente ed oro?

Alfin che spero mai del mio lavoro
altro che sdegno, invidia e disonore
a che vo' consumando i giorni e l'ore
noiando Apollo e de le Muse il coro?

Se quel che del mio stil s'orna ed onora
mi loda in volto, poi con danno fiero
me stessa, l'opra e l'inchiostro divora?

Va mondo sciocco ch'io di certo spero
che 'l mio bel lauro che sovente infiora
sia sempre verde, e di sua gloria altero.* (pp. 169 – 70)

Un sol mi potrà ben farmi voltare
de l'esser mio e tutta avermi seco
quando il ciel mi vorrà spesso donare
ch'abbia quel fior ch'or porto intatto meco.
Ma s'altramenti volesse operare,
ogni ardito pensier sarebbe cieco;
ch'anzi ritorneria su le piante
de l'Alpi il fiume torbido e sonante. † (p. 170)

Chi raccontar le molte   **Desideri Cavalcabò**
bellezze potria mai del largo petto
in cui l'alto diletto
s'annida di quei pomi onesti e cari?
E indarno le parole al vento ho sparte
e invano sospirato e pianto assai
quando con viva voce e quando in carte
risposta al mio pregar non ebbi mai. ‡ ((pp. 170 – 71)

Udito ho già da voi recitar spesso   **Laura Terracina**
di cocenti sospir l'aria accendea,
dir donne contra donne è mal concesso,
ne ragion lo permette giusto o rea.
Ma per gradir vostro desire espresso,
v'ho scritto, ben che scriver non devea.

* *Seste rime*, p. 86.   † *Rime*, p. 17.
‡ Linda Maroi, *Laura Terracina, poetessa napoletana del secolo XVI* (Naples, 1913), pp. 53–54.

So certo, che di donna oltraggio havete,
*ma voi cagione del vostro biasmo sete.** (p. 172)

~

Più giorni è Monsignor che sommi accorta
de l'esser vostro, anzi del vostro intento
ma perchè non rileva, e non importa
non n'ho tenuto, o tengo alcun spavento,
poco stim'io, dove il pensier mi porta,
seguite pur quel che v'è contento
di ciò nulla ansia nel mio cuor lavora
io per me dormo, e voi dormite ancora. † (p. 172)

~

Che la mia Musa abbia valor conforme
a l'eleganza de' bei versi vostri,
chi 'l pensa, non chi'l dice, è stolto, e dorme,
Signor Tansillo, onor de' giorni nostri;
Ma sol da l'ignoranza in tutto torme
vo finalmente oprando carta e inchiostri.
Son femmina, e non ho colpa di questo;
voi potete pensare a tutto 'l resto. ‡ (p. 174)

~

Luigi Tansillo

Se Sapho, se Corinna, se Centona,
si qualunque altra antica età ne diede
se due moderne, il cui gran nome sona
sì, ch'a fama viril punte non cede,
le falde di Parnaso e d'Elicona
non avesser giammai tocche col piede,
voi sola bastereste a darne segno
di quanto alzar si può donnesco ingegno. § (p. 174)

~

Otto dì il sol rotando ha volto
e corso dal levante a l'occidente,
ed io spuntar i rai del vostro volto
non vedo dal balcon ch'è il mio oriente.
Perchè m'avete il cor d'un nodo avvolto,
ch'il tenerà legato eternamente?
Alma real degnissima d'impero
talor mirate il vostro prigionero. ‖ (p. 174)

~

Non consentite, O viva luce mia,
che il mio dolce sperar sul nascer pera
e al comminciar del dì nasca la sera. ¶ (p. 174)

---

* *Rime,* p. 17.   † *Commentary,* p. 50.   ‡ Luigi Tansillo, *Le lacrime di San Pietro* (Venice, 1738), p. 57.   § Tansillo, *Le Lacrime,* p. 58.   ‖ Borzelli, *Laura Terracina,* p. 23.
¶ Borzelli, *Laura Terracina,* p. 22.

Laura Terracina

   Di Tansillo non curo, nè mi duole
de la sua morte, perchè si credeva
*tener de la fortuna la man la rota!** (p. 175)

   Com'esser può giamai ch'un cor gentile
possa mostrarsi al fin superbo et fiero
ne la bugia covrir può tanto il vero
che di lei non rimbombi & Battro e Tile?

. . .

   Com' esser può giamai che questo amore
e questa fede e queste amate carte
possan perder a un tempo il frutto e 'l fiore? † (p. 175)

   Gran duol sent'io qualor veggio il mio conte
soggiorno far nel mio piccolo albergo
che sue tante virtuti altiere e conte
non comprend'egli e il viso ognor n'aspergo,
nè ardisco mai d'alzar la bassa fronte
se non quanto quest'occhi al bel viso ergo;
non potendo far più lungo onore,
io accetto e ricevo mezzo il core. ‡ (p. 175)

. . .

ben me ne pento e me ne doglio assai
d'aver posto un somier, benchè sia d'oro
fra sì animosi e fra sì bei corsieri. § (p. 175)

   Laura quell'alma sete
che di nature ogn'altro pregio havete
perciò si lagna in Cielo
ch'à riposto ogni ben nel vostro velo,
e un Sol è sua bellezza
ma la vostra duo son, di più vaghezza
tal che perfetto è il mondo
havendo il vostro sguardo, almo et giocondo,
per ch'à l'aprir del viso,
dimostrate il valor del paradiso,
onde ciascun che vi contempla, spera
egli non mai veder l'ultima sera ‖ (p. 176)

Giovani Alfonso
Mantegna di
Maida
◉ Track 26,
Reading 25

---

* Benedetto Croce, "La casa di una poetessa," *Napoli Nobilissima*, vol. X, fasc. IX, p. 138.
† *Quarte rime*, p. 60.   ‡ Borzelli, *Laura Terracina*, pp. 21–22.
§ Borzelli, *Laura Terracina*, p. 34.   ‖ *Quarte rime*. p. 39.

Laura Terracina
 ◉ Track 27,
   Reading 26

  Gentil signor tal sete
ch'infinita vertù data vi havete
e un vivo humor del cielo
che m'acqueto il desio del mortal velo
et con questa bellezza
vò di voi contemplando ogni vaghezza
tal che dispregio il mondo
con un ardito veloce alto et giocondo
che rivolgendo il viso
l'aere infiammate, e l'alme al paradiso
onde lo spirito al fin si nudre et spera
non veder egli mai l'ultima sera.* (p. 176)

   ⁓

Giovani Alfonso
Mantegna
di Maida

  Laura gentil che nel divin pensiero
sempre albergaste la più bella idea
perchè regger il mondo si dovea
dal soperno valor del vostro impero.

  Già gran tempo il mio cor puro e sincero
brama adorarvi, qual celeste dea
che sgombrò d'ogni pena acerba e rea
in mirar voi ben sia lieto e altiero,

  Ma perchè sì divin sì chiaro obietto
esser non può ch'ad abbagliar non vegna
non pur' occhio mortal, ma l'intelletto,

  Non ardisce venir ben che disegna
gioirlo eternamente onde interdetto
gli è il passo ch'a vertù la strada insegna. † (pp. 176 – 77)

   ⁓

Laura Terracina

  Il vostro dolce stile è 'l bel pensiero
che non sol'io ma la sacrata Idea
che dotti et toschi dominar dovea
paventar si che men cura l'impero,

  Hor donde havrò pensier tanto sincero
se di voi trema l'una & l'altra Dea,
qual mente sgombra d'ogni nebbia rea,
havrà degno di voi stil tanto altiero?

  Qual'ingegno divin, qual chiaro obietto
vedrò già mai che con timor non vegna
a lasciar dopo voi l'alto intelletto?

---

* *Quarte rime*, p. 29. † *Quarte rime*, p. 29.

Hor d'oggi inanzi io cedo al gran Mantegna
ne brama altro saver poi che interdetto
m'è il passo che d'honor la strada insegna. * (p. 177)

~

Scevra d'ogni amoroso e van desìo
stava un tempo io, salvando 'l mio bel fiore
de la mia verde etate al sacro amore,
ne mi rimossi mai dal esser mio;

Hor mi ritrovo in un camin sì rio,
in un voler si giusto, in un dolore
ch'io mi sento partir dal petto il core,
tal ch'il primiero ardor mando in oblìo.

Ne credete però che gli miei affanni
faccian noto di lasciva alcuno
ma di virtù mi pasco, e d'onor godo

Così a punto havendo' io trenta due anni
à mille e cinquecento, e cinquanta uno
ho posto duo pensieri in un sol nodo. † (pp. 177 – 78)

~

Il cocente desir, l'aura che nacque
ne l'alma di mirar vostra beltade
et del vostro apparir, la maestade
per cui l'honor d'ogni altra bella giacque

Spesso è cagion, che ne le torbide acque
caggia del rio de l'aspra crudeltade
et tal volta poggiar mi fa le strade
del cielo a cui sì rara farvi piaque. ‡ (p. 178)

Giovani Alfonso
Mantegna
di Maida

~

La vostra cortesia che 'l grembo umile
scuopre sovente, et la dimostra aperte
mi fa di tanto amore l'anima certa
ch'io son costretta al fin d'esser virile.

Poscia che 'l puro cor faggio, et gentile
m'ha la sua intera candidezza offerta,
convien che poggi per l'altera, et erta
strada, il suo vago et honorato stile.

Hor canta dunque l'infinite lodi
benche non ponno le tue forze a pieno
Laura, che basta il tuo desìo,

Laura Terracina

---

* *Quarte rime*, p. 27.   † *Seste rime*, p. 162.   ‡ *Quarte rime*, p. 17.

E gli atti e gesti e le virtudi, e i modi
che havranno eternamente il Cielo sereno
senza non mai temer l'onde d'oblìo. * (pp. 178 – 79)

⁓

Giovani Alfonso
Mantegna
di Maida

Se sdegno è quei di gelosia che muove
or, sacro Apollo, il tuo caldo pensiero,
di tormi coi tuoi rai dal viso altero
la bella vista, one'ogni grazia piove,

Spero ch'in te di ciò perdon ritrove
perchè Laura gentil degna d'impero
per cui mi struggo, incenerisco, e pero
mi tiene il cor, nè gir il lascia altrove.

Et Amor, che per lei del mondo è donno
vuol che ne i lacci delle bionde chiome
trema et arda nel sol de'chiari lumi.

Così voi anco il ciel ch'io mi consumi
tra il fuoco e 'l ghiaccio, oimè, che non so come
viva, senza mai dar ricetto al sonno.† (p. 179)

⁓

Laura Terracina

A che, perchè con la saetta d'oro
m'apristi il fianco e m'impiagasti il core
crudel tiranno, e perfido signore
s'hor del nome godo io di Polidoro?
Mi dovevi lasciar col mio tesoro
con la mia propria vita, e col mio honore
e non darmi di poi pianto e dolore
s'ambedue n'annodasti in uno alloro. ‡ (p. 180)

⁓

S'io non son stata e non sarò d'altrui
a che prendete voi tanto dolore?
Se dal cielo, dacchè nacqui, sola a vui,
me diè per sempre, a che affannate il core?
Voi sapete ch'io sono e sempre fui
antiqua serva vostra col mio cuore.
A che vi date poi doglia cotale
se volete morir senza alcun male?. § (p. 180)

⁓

E ch'amor mi consuma e mi distrugge,
pensa di tormi l'honorato pegno
e perch'ogn'hora al mio chiamar mi fugge.
Creda che donna sia di poco ingegno

---

* *Quarte rime*, p. 52.   † *Quinte rime*, p. 35.   ‡ Maroi, *Laura Terracina*, p. 65.
§ Maroi, *Laura Terracina*, p. 64.

e che a modo d'un topo il cor mi rugge,
ruderà tal che non appaia il segno,
non bisogna di ciò pagarmi il fio,
chè quanto amar si può, tanto v'amo io * (p. 180)

~

Voi leggerete come curioso
queste mie rime colme d'ignoranza:
non vi crediate c'habbia al Furiosoo
aguagliato il mio verso o la mia stanza:
l'ho fatto per fuggir l'ocio noioso,
c'ha ne nostri pensieri troppo possanza.
Però col dir donnesco ho accompagnato
che dolce più, che più giocondo stato. † (p. 181)

~

Fanciulla era stamane ed or son vecchia
ogni cose mortal tempo distrugge
sempre nel nostro mal lieto si specchia
sempre ne chiama e poi sempre fugge
e chi goder la vita s'apparecchia
Morte a quell'ora il proprio sangue sugge
talchè ad un tempo il fior si perde e il frutto
perchè la morte ne disturba il tutto. ‡ (p. 186)

~

Voglio morir anco io: a che son viva?
A che seguo più Apollo?
. . .
Chi mi darà più odenza come suole,
poichè s'ha tolto al tempo che viveva
Ottinello, Terminio et Tarcagnota? § (p. 186)

~

O crudel moto, o cosa horrenda et fiera
non successa qui mai nè vista ancora!
Alli sessantatrè nanzi l'aurora,
il dì che Maggio alli vinti un giunt'era

Scesero in questa piaggia nostro altiere
tre vascelli di Turchi a la sesta hora,
gridando salva salva, fuora fuora
Turchi! Turchi! fuggerti alla leggiera.

Fu per certo il timor grande e'l tormento
di tutti nostri cittadini et donne,
ch'il più bel sonno all' improvviso denno.

---

* Luigi Mantella, "Una poetessa del rinascimento, Laura Terracina (Salerno, 1993), p. 107.
† Rime, p. 13.   ‡ Maroi, Laura Terracina, p. 63.   § Croce, "La casa di una poetessa," p. 138.

Piaque a Dio ch'in quel sì fier tormento
che scalze si salvar, che senza gonne,
et quei, che tolti fuor, non hebber senno. * (p. 200 n.18)

The following verses are repeated from the English text for the convenience of the CD listener.

Ariosto
◉ Track 28,
Reading 27

Se come in acquistar qualch'altro dono
che senza industria non può dar Natura,
affaticate notte e dì si sono
con somma diligenza e lunga cura
le valorose donne, e se con buono
successo n'è uscit'opra non oscura
così si fosson poste e quelli studi
ch'immortal fanno le mortalvirtudi. (p. 182)

~

Laura Terracina
◉ Track 29,
Reading 28

Deh fosser molte al mondo come voi,
donne che a gli scrittor mettesser freno
ch'a tutta briglia vergan contra noi
scritti crudeli, e colmi di veleno,
che forsi andrebbe insino a i liti Eoi
il nome nostro, e'l grido d'honor pieno;
ma, perche contra a lor nulla si mostra
però tengono vil la fama nostra. (p. 182 – 83)

~

◉ Track 29,
Reading 29

Non credo non, che gli scrittor, che carte
han scritto in biasmo nostro, e in poco lode
c'habbian si ben compito il mondo, e l'arte
che non si possa oprar contra lor frode
poi c'hanno posto il ben nostro da parte,
e in mal quanto si può per tutto s'ode.
Deh fossero almen dati a un'atto buono,
se come in acquistar qualch'altro dono. (p. 183)

~

◉ Track 29,
Reading 30

Che se da lor medessime potuto
havessero le Donne scriver molto
li Scrittor forse non havrian taciuto
quel c'hor tacendo, han più che infamia occolto,
ma, perchè è vuopo mendicare aiuto
a gli scrittor, per nostro viver stolto
però si fan si caldi in lor scrittura,
che senza industria non pùo dar natura. (p. 183 – 84)

---

* *Seste rime.*

NOTES

1   Included in Terracina's volumes are poems to her from other poets, together with her responses. (Mention should be made of Lucrezia Marinella [1571–1673], who published more books, but several were written and published in the seventeenth century.) Laura's published books, not including reprints, include *Rime* (Venice, 1548), *Rime seconde* (Venice, 1549), *Discorso sopra tutti i primi canti di "Orlando Furioso"* (Venice, 1549), *Quarte rime* (Venice, 1550), *Quinte rime* (Venice, 1552), *Seste rime* (Lucca, 1558), *Sovra tutte le donne vedove di questa città di Napoli* (Naples, 1561), and *La seconda parte de' Discorsi sopra le seconde stanze de' Canti d' 'Orlando Furioso'* (Venice, 1567). We have used a photocopy of her *Rime* held by Harvard College Library and a copy of the *Discorso* bound together with several volumes of her *Rime* in the Spencer Collection of the New York Public Library. We wish to thank the librarians in the Spencer Collection for their exceedingly kind help.

2   Codex CCXXIX. A number of Laura's poems were set to music, only two of which are listed in the New Vogel: "Amore tu causi tutto il penor mio / tu mi fai il torto e non colei ch'io adoro . . . ," set to music by Ghinolfo Dattari (1568, #692), and "Chi mi conduce O ciel crudo a seguire / costei che brama solo il mio morire," set to music by Pietro Havente (1556, #1311). Gian Mario Meriggi of the Department of Music, University of Bologna, found by computer search eight further entries: "Ahi fortuna crudel tu non dovevi / cercar d'allontar mai tanto amore; Che posso far per te più ch'io mi faccio / dimmel crudel che ben crudel ti chiamo; Madonna il dirò pur che non m'inganna / il mil giudizio se altri pur lo danna; Non èrudel sì il mal s'io grido il giorno / se poi la notte intraccio mi tien seco; O dolorosi amanti / che spregiando la vita," set to music by Francesco Menta (1560) and Gio. Andrea Dragoni (1575); "La man mi trema e mi vacilla il core / a por la penna in carta e di voi dire," set by Pietro Vinci (1584); "Chi mi darà la voce e le parole" (this line by Ariosto, followed by verses by Laura) and "Che debb'io amor che mi consigli" (this line from Petrarch, followed by verses by Laura). We wish to thank Dr. Meriggi for sharing this information with us.

3   The *Discorso* (*Commentary*), published by Giolito in Venice in 1549, was reprinted for the tenth time in 1608. We are using the edition of 1582.

4   *Commentary*, canto 11, stanza 4.

5   Two short but important twentieth-century biographies of Laura Terracina offer this basic information about the Terracina family: Linda Maroi, *Laura Terracina, poetessa napoletana del secolo XVI* (Naples, 1913), and Angelo Borzelli, *Laura Terracina, poetessa del cinquecento* (Naples, 1924).

6   In 1549, 1550, 1554, 1556, and 1560; reprinted again in 1692 and 1694.

7   There were two other literary academies in Naples, the Accademia dei Sereni and the Accademia degli Ardenti. They all flourished briefly and were closed in 1547 by order of Pietro di Toledo, who suspected them of being cells of conspiracy against the Spanish rule. The literary academy began to flourish in the sixteenth century; in keeping with the Mannerist taste for the quixotic, the academies took on absurd names such as the Accademia degli Intronati (Academy of the Thunderstruck) in Siena and the Accademia degli Assorditi (Academy of the Deaf) in Urbino. Academicians assumed academic names on becoming members. For a list of sixteenth-century literary academies, see Girolamo Tiraboschi, *Storia della letteratura italiana* (Florence, 1813).

8   Laura was herself praised by many contemporary writers, including Ludovico Dolce, Girolamo Ruscelli, Galeazzo di Tarsia, and Luigi Tansillo.

9   Much has been written about literary Mannerism; see particularly Aldo Scaglione, "Cinquecento Mannerism and the Uses of Petrarch," in *Essays on the Arts of Discourse* (New York, 1998).

10   We do not agree with one writer who believes that Laura's praise was motivated by her desire for gifts and money. See http//www.idn.it/orgoglio/napoleta/storie/laura14.htm.

11   *Lettere à Benedetto Varchi* (Bologna, 1859), p. 47. Laura Battiferra often sent her poems to Varchi for his advice and suggested revisions. We have not identified the poem to which Battiferra refers; possibly it was never sent. Terracina probably wrote to Battiferra after the latter's collection of poems was brought out in 1560.

12   Benedetto Croce, in "La casa di una poetessa," *Napoli Nobilissima*, vol. X, fasc. IX, p. 132, cites Zilioli as the source of the story.

13   Borzelli, *Laura Terracina*, pp. 12–13. Enea Vico made four engravings of Laura. We believe they were made in the following order: the first was for the frontispiece of *Rime* (1548); the second was for the frontispiece of *Discorso* (1549); and the third, which we illustrate, was made for Antonio Francesco Doni's *Le medaglie del doni, la prima parte* (Venice, 1550). We have not seen the fourth, and do not know the date.

14   Laura's insistence on her chastity should be seen in the context of the general view that associated intellectual activity in a woman with unchaste behavior. Aware of this association, any woman engaged in intellectual work would be inclined to belittle herself and her talent while laying great stress on her chastity. When Isotta Nogarola (1418–1466) began to gain fame as a humanist, she was accused of incest, as Letizia Panizza remarks in her introduction to *Lucrezia Marinella, The Nobility and Excellence of Women* (Chicago, 1999), p. xxiv.

15   Laura's image here of the backward-flowing river suggests that she had in mind Euripides's *Medea*, where the chorus, after Creon has sentenced Medea to exile, sings, "Flow backward to your sources, sacred rivers." The suggestion is reinforced by the next stanza, in which the chorus laments that Apollo did not "Bestow the lyre's divine / Power [on women], for otherwise I should have an answer / To the other sex. Long time / Has much to tell of us, and much of them." See Bernard Knox, *Classical Literature* (New York, 1993), p. 408.

16   Jacopo Sannazaro gave his villa to the friars of the Servi di Maria in 1529, which then was dedicated as the Church of Santa Maria del Parto. Carafa acquired the altar where the St. Michael painting is still located in 1542, and gave the commission to Leonardo Grazia sometime later. See Attilio M. Carrella, *La chiesa di Santa Maria del Parto*, pp. 67, 76.

17   Borzelli, *Laura Terracina*, p. 20.

18   Although "Enigma" is in her collection *Seste rime*, published in 1558, it had been written seven years earlier, for the context of the poem shows that she is writing in the present tense, "now I find myself on a path so wicked," that is, in 1551, when, she writes, she was thirty-two years old. This is not a singular case; other poems were written well before they were published, viz: "Prophetia della Signora Laura fatta a tre di Giugno del LII" ("Prophecy of Signora Laura on June 3, 1552"), also in *Seste rime*. At least one poem in this volume indicates that volume six had a publication subsequent to 1558 that is not recorded, for she writes of a Turkish invasion of Naples in 1563. We quote it as exceptional in her oeuvre and as an example of the vivid immediacy that Laura was capable of achieving: "Oh, how cruel, how horrible and fierce / nothing like this has ever been seen / At dawn on May twenty-first / in the year fifteen sixty three / there descended on these proud shores / at six in the morning, three galleys of Turks / shouting and running, get out of here / the Turks are coming, the Turks are coming! Don't wait! / It was in great fear and anguish / that our citizens were awakened from their dreams. / In such fierce turmoil / some ran out barefoot others without clothes saved themselves thanks to God / while others were captured not understanding what happened" (the Turks themselves had been yelling "save yourselves" as a trick to get people to run out of their houses so as to capture them more easily). (pp. 197–98)

19   A number of love poems in Laura's collections are addressed to women. Some writers believe that she was simply writing in the Petrarchan mode and that the poems are not addressed to real women; others interpret the poems as having been written on commission. We tend to believe the latter, whether she was actually paid or wrote as a favor, as for example she did for Leonardo da Pistoia. She also wrote to Vittoria Capanna, at the request of Mantegna (in *Seste rime*, p. 93).

20   Laura's seventh volume, *Sovra tutte le donne vedove di questa città di Napoli titulate et non titulate* (*On all the widows of this city of Naples*) was published in Naples in 1561. This is another example of the perverse wit that marks Laura's poems, especially in her *Commentary*, as we shall see, in that others had brought out books praising "all" the beautiful and "all" the illustrious noblewomen of Naples, whereas Laura's widows were of no special note. If in her early work Laura despaired of human folly and corruption, here she is depressed: life is sad, the dead are gone forever, only God can end our suffering, the world is monstrous, and tears are useless. Those who loved their husbands too well and regret their lost happiness are miserable, everything comes to an end. However, at the end of the volume she returns to her past custom, praising notable men among her contemporaries.

21   Laura adapted this idea from Petrarch's *Canzone* (poem 70), which begins, "*Lasso me, ch'i'non so in qual parte pieghi / la speme ch'è tradita omai più volte!*" (Alas I do not know where to turn the hope

that has been by now betrayed many times; translation by Robert M. Durling, *Petrarch's Lyric Poems* [Cambridge, 1976], pp. 150–151). In this poem Petrarch ends each ten-line stanza with a line from an important poet. Petrarch probably knew a similarly constructed poem by an obscure Latin poet made up of verses from poems of Virgil, since it is mentioned by his friend Boccaccio in *On Famous Women*.

22   Borzelli, *Laura Terracina*, p. 47.

Plate. IV.
Agnolo
Bronzino.
*Portrait of Laura
Battiferra* [?]
ca. 1547-1553.
Palazzo Vecchio,
Florence.
Photo, Art
Resource.

CHAPTER SEVEN

LAURA BATTIFERRA
(1523–1589)

& AGNOLO BRONZINO
(1503–1572)

🖋 A POET, A PAINTER,
A PORTRAIT, AND A POEM

"Iron within, ice without. . . ."

This is the first line of a sonnet by Agnolo Bronzino that has repeatedly, since 1928, been brought to bear on a portrait, also by Bronzino, of a woman seen in profile. The woman is identified in the collection of the Palazzo Vecchio as Laura Battiferra,[1] among the most highly esteemed women poets of the Cinquecento. She is holding a book with sonnets 64 and 240 by Petrarch visible on its facing pages (plate IV).

> *If you were able by some angry signs—*
> *casting your eyes down, bending your head,*
> *or fleeing faster than another would,*
> *or averting your face at my pure and worthy prayers—*
>
> *Ever to escape by these or other means*
> *from out my breast where Love from that first laurel*
> *grafts many branches, I would surely say*
> *this is just reason to show me disdain:*
>
> *A noble plant that grows in arid ground*
> *is badly suited and so naturally*
> *is happy to depart from such a place.*
>
> *But since your destiny prohibits you*
> *from being somewhere else, at least be sure*
> *the place you stay is not always so hateful.*
> (Petrarch, *Sonnet 64*) (p. 226)
>
> *I have begged Love and I beg him again*
> *to beg your pardon for me, my sweet pain,*
> *my bitter bliss, if I with my complete*
> *faithfulness deviate from the straight path.*

I can't deny, I don't deny my Lady
that reason who restrains every good soul
may be at times won over by desire
who leads me where I am forced to follow.

You, with that heart the heavens have lit up
with intellect so bright, with such high virtue
—as much as ever poured from a good star—

Should say with pity and no trace of scorn:
"What choice does this man have? My face consumes him.
Why is he greedy? Why am I so lovely?"
(Petrarch, *Sonnet 240*) (p. 226)

7.1.
Bronzino
signature on the
profile portrait
compared with
the signature
published in
*Dizionario
enciclopedico dei
pittori e degli
incisori italiani
dal XI al XX
secolo.*

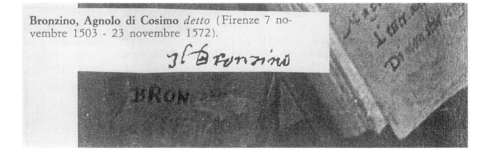

The book is meant to represent Petrarch's *Canzoniere,* although sonnet 64 in an actual volume would not face sonnet 240.[3] The painting's attribution to Bronzino is acceptable, although the block letters on the painting do not resemble other signatures of Bronzino[4] (figure 7.1). But is the sitter Laura Battiferra? We believe there is cause for doubt. The profile portrait has been accepted as representing Laura Battiferra since the 1920s. The identification was made by an American collector of Italian Old Masters, Charles Loeser, who acquired it sometime between 1914 and 1920. Its whereabouts is unknown until the eighteenth century, when it belonged to the Aresi family in Milan. In the nineteenth century it was in the collection of the Duke Maximilian von Leuchtenberg, who had moved, with his art collection, from Munich to St. Petersburg when he married the daughter of Czar Nicholas I. It thus descended to Duke George von Leuchtenberg and remained in St. Petersburg until it came into Loeser's collection. When he died he bequeathed his thirty-odd paintings, sculptures, and bronzes to their present location in the Palazzo Vecchio in Florence.

In its earlier history the painting was thought to be an idealized portrait of Petrarch's Laura, or Vittoria Colonna.[5] Mario Tinti was first in print to accept Loeser's identification, albeit with a question mark, explaining that in Bronzino's literary work "he reveals a platonic attitude and, like Michelangelo, had a platonic lover, Madonna delli Ammannati. Perhaps," he goes on, "the superb portrait in the Loeser collection, in which a rigid and cold woman displays a volume of sonnets by Petrarch is that Laura." Tinti then goes on to provide all future writers on the painting with the neat association of the painting with the first line of a poem by the painter, *"Tutta dentro di ferro e fuor di ghiaccio"* (All iron within, ice without), asking rhetorically if that verse does not "marvelously" fit the expression of the painting.[6]

The next discussion of the painting appears in a book by Arthur McComb, who explains the reason for identifying the sitter as Laura: "It is known that Bronzino and this lady exchanged verses written in the manner of Petrarch. The volume of Petrarch in the hand of the lady of the portrait would therefore point to her as Laura," and continues with the remark that "her personality fits perfectly with Bronzino's description of her in one of his sonnets as '*Tutto [sic] dentro di ferro e fuor di ghiaccio*'."[7] The identification of the sitter as Laura continues in recent scholarly literature on the painting by Victoria von Fleming in *Dichterin und Muse Michelangelos*, Victoria Kirkham in "Dante's Phantom, Petrarch's Specter: Bronzino's Portrait of the Poet Laura Battiferra," and Carol Plazzotta in "Bronzino's Laura."[8]

Although their reasons for accepting the identification are strong, as we will see, there are a number of troublesome questions that make acceptance somewhat less than entirely compelling. Given the importance of both Battiferra and Bronzino, and in view of those troublesome questions, a further discussion including a review of what is known of Laura's life and her relationship with Bronzino seems appropriate.

Capricious fortune seems to have smiled more often than she frowned on Laura Battiferra. Although Laura's obscure mother, whose name is even unknown, was not married to her father, Giovanni Antonio, a nobleman of Urbino, he acknowledged her as his daughter and she was legitimized by Pope Paul III so that she would eventually be his rightful heir. Judging from the esteem she enjoyed as an adult among her intellectual friends, she appears to have been well educated in literature, philosophy, and religion. True, she was not lucky with her first marriage; it ended with the early death of her husband, Vittorio Sereni, who may have died violently, for in a sonnet addressed to her "heavenly companion, with whom my thoughts dwell and share the hours," she refers to divine justice and revenge, and concludes, "like a stroke of lightning, this life disappears and flies to death." Laura was left a young, grieving widow sadly mourning, "alone in the world."

> As the sun disappears and the shadows
> descend from the mountain top
> and human cares drop away, one by one,
> leaving hearts tranquil,
> death and cruel fate fill me with anguish,
> rest refuses to come to my tired heart,
> and I pass my hours and nights crying
> with tears in my heart as well as my eyes.
>
> Alas, when I see the cornucopia filled
> with fruit and flowers, when I see the faithful friends
> Flora and Ceres, the one carrying roses at her breast,
> the other, mature wheat,
> and the peasant boy coming from the fields
> carrying the rewards of his hard work

> *I say with tearful eyes: are loss and mourning now*
> *to be forever the fruit of my hopes?* [9] (pp. 226 – 27)

Destiny's answer was more favorable than she feared. She was still in her twenties when she remarried, probably in 1550. She and her second husband, Bartolomeo Ammannati (1511–1592), lived in Rome during the early years of their marriage, a city that she loved, as her ode tells us:

> *Lofty, sacred hills,*
> *flowering and gentle,*
> *under whose great and glorious empire*
> *your sons embraced the whole world,*
> *may our skies be eternally clear*
> *and may you be ever free from heat and frost;*
> *and you, lovely, flowing, silvery river,*
> *you make Rome even more beautiful;*
> *may your sun be never so strong*
> *as to dry your green tresses.*
> *Let the woeful day never come*
> *that I must leave your warm shelter.* (p. 227)

Bartolomeo was twelve years older than Laura and at the time of their marriage was already a well-established sculptor in Florence and elsewhere. In the early fifties he carried out architectural commissions for Pope Julius III in Rome, which he had secured with the help of Michelangelo and Giorgio Vasari, and his career in both sculpture and architecture flourished from then on. With the pope's death in 1555 Ammannati had no further commissions in Rome, but Vasari had moved by this time to Florence, where he became part of the illustrious circle of artists around Cosimo I de' Medici, and he invited Bartolomeo to join him there. Vasari included him in a tondo on his ceiling decoration in the Sala di Cosimo I in the Palazzo Vecchio; his head is close to Cosimo's left elbow (figure 7.2).[10]

Laura hated leaving Rome, not only because the city meant so much to her but also because she had apparently begun to be known as a poet and was already aspiring to lasting fame, thinking, it seems, of bringing out a collection of her poems. But time was flying by, she notes nervously,

> *I see night coming on and the hours and days,*
> *the lusters, the years, are flying,*
> *and I look back already on more than twenty five,*

> *I hurry so that before nightfall*
> *I can gather up my pile of scattered thoughts*
> *to make them eternally lustrous.* (p. 227)

She was afraid that her budding reputation would not survive in her new surroundings, far from what she felt was the hub of the world.

Here am I, belonging to you, inviolate, noble ruins,
yes, here my very self—oh cruel destiny—
about to leave you; alas, will my deep sadness
ever come to an end?

And you, wandering spirits,
to whom heaven gave such great gifts
as to win for you the bliss
of eternal citizenship above.

Let my humble prayer be heard in heaven:
though I am far away, living in horrible darkness
and buried alive on the Arno,

Make my name, that best part of me
that stays here on the Tiber, purged of all dross,
remain alive among your precious treasures. (p. 227 – 28)

**7.2.
Giorgio Vasari.
*Cosimo I with his
Architects and
Artists.* 1559.
Palazzo Vecchio,
Florence.
Photo, Scala/
Art Resource.**

Again Fortune smiled. Laura found herself quite content in her husband's villa in
Maiano, near Florence, where she went frequently and stayed as long as she could.

At the foot of the proud and ancient walls
unchanged through time and memory,
along the beautiful mountain which, green and lofty,
raises its face to pierce the sky,

I looked into the pure, crystalline water
that makes the fields and grassy countryside bloom,
and that even in the harsh season
fills my heart with sweet hope.

My lovely Fiesole, graced by Mount Cecero,
with your gentle showers, shady, quiet valley,
why can I not stay here with you?

So I say when on scorching days
I put my greedy, happy mouth
again and again to the overflowing spring. (p. 228)

Their marriage was evidently happy. Benvenuto Cellini, in a sonnet addressed to her, conflates Petrarch's "Laura" with Laura Battiferra (a conceit that poetically flattered many a "Laura" of the Cinquecento) and relates her and her husband not only to Petrarch and Laura, who are united in Paradise ("*Lassù v'alzò il Petrarca*"), but also to Orpheus and Eurydice, who, he writes, would have been as happy as Laura-Petrarch/Laura-Bartolomeo had Orpheus obeyed the warning not to look back at his wife as he led her out of Hades.[11] In correspondence with their friends, both Laura and Bartolomeo refer to each other in ways that suggest their mutual concerns. We get a glimpse of their life together at the Villa in her letter of 9 June 1557 to Benedetto Varchi, with whom she had a close friendship until his death in 1565. She was among those to whom he circulated his poems, and she habitually sent him her poems for his opinion and suggested revisions. In an earlier letter she had written of her husband's being ill.

"He is very well, now," she writes, "and so am I, in this beautiful, charming villa. He comes here every morning and evening, and we give ourselves a hundred pleasures, going to see one or another beautiful place or to watch the peasants dancing. If I decide to return to Florence for San Giovanni [the feast of St. John the Baptist, patron saint of Florence], I want to return here to stay another few days."[12]

Laura nevertheless seems to have been somewhat grudging about what would appear to have been her happy situation. In a two-character eclogue, *Europa*, dedicated to Leonora Cibo de' Vitelli in praise of her hero-husband, she claims to feel satisfied, but her tone suggests otherwise. In verses given to Dafne, the character representing herself, she writes,

Without mean and scornful thoughts
that would bar my way to heaven,
far from the multitude, solitary and peaceful,
I live apart, without jealousy or anger.

> Let others have and enjoy a richer, fatter
> herd than mine, which is meager and poor;
> I am satisfied with what my wise shepherd can give me
> for he is faithful above all others.
>
> It is now going on eleven years since I was tied to him
> by Hymen with such a knot
> that neither time nor fortune can loosen it,
>
> And when I shear the sheep and milk the cows,
> the wool and milk are abundant enough
> to keep away hunger and cold. (pp. 228 – 29)

Although she was writing as a shepherdess in the context of a pastoral poem, an autobiographical note of deep discontent is clearly sounded. Laura was indeed a woman of changeable moods, as she plainly describes herself:

> Enveloped in cold hope and hot fear,
> in dubious peace, I live in turmoil;
> I shun death and yet deprive myself of life,
> at once triumphant and defeated.
>
> Now I stop, now I go backward, now pushed forward
> I go ahead, now slowly, now quickly
> I keep going; now how many sheets I write,
> then throw away; now I reveal myself as I am, now I pretend.
>
> I cry, I laugh; I blush and I pale;
> now I love myself, now I hate myself;
> now I lie on the Earth, now I fly through the heavens
>
> So that sometimes I don't want, I reject what I want;
> I hurt myself and I console myself;
> living in such a state, I die. (p. 229)

Granted that we hear the pervasive influence of Petrarch's innumerable oppositions (cold and heat; hate and hope; laughter and tears); nevertheless, she probably *felt* as she described herself and relied on Petrarch for language to express her feelings. Why such despair?

At the time she wrote the poem she had not yet published her work. It was known through private circulation among artist and intellectual friends such as Benedetto Varchi, Annibale Caro, Lelio Bonsi, and Bronzino. But despite her close ties to these men, she was evidently not invited to become a member of the prestigious Florentine Academy, founded under the aegis of Cosimo in 1541, to which they belonged.[13] She did belong to the Accademia degli Assorditi of Urbino and the Accademia degli Intronati of Siena, but if she was excluded from the prestigious academy in the city where she lived, this would understandably have been a cause of feeling some serious disappointment and could have contributed to the unhappiness that is reflected in her poems, leading her to adopt the persona of one whose real home is in nature, indifferent to the attractions of sophisticated urban life—such as membership in the Florentine Academy.

> *In a secluded villa surrounded by sunny slopes*
> *and narrow ravines, near a beautiful murmuring stream,*
> *far from the bustling crowds*
> *I spend my hours and days;*
>
> *And even more do I enjoy hearing the maidens*
> *and shepherds who, when Apollo's light is shining far away,*
> *spring up at the tinkling of love-exciting cowbells,*
> *and begin their amorous dancing,*
>
> *And seeing the thick woodlands all around me,*
> *the lofty mountains and the green fields of Maiano,*
> *and the Mensola flowing here like the Arno through Florence.*
>
> *No matter the music, the palaces, the great buildings*
> *that adorn Florence and the world, all this cannot be taken*
> *from me by jealousy and wicked destiny.* (p. 229)

Surely the most intriguing problem one encounters in writing about Laura Battiferra is raised by the twin questions surrounding the splendid profile portrait probably by Bronzino and her relationship with the artist. "Bronzino's precise relationship with Laura Battiferri has still to be fully investigated," writes Charles McCorquodale, curious as everyone writing about these two must be.[14] Were they lovers? Confronting this question as well as that of the correctness of identifying the sitter of the profile portrait as Battiferra, we must keep in mind that *love, lover, beloved* are words that in the Cinquecento did not necessarily carry the primarily sexual meaning that they have in our modern culture. Neo-Platonism came to rule Italian sensibilities, while Petrarchism dominated Italian poetry until late in the century, and poets yearned for their aloof ladies and lamented their unrequited love with what often appears to be blissful woe. Even women poets adapted the male view although it seems in fact that they had more of the woe, the men, the bliss.[15]

Questioning the nature of the friendship between Bronzino and Laura, we would expect that some clues, some inferences, at least, could be drawn from an examination of the poems they exchanged. In her collection published in 1560, Laura included four poems by Bronzino addressed to her, with her direct responses to each.[16] Three of them follow each other in a sequence of three pages, 69, 70, and 71, while the fourth appears on page 82. In the first, Bronzino writes of his grief over the death of his master. This was Jacopo Pontormo (1494–1557), with whom he worked for many years on important frescoes for a Carthusian monastery and for Medici villas: we can thus date the sonnet to 1557, when Pontormo died. He feels aimless, he writes, like a man who can no longer see, and he feels nothing but pain.

> *If only I could hear his voice, if only he could guide me,*
> *the good Painter who was the mirror of our age,*
> *dead now, and I am consumed in grief.* (p. 229)

Bronzino plays on the words "the good Painter" *(Pittore)*, capitalizing the "P" to associate the words with "the good Shepherd" *(Pastore)* as well as "the good Pontormo." The poem seems not to refer to Laura, but in lines 5–6 we find another play on words when he writes of flowers waving in the breeze (*l'aura*, which he writes *l'Aura*):

> *How sweet it is when I seem to hear the gentle breeze*
> *rustling through the living jewels.* (p. 230)

In her response, Laura first consoles him with the thought that his master is now in heaven and pleased that he, Bronzino, misses him so much, and she begs him to continue writing the lovely poems that raise him above the common herd. She is apologetic for her own "voice like a hoarse bird," but she hopes,

> *Perhaps one day, if death does not take me*
> *before my time, I will be able to go beyond my usual self*
> *to join you in that upper realm.* (p. 230)

In the next exchange of sonnets Bronzino is still mourning for Pontormo, but she assures him that his muse will sing again bringing him new honors; her own steps are faltering, but she hopes to be able to follow him.

In the third of these sonnets Bronzino repeats the play on Laura's name.

> *The aura [l'aura] of your soul—now that the strong*
> *north wind which fades the flowers*
> *and freezes the river to icy silver, and leaves the earth*
> *bare and saddened as a widow, has departed—*
>
> *Seems with its gentle breath, to move the air*
> *with new strength, and bedew the earth, to open up the sky*
> *so that plants, water, grass, and flowers*
> *rejoice with renewed energy.*
>
> *While I, like foliage in bitter winter,*
> *frozen inside and out, bleak and neglected,*
> *deprived of my dear father and leader,*
>
> *I am revived and melt the ice within me,*
> *I dress myself in his mantle and his love*
> *and I rise serene, and reveal my own Light.* (p. 230)

Laura responded, starting with his name, as, in the original Italian, he had started with a play on hers, and assuring him he needed no other guide but God.

> *Bronzino, your beautiful soul shines in heaven;*
> *what other lovely, luminous Power*
> *could create among us greater works, honor, and brilliance*
> *than the world has ever known;*
>
> *The steep path that leads to God*
> *beyond this brief, mortal sojourn*
> *is revealed so clearly to you*
> *that you have no need for a better Guide or Leader,*
>
> *While I, as if on the high seas with no captain,*
> *the sky dark with heavy clouds,*
> *I veer this way and that, seaward or windward,*
>
> *Though I was prey of great, mocking Neptune,*
> *I see not far away the dawning light*
> *and my weary boat takes heart.*[17] (pp. 230 – 31)

In the fourth of the sonnets by Bronzino that she included in her book, he writes,

> *I swear to you by this living wreath*
> *from the tree which once you were, beside the sacred spring,*
> *and I swear by the holy flame of Him*
> *who rules over heaven, the earth, and the waters.*
>
> *I swear in all truth that in its lively, happy shade*
> *I have perceived such that*
> *I disdain what others most prize*
> *and nothing else can give me greater delight.*
>
> *I maintain that as happy Laura and Beatrice*
> *are honored by the world, to the wisdom and works of others*
> *is owed no less than their merit deserves.*
>
> *You by your own gifts triumph over Laura and Beatrice;*
> *you surpass their excellence*
> *and perhaps even their poet-lovers.* (p. 231)

Laura protests, as well she might, at this extravagant praise.

> *If at the baptismal font my stars,*
> *benevolent and favorable when they gave me my name,*[18]

had also given me the art
with which Apollo inspires you, the new Apelles.[19]

Then your lofty poems, in which
truth dresses True Love, freed from its false veil,
would make me worthy of the praise you give me
which they alone deserve.

And perhaps I would not be less happy than those two
whose happiness surpasses all others
with their chaste Lovers who sing their praises eternally.

But since in this world you alone
can give a double life to others, why not do so
for yourself, so that I may live with you? (p. 231)

In the first three of these poems exchanged between Bronzino and Battiferra, there are what might appear to be hints, here and there, of hidden messages, as between lovers whose love must be concealed. In the fourth sonnet he puns lovingly on her name and is filled with renewed energy by the aura of her soul; he sees her as Daphne changed into a laurel tree and swears by a branch of it that he was once happy in its shade where he learned to prize what is most valuable in life; she writes, seemingly, of her desire to live with him. We must note, however, that she was a married woman who most certainly would not make a secret affair public and, moreover, the poems were published with the approval of her husband.[20] We therefore interpret these poems as we believe they were understood at the time, as expressions of platonic love and mutual admiration that were perfectly conventional within their Petrarchist frame. As for the fourth of these poems by Laura to Bronzino, which ends with her question why he does not give double life to himself, as he does to others, we interpret this to refer to the fact that he was a painter who can create images that "double" the living sitter, and she asks why does he not create one of himself, "so that I may live with you." We believe this is a reference—and understood as such by her husband and contemporary readers—to a portrait he had made of her, thus her "double," and her desire for him to give her one of himself, so that the two portraits might "live" together. We find Laura referring to a portrait of herself by Bronzino in the collection of Bronzino's sonnets, published for the first time by Domenico Moreni in 1823, which he found in the Magliabechiana collection, now in the National Central Library in Florence.[21] The editor included poems by some of Bronzino's contemporaries, among which is the following by Laura:

In this shining, lovely face
you clearly show, dear Crisero [22]
how your chaste and sincere heart
happy and peaceful, yearns for your shepherdess.

As in my own new image
the wonderful work of your gifted hand
discovers every feeling, every thought,
however much the heart may desire to conceal it.

And thus the Tree that you,
worthy rival of Apollo, love so much,
rises, evergreen, to the sky, nurtured by you,

While I, thanks to you, doubly praised,
clasp my lowly, humble stem so that it may not be blown away
by the northern or southern winds. (pp. 231–32)

In this important poem, which she did not include in her own volume along with the others by Bronzino, we learn that Bronzino's portrait of Laura represented her as a shepherdess, and, "doubly praised," she held in her hand a "stem," probably a laurel leaf, as suggested by the previous tercet. We infer that her portrait was set in a landscape, with a laurel tree in the background.[23] He apparently did not respond to her suggestion that he make his own double: there is no known self-portrait of Bronzino.

Platonic as this exchange of loving affection may be, a number of poems by Bronzino in *his* collection, *not* published in his or Laura's lifetime, reveal that his feeling for her was different, more fervent that hers for him. On page 5 of the volume edited by Moreni there is a sonnet addressed "To M. Laura Battiferra delli Ammannati" in which he calls her Daphne, the nymph pursued by Apollo whose father, a river god, saved her from capture by changing her into a laurel tree. We have already seen in Bronzino's poem to her (in her collection) beginning

I swear to you by this living wreath
from the tree which once you were, beside the sacred spring,

that Daphne (transformed into a laurel tree) was Bronzino's poetic image for Laura. Daphne is also the name of a shepherdess in pastoral poetry and is the name Laura gave herself in her long poem, *Europa*. On page 6 of the Bronzino collection, in the poem by Laura to Bronzino quoted earlier, she refers to herself has "your shepherdess."

In his direct response on the same page, Bronzino addresses her as beautiful, chaste Daphne and tells her that her virtue has changed him so much that all he desires is honesty and beauty. In an exchange between them on the death of their mutual friend Luca Martini, he addresses her again as Daphne, and in another poem we find "gentle Daphne, my dear Daphne," in whose eyes he sees the woman he loves. She evidently went away for a while, for he writes,

Daphne, fair Daphne, where are you hiding?
no matter where I look I cannot find you,

not in the mountains, or meadows, or valleys do I find
those beautiful eyes, that curly golden hair. (p. 232)

But in the last of the Daphne poems Bronzino seems to have become unplatoni-
cally jealous. He writes that he has seen her with another man who, loving her, has
changed her usual coldness to ardent affection. He warns her that this man will not be
faithful and begs her to flee from him.[24]

Although we cannot date the Daphne poems, we begin to realize with Bronzino's
poem to his "Nymph" that the friendship existed over a long time.

Is it thus that blind oblivion has erased,
oh, gentle nymph, those innocent games
that we played together, you and I,
in our salad days.

What sweet thoughts, what desires
that once lay in your breast were taken from me
by Batto, alas! No longer could you climb the hills
and wander down to the brook with me!

I swear to you that the pure, chaste
pleasure we took in those places, lives
in my memory, which will never die;

And since it seems that in your heart
you also remember that sweet friendship,
I am filled with gladness that doubles my pain. (p. 232)

Batto apparently refers to Bartolomeo Ammannati (possibly the man of whom he
was jealous), and the poem makes evident that Laura and Bronzino had enjoyed an
idyllic friendship "in their salad days" before her remarriage in 1550. Luisa Becherucci, accepting the identification of the profile portrait as Laura, dates the painting to
1555–1560, believing that this was the period of their friendship. Kirkham dates it to
the 1560s because there is no mention of it in Laura's book of poems published in
1560.[25] We believe that the fact that Laura does not refer to it supports the suspicion
that it is not her portrait. However, neither does she refer to her portrait as a shepherdess in her own volume, although she includes other poetic exchanges between
Bronzino and herself: That poem was in Bronzino's collection, unknown until it was
published in the Moreni edition of 1823. Was there a particular reason for omitting it
from her own volume?

It seems clear from the poems they exchanged that the relationship was warm,
even loving, but platonic by her preference, if not by his. Like Petrarch, he accused
his Laura of coldness, he was sometimes content, and sometimes desperately
"through with love." The poems cannot be taken entirely at face value, for the feelings expressed, however real, are also partly attitudinized. However, the truth of
their relationship may be clouded in these poems. It may have been, at least for a

7.3.
Alessandro
Allori.
*Christ and the
Canaanite Woman*
(detail of plate V
showing the
Canaanite
woman
and Laura
Battiferra).
ca.1585-1590.
Church of San
Giovannino,
Florence.
Photo, Scala/
Art Resource.

time, and on Bronzino's part, much more ardent and tempestuous, as we shall presently see.

In our effort to investigate whether or not the profile portrait represents Laura Battiferra, we must look carefully at the painting *Christ and the Canaanite Woman* by Alessandro Allori in the Church of San Giovannino degli Scolopi in Florence (plate V, figure 7.3). Laura was known to be devoutly religious, and indeed she and her husband, under her influence, developed extremely close relations with the Jesuits from about 1570 to the end of their lives. When she came into her substantial inheritance in 1565, the couple began to give large contributions to support the order's activities. As an architect, Ammannati undertook much of the planning and direction of the architectural program of the society, becoming the architect of the Jesuit College in Florence, among other important architectural works including the Church of San Giovannino, where both he and Laura were eventually buried.

For San Giovannino they commissioned an altar dedicated to Ammannati's namesake, St. Bartholomew, and commissioned Allori to paint *Christ and the Canaanite Woman* as an altarpiece. The artist inherited the mantle of Bronzino, who was not only his teacher but almost a surrogate father, for his natural father died when he was young and Bronzino brought him up, making him an assistant in his own painting commissions. He evidently also inherited the mantle of Bronzino as friend of Laura and Ammannati. Bartolomeo Ammannati's likeness is represented in the disciple St. Bartholomew, standing closest to Christ, leaning with both hands on a long cane; behind him are other disciples. The woman kneeling behind the Canaanite woman holding a book pressed against her breast with her left hand has been accepted as representing Laura. Although the attribution has no contemporary documentary evidence to support it,[26] it seems reasonable to accept the tradition that both husband and wife were represented in a painting that they commissioned, and indeed, Bartolomeo as the saint indicates a relationship by looking at this kneeling woman; this pose moreover heightens the woman's importance in the composition by drawing the viewer's attention to her. We thus join the other scholars from the seventeenth century to the present in accepting this identification as Laura.

As recounted by Matthew 15:21–28, Christ encountered a woman who begged him to save her daughter, who had been seized by the devil. At first Christ refused to heed the woman, saying that he was sent only to bring in the lost sheep of the House of Israel. The woman knelt at this feet. "'Lord,' she said, 'help me.' He replied, 'It is not fair to take the children's food and throw it to the house dogs.' She retorted, 'Ah yes, Sir, but even housedogs can eat the scraps that fall from their master's table.' Then Jesus answered her, 'Woman, you have great faith. Let your wish be granted.' And from that moment her daughter was well again." Because the woman was not one of the "lost sheep of Israel" but a Canaanite, it seems likely that Laura and her husband would have chosen the subject because it is particularly compatible with the mission of the Jesuit order to bring the Gospel to the "pagan" world.[27]

The church was completed in 1584, and the painting was probably executed not long after. However, Simona Giovannoni Lecchini "supposes" that Ammannati commissioned the work shortly after Laura's death in 1589,[28] and we are free to suppose that her portrayal in it may have been made either from life or shortly after she died. With regard to the accuracy of the likeness, from life or shortly after does not matter, inasmuch as Allori as a close friend knew her well and could easily have painted her likeness from memory if she had died; we may take it to represent Laura as she looked in her sixties, and although it is almost a full face view (figure 7.3), we ought to be able to recognize in it the thin, long, bony structure of the face in Bronzino's profile portrait if it is of the same woman, even though many years younger. But this woman's face is round, not long. The nose is prominent, as in the earlier painting, but this one feature in itself is not enough to prove an identity between the two; it is characteristic of many Italian faces and is evident in the profile of the Canaanite woman, probably posed by an artist's model. It does not seem to us that the physiognomy of the two faces is similar enough to satisfy fully their identity as unmistakably the same person, and therefore one must hesitate to support the identification of Laura in the profile portrait on the basis of its problematic resemblance to the woman in the Allori painting, although this has been a basic premise among the modern writers to whom we have referred.

We return now to Bronzino's profile portrait, identified as Laura Battiferra. The theme of a woman with an open book is rooted in portrayals of the Virgin such as Ambrogio Lorenzetti's *Annunciation,* and developed more elaborately in Botticelli's *Madonna of the Magnificat,* which has strong similarities with Bronzino's profile portrait.[29] Bronzino's immediate iconographical source was Andrea del Sarto's *Girl with a Petrarchino* in the Uffizi, in which the sitter, disputably identified as Maria del Berrettaio, also holds open a book representing a volume of Petrarch's poems and points to the poem that begins, "Go, warm sighs, to her cold heart" (figure 7.4). Unlike Andrea's young woman, however, who smiles at the viewer, Bronzino's sitter turns her face away: it is as if Bronzino is contrasting the chaste, upright character of his sitter with the pert and possibly teasing nature of Andrea's.

The crucial poem that doubtless influenced those that wrote about it beginning "All iron inside, and ice without" is the last of a group of four poems in which Bronzino uses the metaphor of iron and ice. There is indeed evidence to show that this poem does concern Laura, evidence that we find in the third of this group of seemingly related poems in which he sees the daughter of Peneus, that is, Daphne (his poetic name for Laura), as a laurel tree surrounded by ice (ice on the outside), with roots of iron (iron on the inside), and he fears this condition will cause her to loose her branches.

> *I do not know, certainly, but I fear*
> *that covered by ice, and with roots of iron*
> *she will lose her beautiful branches.* (p. 232)

Laura herself, it seems, although sometimes confident of her gift, sometimes felt bereft of inspiration, as we find in one of her poems in Bronzino's collection where she writes,[30]

> *A sterile tree am I, unskilled and uncultured,*
> *who, though my kind gardener tries always*

7.4.
Andrea del
Sarto.
*Girl with a
Petrarchino.*
1526-1528.
Galleria degli
Uffizi, Florence.
Photo, Alinari/
Art Resource.

to make me beautiful and to flourish,
produces neither fruit in autumn or flowers in May. (p. 233)

Because Bronzino's Laura/Daphne, the laurel tree, is linked to iron and ice, we believe that all four iron-and-ice poems in the group are about her. In the first he writes of

My lady, with the face of an angel, a heavenly soul,
who has a heart of iron and skin of ice.

But, he says to Love,

Do not brag that you have set the stars
against me and her, far more worthy,

so that I am not alone burnt and wounded by you. (p. 233)

In the second he addresses the

Foolish boy [Amor] . . .
now your fire is out, your weapons blunted, truth
reveals you defeated
by living iron and living ice. (p. 233)

The third we have already quoted. In the fourth, whose first line echoes Petrarch's poem 135:59–60: "All inside and outside I feel myself turn to ice," Bronzino writes,

All iron within, ice without,
with a heavy hand and inspiration spent,
her soul enclosed in a hard shell,
I call out, to warm and soothe her.

And trying to reach heaven's summit,
I draw near the sun, but my thoughts aspire to such heights
that every flight, every effort would be too little,
too late, and without wings, crippled, I chase the wind.

Yours the fault, mine the injury, oh foolish desire,
the promises you made to me and to her were false,
and what could we expect?

Now disarmed and defeated,
without struggling, without pay,
one must serve where one fears to run away. (p. 233)

Here in these four ice-and-iron poems we glimpse a relationship that led to disappointment. We believe they were early ones, possibly written during the period of 1546–47 when Bronzino spent some time in Rome, and that the painter was eventually resigned to the platonic friendship reflected in the later exchange of poems we have presented.

Supposing, then, that the poem does refer to Laura Battiferra, is there any evidence to suggest that it refers to the sitter of the profile portrait? There is one possibility— and we must be alert to all possible clues—the word "iron" in Italian is *ferro*, possibly referring to Batti*ferra* in a characteristic Bronzino pun (see note 6). But the clue is somewhat weakened by associating iron with ice, a Petrarchist opposition that may have nothing to do with the sitter's name. Bronzino's por-trait style was characterized by Roberto Longhi as blending the ideal with the "superbly glacial" and Arnold Hauser writes, "The idea of cool, unapproachable *grandezza* . . . is most directly realized in the work of Bronzino, who, with the crystal-clear correctness of his forms, is the born court painter."[31] Thus, the cold elegance of the sitter—evident in his por-traits generally—is no indication that the iron-and-ice poem about Laura must be associated with the portrait. One would expect that artists' paintings and verses would share some of the same imagery, no matter whom they painted.

Can it have been Laura Battiferra? The painting carries a message of love, but Laura was not the only woman Bronzino ever loved: there was one whom he addressed as *"giovanna angioletta,"* who died, another whom he called Milvia, and perhaps even others.[32] Nevertheless, although not necessary, it is plausible, and even enjoyable, to believe that the woman holding a book with Petrarch's poems displayed was named Laura, and because one of the bases for the friendship between Bronzino and Laura Battiferra was the poetry they wrote and exchanged, we might feel comfortable accepting Charles Loeser's educated guess. But the troublesome doubts must be confronted nonetheless.

First, we do have the portrait of Battiferra that can be accepted as her image when she was in her sixties as represented in Allori's painting *The Canaanite Woman.* We do not find a decisive resemblance to the woman in the profile painting. Second, we have evidence of only one portrait of Laura by Bronzino, but the description of her portrait for which she thanks Bronzino in the poem she wrote, beginning "In this shining lovely face" (quoted earlier), is surely not the profile portrait; from her poem we know that he represented her as a shepherdess, holding in her hand a stem (probably of laurel), with a laurel tree included in the composition. To accept the profile portrait we must suppose it to be a second portrait of Laura by Bronzino. Could that second portrait be the one described by Bronzino's contemporary, Anton Francesco Grazzini (known by his academic name, Il Lasca) in his poem, "Sonnet on the Portrait of Laura Battiferri"? He begins with a reference to the painter's name, Agnolo, a variant of Angelo, "angel".

> He must be an angel, otherwise
> all his effort, all his work, all his art would be in vain;
> it is not possible for something so divine
> to be portrayed by a mortal hand.
>
> Thus you alone, angelic, supreme spirit,
> by painting her so accurately, with full particulars,
> can portray the Graces that dwell in all her being,
> where any other brush would fail:
>
> How else would it be possible for a human eye
> to gaze fixed and intent on such
> serene eyes, and saintly face?
>
> Blessed alone are you, on whom heaven bestows
> such insight, to reveal to posterity
> the beauty of Paradise. (pp. 233 – 34)

In this sonnet to Bronzino praising his portrait of Laura Battiferra, Grazzini rhapsodizes over how Bronzino by painting her accurately, with full particulars (*a parte a parte*), was able to reveal in his portrait the Graces that were "diffused" as he says, throughout her being, body and soul. But how are we to understand what Grazzini meant by "full particulars"? It seems to refer to the whole woman, not just her profile, although it is possible that he intended to emphasize the precision of the contours.[33] Furthermore, he is captivated by "the serene eyes" *(occhi sereni)* together with her "saintly face." But in the profile portrait there is only one eye visible. Would a viewer looking at the portrait refer to eyes in the plural? It seems psychologically unlikely. Could Grazzini have given the profiled sitter two eyes in his poem in order to use the plural form of "serene" *(sereni)* as a play on her first married name, Sereni? Name puns were popular in Cinquecento poetry. Was the profile portrait painted in Rome in the mid-1540s while Sereni was still living? This seems possible, stylistically, comparing it with Bronzino's *Portrait of Lucrezia Panciatichi,* dated to 1540. Grazzini's poem is not without ambiguity, and we must wonder if he was praising the profile portrait—or was it a full-face Laura as a shepherdess, or a *different* portrait of Laura that enthralled him?

Third, Bronzino in his collection refers twice to his beloved's "golden hair" as for example in a sonnet that he begins with a familiar play on Laura's name.

> The breeze [L'aura] which gently moves
> the tops of the fresh green laurel
> sweeps across me in such sweet waves
> that I am restored from all my anxiety.
>
> And you, a new shrub with your golden foliage
> abundant with flowers,
> just looking at you Love floods my heart
> with such sweetness that I languish and die. (p. 234)

Here his Laura / Daphne's hair is the laurel tree's "golden foliage," and again in the sonnet quoted earlier, "Daphne, fair Daphne, where are you hiding," he writes that he cannot find "those beautiful eyes, that curly golden hair." The woman of the profile portrait is depicted with brown hair. On the other hand, the Petrarchan beloved lady that ruled sixteenth-century imagery is always a golden-haired blonde.

Fourth, we must recognize that the poems in the book held by the sitter, out of sequence as they are, had to be chosen for a purpose. Kirkham argues that it is Laura who is exhibiting a notebook in which she herself had written some of Petrarch's poems, for she sees that the handwriting in the painting is similar to the handwriting in the manuscript of her poems and therefore believes that Laura chose and wrote the verses. But consider the implications of this speculation: even if the notebook and the writing actually belonged to Laura, the notebook and writing in the painting are only *painted depictions,* as Kirkham acknowledges, so the painted "handwriting" must have been executed by Bronzino, not Laura.[34] Did Laura show him her notebook (how else would he have known it existed?) and ask him to paint her holding it? Did she choose the pages with those verses simply because she liked them particularly, and because the one on the right side of the represented book (on the viewer's left), the more shaded side, refers to the laurel, symbol in Petrarch of his beloved Laura and thus related to her own name? Did she then choose the pose with her face averted? This puts an extraordinary and unnecessary strain on imagining the genesis of the composition. In our view it is more plausible to think that Bronzino was in control of his portrait from beginning to end, that he chose both the pose and the verses of Petrarch because they expressed what he wanted to say to a woman he loved.

Can the sitter be Laura Battiferra? Summarizing the possibilities, we find on one hand that Bronzino's sitter is holding a "volume" of Petrarch's *Canzoniere* addressed to his Laura, so the name of the woman portrayed might have been Laura; Petrarch, moreover, refers to his Laura averting her face, as indeed the sitter for the portrait does, and we have seen that Laura kept Bronzino at a distance. However, Bronzino in using the poem could have meant that the woman, whatever her name, was *his* Laura, averting her face, the archetype of the chaste woman who refuses a would-be lover; we have seen that the woman represented in Andrea del Sarto's *Girl with a Petrarchino,* which, we have pointed out, was the iconographical source for Bronzino's profile portrait, may very well not have been named "Laura." Some writers have agreed with the Laura Battiferra identification partially on the basis of an interesting argument holding that Bronzino, who had compared Battiferra to Dante and Petrarch in a poem, meant to praise Battiferra as a poet by showing her in a pose similar to the way he supposedly had posed Dante, while she was reading Petrarch's poems (see the final tercet in Bronzino's poem, beginning, "I swear to you by this living wreath"). But the attribution of the "Dante" to Bronzino is now not accepted; in the catalogue of the National Gallery, Washington, it is attributed to "Vasari, Giorgio (Circle of)" and dated to 1575/85, which thus undermines the rational for the Dante/Petrarch connection (figure 7.5).[35] This is the Dante type we have seen in Vasari's *Six Tuscan Poets* (see figure 2 in the preface). Nevertheless, the final word is yet to be written on the Washington painting. We must also recognize that a profile view of Dante had a long tradition by the sixteenth century, and a lost portrait of Dante by Bronzino is thought to have been Vasari's model.[36]

From Grazzini's poem, Bronzino is known to have painted her portrait, but his reference to painting the sitter "accurately, with full particulars" does not call up an image of a profile (although this is ambiguous), and his words "serene eyes" do not match the profile portrait with one eye; furthermore, this strong, determined portrayal seems unlikely to have suggested saintliness to him, granted that viewers' reactions are subjective. Moreover, the woman of the thin, long, bony profile does not suggest aging into the softer contours of the more fleshy-faced Laura Battiferra in Allori's *The Canaanite Woman.* And also as we have pointed out, the woman in the portrait is not blonde.

In only one of the two poems by Petrarch in the book held by the profiled sitter is there a reference to the laurel. Because Bronzino, in his poetry, calls Laura "Daphne" and associates her with the laurel, we would expect at least a laurel leaf somewhere in the painting to identify her symbolically. From Petrarch on, the laurel became the iconographical identification of a poet, and we see it in portraits of women poets such as Tullia d'Aragona and Gaspara Stampa and earlier in the portrait of "Laura," who wears a dress decorated with a laurel design and holds a book (see figure 6 in the preface), whom we identify as a poet on the basis of the laurel and the book.[37] Bronzino himself gave laurel symbols to Laura in his portrait of her as a shepherdess as we

7.5.
Anon. (Formerly
attributed to
Bronzino.)
*Allegorical
Portrait of Dante.*
16th century.
National Gallery
of Art,
Washington,
D.C. Photo,
National Gallery.

know from her poem (see pages 213 – 14). Because the woman portrayed in profile is
not holding her own book and there is no laurel in the painting, we do not even have
evidence that she was a poet.

From what we have presented in the foregoing pages, we believe the arguments in
favor of accepting the profile portrait as Laura Battiferra (her name, her friendship
with Bronzino, the imputed identity of the profile sitter with the elderly Battiferra in
Allori's painting, the supposed reference to the portrait in the iron-and-ice poem) are
not entirely persuasive. With luck, some day the portrait of Laura Battiferra by
Bronzino that was copied by Hans van Aachen may be located, or firm evidence will
be found in one archive or another that will answer our questions; it would be very

satisfying to find that this impressive painting portrayed Laura Battiferra.[38] For the present, there are too many reasonable doubts, and we believe the painting should be labeled "Laura Battiferra?"

POEMS IN THE ORIGINAL ITALIAN

Francesco
Petrarch[39]

Se voi poteste per turbati segni,
per chinar gli occhi, o per piegar la testa,
o per esser più d'altra al fuggir presta
torcendo 'l viso a' preghi honesti et degni,

uscir già mai, over per altri ingegni,
del petto ove dal primo lauro innesta
Amor più rami, i' direi ben che questa
fosse giusta cagione a' vostri sdegni:

chè gentil pianta in arido terreno
par che si disconvenga, et però lieta
naturalmente quindi si diparte;

ma poi vostro destino a voi pur vieta
l'esser altrove, provedete almeno
di non star sempre in odiosa parte. * (p. 203)

⏺ Track 30,
Reading 31

I' ò pregato Amor, e 'l ne riprego,
che mi scusi appo voi, dolce mia pena,
amaro mio dilecto, se con piena
fede dal dritto mio sentier mi piego.

I' nol posso negar, donna, et nol nego,
che la ragion, ch'ogni bona alma affrena,
non sia dal voler vinta; ond'ei mi mena
talor in parte ov'io forza il sego.

Voi, con quel cor, che di sì chiaro ingegno,
di sì alta vertute il ciel alluma,
quanto mai piovve da benigna stella,

devete dir, pietosa et senza sdegno:
che pò questi altro? Il mio volto il consuma:
ei perché ingordo, et io perché sì bella? † (pp. 203 – 4)

Laura Battiferra ‡

Quando dagl' alti monti umida, e bruna
da noi partendo il sol l'ombra discende

---

* Sonnet 64.   † Sonnet 240.   ‡ All Laura's poems are from *Il primo libro dell'opere toscane* (Florence, 1560) except where noted.

VITORIACOLVMNA

Pl. I. Cristoforo dell'Altissimo.
Portrait of Vittoria Colonna.
16th century. Galleria degli Uffizi, Florence. Photo, Museum.

QVAE SA... ...
CAPVT SALTANDO
OBTINVIT

ABOVE **Pl. II. Alessandro Bonvicino (Moretto da Brescia).**
Tullia d'Aragona (?).
**16th century. Pinacoteca Civica Tosio Martinengo, Brescia. Photo,
Museum.**

OPPOSITE **Pl. III. Alessandro Ardente/ Francesco Cellini.**
Emperor Augustus and the Sibyl.
ca. 1545?-1576. Villa Guinigi, Lucca. Photo, Museum.

ABOVE **Pl. IV. Agnolo Bronzino.**
Portrait of Laura Battiferra [?]
ca. 1547-1553. Palazzo Vecchio, Florence. Photo, Art Resource.

OPPOSITE **Pl. V. Alessandro Allori.**
Christ and the Canaanite Woman.
ca.1585-1590. Church of San Giovannino degli Scolpi, Florence. Photo, Scala/Art Resource.

ABOVE **Pl. VI. Giovanni Battista Moroni.**
Portrait of Isotta Brembate.
ca. 1550. Accademia Carrara, Bergamo. Photo, Museum.

OPPOSITE **Pl. VII. Anon. (Giovan Paolo Lolmo?).**
Portrait of Isotta Brembate, Seated.
ca. 1590? Collection, Counts Moroni, Bergamo. Photo,
Count Antonio Moroni.

Pl. VIII. Jacopo Tintoretto (School of)
Portrait of Veronica Franca. ca. 1575.
Worcester Art Museum, Worcester, Massachusetts. Photo, Museum.

e che l'umane cure ad una ad una
sgombra chi i petti altrui tranquilli rende,
di nojosi pensier morte e fortuna
m'empie, e riposo al cor lasso contende:
onde dentro col cor per gli occhi fuore,
piangendo spendo le mie notti e l'ore.

. . .

   S'io miro, oimè! di fior, di frutti pieno
   di copia il corno, aver le fide amiche
Cerere e Flora l'una carca il seno
di rose, e l'altra di mature spiche,
e il villanel che dal colto terreno
riporta il premio delle sue fatiche,
dico cogli'occhi molli: Or danno e lutto
dunque del mio ben far sempre fia il frutto? * (pp. 205 – 6)

   〜

   Superbi e sacri colli,
sotto il cui glorioso e grande impero
tennero i figli vostri il mondo intero,
così fioriti e molli
vi serbi largo e temperato cielo,
nè vi offenda giammai caldo nè gelo,
e tu, vago, corrente, e chiaro fiume,
che fai più adorna Roma,
così tua verde chioma,
del Sol non secchi il troppo ardente lume;
Fate che mai non sia quel crudo giorno
ch'io lasci il vostro dolce almo soggiorno. † (p. 206)

   〜

   Et io che veggio avvicinar la notte
e volar l'ore e i giorni, gli anni e i lustri,
e già dal quinto indietro mi rivolgo,

   Il passo affretto, e prima che s'annotte,
lo stuol de' pensier miei sparsi raccolgo
per fargli in cielo eternamente illustri. ‡ (p. 206)

   Ecco ch'io da voi, sacre alte ruine,
anzi da me medesma—ahi, crudel fato!—
pur mi diparto: or lassa, in quale stato
il mio grave dolor troverà fine?

---

* *Il Primo Libro*, Stanza, p. 31, lines 1–8, 25–32.

† Jolanda Bergalli, *Antologia della poesia italiana* (Parma, 1954), p. 190.

‡ *Il Primo Libro*, p. 28 ("Quando nell'ocean l'altera fronte"): p. 28, lines 9-14.

O voi, anime sante e pellegrine,
a cui sì largo don dal ciel fu dato,
che in pregio del valor vostro beato
siate or lassuso eterne cittadine,

fate s' umil preghiera è in ciel udita—
mentre lontan su l'Arno in cieco orrore
starà vivo sepolto il mio mortale,

che il mio nome sul Tebro, il mio migliore
ch'or con voi resta, scevro d'ogni male,
*fra i vostri alti tesor rimanga in vita.** (p. 207)

◉ Track 31,
Reading 32

A piè dell'onorate antiche mura
da cui memoria ancora il tempo serba,
lungo il bel monte che verde e superba
alza la fronte sì che il ciel ne fura,

vidi quell'aqua cristallina e pura
che i prati infiora e le campagne inerba,
e ch'a me già nella stagione acerba
empie il petto di dolce onesta cura.

Fiesole mio gentil, Cecero adorno,
roccia serena, ombrosa valle e queta,
perchè non poss'io far teco soggiorno?

Così diss'io, mentre, al più caldo giorno
porsi la bocca disiosa e lieta
più volte al fonte ch'innondava intorno. † (p. 208)

◉ Track ?

Scarca d'ogni pensiero indegno, e vile,
che di salire al ciel la via ne chiude,
lungi dal volgo in soletaria e queta
parte mi vivo, senza invidia o sdegno,
ch'altri habbia e goda, o più grasso o più ricco
gregge del mio, ch'è così magro e povero;
ch'io mi contento, ch'ei sia tal che possa
al mio saggio pastor, più d'altro fido,
a cui santo Himeneo con nodo tale
che sci, no 'l potrà tempo o fortuna
mi legò, corre homai l'undecim' anno.
Et a me sol (quand'io lo mungo, e toso)

---

* *Il Primo Libro*, p. 27.   † *Il Primo Libro*, p. 49.

dar di latte e di lana una tal copia
che basti a discacciar la fame e'l freddo. * (pp. 208 – 9)

~

Di fredda speme e calda tema cinta,
in dubbia pace, e in certa guerra io vivo,
me stessa a morte tolgo, e tolta privo
di vita, a un tempo vincitrice, e vinta.

Or mi fermo, or m'arosso, or risospinta
cammino innanzi, or lento, or fuggitivo
il passo movo; or quanto in carta scrivo
dispergo; or vera mi dimostro, or finta.

Piango e rido; or m'arosso, or mi scoloro;
or vo cara a me stessa, or vile; or giaccio
in Terra, or sovra il Ciel poggiando volo.

Talor quel, ch'io vorrei disvoglio, e scaccio;
me stessa affliggo, e me stessa consolo;
in tale stato ognor vivendo, moro. † (p. 209)

~

Fra queste piagge apriche e chiusi orrori,
presso un bel rio che mormorando stilla,
lungi dal volgo in solitaria villa
compart'io il tempo e i giorni miei migliori;

e più m'aggrada udir ninfe e pastori
quando Apollo da noi lontan sfavilla,
che desti al suon dell'amorosa squilla
van palesando i lor graditi amori;

e Maiano veder con tanti intorno
folti boschi, alti monti, e verdi campi,
e Mensola ch'al par del'Arno corre,

che quante melodie, palazzi ed ampi
tetti rendon Fiorenza e il mondo adorno
ch' invidia e reo destin non mi può torre.. ‡ (p. 211)

~

Ma ch'io sol la sua voce oda, e mi guide   Agnolo Bronzino
lo buon Pittor, che fu dell 'età nostra
specchio e già fermo, e'n doglia mi consume (p. 210)

. . .

---

* *Il Primo Libro*, eclogue, pp. 111–112.   † *Il Primo Libro*, p. 48.
‡ *Il Primo Libro*, p. 34.

Sì dolce udir mi par l'Aura ir destando
le vive gemme, e sì bel raggio intenta * (p. 211)

～

Laura Battiferra

Che forse un dì, se Morte non recide
anzi tempo il mio starne, all'alta chiostra
con voi sarrò fuor d'ogni mio costume. † (p. 211)

～

Agnolo Bronzino
● Track 32,
Reading 33

L'Aura vostr' alma, hor ch'l fier Borea ammorza
alle campagne i più vaghi colori,
e 'l corso impetra a i vivi argenti, e fuori
vedova, e attrista ogni terrena scorza;

Col suo dolce spirar, di nuova forza
par ch'aer muova e nuova terra irrori.
Nuovo ciel n'apra e Piante, acque, herbe, e fiori
ne renda, e tal ch'à rallegrar ne sforza.

Ond' io qual fronda al più nemico verno,
dentro agghiacciato, e fuori, atro, e negletto,
orbo del caro mio buon padre, e duce,

Vigor riprendo, e 'l giel distruggo interno,
de gli honor suoi mi vesto, e 'l suo diletto
seren m'innalza, e scuopre la mia Luce. ‡ (p. 211)

～

Laura Battiferra
● Track 33,
Reading 34

Bronzino, in Ciel l'alma beata luce
quant'altro vago, e luminoso aspetto
atto à produr fra noi più degno effetto
come fu già del Mondo honore, e luce;

Tal che l'erto sentier, ch'à Dio conduce
fuor di questo mortal breve ricetto
mostra si piano al vostr'alto intelletto
ch'vuopo non ha di miglior Guida, o Duce.

Et io, ch'en alto Mar senza governo
quando è più nudo il ciel de'suoi splendori
erro sempre alternando hor Poggia hor Orza,

---

* All Bronzino's poems in this chapter are from *Sonetti di Angiolo Allori, detto Bronzino ed al-*
tre Rime inedite di più insigni poeti (Florence, 1823), except where noted. This poem is from
the sonnet beginning "Mentre Sepolto. . .," p. 59, ll. 12–14.
† *Il Primo Libro* ("Se fermo è nel destin, che lacrimando"), 12–14.
‡ *Il Primo Libro*, p. 71.

Già fatta Preda al gran Nettuno, e scherno,
scorgo non lunge i suoi lucenti albori,
si, che la stanca Nave si rinforza.* (p. 212)

~

Io giuro à voi che quella viva fronde
di cui voi fuste al sacro fonte Pianta,
e per quella di lui, cortese, e santa
fiamma, che regge il Ciel, la terra, e l'onde,

Ch'alla sua felice ombra in sì gioconde
note, ho veduto tal, c'honesta canta
ch'io tegno à vile homai qual più si vanta,
e dolcezza maggior non viemmi altronde.

Che se le fortunate Oretta, e Bice
honora il Mondo, all'altrui senno, ed' opra
si dee non men ch'a i lor merti dar vanto.

Voi per proprio valor Laura e Beatrice
vincete, e siete ai lor pregi di sopra,
e forse ai loro amanti in stile, e canto. † (p. 212)

~

Si come al fonte hebb'io larghe, e feconde
le stelle à impormi il nome, havess'io tanta
grazia dar lor pur'anco havuta quanta
a voi novello Apelle Apollo infonde;

Ch'oggi le vostre altere rime donde
verace Amor di falso velo ammanta
il vero, à me con gran ragion cotanta
lode darian, ch'a lor sol corrisponde,

E forse delle due non men felice
sarei, che stanno à tutte l'altre sopra
co' lor casti Amator per sempre à canto,

Ma poi che'n questa etate à voi sol lice
dar doppia vita altrui, perchè non s'opra
per voi si, ch'io con voi viva altrettanto? ‡ (pp. 212 – 13)

~

Così nel volto rilucente, e vago
la Pastorella tua, chiaro Crisero,

Agnolo Bronzino
◉ Track 34,
Reading 35

Laura Battiferra
◉ Track 35,
Reading 36

---

* *Il Primo Libro*, page 71.   † Bronzino, *Sonetti*, p. 45; also in *Primo libro*, p. 82. See Laura's response immediately below, with matching rhyme endings.   ‡ *Il Primo Libro*, page 82.

quanto brama il tuo cor casto, e sincero,
ti mostri aperto, e sii contento, e pago,

Come la propria mia novella imago
della tua dotta man lavoro altero,
ogni mio affetto scuopre, ogni pensiero,
quantunque il cor sia di celarlo vago.

~

E così l'Arboscel, ch'ami cotanto,
degno rival d'Apollo, in fino al cielo
colto da te, mai sempre verde, s'erga,

Com'io, la tua mercè, di doppio vanto
cingo il mio basso oscuro umile stelo,
perch'Austro, od Aquilon non lo disperga. * (pp. 213– 14)

~

Agnolo Bronzino   *Dafne, oppur chiara Dafne, ove t'ascondi,*
e dov'io più ti credo ivi più falle?
nè per monte cercar, campagna, o valle
veggio i begli occhi, e i capei crespi e biondi. † (pp. 214 – 15)

~

Dunque non son però da cieco oblìo
spenti, o Ninfa gentil, quei giochi onesti,
ch'io di te vago, e tu di me prendesti
mentre tu acerba, e non maturo er'io?

Quanti dolci pensier, quanto desìo,
tolti ne fur poi, che nel sen giacesti
di Batto oimè, da che più non potesti
salire al poggio, o scender meco al rio!

Ben ti giur'io, che in quanti lochi, e modi
piacer prendemmo, e puri, e casti, vive
memoria in me, che non morrà giammai;

E poi, che tu de'dolci onesti nodi
hai rimembranza, in cor par, che m'arrive
diletto, ahimè, che mi raddoppia i guai. ‡ (p. 215)

Nè so per quanto, ma tem'io, che'l ghiaccio,
che la circonda, e 'l ferro ond' ha radice,
la faccia scarsa ancor de'suoi bei rami. § (p. 218)

~

---

* Bronzino, *Sonetti*, p. 6.   † Bronzino, *Sonetti*, p. 103, ll. 1–4.   ‡ Bronzino, *Sonetti*, p. 107.
§ Bronzino, *Sonetti*, ("Vano è certo il desir, e la speme, onde"), p. 121 : 9–11

Steril arbor son io, rozzo e selvaggio *Laura Battiferra*
ch'al mio sì buon cultor, che tanto ognora
m'orna, e m'abbella, non produssi ancora
frutti nel Autunno, o fiori al Maggio * (pp. 218 – 19)

⁓

mia Donna, Angelo il volto, alma celeste *Agnolo Bronzino*
ebbe, e di ferro il cor, di ghiaccio il lato?

Nè ti vantar poi, che le Stelle hai preste
contra me teco, e lei, ch'assai più vale,
ch'io non son da te solo arso, e piagato. † pp. 219 – 20)

⁓

Folle garzon . . .
Freddo è 'l tuo foco, ottuse l'armi . . .
Nel vivo ferro, e vivo ghiaccio, il vero
ti scuopre vinto. . . . ‡ (p. 220)

⁓

tutto dentro et di for sento cangiarme, *Francesco Petrarch*
et ghiaccio farme, così freddo torno . . . §

⁓

Tutta dentro di ferro, e fuor di ghiaccio, *Agnolo Bronzino*
con lenta mano, e con già spento foco, ◉ Track 36,
e'n dura scorza alma rinchiusa, in roco Reading 37
suon chiamo, scaldo, e mansueta faccio;

E poter più del Ciel giugnere al laccio
il Sol tento, e tant'alto il pensier loco
ch'ogni volo, ogni ardir sarebbe poco,
tardo, e senz'ali, e zoppo l'aura caccio;

Tua colpa, e danno mio, folle desire,
che di lei qual di me, falsa credenza,
far promettesti, e 'n che ponemmo speme?

Or disarmato, e vinto meco, e senza
alcun contrasto, converrà servire
fuor di mercede, ove scampar si teme. || (p. 220)

⁓

Angelo esser devea, se non che 'nvano
era ogni sua fatica, ogni opra, ogni arte; *Anton Francesco*
Grazzini (Il Lasca)

* *Il Primo Libro*, p. 19, ll. 1–4.
† Bronzino, *Sonetti*, ("Amor senza fatal possente aita"), p. 120: 10–14.
‡ Bronzino, *Sonetti* ("Folle garzon, che vanamente imperi"): p. 120, ll. 5, 7–8.
§ Stanza 135, ll. 59–60. || Bronzino, *Sonetti*, p. 121.

non può cosa divina in nulla parte
esser ritratta mai da mortal mano.

Dunque voi, spirto angelico, e sovrano,
potete sol pingendo a parte a parte
ritrar le Grazie in lei diffuse, e sparte,
ove ogni altro pennel sarebbe vano:

come gli occhi sereni, e 'l santo viso,
occhio terren saria stato possente
poter mai rimirare, intento, e fiso?

Beato voi, cui solo il Ciel consente
il senno, e la beltà di Paradiso
far conta, e chiara alla futura gente. (p. 221)

Agnolo Bronzino

L'Aura, che dolcemente al verde alloro
move l'altere, e sì benigne fronde
l'aere percote in me con sì dolci onde,
che fora ad ogni affanno ampio ristoro.
E voi nuovo arboscel, ch'avete d'oro
la chioma, e sì bei fior par, che v'abbonde,
a sol mirarvi Amor dolcezza infonde
nel mio cor tal, ch'io ne languisco, e moro. † (p. 222)

---

* Edi Baccheschi, *L'opera completa del Bronzino* (Milan, 1973), p. 11.
† Bronzino, *Sonetti*, p. 107.

NOTES

1   We follow Victoria Kirkham in spelling the poet's name ending with "a" instead of "i," as it was generally spelled before her article in "Dante's Phantom, Petrarch's Spectre: Bronzino's Portrait of the Poet Laura Battiferra," *Lectura Dantis* 2–23 (Spring–Fall 1998): 63–139. Laura, she points out, signed her full name Laura Battiferra degli Ammannati (pp. 63–64). Luisa Bergalli, ed., *Componimenti della più illustri rimatrici di ogni secolo* (Venice, 1726), pp. 189–204, also used the "a" ending.

2   The English renderings here are from Petrarch, *The Canzoniere* (translated with notes and commentary by Mark Musa, Indiana University Press, 1996). In sonnet 64, however, we have altered Musa's translation of *"pieghar la testa"* in line 2 from "turning the head" to the more literal "bending the head."

3   John Pope-Hennesy, in *The Portrait in the Renaissance* (New York, 1988), p. 244, incorrectly gives numbers 49 and 182 for the sonnets, noting correctly, however, that they could not be on contiguous pages. The sonnets have been in unbroken numerical order since the sixteenth century.

4   See the *Dizionario Enciclopedico dei Pittori e degli incisori Italiani dall' XI al XX secolo* (Turin, 1972), vol. II, p. 305. We accept, with some reservations, the attribution of the painting to Bronzino, although not on the basis of the signature which was discovered some forty years ago when it was cleaned by the museum conservators. It seems possible that this painting is a copy of an original by Bronzino: the placement of the right shoulder appears faulty. However, this may be a consequence of paint loss and faulty repainting at some time during the portrait's career. Jonathan Nelson, in "Dante Portraits in Sixteenth-Century Florence," *Gazette des Beaux-Arts* (September 1992): 59–77, considers that the attribution to Bronzino of the "Allegorical Portrait of Dante" in the Washington National Gallery is problematic because it reveals artistic weaknesses similar to those we see in the profile portrait identified as Laura Battiferra, weaknesses that point to "a less-skilled artist."

5   Bibliography on this painting includes references to it in a number of books and articles, such as *Il Petrarca* (Venice, 1805), vol. 2; *Die Gemaldesammlung in der Kaiserlichen Ermitage zu St. Petersburg nebst Bermerkungen uber andere dortie Kunstsammlungen* (Berlin, 1864), p. 371; Albertina Furno, *La vita e rime di Angiolo Bronzino* (Pistoia, 1902); A. Néoustroieff, *L'Arte* 6 (1903): 330–332; Arthur McComb, *Agnolo Bronzino: His Life and Works* (Cambridge, 1928), pp. 66–67; Edi Baccheschi, *L'opera completa del Bronzino* (Milan, 1973); Luisa Becherucci, *Manieristi Toscani* (Bergamo, 1944); and Charles Mc-Corquodale, *Bronzino* (New York, 1981). For recent bibliography, see Kirkham, "Dante's Phantom," and others in note 8.

6   Mario Tinti, "Agnolo Bronzino pittore 'platonico'?" *Dedalo* I (September 1920): 247. Although Tinti does not suggest it, it has occurred to some readers that the word *ferro* suggests a reference to Batti*ferra*. While this could be significant, the connection between the poem and the portrait seems too facile. As Arnold Hauser remarks, "In [Bronzino's] art, it is very evident that physiognomy becomes not only a mirror, but also a mask of the personality . . . a figurative form that both reveals and hides the character" (Baccheschi, *Opera completa*, p. 14).

The hidden iconography of this painting has never before been detected. As previously pointed out, making puns was a very popular amusement in in *cinquecento*. The double meaning of many words in poetry of this period is often sexual. According to a list of love positions made by Aretino, the word "profile" alluded to position 31, as revealed in the *Dizionario letterario del lessico amoroso: Metafore, Eufemismi, Trivalismi* (Literary Dictionary of amorous words), Walter Boggione and Giovanni Casalegno (Turin, 2000); an open book showing two pages refers to "woman," the pages alluding to the cheeks of the buttocks; "lauro" refers to the anus, and the metaphor compares a plant that does not bear fruit (male) in contrast with the female. See here also, the portrait of Dante (fig. 7:5), p. 224. In addition to the profile portrait, the poems between Laura Battiferra and Bronzino, and, indeed, much of the poetry in this book, should be read and checked with this *Dizionario*.

7   McComb, *Agnolo Bronzino*, pp. 66–67. Neither Tinti nor McComb mentions that Bronzino's first line echoes Petrarch's poem 135, lines 59–60. Note that Bronzino changed *"tutto"* (masculine) to *"tutta"* (feminine).

8   See Sylvia Ferino-Pagden, ed., *Dichterin und Muse Michelangelos* (Vienna, 1997), pp. 219–220; Carol Plazzotta, "Bronzino's Laura," *Burlington Magazine* 141 (April 1998): 251–263; and Kirkham, "Dante's

Phantom." I wish to acknowledge the kind courtesy of Professor Kirkham in replying to a letter in which I brought up the questions discussed herein. She acknowledges that there is no documentary evidence that the profile portrait is a likeness of Battiferra; she does not share our doubts, however.

9   Laura Battiferra, *Il primo libro dell'opere toscane* (Florence, 1560). All Battiferria poems are from *Il Primo Libro* except where noted.

10   For identification of the men represented in the tondo, see W. Chandler Kirwin, "Vasari's Tondo of Cosimo I with his Architects, Engineers, and Sculptors," *Mitteilungen des Kunsthistorischen Institutes in Florenz* XV (1971): 105–122.

11   Cellini's sonnet (the first line of which is "Con soave canto, e dolce legno") is included in Battiferra, *Libro*, p. 75.

12   Laura Battiferra, *Lettere a Benedetto Varchi* (Bologna, 1879), letter VI, p. 28: "M. Bartolomeo sta benissimo . . . come anco io, in questa sì bella e piacevol villa. Egli se ne vien, quando ogni sera e quando in terza, e ci diamo cento piaceri, ora con l'andar veggendo questi bei luoghi e abitazioni, e ora in veder ballare queste contadine; di modo che, se ben presto tornar in Fiorenza per questo San Giovanni, voglio ritornarmene a star qui qualche giorno di più."

13   It should be noted that Bronzino was expelled from the Academy in 1547. Readmitted 1566.

14   McCorquodale, *Bronzino,* p. 139.

15   For a useful and succinct discussion of the affects created by the combination of Platonic philosophy and Petrarch's *Canzoniere,* see Fortunato Rizzi, *L'anima del cinquecento e la lirica volgare* (Milan, 1928), especially chapter III, "La Vita del Petrarchismo."

16   By direct response we mean a poem written in response to one received, in which the rhyme endings in Italian match the received poem line for line as previously explained in chapter 2 note 15; see also such epistolary exchanges between Tulla and Muzio, chapter 3.

17   Line 12 of this sonnet possibly throws light on an intriguing passage in the autobiography of Cellini, Laura's sometimes friend. The sculptor had been commissioned by the duchess, Eleonora da Toledo, wife of Cosimo I, to make a giant statue representing Neptune, and had been given a great slab of marble for it. It was a major commission, and all Florence knew Cellini was working on a huge model in wood and clay during 1556–57. He became ill, however, and, the duchess decided to give the commission to Ammannati, according to the manuscript of Cellini's autobiography, "who then sent a Mister . . . to tell me that I could do what I liked with the model I had begun . . . for he, Ammannati, had won the marble. This Mister . . . was one of the lovers of the wife of the said Bartolomeo Ammannato: and because he was the most favored, since he was polite and discreet, this said Ammannato gave him every opportunity." In this passage in the manuscript as described by Robert H. Hobart Cust, ed., *The Life of Benvenuto Cellini* (London, 1910), p. 421, n. 1, there are complete and destructive erasures where the name following "Mister" is deleted, even so far as to destroy the very paper itself. We have translated the direct quotation from Guido Bonino, ed., *Benvenuto Cellini, La Vita* (Turin, 1973), p. 483. We tend to believe that line 12 suggests that Cellini himself was giving Laura his unwelcome attention and that his gossiping remark about her "lovers" was provoked by her rejection of him, and by his personal and professional envy of Ammannati. In an apparently laudatory sonnet to Ammannati, Cellini addresses him: "Bartolomeo . . . a voi'l divin sculpire, e quanto vale / sento eccelenzia in vostra onesta moglie / che portando passa le gran soglie / qual mai fè donna, o qual degn'uom mortale." Guido Ferrero, the editor of *Opere di Benvenuto Cellini* (Milan, 1959), notes (p. 896) that this poem might be meant ironically, inasmuch as, given Cellini's temperament, he was capable of praising Ammannati publicly while insulting him privately.

18   According to Giulio Negri, S.J., *Istoria degli scrittori fiorentini* (Ferrara, 1722), Laura's full name was Maddalena Laura Battiferri. We have not been able to confirm this, but if true it is interesting inasmuch as it shows that she chose to be known by her poetically laden name.

19   Varchi called Bronzino "great Apelle and not second to Apollo" (Benedetto Varchi, *Sonetti Spirituale* [Florence, 1573], p. 992, sonnet 89), and "the new Apelle and new Apollo" (Domenico Moreni, ed. *Sonetti di Angiolo Allori detto il Bronzino ed altre rime inedite di più insigni poete* [Florence, 1823], p. 122).

20   Battiferra, *Libro,* in the dedication of her volume to Eleonora da Toledo. Ammannati sent a copy of her book to Michelangelo, so he was obviously proud of it. See Kirkham, "Dante's Phantom," p. 79.

21   *Sonetti di Angiolo Allori, detto Bronzino ed altre Rime inedite di più insigni poeti* (Florence, 1823) (hereinafter Bronzino, *Sonetti*). Moreni also published a collection of poems by Bronzino in other than sonnet form in a separate volume, in 1822. The codex number for the Bronzino collection is II. IX. 10. All following quotations from Bronzino's poems herein are from this volume except where noted.

22   According to the *Enciclopedia italiana* (Milan/Rome, 1931), vol. XI, p. 912, excavations in Rome in 1886 brought to light a figural sculpture group with three signatures on the base, presumably the names of the sculptors, one of which is "Crisero." The style is second century A.D. Bronzino was, of course, a painter, so it is curious, if this name were known to Italians in the sixteenth century, that Laura calls him "Crisero," and interesting that Varchi likewise addressed him in a poem quoted in Bronzino's collection of poems. See Moreni, *Sonetti*, p. 4. Kirkham suggests several possibilities to explain this nickname, the most interesting and possible connecting it to the Greek word for gold, *chrysos*, meaning that Bronzino was somehow associated with something gold: his copper-colored hair, perhaps, or his "golden words." It seems likely that this was the name he chose as his academic name.

23   In our correspondence with her, Victoria Kirkham agreed that the portrait by Bronzino representing Laura as a shepherdess cannot be the profile painting here under discussion.

24   In the poem beginning, "Altera fronda. Che dal quarto Ciel," he writes, "Invidia, e gelosia m'arde" (I burn with envy and jealousy; line 5), "fors' or v'innamora" (perhaps now he loves you; line 7), "ma sì poco regna / in lui fede d'amor, ch'io più vi lodo / se la fuggite" (but faithful love means so little to him that I would praise you more if you fled from him; lines 12–14).

25   Luisa Becherucci, *Manieristi Toscani*, pp. 50–51. If the painting does represent Laura, a date "in the sixties" would make her more than thirty-seven years old. Judging from the appearance of the woman (a subjective judgment in any case), she seems to be quite young, in her twenties. This would date the painting to 1547–1553.

26   Carol Plazzotta, "Bronzino's Laura," p. 253, quotes from Filippo Baldinucci's *Notizie de' professori del disegno da Cimabue in quà* (1681), and p. 254, Karel van Mander's *Schilderboeck* (1604), where the authors refer to the woman as Laura Battiferra.

27   *The Jerusalem Bible: Reader's Edition* (New York, 1966). For the ancient Hebrews, "dog" was a symbol for nonbelievers. See M. J. La Grange, *Sintossi dei quattro evangeli* (Brescia, 1948), p. 55. The woman's persistence showed her faith; her answer makes the story especially appropriate for a Jesuit-inspired painting inasmuch as it underlines the relatively new practice, developed by the Jesuits, of traveling to faraway places to bring the Gospel to the "pagans." We wish to thank Patrick A. Heelan, S.J., professor of philosophy at Georgetown University, who read this chapter and agrees with our interpretation of Allori's painting with reference to the Jesuits.

28   Giovannoni Simona Lecchini, ed., *Mostra di disegni di Alessandro Allori* (Florence, 1970), p. 272.

29   Ambrogio Lorenzetti, *Annunciation*, 1344, Pinacoteca, Siena; Botticelli, *Madonna of the Magnificat*, ca. 1485, Uffizi, Florence. We want to thank Professor Yvonne Korshak for bringing our attention to the Botticelli as particularly suggestive of Bronzino's profile portrait.

30   Moreni, *Sonetti*, p. 19. The context makes it clear that she was not referring to being childless.

31   Arnold Hauser, *The Social History of Art* (New York, 1957), vol. 2, p. 136.

32   According to Kirkham, Bronzino is said to have been homosexual.

33   The *Grande Dizionario della Lingua Italiana* (Torino, 1984), vol. XII, p. 652, defines *A parte a parte, a parte per parte, di parte in parte, parte per parte* as acting analytically, very accurately, with extreme attention and precision, point by point, minutely, precisely: "Con procedimento analitico molto accurato, con estrema attenzione e precisione, punto per punto, per filo e per segno." In Petrarch we find two instances of *a parte a parte:* in sonnet 151, line 13, which Robert Durling translates as "bit by bit," and in the sestina, line16, as "place to place." In both instances the context suggests parts adding up to a whole. In *Del Secondo Libro delle Rime Di M. Diomede Borghese Gentil'Huomo Senese* (Padua, 1567), p. 26, line 1, stanza 2, begins "Musa Mia, s'io volessi à parte à parte / l'allegrezza commun chiudere in versi" (If I were to try to enclose in verses one by one the common happiness): the phrase is rendered "one by one" again as if to achieve a wholeness.

34   Kirkham published an article on Laura's autograph manuscript in *Rinascimento*, "Laura Battiferra degli Ammanati" (vol. 36 [1996]: 351–391). Plazzotta, "Bronzino's Laura," p. 256, n. 38 writes, "The hand is certainly not that of Battiferri. . . . It is most like Bronzino's own italic script."

35   See note 4.

36   See Jonathan Nelson and Fern Rusk Shapley, *Catalogue of the Italian Paintings, National Gallery of Art,* vol. I, p. 514. The most extended discussion of the Dante connection with the supposed Battiferra portrait is in Kirkham, "Dante's Phantom." See also Camille Shenouda, "The Portrait of Laura Battiferri" (M.A thesis, George Washington University, 2000).

37   This is not to say that *all* women poets are pictured with a laurel symbol, as can be seen in some of our illustrations. Bronzino, however, constantly associates the laurel with Battiferra in his poems, and we therefore believe he would have included the symbol in this profile portrait, as he did indeed in the portrait he made of Laura as a shepherdess. For Gaspara Stampa's portrait see chapter 8, figure 8.1; for Tullia, see plate II.

38   Baldinucci, *Notizie dei professori del disegno,* vol. III, p. 339, mentions that Hans van Aachen made a portrait of Battiferra in Florence. Karl van Mander also refers to a portrait of Battiferra by van Aachen. According to Saur's *Allgemeines Kunstler Lexicon,* the portrait was known in the twentieth century to be in the Schloss Werenwag (Werenwag Castle), which we traced to Beuron-Hausen im Tal with the help of the German consulate in New York, help that we acknowledge with many thanks. Information from the castle indicates that the paintings in the castle were dispersed at some unknown time. The location of van Aachen's painting is thus now unknown—unfortunately, inasmuch as it might very well clear up the mystery of the profile portrait if it were found.

39   Petrarch, *Canzoniere* (Torino, 1992).

CHAPTER EIGHT

GASPARA STAMPA
(CA. 1523 – 1554)
 ### IN LOVE WITH LOVE

> For the sake of love I live in flames
> like some kind of salamander or
> other strange creature
> that lives and breathes in fire.
>
> My delight, my desire
> is to live ablaze yet not feel the pain,
> not caring whether he who set me afire
> pities me or not.
>
> Hardly had my first love died
> when Love's torch began again to burn in me
> more intense than ever.
>
> And I do not regret my ardent passion
> as long as he who has taken my heart from me
> is happy and content with my love.[1] (p. 265)

his "passionate affirmation" of love is Gaspara Stampa's most famous sonnet; it was quoted by Gabriele D'Annunzio in his novel *Il
Fuoco* and has provided verses for a number of musical compositions, including Gilberto Bosco's *Dedica* for soprano, flute, clarinet,
and horn (1982).[2]

Her relationships with a number of men led Abdelkader Salza to believe that Gaspara (or Gasparina, as she was usually called) was a courtesan. His article *Madonna
Gasparina Stampa secondo nuove indagini* (New research on Miss Gasparina Stampa)
triggered a polemic that filled hundreds of pages of Italian literary journals for several years.[3] Salza cites as evidence a long letter from a nun, Sister Angela Paolo, who at
the time that Gaspara was grieving over the death of her brother pleaded with Gaspara to give up her style of life with its meaningless pleasures and turn to religion for
consolation. There is nothing in the letter, however, to suggest that Gaspara was sexually promiscuous; for the nun, any activity not devoted to Christ was vain. Further,
as a late Victorian, Salza believed that no man would presume to send a respectable
woman the kind of literary material she received from her contemporaries such as
Francesco Sansovino, whose *Ragionamento* (1545), an essay on the art of love, he considered salacious: Pretending, Salza believed, to warn Gaspara and her sister about
men who would try to fool them in order to win their "love," his dialogue actually

presents two speakers who talk suggestively about "the kisses, the laughter, the words, the playful games, the embraces of those who have tasted the fruit of that desire that we call love," and reveal their concept of a woman "born only for our pleasure . . . a pleasing animal."[4] He goes on to list the large number of men documented as Gaspara's friends, some of whom, according to Salza, were womanizers, and frequented women of "easy virtue," and he quotes Sperone Speroni, who is said to have made a vulgar joking rhyme to a friend about Gaspara and her sister Cassandra, asking, first,

> Tell me, who is more divine
> Cassandra or Gasparina?

then altering the question, asking,

> Tell me, who is the easiest lay
> Gasparina or Cassandra?[5] (p. 265)

Salza cites in support of his argument a scurrilous "epitaph," one of twenty-one written by an unidentified author.

> Stop, passerby, if you wish to know
> the end of my wretched life;
> I was Gaspara Stampa, woman and queen
> of how many whores among you.

> Gritti had me first, as a virgin, and since then
> I have ruined thousands of cocks;
> I lived by cheating and robbing
> I was killed by violent fucking.

> I ruled paper that I filled with love letters
> that I copied from others
> and the verses written for me
> by Fortunio * appeared to be my own

> Go in peace, and to soothe my terrible pain,
> screw me with your strong pecker
> which was the only thing in my life that pleased me. (pp. 265 – 66)

The poem reeks of hatred and suggests the bitterness of a rejected would-be lover such as a certain Orazio Brunetti, who was angered because he came repeatedly to her door but was refused.

As Eugenio Donadoni and others show, Salza's evidence overlooked the mores of

---

* This was either Gianfrancesco Fortunio (according to Salza) or Fortunio Spira (according to Donadoni), who helped her learn to write poetry.

the circle of intellectuals and writers among whom Gaspara lived. Unconventional, indifferent to the manners and morals of Venetian society, they congregated among themselves, self-consciously elite, sophisticated, engaged in the kind of literary issues, witty gossip, extravagant praise that lorded over professional jealousies, and casual sex that seems always and everywhere to have been characteristic of such groups. Donadoni thought of them as "irregulars" and recognized Gaspara as such a one. Although she perhaps entered freely into love affairs, not even Salza claims that she was ever paid for a sexual relationship as a courtesan would be; she certainly did not comport herself as Tullia d'Aragona did, wearing high-fashion clothes and precious jewelry. Laura Terracina, we remember, also had many men friends among the intellectual community where she lived, but she advertised her chastity, and in her poetry she insisted on her conventional respectability.

Authentic information about Gaspara's life is limited to a few contemporary documents and what can be gleaned from her poetry. Her date of birth (put between 1523 and 1525) is only a conjecture based on circumstances, but that Padua was her birthplace is known from one of her sonnets, where she writes,

> You went, my lord, without me
> where the great Trojan stopped with his wandering bands,*
> where I was born, where I first saw the light of day,
> a place so charming I would never desire to be elsewhere.

> You will see lively fiestas
> lovely young women and merry lovers
> and many who come to honor
> the saint most beloved of God. †

> And I, remaining here on the Adriatic shore,
> follow you to my birthplace,
> not held back in my thoughts,

> But I cannot go with you for my lord
> does not permit it, and since it is he who sets me on fire
> Love forbids me freely to come and go. (p. 266)

Gaspara's father, Bartolomeo Stampa, was a successful jewelry and gold merchant. Whether or not he was related to a minor branch of a noble Milanese family, as some writers believe, he apparently had an aristocratic taste for humanist learning. He not only provided a comfortable living for his wife, Cecilia, and three children, Cassandra, Baldassare, and Gaspara, but he also arranged for the children's private education

---

* Although the man to whom this poem is addressed has not been identified, we hazard the guess that it was Sperone Speroni, who was also born in Padua. Gaspara addressed a poem to him (CCLIII) in which she writes of following him as a poet and also associates him with Antenor, the "Trojan" who led his followers to Padua after the fall of Troy.

† Padua honors the feast day of Saint Anthony, the patron of the city.

along the lines established by Vittorino da Feltre. They learned some Latin and read the classical philosophers and poets and the canonical writers of Italian vernacular literature, and thus made familiar with the high style of the great literary tradition, they learned to speak and write well. Baldassare showed early promise as an accomplished poet, unfulfilled because of his early death, probably not much more than twenty years old. Of paramount importance in their training was music, and both Cassandra and Gaspara sang well, although by all accounts, it was Gaspara who had the more beautiful voice and deeper understanding of music: Her teacher, Perissone Cambio (Pierre de La Rue), himself a much admired vocalist and composer, dedicated to her a collection of his madrigals in which he wrote that everyone agreed that "no other woman in the world loves music as you do nor is there one who understands it better."[6]

Bartolomeo died around 1530, and Cecilia moved with her children to Venice. By 1545, when Sansovino sent Gaspara his *Ragionamento*, the Stampa home had become one of the salons where the intellectuals of the city gathered informally to enjoy their sophisticated conversations on their favorite subjects—not politics or war, apparently, which absorb the intellectuals of our own time, but literature or personal matters such as love, honor, and virtue, as reflected in Castiglione's *The Courtier* and the many "Dialogues" that followed. They were drawn there also by the charm of the two sisters and their singing, and they wrote poems and letters praising them. We may take as typical Girolamo Parabosco, an organist at St. Mark's basilica, whom Salsa describes as "carefree," an "interesting writer," a young man "inclined to pleasure and liberal manners . . . passing from one love affair to another." Parabosco avowed in a sonnet to Gaspara that she was "Venus herself, the beauteous mother of us all," and in a letter swore with Petrarch's familiar image that he had never before felt himself "burning and freezing at one and the same moment." "Believe me," he wrote, "I never believed that the Siren's song could have had the power to draw her listeners out of themselves." Gaspara certainly flirted with him, for, looking into her eyes he was overwhelmed with emotion and would have called for help, he assured her, had her sweet glance not come to his aid: "Oh, my lady, beloved and favored by the stars above, this is the fire that will never cool, thanks to your great virtue. Who ever saw elsewhere such beauty, such grace, such sweetness of manner? Who has ever listened to such soft, sweet words? Who has ever heard more noble thoughts? What can I say of that angelic voice that fills the air with its divine sound that, unlike the Siren, floods the spirit and life of those who hear, bringing them to tears."[7]

Parabosco's extravagant adulation was not unusual in the sixteenth century, as we have seen; it can be understood as an aspect of the Mannerist taste for exaggeration and artifice, for style above content, and offers insight into how to read Gaspara Stampa's *Canzoniere*. Much has been made of her great love for Collaltino di Collalto, which, however romanticized during the nineteenth century and then demythicized by Salza, has been widely taken for the driving force of her passionate verse and the content that structured her *Canzoniere*. But this interpretation takes the work as a kind of diary—indeed, Benedetto Croce calls it nothing more than a body of correspondence and a diary recording the great love of her life,[8] as if Gaspara's poems described faithfully as they occurred the events and her emotions centered on Collaltino. Flora

Bassanese has provided the necessary corrective to this view in her *Gaspara Stampa*, published in 1982 and still the most complete and authoritative account of Stampa's life and art. As she observes, Stampa's *Canzoniere* is a literary work in the tradition of Love as the inspiration of art, carefully crafted, and not at all a spontaneous outpouring of raw emotion.[9] Facts, like driftwood, change their character and become art when placed in an artistic context. Stampa's studied reading of Petrarch is evident in the theme, the technique and the vocabulary of her poems.

Petrarch's influence has been noted by Bassanese and most writers on Gaspara, although little attention has been given to the way that she uses his very words but profoundly changes their meaning. We will offer one highly important example, the opening stanzas in her *Canzoniere*. It has often been shown to echo Petrarch's opening in his, but comparison reveals not only Stampa's debt but her very different intentions. Stampa writes, *"Voi, ch'ascoltate in queste meste rime . . . il suon degli amorosi lamenti,"*

> *Hear, all of you, in these sad verses*
> *in these sad, dark tones,*
> *the sound of my amorous laments*
> *the pain I feel, sharper than any others,*

> *Where there is one among well-born people*
> *who appreciates and esteems courage*
> *I hope to find not only pardon*
> *but glory for my laments, for their cause is so sublime.*

Stampa thus announces at the very beginning her large ambition, the motivation for her *Canzoniere*: she is reaching for fame, "glory." The "sublime cause" for which she has suffered and deserves glory is not the man who is her ostensible subject—as it is usually taken to be—but poetry, which gives voice to the most noble of human thoughts and feelings. With this interpretation, we shift the meaning of her poems from an emphasis on the love story of a woman to her fundamental ambition to attain the immortality of the poet. In the final six lines of this opening sonnet she writes,

> *And hope also that some woman might say*
> *"Happy is she who has endured*
> *such blessed injury for such a noble cause."*

> *Oh why has not such love*
> *from a noble lord been my good fortune*
> *so that I could be like that happy woman?* (p. 266)

In this, her first poem in the *Canzoniere*, she has not yet met the man who will inspire her muse, but the question suggests that she will. And she did, as we will presently read in her second sonnet.

Comparing her opening with Petrarch's, we can find many of the identical words:

> *You who hear in these verses the varied sound*
> *of the sighs that nourish my heart*
> . . .
> *where there is one who from experience understands love*
> *I hope to find not only pardon but compassion.*

Without a comma after *voi* (you), however, the line must be translated quite differently, with the verb *ascoltare* (to hear or to listen) not imperative, as in Stampa, but discursive, and Petrarch's hope is directed to compassion, not fame. The difference in their stated ambitions underlies the entire two *Canzonieri*. Petrarch hoped to ascend from earthly to divine love; he regretted the pleasure fame had given him, as his opening poem continues,

> *For I well see how*
> *for a long time I was on every tongue*
> *for which now often I feel ashamed*
>
> *For my pride, shame is the fruit*
> *and remorse, and the clear understanding*
> *that pleasure in the world is a brief dream.* (pp. 266 – 67)

Gaspara never attained that state of renunciation. She remained, despite a few addresses to God and the Virgin, a woman yearning for love and glory, as she proclaims from the first. Love was her inspiration but fame was her motivation for writing.

In a sense, although she doubtless loved him passionately, Gaspara invented Collaltino and, as Anassilla, invented herself.[10] We see this woman as a poet in need of an epic.[11] War and great adventures were beyond her ken, but a grand passion could also have epic dimensions if the protagonists were heroic, the beloved gloriously worthy of all sacrifice, a conflict arose of titanic proportions, and the lover were superbly faithful. And so Gaspara, dramatically reversing the customary gender roles, made herself the suitor and transformed her beloved Collaltino from the charming, handsome young nobleman that he probably was, to the perfect beloved knight, unmatched and unmatchable in all the arts and skills of war and peace.

> *Would you, ladies, wish to know something of my lord,*
> *picture a handsome, refined gentleman,*
> *young in years but mature in intellect,*
> *the very image of martial glory and courage?*
>
> *Picture blond hair, a ruddy complexion,*
> *a tall man, broad-chested,*
> *all in all perfect in everything he does.* (p. 267)

Perfect, that is, except for a grievous flaw, as she tells us in the fourth line of this quatrain: "except, alas, that he is cruel in love." As with legendary great figures in history, the cosmos itself was involved in his conception (p. 267).

When my lord was conceived,
all the planets, all the stars in the sky
gave him their favors, bestowed their gifts
so that he alone among us might be perfect.

Saturn gave him superb intellect,
Jupiter the taste for everything beautiful and worthwhile,
Mars made other men seem weak by comparison with him,
Phoebus filled his heart with style and wisdom,

Venus gave him beauty and grace,
Mercury, eloquence,

but, Gaspara confesses,

the pale Moon
made his heart colder than my warm desire . . . . (p. 267)

Even the day she met him, possibly at one of the literary gatherings in the salon of Domenico Venier, the "dean" of Venetian intellectuals at the time, even the day itself was charged with epic significance, for it was near Christmas.*

It was near the day when the Creator,
who could have remained in the highest realm
came in human form to reveal himself
born from the virginal womb,

When my illustrious lord
for whom I have so often sighed in verse
came to nestle in my welcoming heart
though he could have found a higher place to nest.

This rare and most fortunate chance
I happily embraced, regretting only that fortune
delayed so long in making me worthy of her kindness.

From that day to this, long as the sun may shine,
my every glance, my every thought and hope turns on him
who is brilliant and cultured beyond measure. (pp. 267 – 68)

And so begins Gaspara's *Canzoniere*, the collection of lyric poems that she hoped might bring her everlasting fame in the pantheon of literary heroes. Most of these

---

* Gaspara is reminding the reader that Petrarch recorded seeing Laura for the first time on the day of Easter: "It was the day when the sun was darkened by grief for the Creator" (3:1).

verses relate to her love affair with Collaltino, presented in a sequence arranged primarily by her sister, Cassandra, and published in 1554. When Gaspara died, Cassandra was overwhelmed with grief and wanted to remove from her sight those things of her sister that pained her to see or touch. At the insistence of some of Gaspara's gentlemen friends, however, she collected *those poems that could be found*, as she noted in her dedication of the volume to Archbishop Giovanni Della Casa, and submitted them to the Venetian publisher, Plinio Pietrasanta, where they were edited by Giorgio Benzone.[12] Only three of these poems, LI, LXX, and LXXV, had been published during Gaspara's lifetime, included in an anthology of 1553, *Il sesto libro delle rime di diversi eccellenti autori* (The Sixth Book of Poems by Various Important Authors).[13] There is no mention of her volume after it appeared in 1554; it, and its author, sank into oblivion for 184 years.

In 1738, a descendant of the noble Collalto family, Count Antonio Rambaldo di Collalto, who preserved his family archives, decided to reprint the book of the illustrious poet "in order to satisfy somehow his obligation to her memory" and appropriately commissioned a woman, Luisa Bergalli, who had published her *Componimenti poetici delle più illustri rimatrici d'ogni secolo* (Poetic Compositions of the Most Illustrious Women Poets of All Time) in 1726, to edit a new edition, which she did in collaboration with a learned scholar, Apostolo Zeno. For the new volume Count Rambaldo ordered engraved portraits of both Gaspara and Collalto (figures 8.1, 8.2).[14] The first edition of 1554 carried an engraving of the poet only (figure 8.3). Comparing the portraits in the two editions we note that in both, Gaspara is shown with a laurel wreath crowning her head which is turned to her right. She is seated with her left arm raised so that the fingers of her left hand are curled against her neck and is leaning her left elbow on a book. Her right arm crosses her waist. Clearly the 1738 engraving was taken from the earlier image. But the pictures differ.

In the 1738 engraving the right hand is fully rendered; in the 1554 image the arm is cut off at the wrist by the margin of the print. It could not have been painted that way in the portrait that served for the engraving—no artist in the sixteenth century would have posed a sitter so that the hand would be cut off by the edge of the pictorial ground. We must therefore conclude that the engraver of this image drew from a portrait in which the right hand was fully rendered, but that his/her engraving was cropped. Because the engraving of Gaspara in the new edition of 1738 was clearly drawn from the same source, but has the added feature of the lyre at her right side, and her right hand is fully rendered, we realize that the cropping was not limited to the bottom of the print but also cut off the lyre beside her: Gaspara's upper right arm is tight up against the margin of the 1554 engraving, so that she is squeezed into a space too small for her buxom figure. We conclude then that the original image included both the lyre and the hand.

According to Count Rambaldo in his preface to the new volume, the engraving of Gaspara that he commissioned was after a painting that had been copied by Guercino from a portrait by an unknown artist; it had been given to him by Charles VI, the Holy Roman Emperor (1711–1740).[15] He commissioned Daniel Antonio Bertoli, in charge of the emperor's art collection, to make the new engraving. But we are left to wonder who made the original portrait that Guercino copied. The probable answer comes from a curious source. It was Gaspara Stampa's fortune to become a nineteenth-cen-

CASPARA   STAMPA

Clarior ingenio, forma   virtutis amore,
Heroisque sui   nulla fuit, nec erit.

Dan. Ant. Bertoli del.   Felicitas Sartori sculpsit.

8.1
Daniel Antonio Bertoli/ Felicitas Sartori
Portrait of Gaspara Stampa. **1738.**
Achille Bertarelli Print Collection, Castello Sforzesco, Milan. Photo, Bertarelli Collection.

tury romantic heroine, a woman who died for love. At least two plays were written with Gaspara as the leading character, one of which was by Jacopo Cabianca.[16] In Cabianca's play, the cast of characters includes Gaspara Stampa, Cassandra, her sister, Collaltino di Collalto, Bice Contarini; a friend of Gaspara, Lorenzo Venier; and an artist, Cesarino da Murano. The play opens with the artist painting Gaspara's portrait.

Because the characters bear their actual names, we would expect that the artist's name was real. Disappointingly, there is no trace of a Cesarino da Murano in any of the reference works we have searched. But there was a Natalino (Nadalino) da Murano, a Venetian artist, pupil of Titian, contemporary with Gaspara. We believe we have discovered in Natalino da Murano the artist who painted her from life and provided the image for the 1554 engraving, which was cropped.[17] The portrait after

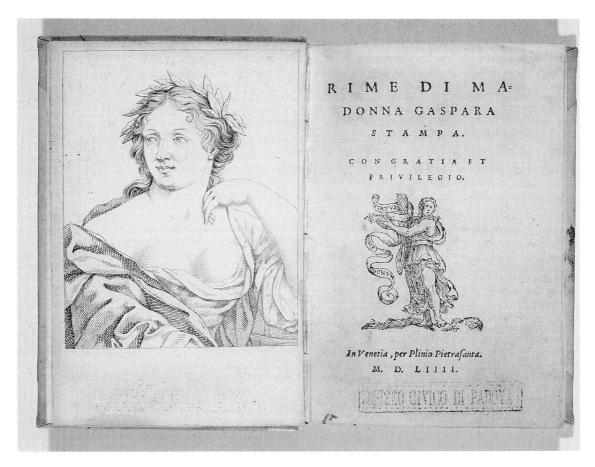

which the engraving of Collaltino di Collalto was made was by Titian himself.[18] There is a further discovery that we will eventually reveal about this portrait, but for the moment we will let our readers look for this discovery themselves, since it is in plain view!

Since that edition of 1738, a number of editions have been brought out, with variations in the contents.[19] The authoritative edition now in use is that edited by Abdelkader Salza. Salza divided the poems into two sections, the first of which included I–CCXLV, which he labeled *"Rime d' Amore"* (Poems of Love), the second, CCXLVI–CCCXI, he called *"Rime Varie"* (Miscellaneous Poems). The love story can be followed through most of the first section.

Given the history of the 1554 volume, it is evident that "Gaspara Stampa's" *Canzoniere* is actually a collaboration of Gaspara and Cassandra. As a kind of memoir, a literary form that pretends to record what actually happened, it is in fact an artfully arranged series of skillfully crafted poems, with a beginning, a narrative, and an ending, and while the poems were Gaspara's creation, the structure was Cassandra's. Gaspara had sent a collection of her poems, perhaps one hundred, to Collaltino in the summer of 1549 [20] but we do not know if some or all of them were among the ones we now have, or how Gaspara arranged them; the last of the love poems as we have them now, CCXLV, is addressed to Collaltino, and speaks of "this harsh and bitter

8.3.
Anon. (after Natalino da Murano?). *Portrait of Gaspara Stampa,* **frontispiece,** *Rime di Madonna Gaspara Stampa* **(1554). Photo, Biblioteca Civica, Padua.**

parting" as recent, and of her heart "dwelling in Lendenara," but this cannot have been Gaspara's intention because, according to Cassandra's own arrangement of the series, she fell in love again after the end of her affair with him. From Cassandra's letter we may infer that there were additional poems, for she mentions that she collected "those she found." The *Rime* as published now should therefore be considered a kind of "autobiography of Gaspara Stampa by Cassandra Stampa." We have therefore taken the liberty of selecting and ordering the poems so as to offer an account of her emotional rather than her chronological life.

It was love at first sight, as Gaspara tells us in sonnet II, quoted earlier, but more than her heart was set aflame: falling ecstatically in love with Collaltino, she found her poetic voice.

> *If living at the foot of Mount Helicon*
> *could make of a coarse shepherd a poet*
> *who rose to such heights of praise*
> *that almost all others were eclipsed,*
>
> *What marvel is it if low class though I may be*
> *I am inspired by my green, high-rising hill,*
> *more than by study or some planet,** *
> *to write with great emotion?*
>
> *The sacred, enveloping shade of that hill*
> *frees my tumultuous heart*
> *from ignorance and all that is vulgar.*
>
> *I am uplifted,*
> *my pen, become faint, now has renewed vigor,*
> *and such strength revives my soul.* (p. 268)

Gaspara shows herself perfectly aware that her great love is not an end in itself but a means of opening her imagination to her muse. Again and again she reveals her ambition. When she laments,

> *Why did it take so long for my eyes*
> *to be opened, to see this divine face . . .*

it appears that she regrets time lost not only for love, but for fame.

> *I might have been already so famous*
> *thanks to the style he has inspired in me, that today*
> *the Adriatic and its shores would resound with my name.*

---

* The hill refers to Collalto, literally "high hill." "Some planet" refers to her sonnet IV (see p. 000), in which she imagines the planets had endowed Collaltino with their gifts at his birth; she, by contrast, had no such planetary endowment. The shepherd-poet refers to Hesiod.

And now I lament the time I wasted
looking elsewhere; but perhaps I can still dare
to make my fire celebrated. (p. 268)

And again,

If I am but a humble woman
yet able to carry within me such a high torch,
such force and expression,
why should I not give the world some small part of it?

If love, with such extraordinary power
can raise me to where, before, I could never go,
why cannot I invent some way
to match my pen with my pain?

And if love who often conquers and goes beyond
every limit cannot bring me to do this naturally,
let him perform a miracle.

How this might be done I cannot exactly say,
yet, to write of my great destiny,
I feel my heart touched by a new pen. (pp. 268 – 69)

Gaspara's references to her low estate here and elsewhere arise from her realistic perception of the difference between her social rank and her beloved's; Collaltino was a nobleman, she, whatever connection her family might once have had to the nobility, was a commoner.

"You are not equal"—Love tells me—
"He is noble and handsome, you are ugly and low-class,
heaven was generous to him, stingy to you"

she writes, and blames herself, for her wishes were not sensible.

I was the minister of my misery
For, considering my low estate,
I should have looked to a less grand place
to be able to hope for greater sympathy.

Phaeton, Icarus in their time, and I in mine, for
having little power and daring much,
we have been extinguished by a greater fire. (p. 269)

The real and the fictive in Gaspara's story are so tightly interwoven that even the imagery changes places: sometimes the "noble object," "the greater fire" of which she writes and for which she is happy to suffer, is her nobleman lover, sometimes, poetry, and sometimes, as in the above, both.

From the beginning, their relationship was tense and, for Gaspara, unsatisfying. He could be loving, he could be cruel.

> Sometimes I compare my beloved to the heavens:
> his handsome face is the sun,
> his eyes the stars; and the sound of his voice
> is the harmony created by the Lord of Delos.
>
> Tempests, rains, thunder and ice
> when he is angry,
> friendly and serene, benign he is when he wishes
> to tear off the veil of his anger.
>
> Springtime, when flowers begin to bloom,
> is when he makes my hopes blossom
> promising to keep me in this state.
>
> Then horrid winter comes when, changing face,
> he threatens to change his thoughts of me and leave,
> taking from me my dearest hopes. (p. 269)

That she would lose him was her constant worry, even in her happiest moments.

> When I see my handsome one approaching
> he seems to me like the beams of the sun as it rises,
> and when he stays with me for a sweet while
> it is like the sun in its journey.
>
> And I feel in my heart and reveal in my face
> as much joy and vigor
> as does the grass at midday
> painted by the sun in the lovely month of May.
>
> Then, when at last my sun leaves me,
> it is like seeing the shadow that darkens the earth
> as it travels to the west.
>
> The sun will return, life-giving with its light,
> but the return of my own bright shining sun
> is doubtful; leaving is certain. (p. 270)

The Collalto fief, which the family had held since the Middle Ages, was in the Friuli area under the domain of Venice. It included several castles, the largest of which were Collalto and San Salvatore.[21] Collaltino divided his time between his castles and Venice, when he was not engaged in one or another military campaign. To her delight, he sometimes took Gaspara with him to his estates, and at those times it seemed she wanted nothing more from life than to stay there with him forever.

> Oh, sir, in this flourishing time of your life,
> give up chasing after grand victories,
> high honors, good fortune at the cost of such trials
> and the risk to your life.

> In these hills, in this safe and peaceful valley
> and countryside, where Love invites us,
> let us live together, happy and satisfied,
> until the sun fades from our eyes forever.

> Such endeavors, such strains
> make life hard, and such honors
> are soon emptied by death.

> Here let us gather flowers and fruit,
> foliage and ferns, and in sweet harmony
> let us sing with the birds of our love. (p. 270)

Spring 1549 was a more or less happy time for Gaspara, depending on the moods of her lover

> who, whether the sun rises or sets,
> whether it be day or night, summer or winter,
> himself brings me light or shadow (p. 270)

so that even when she thinks of joyous times spent together, her thoughts turn bitter, as in a long *canzone* which begins happily,

> Sparkling, famous sea,
> on whose broad back
> my lord lay with Love's desire,
> beloved banks
> (I must say with a sigh)
> that saw my soft breasts;
> gentle shore and hills
> that heard me sing
> my amorous song,
> no anger, no scorn was there
> but only delight and peace,
> now hear with all attention
> the sound of my bitter lament . . .

but continues with Gaspara, angry and yearning for his return from San Salvatore where in her mind's eye she can see him "going his usual way" hunting birds and hares, living a life of freedom and calm, happily gazing at the sea and countryside, without his "miserable Anassilla":

> *now hear with all attention*
> *the sound of my bitter lament*
> . . .
>   *I am angry*
> *and I call Love thankless*
> *for stealing from me so soon*
> *the beloved that is now far away*
> *and will not return for pity's sake;*
> *he keeps to his usual ways,*
> *while I fall apart and suffer.*
>   *Oh if only he was less distant,*
> *he who makes me cry,*
> *the cause of my just complaints,*
> . . .
>   *and I would call Love wicked and cruel*
> *who made me taste*
> *bitter wormwood and bile*
> *after such a sweet feast.* (pp. 270 – 71)

To judge by the number of her poems in which she writes of his arrogance, his cruel, icy heart, she had pitifully little joy from their affair.

> *With some mercy, turn your eyes now and then*
> *from your beauty to my pain,*
> *so that your heart may be touched by pity*
> *equal to the haughtiness in them.* (p. 271)

> *I am formed of fire, you of ice,*
> *you are free, I am in chains* (p. 271)

Even love cannot help to melt "the solid ice that lies in his heart" (p. 271). She is certain that her passionate suffering is greater than anyone has ever known.

> *There has never been a fire, prison or knot*
> *so hot, so sharp, so harsh and tight, no heart*
> *burnt, wounded, restricted and bound so*
> *painfully, piercingly, bitterly, firmly as mine.* (p. 271)

But the suffering, the terrible anguish, were all worthwhile, not only because

> *Those tormented by love are blessed* (p. 271)

but because it is better

> To struggle for a noble reason
> that makes savage life gentle and blessed
> than to enjoy vulgar, common pleasures,

and because, she continues, Love has endowed her with such a fire

> that from Bactria to Thule I may
> hope one day to be famous and praised.6* (p. 272)

Then the first terrible blow fell. At the end of May Collaltine went off to France to fight for King Henry II in his struggle to take back Boulogne-sur-Mer from the English, and for Gaspara the sunshine of spring disappeared into foggy night.

> Guide me, Love, for alas I have lost my sun
> that once not only made my day bright
> but also lighted my night
> and I scorned the coming of dawn
> for the lovely light of his eyes
> dispersed the shadows and the fog. (p. 272)

The nights of joy are over, and she fears she will be forgotten.

> Oh, alas, my nights full of joy,
> my tranquil days, why has that serene life
> been taken from me by this bitter parting
> and brought me to such a state of suffering.

> And why do I fear (which hurts me most)
> that I will disappear from the memory
> of that cruel count who has wounded me
> beyond healing, even to death? (p. 272)

Her pain is boundless,

> A new, strange miracle of nature
> but not new or strange to that Lord
> whom all the world calls Love
> who can do anything, beyond any limit.

> The valor of my lord, who with his greater valor
> takes the prize from all others

---

* Bactria: Persia. Thule is a legendary island identified as Iceland. Thus, from one end of the earth to the other, as in Petrarch, sonnet 146.

> is conquered, alas, only by my sorrow,
> an everlasting sorrow in my heart.
>
> As much as he exceeds all other knights
> in beauty, nobility and daring
> by so much is he conquered by me, by my fidelity.
>
> A miracle never heard of except in love!
> Grief that no one can believe but one who has felt it!
> Alas, that I alone conquer infinity! (p. 272)

She was miserable without him; she faults him for ignoring his promise to write and taunts him for his love of glory.

> Oh what a brave courteous knight
> to have carried off to France the heart
> of a young, imprudent woman whom Love
> captured with the splendor of his beautiful eyes!
>
> At least you might have kept your promise
> to soften my pain with a few lines
> my lord, but seeking honor,
> you put all your thought to that end. (p. 273)

Then, marked by her most passionate, exultant poems, at last came the day she had hardly dared hope for,

> Oh blessed, sweetest of all news
> oh beautiful message with your promise
> that soon I will see again those dear, shining eyes
> and that benign and handsome face;
>
> Oh my good fortune, my lucky star
> that has so kindly preserved me
> Oh faith, oh hope, who have always been
> my friends through the terrible storm;
>
> Oh changed in a flash is my life
> from sad to happy, turned calm and serene now
> from dark and cruel winter.
>
> When will I ever be able to praise you enough?
> How can I say what is in my heart
> so full and overflowing with happiness? (p. 273)

and the night.

> *Oh, night, more shining to me, more blessed*
> *than the brightest most blessed day,*
> *night that should be praised by the rarest,*
> *most brilliant minds, not indeed by me;*
>
> *You took faithful care of my joys,*
> *you have made sweet and dear*
> *all the bitter stings of my life*
> *bringing back to me the one to whom you tied me.*
>
> *I only lacked the favor given to*
> *that fortunate Alcmena, with whom you stayed*
> *far past the usual time for dawn's returning.*
>
> *But so much praise I can never give you,*
> *oh shining night, that might make you*
> *greater than my song.* (p. 273)

So, after six months, it began again, days and nights of love,

> *Who can describe my happiness,*
> *the height of my joy and my delight?*
> . . .
> *Now I have him always at my side*
> *to enjoy the sparkle of his eyes, the sound of his voice . . .* (p. 274)
>
> *A thousand times, my lord, I move my pen*
> *to express what is in my heart*
> . . .
> *To tell how Love is enthroned in your beautiful eyes* (p. 274)

days and nights of accusations,

> *With what signs, my lord, do you wish*
> *that I show my love for you*
> *if now loving, now dying*
> *you do not believe I am dying for you?*
>
> *. . . why do you wrongly stab*
> *My soul with such cruel hooks*
> *saying that I do not love you?* (p. 274)

recriminations,

> *Oh misfortune, oh perverse fate,*
> *oh wrongful verdict passed against me*

for no fault of mine, making me
suffer the punishment of another's crime.
. . .
   I will scream, sir, so long and loud
that, if you do want to listen to me,
either Love or Death will hear my cries;

   Perhaps some merciful soul will say
"This woman unfortunately placed her hopes
in too harsh a place." (p. 274)

disappointment when he left her again to visit his estates,

   How harsh and savage now becomes
this lovely sea that was once so serene!
Since you left us
I feel as much sympathy for myself

   As envy for the beautiful hill, the pines,
the beeches that shade you, the river that bathes
your feet and gives me my name,
that now enjoy your shining presence.

and anger,

   Were this not the lovely nest
where you were born, I would beg heaven to dry
the woods, ruffle the river, and leave you desolate. (pp. 274 – 75)

Yet, Gaspara never lost her vision of herself. When, lamenting, she asks Love

   "How can it be, since I gave my heart and soul
to my lord that day when I took them out of me
. . .
   That I feel cold jealousy and fear,
deprived of all joyousness,
if I live in him, and am myself without life?"

Love answers her, and pronounces his final sentence,

   "I bid you die for joy and live for grief,"
"Let it be enough that this is what makes you write." (p. 275)

She had good reason to fear. Collaltino enjoyed her beauty, her charm, her talent, and her adulation, but, despite her irresistible hopes, she knew he had no intention of marrying her. And finally, the last blow came.

> *It is no wonder that in one brief moment*
> *you have withdrawn your thoughts and desires from me,*
> *for, once a lover, you have decided*
> *to marry, to become a husband.*

> *A knot not firm, a faith not constant*
> *is easily loosened and broken:*
> *but my knot is stronger than a Gordian knot,*
> *my faith more perfect than a diamond.*

> *Thus it will never be that the one will loosen,*
> *the other shatter, unless cruel death*
> *for which now I pray, sir, should soon come to me.*

> *May I never really see*
> *the miserable fate that my horrible thoughts*
> *present now to my mind's eye.* (p. 275)

Whether Collaltino was already engaged or only told her that he intended to marry in order to break off their relationship is unclear; he did not actually marry until 1557. She felt the rupture was more than she could bear.

> *All the torments of hell*
> *are small, nothing*
> *compared to my great fire,*
> *for where there is no hope*
> *the soul is resigned to suffer forever*
> *and grows accustomed to the pain that can never change.*
> *My sorrow is all the greater*
> *because once it enjoyed the shade of joy,*
> *thanks to hope,*
> *and this constant shift*
> *between joy and misery*
> *increases my suffering.* (pp. 275 – 76)

She thought constantly of death.

> *Cry, ladies, and may Love cry with you*
> . . .
> *Soon my soul shall leave*
> *this tormented body*

and she wrote her own epitaph,

> *here lies the most faithful lover*
> *that has ever lived;*

> *she loved too well and was loved too little.* (p. 276)

Though he was faithless, she was constant.

> *Count, where has it gone so soon,*
> *the faith you swore to me,*
> *what does it mean*
> *that mine is more constant than ever?*
> *. . .*
> *Do you know what people will say? . . .*
> *"Oh what a cruel count!*
> *Oh, what a loyal woman!"* (p. 276)

She begged for death but she struggled to survive, and turned her infinite need of love to God.

> *Since by the will of destiny you turned*
> *yourself and your desire away from me, I have lost hope*
> *of seeing ever again those serene eyes*
> *that I have praised in so many poems,*
>
> *I have turned to the Sun, and with the insight*
> *and light that comes from Him alone,*
> *I have steered my boat with oars and sails,*
> *from the quicksand and shoals.*
>
> *Reason became my sails, the oars were*
> *my will with which I built a dike and wall*
> *against the wrath and pride of Love.*
>
> *Thus, without fear of rocks or reefs*
> *I live in this safe and secure harbor,*
> *praising one sun only, and grieving for no one.* (p. 276)

She would no longer sing of the beauty of that face she had loved, but to a "higher wisdom"; her inspiration, her Parnassus, would no longer be clouded over with gloom.

> *This is the way to rise to true glory,*

she tells her muse, revealing once again her unswerving ambition,

> *this will make you known from west to east*
> *and bring you true honor.* (p. 276)

Gaspara had lived for three years in the turbulent sea of love, she had saved herself with desperate determination, and felt at last she was safe. But she was mistaken.

> Hardly had I arrived in port when Love,
> always ready to worsen my troubles and distress,
> brought me back to the middle of the sea where
> for three years I survived among baffling winds,
>
> And to double the wings of my desire
> he has presented to my eyes such a bright dawn
> that seeing it again, I am comforted
> and it seems I am without anxiety or pain.
>
> I feel a fire equal to my first flame,
> and if, in such a short time, this can happen,
> I fear that it may be greater than the other.
>
> But what can I do, if I am destined to burn,
> if willingly I consent to go
> from one painful fire to another. (p. 277)

In love with love, she was helpless as the chubby archer struck her again and again.

> Like Sagittarius who is always ready
> to aim at a target and never misses,
> drawn either by his own loveliness
> or his hope of gaining by it honor and triumph,
>
> Love, never satisfied with my troubles,
> returns to stab my heart, and never stops,
> and reopens the scars once healed;
> nor does it help if I fear or scorn him.
>
> He takes great delight in wounding me
> expecting to gain great honor from
> the way I feel, and has no other interest.
>
> The bright fire that for many years
> made me burn and sing was almost spent, but he
> who knows no truce has relighted my heart from another. (p. 277)

But she seems, perhaps at last, to have found a satisfying love. We know his name, for she spelled it out in an acrostic poem that we must present in Italian because the acrostic depends on the language:

Ben si convien, signor, che l'aureo dardo
Amor v'abbia aventato in mezzo il petto,
rotto quel duro e quel gelato affetti,
tanto a le fiamme sue ritroso e tardo
havendo a me col vostro dolce sguardo
onde piove disir, gioia e diletto,
l'alma impiaga e 'l cor legato stretto
oltre misura, onde mi struggo ed ardo.
Men dunque acerbo de' parer a vui
esser nel laccio aviluppato e preso
ov'io sì stretta ancor legata fui.
Zelo d'ardente caritate acceso
esser conviene eguale omai fra nui
nel nostro dolce ed amoroso peso.*

Bartholomeo Zen has not been identified.

What love meant to Gaspara is fully and blazingly clear in a long poem that she addressed to still-innocent young women to warn them of what Love, "this lord and master," will give them.

> *A burning feeling, vain desires,*
> *Searching anxiously, despite yourself*
> *for what you will never find, of if you do,*
> *will bring injury and remorse.*

Love is

> *A kind of death, without knowing why you die*
> . . .
> *Degrading yourself, before your lover,*
> *you, a frank and daring person,*
> *unable to stop crying,*
>
> *Despising your own life*
> *while loving another,*
> . . .
>
> *Sleepless . . .*
> *waking frustrated from dreams*
> *always contrary to your desires*

---

* "It is well, sir, that Love, / shy and arriving late, / has sent his golden arrow / and broken the hard ice in my heart; / he has turned your loving eyes to me, / flooded with desire, joy, and delight, / he has pierced my soul / and tightly bound my heart / and I burn and melt in his flames. / Less harsh are the laces / which hold me to you now / than those which once tied me. / It is fine to be set aglow / with the ardent zeal that we share equally." The acrostic was discovered by Salza.

> *Suffering, but not wishing to complain*
> *to the offender, turning your anger*
> *against yourself, abasing yourself.*

And yet, despite the misery, love is

> *Seeing only one face,*
> *gazing fixedly, although it is far away,*
> *a joy of the soul that brings a sigh.*

> *And finally, a pang that stings and soothes.* (pp. 277 – 78)

Stampa's poetry is pervaded by the Platonic idea of love as the desire for beauty, truth, and goodness, one of the most decisive components, as we have seen, in creating the sensibility of the sixteenth century. With Collaltino as the flawed ideal, Stampa's desire for him is the central conflict of her *canzoniere.* She loved his physical "veil," his handsome human body, but she wanted to believe, she *did* believe, that this beauty was the appearance of his flawless soul. Her tempestuous passion, her obsession with suicide, her total surrender to love, have led some writers to see her as a precursor of nineteenth century romanticism. As we have seen, she did indeed appeal to the nineteenth century, as evidenced by publications of a number of fictions based on her life.[22] But far from that sensibility as mainstream writing is today, far from the taste of the sixteenth century as well, the modern reader is still moved by the pulsing energy of Stampa's songs of the joy and anguish of being in love.

Love and song died in Gaspara Stampa's heart only when they were conquered by death on 23 April 1554.

The other "discovery" promised earlier (p. 249, lines 2 – 3) is this. Simon Vouet (1590– 1642), an important seventeenth-century French painter who spent many years of his career in Italy and is known for using images created by celebrated painters, saw Guercino's painting of "a poet" and used it for his image of Calliope in his painting *Apollo and the Muses on Parnassus* (frontispiece and figure 8.4). There in the Museum of Fine Arts, Budapest, never previously recognized, is Gaspara Stampa with her head crowned with a laurel wreath, turned toward her right while she leans her elbow on a book, her forearm raised. In the end, Gaspara achieved what she most wanted: she dwells among the muses on Parnassus.[23]

8.4.
Simon Vouet.
Apollo and the
Muses on Mt.
Parnassus, detail,
Calliope
(Gaspara
Stampa) among
the muses,
Pegasus in
background.
ca. 1635.
Budapest
Museum of Fine
Arts. Photo,
Art Resource.

POEMS IN THE ORIGINAL ITALIAN*

Amor m'ha fatto tal ch'io vivo in foco
qual nova salamandra al mondo, e quale
l'altro di lei non men stranio animale,
che vive e spira nel medesimo loco.

Le mie delizie son tutte e 'l mio gioco
viver ardendo e non sentire il male,
e non curar ch'ei che m'induce a tale
abbia di me pietà molto né poco.

A pena era anche estinto il primo ardore
che accese l' altro Amore, a quel ch'io sento
fin qui per prova, più vivo e maggiore.

Ed io d'arder amando non mi pento,
pur che chi m'ha di novo tolto il core
resti de l'arder mio pago e contento.† (p. 239)

◉ Track 37,
Reading 38

⁓

Dimmi: qual più è divina
Cassandra o Gasparina?

Dimmi qual ì più landra
Gasparina o Cassandra? ‡ (p. 240)

⁓

Fermati, viator, se saper vuoi
l' essito de la mia vita meschina:
Gaspara Stampa fui, donna e reina
di quante unqua p . . . . . . fur tra voi.

M'ebbe vergine il Gritti, ed ho da poi
fatto di mille e piu c . . . . ruina;
vissi sempre di furto e di rapina,
m'uccise un c . . . . con gli empiti suoi.

Vergai carte d'amor con l'altrui stile,
che per quel fatto i versi mi facea
il Fortunio, compare mio gentile.

---

* Salza (as in note 1) is the source for Gaspara's poems, except where noted..
† CCVIII.
‡ Giulio Dolci, *Letteratura Italiana: I Minori* (Milan, 1961), p. 1319.

Va' in pace, e, per temprar mia pena rea,
inestiami col m . . . . . tuo virile,
che sol quel, mentre vissi, mi piacea. * (p. 240)

⁓

Voi n'andaste, signor, senza me dove
il gran troian fermò le schiere erranti,
ov'io nacqui, ove luce vidi innanti
dolce sì, che lo star mi spiace altrove.

Ivi vedrete vaghe feste e nove,
schiere di donne e di cortesi amanti,
tanti, che ad onorar vengono, e tanti,
un de li dèi più cari al vero Giove.

Ed io, rimasa qui dov'Adria regna,
seguo pur voi e 'l mio natio paese
col pensier, chè non è chi lo ritegna.

Venir col resto il mio signor contese;
ché, senza ordine suo, ch'io vada o vegna
non vuol Amor, poi che di lui m'accese. † (p. 241)

⁓

⦿ Track 38,
Reading 39

Voi, ch'ascoltate in queste meste rime,
in questi mesti, in questi oscuri accenti
Il suon degli amorosi miei lamenti
e de le pene mie tra l'altre prime,

Ove fia chi valor apprezzi e stime,
gloria, non che perdon, de'miei lamenti
spero trovar fra le ben nate genti,
poi che la lor cagione è sì sublime.

E spero ancor che debba dir qualcuna:
"Felicissima lei, da che sostenne
per sì chiara cagion danno sì chiaro!"

Deh, perchè tant'amor, tanta fortuna
per sì nobil signor a me non venne,
ch'anch'io n'andrei con tanta donna a paro? ‡ (p. 243)

⁓

Francesco Petrarch

Voi ch'ascoltate in rime sparse il suono
di quei sospiri ond'io nudriva 'l core

. . .

---

* Appendix, XVIII.   † CCL.   ‡ I.

ove sia chi per prova intenda amore
spero trovar pietà nonchè perdono.

Ma ben veggio or sì come al popol tutto
favola fui gran tempo, onde sovente
di me medesmo meco mi vergogno;

Et del mio vaneggiar vergogna è 'l frutto,
e 'l pentersi, e 'l conoscer chiaramente
che quanto piace al mondo è breve sogno.[14]* (p. 244)

~

Chi vuol conoscer, donne, il mio signore,   Gaspara Stampa
miri un signor di vago e dolce aspetto,
giovane d'anni e vecchio d'intelletto,
imagin de la gloria e del valore,

Di pelo biondo, e di vivo colore,
di persona alta e spazioso petto,
e finalmente in ogni opra perfetto,
fuor ch'un poco (oimè lassa!) empio in amore.
. . .[†] (p. 244)

~

Quando fu prima il mio signor concetto,
tutti i pianeti in ciel, tutte le stelle
gli dier le grazie, e queste doti e quelle,
perch'ei fosse tra noi solo perfetto.

Saturno diègli altezza d'intelletto;
Giove il cercar le cose degne e belle;
Marte appo lui fece ogn'altr'uomo imbelle;
Febo gli empì di stile e senno il petto;

Vener gli diè bellezza e leggiadria;
eloquenza Mercurio; ma la luna
lo fe' gelato più ch'io non vorria.[‡] (p. 245)

~

Era vicino il dì che 'l Creatore,   ● Track 39,
che ne l'altezza sua potea restarsi,   Reading 40
in forma umana venne a dimostrarsi,
dal ventre virginal uscendo fore,

Quando degnò l'illustre mio signore,
per cui ho tanti poi lamenti sparsi,
potendo in luogo più alto annidarsi,
farsi nido e ricetto del mio core.

---

* Petrarch I.   † VII.   ‡ IV.

Ond'io sì rara e sì alta ventura
accolsi lieta; e duolmi sol che tardi
mi fe' degna di lei l'eterna cura.

Da indi in quà pensieri e speme e sguardi
volsi a lui tutti, fuor d'ogni misura
chiaro e gentil, quanto 'l sol giri e guardi. (p. 245)

~

Se di rozzo pastor di gregge e folle
il giogo ascreo fe' diventar poeta
lui, che poi salse a sì lodata meta,
che quasi a tutti gli altri fama tolle,

Che meraviglia fia s'alza ed estolle
me bassa e vile a scriver tanta pièta,
quel che può più che studio e che pianeta,
il mio verde, pregiato ed alto colle?

La cui sacra, onorata e fatal ombra
dal mio cor, quasi sùbita tempesta,
ogni ignoranza, ogni bassezza sgombra.

Questa da basso luogo m'erge, e questa
mi rinnova lo stil, la vena adombra;
tanta virtù nell'alma ognor mi desta! † (p. 250)

~

Deh, perchè cosi tardo gli occhi apersi
nel divin, non umano amato volto,
. . .

E sarei forse di sì chiaro grido,
che, mercé de lo stil, ch'indi m'è dato,
risoneria fors'Adria oggi, e 'l suo lido.

Ond'io sol piango il mio tempo passato,
mirando altrove; e forse anche mi fido
di far in parte il foco mio lodato. ‡ (pp. 250–51)

~

● Track 40,
Reading 41

Se, così come sono abietta e vile
donna, posso portar sì alto foco,
perchè non debbo aver almeno un poco
di ritraggerlo al mondo e vena e stile?

S'Amor con novo, insolito focile,
ov'io non potea gir m'alzò a tal loco

---

* II.   † III. Ascrio is at the foot of Mount Helican.   ‡ XII.

perchè non può non con usato gioco
far la pena e la penna in simìle?

   E, se non può per forza di natura,
puollo almen per miracolo, che spesso
vince, trapassa e rompe ogni misura.

   Come ciò sia non posso dir espresso;
io provo ben che per mia gran ventura
*mi sento il cor di novo stile impresso.** (p. 251)

   ⁓

   —Non son—mi dice Amor—le ragion pari;
egli è nobile e bel, tu brutta e vile;
egli larghi, tu hai li cieli avari. †

. . .

accuso me sol de la mia sorte
. . .

   Perchè, vedendo la mia indegnitade,
devea mirar in men gradito loco,
per poterne sperar maggior pietade.

   Fetonte, Icaro ed io, per poter poco
ed osar molto, in questa e quella etade
restiamo estinti da troppo alto foco. ‡ (p. 251)

   ⁓

   Io assimiglio il mio signore al cielo
meco sovente. Il suo bel viso è 'l sole;
gli occhi, le stelle, e 'l suon de le parole
è l'armonia, che fa 'l signor di Delo.

   Le tempeste, le piogge, i tuoni e 'l gelo
son i suoi sdegni, quando irar si suole;
le bonacce e 'l sereno è quando vuole
squarciar de l'ire sue begnino il velo.

   La primavera e 'l germogliar de' fiori
è quando ei fa fiorir la mia speranza,
promettendo tenermi in questo stato.

   L'orrido verno è poi, quando cangiato
minaccia di mutar pensieri e stanza,
spogliata me de' miei più ricchi onori. § (p. 252)

   ⁓

---

* VIII.   † CL.   ‡ CLXVI.   § V.

● Track 41,
Reading 42

Quando i' veggio apparir il mio bel raggio
parmi veder il sol, quand'esce fòra;
quando fa meco poi dolce dimora
assembra il sol che faccia suo viaggio.

E tanta nel cor gioia e vigor aggio,
tanta ne mostro nel sembiante allora,
quanto l'erba, che pinge il sol ancora
a mezzo giorno nel più vago maggio.

Quando poi parte il mio sol finalmente
parmi l'altro veder, che scolorita
lasci la terra andando in occidente.

Ma l'altro torna, e rende luce e vita;
e del mio chiaro e lucido oriente
è 'l tornar dubbio e certa la partita. * (p. 252)

⌒

Deh lasciate, signor, le maggior cure
d'ir procacciando in questa età fiorita
con fatiche e periglio de la vita
alti pregi, alti onori, alte venture;

E in questi colli, in queste alme e sicure
valli e campagne, dove Amor n'invita,
viviamo insieme vita alma e gradita,
fin che 'l sol de' nostr'occhi alfin s'oscure.

Perchè tante fatiche e tanti stenti
fan la vita più dura e tanti onori
restan per morte poi subito spenti.

Qui coglieremo a tempo rose e fiori,
ed erbe e frutti, e con dolci concenti
canterem con gli uccelli i nostri amori. † (p. 253)

⌒

Che, quando viene, e quando parte il sole,
la notte e 'l giorno ognor, la state e 'l verno,
tenebre e luce darmi e tormi suole . . . ‡ (p. 253)

⌒

Chiaro e famoso mare
sovra 'l cui nobil dosso
si posò 'l mio signor, mentre Amor volle;
rive onorate e care

---

* XVIII.   † CLVIII.   ‡ XXVI.

(con sospir dir lo posso)
che 'l petto mio vedeste spesso molle;
soave lido e colle
che con fiato amoroso
udisti le mie note
d'ira e di sdegno vòte
. . .
udite tutti intenti
il suon or degli acerbi miei lamenti.

. . .
e, perch'io pur m'adiri
e chiami Amor ingrato,
che m'involò sì tosto
il ben ch'or sta discosto,
non per questo a pietade è mai tornato;
e tien l'usate tempre,
perch'io mi sfaccia e mi lamenti sempre.
    Deh fosse men lontano
almen chi move il pianto
e chi move le giuste mie querele!
. . .
e chiamerei Amor empio e crudele
ch'amaro assenzio e fele
dopo quel dolce cibo
me fe', lassa, gustare . . .* (pp. 253 – 54)

⌣

Rivolgete talor pietoso gli occhi
da le vostre bellezze a le mie pene,
sì che quanta alterezza indi vi viene,
tanta quindi pietate il cor vi tocchi. . . † (p. 254)

⌣

. . . io son di foco e voi di ghiaccio,
voi sète in libertade ed io 'n catena . . . ‡ (p. 254)

⌣

quel saldo ghiaccio, che nel cor si trova . . . § (p. 254)

⌣

Altri mai foco, stral, prigione o nodo
sì vivo e acuto, e sì aspra e sì stretto
non arse, impiagò, tenne e strinse il petto,
quanto 'l mi'ardente, acuto, acerba e sodo. . . . || (p. 254)

⌣

perchè i martir d'Amor son benedetti. ¶ (p. 254)

⌣

---

* LXVIII.   † XXII.   ‡ XLI.   § XXI. || XXVII.   ¶ XXIV.

Chè l'arder per cagion alta e gentile
ogni aspra vita fa dolce e beata
più che gioir per cosa abietta e vile.

Ed io ingrazio Amor, che destinata
m'abbia a tal foco, che da Battro a Tile
*spero anche un giorno andar chiara e lodata.** (p. 255)

⁓

Menami, Amor, ormai, lassa! Il mio sole,
che mi solea non pur far chiaro il giorno
ma non men che 'l dì chiara anco la notte,
tal ch'io sprezzava il ritornar de l'alba,
sì di quest'occhi la sua vaga luce
*disgombrava le tenebre e la nebbia. . . . † (p. 255)

⁓

Oimè, le notti mie colme di gioia,
i dì tranquilli, e la serena vita,
come mi tolse amara dipartita,
e converse il mio stato tutto in noia!

E perchè temo ancor (che più m'annoia)
che la memoria mia sia dipartita
da quel conte crudel, che m'ha ferita,
*che mi resta altro omai, se non ch'io moia? ‡ (p. 255)

⁓

Novo e raro miracol di natura,
ma non novo né raro a quel signore,
che 'l mondo tutto va chiamando Amore,
che 'l tutto adopra fuor d'ogni misura:

Il valor, che degli altri il pregio fura,
del mio signor, che vince ogni valore,
è vinto, lassa, sol dal mio dolore
dolor, a petto a cui null'altro dura.

Quant'ei tutt'altri cavalieri eccede
in esser bello, nobile ed ardito,
tanto è vinto da me, da la mia fede.

Miracol fuor d'amor mai non udito!
Dolor che chi nol prova non lo crede!
*Lassa, ch'io sola vinco l'infinito! § (pp. 255 – 56)

⁓

---

* LXXXIX.   † XCV.   ‡ LXXXIII.   § XCI.

O gran valor d'un cavalier cortese,
d'aver portato fin in Francia il core
d'una giovane incauta, ch'Amore
a lo splendor de'suoi begli occhi prese!
Almen m'aveste le promesse attese
di temprar con due versi il mio dolore,
mentre, signore, a procacciarvi onore
tutte le voglie avete ad una intese. . . .* (p. 256)

~

O beata e dolcissima novella,
o caro annunzio, che mi promettete
che tosto rivedrò le care e liete
luci e la faccia grazioza e bella;

O mia ventura, o mia propizia stella,
ch'a tanto ben serbata ancor m'avete,
o fede, o speme, ch'a me sempre sète
state compagne in dura, aspra procella;

O cangiato in un punto viver mio
di mesto in lieto; o queto, almo e sereno
fatto or di verno tenebroso e rio

Quando potrò giamai lodarvi a pieno?
come dir qual nel cor aggio disio?
di che letizia io l'abbia ingombro e pieno? † (p. 256)

~

O notte, a me più chiara e più beata
che i più beati giorni ed i più chiari,
notte degna da'primi e da' più rari
ingegni esser, non pur da me, lodata;

Tu de le gioie mie sola sei stata
fida ministra; tu tutti gli amari
de la mia vita hai fatto dolci e cari,
resomi in braccio lui che m'ha legata.

Sol mi mancò che non divenni allora
la fortunata Alcmena, a cui stè tanto
più de l'usato a ritornar l'aurora.

Pur così bene io non potrò mai tanto
dir di te, notte candida, ch'ancora
da la materia non sia vinto il canto. ‡ (p. 257)

● Track 42,
Reading 43

---

* XCVII.   † C.   ‡ CIV.

Chi può contar il mio felice stato,
l'alta mia gioia e gli alti miei diletti?

. . .

Io mi sto sempre al mio signor a lato,
godo il lampo degli occhi e 'l suon dei detti . . .* (p. 257)

~

Mille volte, signor, movo la penna
per mostrar fuor, qual chiudo entro il pensiero

. . .

Come Amor ne' be' vostr'occhi tiene
il seggio suo . . . † (p. 257)

Con quai segni, signor, volete ch'io
vi mostri l'amor mio
se, amando e morendo ad ora ad ora
non si crede per voi, lassa, ch'io mora?

. . .

A che pungermi invano
l'alma di sì crudi ami
con dir pur ch'io non v'ami? ‡ (p. 257)

~

O mia sventura, o mio perverso fato
o sentenzia nemica del mio bene,
poi che senza mia colpa mi conviene
portar la pena de l'altrui peccato.

. . .

Io griderò, signor, tanto e sì forte
che, se non li vorrete ascoltar voi
udranno i gridi miei Amore o Morte;

e forse alcun pietoso dirà poi:
—questa locò per sua contraria sorte
in troppo crudo luogo i pensier suoi. § (pp. 257 – 58)

~

Quanto è questo fatto ora aspro e selvaggio
di dolce, ch'esser suole, e lieto mare!
Dopo il vostro da noi allontanare
quanto compassione a me propria aggio,

Tanto ho invidia al bel colle, al pino, al faggio,
che gli fanno ombra, al fiume, che bagnare
gli suole il piede ed a me nome dare,
che godono or del vostro vivo raggio.

---

*CX.   † CXIV.   ‡ CCXXXVIII.   § CXXIX.

E, se non che egli è pur quell'il bel nido,
dove nasceste, io pregherei che fesse
il ciel lui ermo, lor secchi e quel torbo
. . .* (p. 258)

Quando io dimando nel mio pianto Amore,
. . .

—Come esser può, s'io diedi l'alma e 'l core
al mio signor dal dì ch'a me l'ho tolta,
. . .

Ch'io senta gelosia fredda e temenza,
e d'allegrezza e gioia resti priva,
s'io vivo in lui, e in me di me son senza?

—Vo' che tu mora al bene ed al mal viva—
mi risponde egli in ultima sentenza—
questo ti basti, e questo fa' che scriva. † (p. 258)

~

Meraviglia non è, se 'n uno istante
ritraeste da me pensieri e voglie
chè vi venne cagion di prender moglie,
e divenir marito, ov'eri amante.

Nodo e fè, che non è stretto e costante,
per picciola cagion si rompe e scioglie;
la mia fede e 'l mio nodo il vanto toglie
al nodo gordiano ed al diamante.

Però non fia giamai che scioglia questo
e rompa quella, se non cruda morte,
la qual prego, signor, che venga presto;

Sì ch'io non vegga con le luci scorte
quello ch'or col pensier atro e funesto
mi fa veder la mia spietata sorte. ‡ (p. 259)

~

Le pene de l'inferno insieme insieme,
appresso il mio gran foco,
tutte son nulla o poco;
perch'ove non è speme
l'anima risoluta al patir sempre
s'avezza al duol, che mai non cangia tempre.
La mia è maggior noia
perchè gusto talor ombra di gioia
mercé de la speranza

---

* CXXXV.   † CXXXII.   ‡ CLXXIX.

e questa varia usanza
di gioir e patire
fa maggior il martìre * (p. 259)

⁓

Piangete, donne, e con voi pianga Amore
. . .
sì che l'alma farà tosto partita
da questo corpo tormentato fuore.
. . .

Per amar molto ed esser poco amata
. . . qui giace
la più fidel amante che sia stata. . . . † (pp. 259 – 60)

⁓

Conte, dov'è andata
la fé sì tosto, che m'avete data?
Che vuol dire che la mia
è più costante, che non era pria?
. . .
Sapete voi quel che dirà la gente? . . .
—O che conte crudele!
O che donna fedele! ‡ (p. 260)

⁓

Poi che per mio destin volgeste in parte
piedi e voler, onde perdei la spene
di riveder più mai quelle serene
luci, c'ho già lodate in tante carte,

Io mi volsi al gran Sole, e con quell'arte
e quella luce, che da lui sol viene,
trassi fuor da le sirti e da l'arene
il legno mio per via di remi e sarte.

La ragion fu le sarte, e remi furo
la volontà, che a l'ira ed a l'orgoglio
d'Amor si fece poi argine e muro.

Così, senza temer di dar in scoglio,
mi vivo in porto omai queto e securo;
d'un sol mi lodo, e di nessun mi doglio. § (p. 260)

⁓

Quest'è via da salir a gloria vera,
questo può farti da l'orto a l'occaso
e di verace onor chiara ed altera. || (p. 260)

⁓

---

* CCXXXI.   † CLI.   ‡ CCXXXV.   § CCII. || CCVI.

A mezzo il mare, ch'io varcai tre anni
fra dubbi venti, ed era quasi in porto,
m'ha ricondotta Amor, che a sì gran torto
è ne' travagli miei pronto e ne' danni;

E per doppiare a' miei disiri i vanni,
un sì chiaro oriente agli occhi ha pòrto,
che, rimirando lui, prendo conforto,
e par che manco il travagliar m'affanni.

Un foco equale al primo foco io sento,
e, se in sì poco spazio questo è tale,
che de l'altro non sia maggior, pavento.

Ma che poss'io, se m'è l'arder fatale,
se volontariamente andar consento
d'un foco in altro, e d'un in altro male? * (p. 261)

~

Qual sagittario, che sia sempre avezzo
trarre ad un segno, e mai colpo non falla,
o da propria vaghezza tratto o dalla
spene, c'ha da trarne onore e prezzo,

Amor, che nel mio mal mai non è sezzo,
torna a ferirmi il cor, né mai si stalla,
e la piaga or risalda apre e rifalla;
né mi val s'io 'l temo o s'io lo sprezzo.

Tanto di me ferir diletto prende,
e tal n'attende e merca onor, ch'omai
per quel ch'io provo, ad altro non intende.

Il vivo foco, ond'io arsi e cantai
molti anni, a pena è spento, che raccende
d'un altro il cor, che tregua non ha mai. † (p. 261)

~

È un affetto ardente, un van disìo
. . .
Un cercar suo malgrado con affanno
quel che o mai non si trova, o, se pur viene,
avuto, arreca penitenza e danno,

. . .
Un avilirsi al viso amato innante
un esser fuor di lui franca ed ardita
un non saper tener ferme le piante

. . .

● Track 43,
Reading 44

● Track 44,
Reading 45

---

* CCXXI.   † CCXI.

Un non dormire . . .
Un destarsi sdegnosa ed un sognarsi
sempre cosa contraria a quel che vuoi,

Un aver doglia e non voler lagnarsi
di chi n'offende, anzi rivolger l'ira
contra se stesso e sol seco sdegnarsi.

Un veder sol un viso ove si mira,
un in esso affissarsi, benchè lunge,
un gioir l'alma, quando si sospira,

e finalmente un mal che unge e punge.* (pp. 262 – 63)

---

* CCXLI.

NOTES

1   Our translations of Gaspara's poems are drawn from the edition of her collected works brought out by Abdelkader Salza in *Gaspara Stampa-Veronica Franco, Rime* (Bari, 1913), which is based on the first edition, published in 1554. For an annotated list of all the editions see Flora Bassanese, *Gaspara Stampa* (Boston, 1982), pp. 137–38.

2   In the notes to his edition of Stampa's *Rime* (Milan, 1954), reprinted as footnotes in Maria Bellonci, ed., *Gaspara Stampa, Rime* (Milan, 1994), Rodolfo Ceriello points out (p. 212) that this "passionate affirmation" of love was quoted by Gabriele D'Annunzio in his novel *Il Fuoco* (translated as *The Flame of Life*).

3   Abdelkader Salza, "Madonna Gasparina Stampa secondo nuove indagini," *Giornale Storico della Letteratura Italiana* 62 (1913): pp. 1–101. Together with his later article "Madonna Gasparina Stampa e la società veneziana del suo tempo," *Giornale Storico della Letteratura Italiana* 70 (1917): 281–299, Salza has provided the most minutely detailed study of Stampa and her circle. For the controversy, see, in her defense, G. A. Borgese, "Il processo di Gaspara Stampa," *Studi di letterature moderne* (Milan, 1915), pp. 20–28; E. G. Innocenzi, "In difesa di Gaspara Stampa," *L'Ateneo Veneto* 38 (1915): pp. 1–160, 280–88; G. A. Cesareo, *Gaspara Stampa donna e poetessa* (Naples, 1920). B. Croce, writing in the *Giornale Storico della Letteratura Italiana* (pp. 390–392), agreed with Salza, as did G. Brognoligo, "Gaspara Stampa," *Giornale Storico della Letteratura Italiana* 76 (1920): pp. 134–35. Croce later softened his view, tending to agree with E. Donadoni, *Gaspara Stampa: Vita e opere* (Messina, 1919), that Stampa was "una irregolare."

4   Salza, "Madonna Gasparina Stampa," p. 10.

5   Quoted by Giulio Dolci in *Letteratura Italiana: I Minori* (Milan, 1961), p. 1319.

6   Salza, "Madonna Gasparina Stampa," p. 18.

7   Salza, "Madonna Gasparina Stampa," p. 16. On the role of music in these gatherings, see Sheila Schonbrun, "Ambitious Artists: Music-Making among Italian Renaissance Courtesans (with particular reference to Tullia d'Aragona, Gaspara Stampa, and Veronica Franco)" (Ph.D. dissertation, City University of New York, 1998).

8   Benedetto Croce, *Poesia popolare e poesia d'arte* (Bari, 1933), pp. 366–367.

9   F. Bassanese, *Gaspara Stampa*, especially pp. 39, 122 and passim.

10   As we have noted earlier, it was the custom to take an academic name when becoming a member of one of the *accademie*. That she began to call herself Anasilla therefore supports the supposition that Gaspara was invited to join an *accademia*. It is not known to which academy she belonged; the Accademia dei Dubbiosi, the Accademia degli Infiammati, and the Accademia dei Pellegrini have all been suggested. She chose the name Anasilla because she wished to identify herself with Collaltino; the name Anasilla is derived from Anaxum, the ancient name of the Piave River, which ran through the Collalto estate. Ceriello in Bellonci, p. 120, note 1 and p. 167, note 2. In her sonnet LXV, for example, she writes to Collaltino, "Deh, se vi fu giamai dolce e soave / la vostra fidelissima Anasilla . . ." (Oh, if ever there were anyone so sweet and tender as your Anasilla. . .). See also the dissertation of Catherine Allen Carlson, "Gaspara Stampa and Cinquecento Petrarchism" (Yale University, 1978), p. 61, n. 60.

11   See Patricia L. Natalicchi, "Woman as Hero: The Legend of Gaspara Stampa" (Ph.D. dissertation, Johns Hopkins University, 1986), with which we most closely agree in our interpretation of Stampa's fundamental desire for fame as a poet.

12   Cassandra's account is given in her dedication of the volume to Archbishop Giovanni Della Casa, dated 13 October 1554.

13   Maria Zancan, "Rime di Gaspara Stampa," in *Letteratura Italiana: Le opere dal cinquecento al settecento* (Turin, 1993), vol. II, p. 410.

14   *Rime di Madonna Gaspara Stampa, con Alcune Altre di Collaltino, e di Vinciguerra, conti di Collalto: e di Baldasare Stampa* (Venice, 1738), p. x.

15   Count Rambaldo in *Rime* (1738), pp. xx–xxi. This painting by Guercino is now unlocated.

16   *Gaspara Stampa* was a drama in verse performed at the Eretenio Theatre in Vicenza in 1857. It has now been totally forgotten, but it seems to have made a lasting impression on Arrigo Boito,

Verdi's librettist for *Otello*: In the last scene, Gaspara, having taken poison because of her despair at losing Collaltino, bids her sister goodbye with the words, *"Un bacio ancora, un altro bacio!"* ("Another kiss, one more kiss!") the words Boito famously gave to Otello to end the opera—thirty years later. The play was published in Venice in 1857. Othello's last words in Shakespeare's play were: "I kissed thee ere I killed thee: no way but this; killing myself I die upon a kiss."

17   It seems likely that Cabianca got the name wrong from his unknown source for his play.

18   Count Rambaldo in *Rime*, 1738, p. xxii.

19   See Bassanese, above, note 1.

20   Bassanese, *Gaspara Stampa*, p. 17. Presumably she sent them to him in France for, as we will see, he left Venice for France at the end of May to take up military service for Henri II.

21   Bassanese, *Gaspara Stampa*, p. 13.

22   In addition to the drama by Jacopo Cabianca, see also Diodata Saluzzo-Roero (1774–1840), *Gaspara Stampa*, included in *Versi di Diodata Saluzzo-Roero* (Turin, 1817) and Luigi Carrer, "Gaspara Stampa," in *Anello di sette gemme o Venezia e la sua storia* (Venice, 1838), republished in 1851 as *Amore infelice di Gaspara Stampa*. See also Bassanese, *Gaspara Stampa*, especially pp. 25–27.

23   Even the curators of the Budapest Museum of Fine Arts did not realize that the museum owns a portrait of the poet Gaspara Stampa. The discovery was made by Gernando Colombardo.

CHAPTER NINE

ISOTTA BREMBATE

(CA. 1530 – 1586)

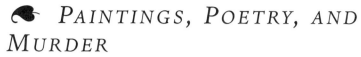 *PAINTINGS, POETRY, AND MURDER*

ergamo Alta, the setting for the portraits, poetry, and the 1563 murder of this account, is an ancient city spread over the top of an alpine foothill, about one thousand feet above the Lombard plain of northern Italy.* Still redolent of its Gothic and Renaissance past, its spacious Piazza Vecchia (figure 9.1) is today almost exactly as it was in the sixteenth century. Behind the piazza is the church of Santa Maria Maggiore. Despite its tumultuous, violent history of constant family feuds and atrocious foreign invasions, Bergamo, like much of Italy, maintained a highly cultivated society and contributed a number of humanist-grounded artists and writers to European Renaissance culture; its popular *bergamasque*, a lively country dance with its own music, was widely known in the late sixteenth and early seventeenth centuries: far away in England, the audience at *Midsummer Night's Dream* heard Bottom ask, in the play's final scene, "Will it please you to see the epilogue, or to hear a Bergomask dance between two of our company?" Theseus answers, "No epilogue, I pray you . . . but come, your Bergomask."

Intrigue, betrayal, and violence were part of daily life in Bergamo. So were family feuds, one of the most famous of which took place among the Brembati and Albani. Fortunately, we have portraits of some of the actors in the drama of the fierce Brembate-Albani feud.[1]

Prominent among the literary figures of Bergamo in the second half of the Cinquecento was Isotta Brembate (plate VI), member of an illustrious, noble Bergamo family that we will see involved in the murders. She was highly esteemed in her lifetime for her poetic and linguistic gifts, and when she died in 1586, "a glory to her feminine sex, an eloquent speaker, an eminent poet," Torquato Tasso (figure 9.2) was one of the thirty-one poets who contributed poems to the volume of verse in her honor.

> *New victims are every moment led to Death*
> *Who unfurls his black banner and wields his triumphant scepter*
> *over all mortals,*
> *the high as well as the low, the weak as well as the strong.*
>
> *But you, my lady, never surrendered*
> *to the shadows of death and his horrible triumph*
> *which you, more noble, trample underfoot,*

---

* This chapter is dedicated to Carlo Cassinari, who encouraged me to take up this project when we were in Bergamo but did not live to see it completed.

9.1.
Bergamo in the
16th century: La
Vecchia Piazza.
Laura B.Colombi
and Maria
Mencaroni
Zoppetti,
*Storie di botteghe,
mestieri e
commerci nella
Piazza Vecchia di
Bergamo e
dintorni tra XVI e
XVII secolo. n.d.*

disdaining Hell, the Styx and the gates of Tartarus

> *Only a part of you, weak and tired, was defeated,*
> *—you who deserve roses, and laurel and myrtle,*
> *even the Serio and Brembo must mourn—**

> *Not the other part, the spirit, which rises to heaven,*
> *for your fame on earth is neither diminished nor forgotten,*
> *nor can death overcome your name and poetry.*[2] (p. 299)

All but forgotten, nevertheless, Isotta was saved from total oblivion not by her poems, of which only one *canzone* and three sonnets have survived, but by two portraits,
one bust-length, the other a full-length seated figure, and possibly a third, all of which
we will discuss.

Isotta was the daughter of Geronimo Brembate's third wife, Daria Roata, and the
granddaughter of Lucina and Leonino Brembate (figures 9.3, 9.4), whose portraits
had been painted about 1520 by Lorenzo Lotto. Both have visual puns and abstruse
references, characteristic of sixteenth-century taste, and these portraits kept their se-
crets for many years—centuries, in fact. It was not until 1913 that a scholar identified
the subject of *Portrait of a Lady* (as the painting had been labeled), as Lucina Brembate
on the basis of the ring she wears that bears the Brembate crest. This scholar then
solved the rebus in the upper left. In the crescent moon appear the letters "c i"; the let-

---

* These are the two rivers that water the Bergamo plain.

9.2.
Alessandro
Allori.
*Portrait of
Torquato Tasso.*
ca. 1590.
Galleria degli
Uffizi, Florence.
Photo,
Alinari/Art
Resource.

ters are literally inside the *luna* (moon), Lu-ci-na, spelling her name. Almost eighty years later, another scholar pointed out that in Leonino's portrait he is shown holding a gold lion's paw in his left hand, a punning reference to *his* name. His right hand is pressed against his chest in an identifying gesture, as "Leo" the lion. She pointed out, moreover, that the husband and wife paintings, as a pair, hold a further significance: Leonino's portrait with its gold lion's paw represents gold, symbolizing the sun, complementing Lucina's moon, which reflects the light of the sun.[3]

Their granddaughter, Isotta, one of the brightest stars in Bergamo's social and humanist firmament, was well educated probably by private tutors or in a convent. She is said to have written verse in Latin, French, and Spanish in addition to her native tongue, and it was in Spanish that she wrote the motto for the *impresa* (devise) she invented as her personal symbol, a walled garden enclosing a tree bearing golden apples and guard-

9.3.
Lorenzo Lotto.
*Portrait of Lucina
Brembate.*
ca. 1520.
Accademia
Carrara,
Bergamo.
Photo, Museum.

ed by a dragon in front of the garden portal (figure 9.5). Across the top of the *impresa* are the words *yo meior las guardarè* (I will guard them better). A poem written in Spanish by Giovanni Battista Brembate, a distant cousin of Isotta and a major figure in one of the murders, identified the image as referring to the Garden of the Hesperides, from which Hercules managed to steal the golden apples after slaying the dragon.

> *Yours is the beauty, beautiful Isolde,*[*]
> *Of the famed Hesperides garden.*
> *the tree bearing its golden fruit, I see,*
> *is your resolute chastity.*
>
> *But the lurking serpent is dead,*

---

[*] Isolde: Isotta.

9.4.
Lorenzo Lotto.
*Portrait of
Leonino Brembate.*
ca. 1520.
Kunsthistorisches
Museum,
Vienna. Photo,
Museum.

worldly pride is overcome;
over the door is written with obscure elegance
"I will guard them better",

    Because you look not to the honor
in which the vain world struts
but to the Lord who has given you so much.

> *And thus trusting to His divine power,*
> *señora, you would rather await Him*
> *whom your ardent soul desires.*[4] (p. 299)

Girolamo Ruscelli, abbot of Monte Cassino and an important contemporary writer, was not completely satisfied with Giovanni Battista's interpretation. He believed the golden apples symbolized chastity *and* honor and that the dragon signified the physical and irrational in human beings which must be vanquished by the power of elevated thought.[5] Ruscelli's reading of Isotta's enigmatic motto is supported by the poet's concerns as she expressed them in her poetry:

> *Sublime thought always*
> *unburdens my heart of other thought*
> *like the brilliant sun lightens dark clouds*
> *shows me the true path to heaven.*

> *This alone rules my breast*
> *and creates desire, forms rose and violet words,*
> *as changing as April*
> *under the majestic sun*

> *Now, if Heaven and Nature*
> *wish that the sun be within me*
> *who is powerful enough then to take it away?*

> *However much cruel Fortune might oppose this*
> *she can never challenge*
> *the mindful care of heaven.* (p. 300)

Isotta's year of birth is not known, but circumstances point to about 1530. In her portrait by Giovanni Battista Moroni, stylistically belonging to his work of ca. 1550, she appears to be about twenty years old.[6] Scholars have held that the style of her dress and the pearls decorating her hair suggest that she was a married woman, which seems doubtful inasmuch as even very young children were dressed with similar elaborateness. In any case, at that time or shortly after, she was married to Lelio Secco d'Aragona, about whom very little is known; his name, however, identifies him as a member of the family of Aragonese rulers of Spain and southern Italy. Lelio died around 1560, and in 1561 Isotta married Gian Girolamo Grumelli, whose portrait, also by Moroni, we will also discuss.

The bust-length portrait of Isotta gives us an arresting face, turned three-quarters to the viewer's left, with a knowing and somewhat mischievous expression, the face of a witty, intelligent young woman, framed by a high, crinkled collar with red rick-rack trim. It is that collar, in fact, that leads us into a puzzle.

In the collection of the Conti Moroni in Bergamo there is another portrait of Isotta Brembate (plate VII). This is a seated whole length with Isotta facing to our right, now, more mature, richly attired with a fur piece around her shoulders. The most

YO MEIOR LAS GVARDARE

9.5.
Impresa of Isotta
Brembate. n.d.
Girolamo
Ruscelli,
*Le imprese
illustri.*
Venice, 1566.

recent scholar concerned with Brembate has pointed out that the stand-up collar around her neck is identical with that of the earlier portrait, without, however, finding anything curious about a woman wanting to be portrayed twice wearing the same inconsequential article of clothing.[7] It is, however, passing strange, and surely requires an explanation.

We begin by noticing that the position of the head and the collar in the two paintings is reversed as if one were the mirror image of the other. We then notice that, in the earlier portrait, the collar with its red trim obviously matches the dress while it has nothing to do with the green and gold damask dress in the later one. The artist obviously placed the earlier portrait in front of a mirror and painted the reflected head and collar, the head now turned to the viewer's right, adding the seated figure.[8] Furthermore, it has been noted by all scholars writing about this painting that there is something awkward about the pose of the seated figure. How does one account for this in view of the fact that Moroni was an excellent artist, a realist who was perfectly in control of the representation of objects in space? He had, in fact, painted another woman, Lucia Albani Avogadro, also a poet (see the appendix) and also a figure in the murder story (figure 9.6), seated in the same pose, in the same chair, as can be seen by its shape and the same three pegs on the side of the chair arm, but without any awkwardness. In view of these anomalies we are forced to the conclusion that Moroni did not paint the seated portrait. There would have been no reason for him to have used a mirror image of his first portrait of Isotta for a second one, painted some years later.

The most reasonable explanation for why the head and collar are mirror images is that they were painted by some other artist when the subject was no longer living. This was probably Giovan Paolo Lolmo (ca.1550–1593), a Bergamo artist to whom is attributed a bust length *Portrait of a Woman with a Fur Scarf* in the Accademia Carrara. This portrait duplicates the head and bust of the seated Isotta, wearing the same collar and the gold-headed fur scarf, and it can hardly be doubted that the same artist did this bust and the seated Isotta.

Moroni died in 1577, Isotta nine years later. Let us imagine that her husband, Gian Girolamo Grumelli, wanted a portrait of his wife, not as a young girl but as the more mature woman she was when they married. Furthermore, he had himself been portrayed by Moroni in 1560 in a large full-length (figure 9.7) and might well have wanted a large full-length of Isotta. Because there was probably no artist who had known her and remembered her as she was twenty-five years earlier, Grumelli would have had to provide an image. There was the bust portrait of the young Isotta, now in the Accademia Carrara, and one other, now in the same museum where it is exhibited with the title *Busto di dama con gorgiera* (Portrait of a Lady with a Frilled Collar), formerly identified as Isotta Brembate (figure 9.8). The identification was withdrawn after it was disputed and discarded by modern scholars. However, the evidence before our eyes suggests that the original identification is correct. There is a strong resemblance between the two bust portraits, and in the second one the sitter is wearing the fur piece seen in the seated *Isotta* with the identical animal's head magnificently mounted in gold and its mouth holding the double gold chain. Let us assume that the artist had both portraits available to copy. Why did he need to make an image from a mirror or a camera obscura? Since it is likely that Grumelli would have wanted the Isotta portrait as a pendant to his own, it would have to be turned to the right, to respond to his own, turned to the left. The new artist therefore took as his model for the figure Moroni's seated portrait of Lucia Albani Avogadro who is turned toward the right. This artist thus painted from a mirror-image of the head and shoulders of the first bust of Isotta so that it, too, would face to the right, altered the face so that she would look somewhat older, and painted the rest of the figure in Lucia's pose, with a typically Moroniesque background to harmonize with the Grumelli portrait. That is why the figure looks awkwardly posed. It is an image composed from the two previous portraits of Isotta plus the one of Lucia Albani Avogadro.[9]

The Brembate-Grumelli connection confronts us with another puzzle, albeit of a very different kind. The portrait of Grumelli (whose cousin was one of the murder victims) is a masterpiece in Moroni's oeuvre; it is signed and dated MDLX on the broken piece of stone at the lower right, which would make him twenty-four years old at the time.[10] Standing in an architectural space, he is wearing a superb reddish-colored attire in Spanish style, set off brilliantly against the grey stone. At the joints of the wall buttress the stone is chipped. The flat wall behind Grumelli is interrupted by a half-seen concave niche which formerly held a statue—a fragment of the statue's foot remains on a base within the niche. The niche itself has lost its upper wall allowing a view beyond into the blue sky. Ivy grows out of the ruined wall. On the floor below the niche lies a classical torso, which has apparently fallen from its base. All of these

9.6.
Giovanni
Battista Moroni.
Portrait of Lucia
Albani
Avogadro (The
Lady in Red).
ca. 1550.
National Gallery,
London.
Photo, National
Gallery.

details point to time past. In the wall under the niche there is represented a figurative sculptural relief with the scene of Elijah rising to the heavens in the fiery chariot, throwing his mantle to his follower, Elisha. Under the scene are the words in Spanish,

> Más el Caguero
> Que el primero

These words, which lend to the portrait an abstruse meaning, have perplexed

9.7.
Giovanni
Battista Moroni.
*Portrait of Gian
Gerolamo
Grumelli*. 1561.
Collection of
Count Antonio
Moroni,
Bergamo.
Photo,
Count Antonio
Moroni.

ANNO AETATIS XXX·

9:8.
Giovanni
Battista Moroni.
*Portrait of a
Woman with a
Frilled Collar (A
Woman of Thirty
Years).*
ca. 1560-1565.
Accademia
Carrara,
Bergamo.
Photo,
Accademia.

scholars, and have been translated variously, the closest as "più quel che vien dopo che il primo" (rather the one that comes after than the first), and interpreted as referring literally to the scene above, which it evidently does. However, the words have also been said to express only a general ethical meaning and to be a declaration of humility. This interpretation seems inadequate for two reasons: although the phrase resonates with the words of Jesus Christ, "The last shall be first," Grumelli does not look humble, and it leaves out of consideration the relevance of the biblical scene to the portrait as a whole. Perhaps a new approach may come closer to the intended meaning.

There are two very strong emphases in Grumelli's portrait. One is on the Spanish taste and affiliation—he is dressed as a Spanish nobleman and was, indeed, one of the many Hispanophiles among the nobility in Bergamo—and the motto, which is given in Spanish. The other emphasis is double-edged; it is on the unlamented past on which Grumelli turns his back, and on the passing of power from an earlier prophet, Elijah, to the one who came after, Elisha: Grumelli's sword slices diagonally across the biblical scene exactly along the line that separates the two prophets, thus making a very strong visual statement that stresses the importance of the division between the prophets, between what *was* and what *is or will be*. Biblical references in a secular work of visual art usually provide a signal that suggests to the viewer a context deeper than the apparent subject. One must look for a content that concerns large, important issues—possibly war and peace. Let us glance back to what we have written in earlier chapters about the military-political situation in Cinquecento Italy up to 1560 when the portrait was painted.

France and Spain had made Italy a battleground for sixty-five years. The so-called Italian Wars had started when Charles VIII of France invaded Italy in 1495. His successor, Louis XII, occupied Milan in 1499. A Swiss army stormed the city in 1512 and wrested Lombardy away from the French. The year after Francis I became king of France in 1515 and embarked on his campaign to recoup France's losses in Italy, he faced the immense power of his rival, Charles I of Spain, who in 1519 became Emperor Charles V of the Holy Roman Empire. The pope, Clement VII, formed a league with France, Venice, and Florence against Charles in 1526, and the Spanish army with German mercenaries marched on Rome and sacked the city in 1527. In the following decades alliances were made, reshuffled, constantly betrayed among the power players—the emperor, the pope, the French kings, and their ever-changing alignments with Venice, Florence, and the Turks. Italy was devastated.

> *What crimes have they committed,*

Leonora Ravira Falletti asks,

> *Our unfortunate abodes*
> *our old people, our fertile plains,*
> *that they must suffer the stubborn, cruel, insane ambitions*
> *Enclosed in those illustrious breasts?*
>
> *These nests were chosen by our ancestors,*
> *without honoring Caesar more than Janus*
> *and now, miserable, we must be servants and subjects*
> *to France and Spain.*
>
> *If at least this painful struggle*
> *that has lasted more than twenty years and is worsening*
> *might end so that we would be under only one yoke.*
>
> *What I fear, with good reason, is*
> *that we will be forced to abandon our ancestral homes*
> *or be vanquished by hunger.*[11] (p. 300)

Bergamo had been invaded time and again by French and Imperial-Spanish armies in turn. At last, in 1559, the hostilities ended with the peace of Cateau-Cambrésis. Spain was the big winner, firmly in control of the Kingdom of Naples, Sicily, and Sardinia, with coastal fortresses on the Tyrrhenian Sea and now controlling the duchy of Milan and all of Lombardy. Falletti must have been somewhat relieved that Italy was under "only one yoke." The Hispanophiles in Bergamo must have exulted. Grumelli's portrait was painted the following year.[12]

Turning now to Grumelli's portrait and the detail of Elijah and Elisha, we remember that Elijah gave his mantle twice to Elisha, the first when the older prophet took Elisha as his follower, the second, the scene actually represented, when Elijah ascends to heaven in the fiery chariot, throwing his mantle to Elisha and granting to his spiritual heir his request for a double share of Elijah's spirit. Is the "double share" the subject of the preference expressed in the motto? Or is it more likely that the Elijah-Elisha story is linked to the historical account we have just given?

During the lifetimes of the two prophets there was constant war between Israel and Judah, with sieges and starvation, massacres and endless suffering, just as Bergamo had suffered so often, torn between France and Spain. But while in Ecclesiasticus 48:1–2 we read, "Then the prophet Elijah arose like fire, his word flaring like a torch. It was he who brought famine on [Israel's enemies] and who decimated them in his zeal," when Elisha captures the Aramaean army and delivers his prisoners to the king of Israel who asks, "Shall I kill them?" Elisha answers "Do not kill them. Do you put prisoners to death when you have taken them with your sword and your bow? Offer them bread and water for them to eat and drink, and let them go back to their master." After this, "Aramaean armies never invaded the territory of Israel again" (2 Kings 6:18–23). Comparing the two prophets, it appears that Elisha, having triumphed over the enemy, was the one through whom peace was won, and it seems plausible to believe that this is the thought expressed in that enigmatic motto under the representation of the biblical scene, in a portrait painted not long after the peace of Cateau-Cambrésis.

Now that we have seen some of the cast of characters, let us take up three of the crimes that throughout Italy were the down side of the "splendid and cruel" Renaissance, as Silvana Milesi has characterized it.[13] In Bergamo, civic life had often been disturbed not only by foreign invasion but also by violent outbreaks of family feuds, none more violent, and tragic, than that between the Brembate and Albani families. In the decade before the murder in 1563 mentioned at the beginning of this chapter, the authorities of the city had tried repeatedly to stop the hostility—the origins of which no one is certain—between Giovanni Battista Brembate, a relative of Isotta from another branch of the family, and Giovanni Gerolamo Albani. Both men, born around 1509, had won many high honors, and in 1555 Albani had been named *collaterale generale*, a commander in the Venetian army, while Brembate had been given the rank of colonel by the Spanish duke of Alba in 1556 in recognition of his valiant service in the imperial forces against France, sometime ally of Venice. The feud, indeed, unfolded against the background of mutual hostility between Spanish Milan and the Francophile Venetian Republic, to which Bergamo belonged. In addition to his military career, Giovanni Battista Brembate was also known as a poet (see p. 284), and even won praise from Pietro Aretino, although this might be owed to Brembate's having provided him with *confetti* (sugared almonds), at that time a prized product of Bergamo.

Albani, commander in the Venetian army, had seven children, of whom four are of interest to us: Francesco, Domenico, Giovanni Battista, and Lucia, the same Lucia whose portrait by Moroni was used as a model for the seated Isotta. He denounced Brembate as a spy for Spain, claiming that the colonel had won his rank in the Spanish army as a reward for that service. Fighting between the factions continued, and in 1560 Giovanni Battista was assaulted by a gang as he was leaving the house of Francesco Secco d'Aragona with his usual company of bodyguards. An excellent swordsman, Brembate escaped. He accused Francesco Albani, Gio. Gerolamo's son, of instigating the attack. Francesco was found guilty by a Venetian court and sentenced to two years of confinement in Venice. Francesco's hired assassins were sentenced to the galleys for eighteen months. The entire city of Bergamo was angrily divided between partisans of each family.

Brembate, dissatisfied with Francesco's light sentence, sent a group of *bravi* to Venice to assassinate Francesco. The plot was discovered, but Brembate was warned that his arrest was imminent, and he fled to Spanish protection in Milan. He was sentenced in Venice, however, to perpetual banishment from the Republic.

In 1563, during Lent, Francesco Albani, returned from his confinement in Venice, informed the mayor of Bergamo that he and his family wanted to make peace with the Brembati and proposed a meeting. Because Giovanni Battista was still living in Milan, the mayor asked his brother, Achille, to go to the meeting in his place. Francesco Albani with his brother, Domenico, suggested that they meet on 1 April at the mayor's office, going first to Santa Maria Maggiore to ask God's pardon and advice, and to hear the mass. Achille arrived at the church, listened to the sermon, and knelt when the mass began. As the priest raised the consecrated host, a gunshot rang out. Achille was hit but not killed. He rose to his feet and the assassins fell on him with daggers; more shots were heard, and the attackers fled. Achille was carried outside the church to a shop nearby on the Piazza Vecchia, where there is today a bookstore, and there he died.

The Albani, father and sons, their accomplices and hired assassins, were found guilty by a tribunal in Venice, where Emilia Brembate, Achille's sister and also a poet (see the appendix, pp. 306 – 7), spoke with apparently unforgettable fervor of the betrayal and the sacrilege of the murder. They were condemned to banishment in various places, the sons perpetually banished from Venice, although not the father who was sentenced to a five-year confinement on the island of Lesina, off the Dalmatian coast, where he wrote poems lamenting his exile and fallen state, Venice having taken from him his title of *collaterale generale*. The hired assassins were sentenced to hideous executions, carried out immediately. The assassination had tragic consequences for many Bergamese, including Lucia Albani Avogadro and her husband, who after the murder left Bergamo to live in Ferrara, where they both died within a few years. We have included in the appendix a poem by Lucia expressing her misery.

Giovanni Brembate, still vengeful, organized another attack, this time successful; the victim was an accomplice of the Albani faction and the elder Albani's cousin by marriage, Giovanni Battista Grumelli, cousin also to Isotta Brembate's husband. Shot and killed by "parties unknown," the murder was quickly traced to Giovanni Brembate as the instigator. Venice condemned him for the second time to perpetual banishment, vainly, of course, for he was living in Milan with a large escort of bodyguards provided by the Spanish governor of the city. But although the principals were no

longer in Bergamo, their supporters carried on the vendetta with frequent occurrences of violent incidents.

In 1568 Giovanni Gerolamo Albani, his five-year exile over, went to Rome to see his
friend Pope Pius V, who owed him a favor: in 1550 Pius V, at that time Father Inquisi-
tor Michele Ghisleri, had aroused the ire of the Bergamese by investigating their Bishop Soranzo for heresy. The convent of Santo Stefano, where Ghisleri was staying, was
attacked, but Ghisleri got away and managed to get to Urgnano, an Albani castle that
belonged to Gio. Gerolamo, who hid him until it was safe for him to leave. Pius remembered his debt to Albani. In 1570 the erstwhile banished conspirator became *Cardinale di San Giovanni ante portam latinam* and his sons were named to the Roman
nobility. Through the interventions of the kings and queens of France and Spain, the
Pope, Don Giovanni of Austria, and the Pasha of Turkey, by 1573 Venice and Spain
had canceled all of the banishments and death sentences, with the sole proviso that
the Albani sons could not return to Bergamo. The Brembati had to face the fact that
their enemy had triumphed brilliantly. There was no choice but to make peace.

Giovanni Battista Brembate died in Milan in 1573; Francesco Albani died in 1575.
In the following years Emilia Brembate resisted fiercely every attempt of Giovanni
Gerolamo Albani to have the ban on his sons lifted. It was a frustrated and angry cardinal who wrote to the Venetian authorities that unless they used force, "the stub-
bornness of a woman would succeed in keeping his sons exiled." Finally, in 1580,
perhaps after her death, he had his final triumph over the Brembati; Giovanni Battista
and Domenico were allowed to enter Bergamo. The cardinal died in 1591 in Rome.

But the Brembate family was not finished with murder. In 1577, Isotta's brother,
Leonino, the grandson of the Leonino portrayed by Lotto, was killed by Ottavio
Brembate, Isotta's son-in-law, married to Flaminia, her daughter by her first marriage.
Ottavio was apprehended and sentenced to banishment.

Ottavio and Leonino descended from different lines of the family, which had a
common ancestor in one Aiolfo who flourished in the thirteenth century. Leonino
had no children, so Isotta as his nearest relative inherited his very large estate, worth
many millions of dollars today. Ottavio's father, Giovanni Davide, brought a suit
against Isotta, challenging her right to the inheritance on the grounds that his son was
the nearest *male* relative, although he was nine generations removed from Aiolfo.
However, the will of Isotta's great-grandfather, Luca, stipulated not only that his
wealth must always remain in the Brembate family but that future heirs must always
bear the arms of his family. Giovanni Davide had to admit that his family arms dif-
fered from that of the other family. In a document that seems to be Isotta's deposition
she remarked that Ottavio had killed Leonino "without legitimate [!] cause." She apparently did not accuse the father and son of killing Leonino for the inheritance they
thought would be theirs.

On 6 February 1582 a notary, Giovanni Antonio Suardo, wrote Isotta's will for her
because she was somehow unable to write: from what we can infer from various
sources, including her doctor's letter to a priest requesting that she be allowed to eat
meat on Friday because she needed "plenty of red meat," she was ill during the last
years of her life. Although she had had ten children, a son and three daughters with
Lelio, and three daughters and three sons with Grumelli, when she made her will her
only son by Lelio was dead, the other children were nuns or married except one of her

daughters with Grumelli, Virginia, whom she made heir of her estate after the death of Grumelli, who had the use of it as usufructuary.[14]

One of the few surviving poems by Isotta is a long *canzone* written sometime before 1571:

> *The lovely Aurora*
> *had already spread her beautiful golden hair*
> *and the resplendent Apollo on his daily journey*
> *swiftly rose toward the sky*
> *then with my mind free from earthly thought*
> *I saw a woman*
> *adorned around her fair face and neck*
> *with flowers of every kind*
> *which, singing, formed a crown as they fluttered*
> *like bees amid those sweet flowers*
> *over nymphs and cupids,*
> *filling all with marvelous delight;*
> *their garments of infinite variety*
> *were strange, delightful.*
> *Curious, I turned to hear what was going on, and to see*
> *if I recognized any of this lovely multitude*
> *that never craves amorous pleasure*
> *but even less does my mortal self,*
> *troubled by such knowledge,*
> *recognize its divine nature.*
>
>   *Thus filled with desire and sweetness,*
> *I turned my uncertain steps from their usual end*
> *urged and swayed by my pleasure.*
> *Then that woman whose subtle beauty*
> *sometimes blinds and overwhelms human will*
> *and sometimes raises it from base thoughts, to heaven*
> *addressed me, her voice angelic and divine:*
> *"You, seeking the good,*
> *which is close by*
> *and which burns away mortal afflictions, naked and weak,*
> *search for the principle and the purpose of my destiny*
> *under my guidance*
> *follow the solitary, lonely path*
> *that one perceives as the true aim of all joy.*
> *And because it may be difficult for you*
> *to spend many hours, days, years*
> *following me through the sacred labyrinth*
> *made by Daedalus, keep your spirits high*
> *knowing that this sweet anxiety calls to you*
> *the favor of your lucky star."*

Like a timid bird trying its wings for the first time
still doubtful of its weight
I shook my new wings and started off
behind this lovely woman who, following the sun,
soared between the two poles.
She began to speak to me again
in language I could hardly understand.
"Before the beginning of Time,
in darkness I was born,
naked, and without beauty, as willed by the Creator,
but desiring divine light
and following my destiny,
I turned, and his divine light
impressed on my breast
designs that were colored and shaped by the hollow sky.
But this is the least of it: You will soon see and understand
The art of the ancient saints toward whom we are traveling."
So saying, she led me past the limits of the Atlantic,
The new lands, and the Ganges,
Descending where the Hippocrene murmurs and splashes.

"Then," she continued, "after Argo, the superb ship,
brought back from Colchis
the Golden Fleece,
Jove affixed it to the sky
between Hydra and the constellation of the Great Dog."
At the will of the muses we moved on.
I enter then their sphere where they welcome me as a pilgrim,
ready to take me to the beautiful beyond
where the soul rejoices and is full of love.
Then, ignoring the center rim,
we press on toward the sky with long swoops
and the goddesses, honored and revered by Parnassus,
heighten my awareness and my desire for the good
with their divine songs and words.
Looking down now from strenuous flight
upon the little globe where the sun sets
and encloses both the glorious earth and human follies
I disdain the long weariness which on earth,
where the sun is lower and colder, overwhelms one,
and we enter the heavens with light steps.

Overcome by these marvels,
I gaze at the sublime lights and from the rhythm of some
strange and divine harmony, unlike any earthly song,
I perceive that I am moving

while, from one of my noble companions I heard:
"I notice your hesitation, but your devoted desire
to turn to the good must not pause here;
loving the Creator for his greatest work
aspire with us to reach the supreme sphere."
Thus rising toward heaven from circle to circle
my spirit becoming freer from earthly ties
now becomes angry against its pride and vainglory.
Thus coursing through the upper regions
on the slanted pathway from where Phaeton fell
because of the dreadful appearance of his monsters
and from where Apollo,
rising or descending,
sends out his sun rays
to the most distant and the nearest lands,
amazed, I rose over the sky and I was inflamed.

    "Now you filter into me, courteous goddesses,
The elixir that the winged horse
carried from the sacred mountain
so that I might sing of the
high purpose that directs our knowledge,
that part that I already understood.
While in that state, I saw, thanks to you,
The eternal mantle of him who instills sacred thoughts."
Nine circles of living flame
surrounded as its own circle that great light
which like a fountain or a river,
forever clear and shining
sends rays among the elected spirits
and rekindles their light so that they perceive
ultimately, the beautiful symbol of the
ineffable King who alone is eternal:
That powerful gaze still burns brightly in my thought,
freeing me from every stress.
I fell, longing to remain always in this
sweet and happy state.

    Oh, my song, you sense that, human, I lack the power
to put my sacred purpose to the highest trial
even though I return as a new phoenix.
If you find in heaven a great flame of merciful love,
I beg that my light which now is forced
might shine with splendor,
and may it be seen that the true God
lives in my mind
which is his temple. (pp. 300 – 3)

POEMS IN THE ORIGINAL ITALIAN
AND SPANISH

[On the death of Isotta Brembate]

Ogn'hor condotta è nova preda à Morte,   *Torquato Tasso*
ch'à tutti spiega la sua negra insegna   ● Track 45,
dal Mauro al'Indo, e tien lo scettro, e regna,   Reading 46
e l'alto al basso, e'l frale agguaglia al forte.

Ma l'horribil trionfo, e l'ombre smorte,
non seguì Donna mai d'honor più degna
di lei, che sotto i piedi hor pone, e sdegna
Averno, Stige, e le Tartaree porte.

Pur vinta è solo inferma parte, e stanca,
che meritava rose, e lauro, e mirto,
tal chè dee Serio, e Brembo anco dolersi.
L'altra non già: ma vola in Ciel lo spirto,
nè la sua fama in terra è spenta, ò manca,
*nè trionfa la Morte il nome, ò i versi.** (pp. 281 – 82)

~

De las esperidas la famosa huerta   *Giovanni Battista*
la hermosura es de vos hermosa Yseo   *Brembate*
y el arbol de las fructas d'oro veo
que la castidad es, que en vos resuerta.

Mas la serpiente aguardadora, muerta
la honrra es del mundo que perdida creo;
però es escripto en muy gentil rodeo,
mejor las guardarè, sobre la puerta.

Por que os mirais nò en l'hõrra en que vanea
el mundo vano, mas à la deuda
en que sois al Señor, que os donò tanto

Y ansì os fiando en el poder su santo
Señora, a guardareis mejor sin duda
El, que celosa ansì l'alma dessea.† (pp. 284 – 86)

~

---

* Giovanni Battista Licinio, ed., *Rime funerali* (see note 2), p. 86.
† Girolamo Ruscelli, *Le Imprese Illustri con esposizioni et discorsi* (Venice, 1566), p. 452 (as printed).

Isotta Brembate
◉ Track 46,
Reading 47

L'alto pensier, ch'ogn'altro mio pensiero
dal cor mi sgombra ogn'hor, come far suole
oscura nube chiaro ardente Sole
di gir' al Ciel mi mostra il camin vero.

Questo sol tien di petto mio l'impero
e'n mi cria desir, forma parole,
come suol vago April rose, e viole
con la virtù del Re de' lumi altero.

Dunque, se'l Ciel concorde a la natura,
consente, e vuol, che sol'ei meco stia
chi sia possente indi levarlo mai?

Si a mi, pur quanto può, Fortuna ria
contraria ogn'hor, ch'a la celeste cura
non potrà contrastar' ella giamai.* (p. 286)

〜

*Eleonora de la
Ravoire Falletti*[15]
◉ Track 47,
Reading 48

Che colpa han nostri sfortunai tetti:
gli antichi abitatori e il fertil piano,
de l'ostinato e rio desir insano
chiuso, per altro, in due si chiari petti?

Fur da' nostri avi questi nidi eletti
senza onorar più Cesare che Giano
ed or convien ch'al Franco ed all'Ispano
siamo, miseri noi, servi e soggetti,

Si terminasse almen la dura impresa
che passa il quarto lustro e più rinforza,
acciò un sol giogo ci tenesse avvinti.

Che così temo, e'l mio timor non erra,
ch'i patrii lari abbandonar sia forza,
o, che sarem da lunga fame vinti. † (p. 292)

〜

Isotta Brembate

Havea già sparsi à l'aria i bei crin d'oro
la vaga Aurora, e con spedito corso
inverso il Ciel salia l'aurato Apollo,
seguendo nel suo antico alto lavoro;
quando àlhor, che la mente in se ritorna,
sciolta d'ogni terreno human discorso,

---

* Luisa Bergalli, *Componimenti delle più illustri rimatrici di ogni secolo* (Venice, 1726), p. 241.
† Agne sod (as in note 11), p. 249.

donna vid'io fuor che 'l bel viso, e 'l collo,
tutta di varii fior cinta, e adorna:
cui, cantando, facean lieta corona
ninfe leggiadre e pargoletti amori:
Tra que' soavi fiori,
come l'api, volando, ogni persona
empiean di non usato alto diletto;
l'habito novo, e 'n mille guise schietto.
Vaga d'udir sua condition qual'era,
oltra mi trassi, e di veder s'alcuna
riconoscessi de la bella schiera
d'amoroso piacer non mai digiuna:
ma poco ancor del suo divin comprese
il mio mortal, cui troppo lume offese.

    Così di desir colma, e di dolcezza,
volgo del proprio fin l'incerti passi,
ove il mio bel piacer mi sprona, e 'n inchina:
indi costei, la cui vaga bellezza
hor tien l'human voler cieco e oppresso,
hor lo solleva al Ciel da pensier bassi,
dissemi in voce angelica, e divina,
tu, che seguendo il ben, ch'è qui dapresso
arde il mortal affetto ignudo, e 'nfermo,
cerchi il principio, e 'l fin de la mia sorte,
sotto mie fide scorte
segui l'erto sentier al vero solingo, e hermo,
c'huom scorge forse al vero fin d'ogni gioia:
et perchè forse à te sarà gran noia
il consumar molti anni, e giorni, e hore
dietro a miei passi; questi sacri vanni
che di Dedalo fur, con alto core
spiega felice, che à si dolci affanni
t' è favor chiama di benigna stella,
disposta à farti ancor beata, e bella.

    Come timido augel, che il primo volo
tenta, dubbioso ancor del proprio peso,
scossi le nove piume, e 'l corso presi,
che dietro al Sol fra l'un, el'altro Polo
tenea questa gentil Donna, che sciolse
ver me novo parlar fa pochi inteso.
Prima che il Sol girasse gli anni, e i mesi,
in ombra oscura, come il Fattor volse,
ignuda nacqui, e di bellezza priva;
ma desiando il bel raggio divino

seguendo il mio destino,
mi volsi, e da sua luce altiera, e diva
s'impresse nel mio sen la varia forma,
che il concavo del Ciel depinge e'informa.
Questo è del vero ben la minor parte.
Vedrailo à pien, se le vestigie sante
di quelle, à cui n'andiam, tu se qui, e l'arte.
così dicendo i termini d'Atlante
lasciamo adietro, e i novi Regni, e'l Gange,
scendendo ù l'Hippocren mormora, e range.

Poscia, che del Monton l'aurate spoglie
da Colchi riportò il superbo legno,
fra l'Idra e'l maggior Can di stelle adorno
l'affisse Giove in Cielo; e à le sol voglie
de le Muse hor si move; ivi entro à l'hora
pellegrina m'accolser nel suo regno,
preste à condurmi al bell'alto soggiorno,
v'l'alma in se gioiendo, s'innamora.
Quivi obliando la primiera scorza,
poggiammo verso il Ciel con larghi giri,
e alzando i miei desiri,
così del proprio ben la mente accorta
feron con divin canto, e con parole
le Dive, cui Parnaso honora, e cole:
che riguardando da l'ardente giro
il picciol globo, v'sol si chiude, e serra
terrena gloria e folle human desiro;
il lungo affaticar sdegnai, che in terra
n'affligge; e dove il Sol più freddo, e basso
si mostra, entrammo in Ciel con lieto passo.

Mentre, che presa d'alta meraviglia,
miro gli eccelsi lumi, e dal suo moto
raro, e divin concento uscir m'accorgo,
a cui nullo mortal canto simiglia;
d'una de le mie nobili Compagne
udì, Quì non s'arresti il tuo devoto
desìo di gir al bene, ov' io ti scorgo;
ma, amando il lor Fattor ne l'opre magne,
con noi fin al supremo giro aspira.
Così di cerchio in cerchio il Ciel salendo,
lo spirto mio perdendo
giva i terreni affetti, ond'hor s'adira
contra l'imperio lor superbo, e fiero:
indi scorrendo l'alto magistero

del Calle obliquo, onde cadeo Fetonte
per l'horribil aspetto de' suoi mostri,
et onde Apol comparte, o saglia, o smonte,
a più lontani, et a' paesi nostri
eguali i raggi suoi, per tutto sparsi;
stupida sopra il Ciel m'alzai, e arsi.

Hor voi stillate in me, cortesi Dive,
l'almo liquor, che già il destrier alato
trasse dal Monte aventuorso, e santo;
acciò de l'alto obietto, che prescrive
il saper nostro, quella parte io canti
che già compresi, mentre in quello stato
vidi (vostra mercè) l'eterno manto
di lui, che infonde in voi concetti santi.
Nove cerchi di vive fiamme ardenti
cingean, qual proprio centro, quel gran lume
che, come fonte, o fiume,
senza arrestarsi mai chiari, e lucenti
rotando i raggi suoi tra spirti eletti,
rischiara il lume loro; onde perfetti
scorgon nel proprio fin la bella stampa
del ineffabil Rè, che è solo eterno:
al cui possente sguardo, ch'anco avampa
nel mio pensier, ogni vigor interno
si sciolse, e mi cadei, bramando sempre
Starmi in sì care, e sì felici tempre.

Canzon, ch'al santo obietto humana forza
senti marcar, ardend'io, benchè i torne,
qual novella Fenice, à l'alta prova;
se gran fiamma d'amor mercè ritrova
nel Ciel, m'impetra, che mie luci adorne
de lo splendor, che à la primiera scorza
diè lume, on d'hor il suo poter si sforza,
veggan nel mio pensier con chiaro essempio
il vero Dio habitar, ch'è pur suo tempio.* (pp. 296 – 98)

---

* *Rime funerali* (see note 2), pp. 87 – 93. The imaginary tour of the author suggests not only Dante's *Divine Comedy*, which Isotta assuredly knew, but more surprisingly, Christine de Pisan's *Le Chemin de Longues Études*, in which the guide is also a woman.

APPENDIX

Only four of Isotta Brembate's poems have survived. Two are included in the main text of this chapter; the other two follow.

❧ To Astorre Baglioni

A shout of honor echoes all around in
thousands of words to that great Hero
on whom Mars has bestowed the highest honor;
he has become a new star in the Fifth circle of Heaven.

What torture and scorn and sacrilege
he suffered at the hands of the godless Scythians,
now let my Brembo take away those memories,
let the trumpets be sounded.

Oh fortunate Hestor, that both Belgrade and Istria
raise their trophies to your great name,
to your invincible right hand and your strong heart

That cast down Cyprus and weakened
the Ottoman armies. Now, rise among the gods,
take the martyr's crown and palm for your vile death.

❧ A Astorre Baglioni

◉ Track 48,
Reading 49

A quel grido d'honor, che d'ogni intorno
alto rimbomba in mille e mille carte;
del grande Heroe, che tolto il pregio a Marte
fa il quinto Ciel d'un novo lume adorno;

Di quanto al fin sostenne, e strazio e scorno
da Scytha empio, e pergiuro; homai da parte
pongo il mio Brembo ogni memoria, e parte
sciolga in tal note e l'uno, el'altro corno.

O fortunato Hestor, ch'al tuo gran nome
a la tua destra invitta, al petto forte
et la Bagrada e l'Histro alzar trofei

Che in Cipro afflitte, e poco men che dome,
l'armi Othomanne; hor sù trà gli alti Dei
corona e palma hai di tua indegna morte.[16]

❧ To the Very Illustrious Signora Donna Girolama Colonna

Love, whose ardent fire
renders Juno less envious,
who ignites the waves of great Father Ocean
where Venus arose on his beautiful breast

To restore your flames in the brilliant, divine rays
and to raise creative inspiration to where
all beauty and truth is hidden
from the base and vile earthly prison

Now take your place
above this lovely Colonna
and thence let every burning soul hear your sacred words

That she may know from whom we receive our splendid gifts
and that she may perceive a higher path
from which to contemplate the eternal lover

～

(Alla Illustrissima Signora Donna Girolama Colonna)

Amore, à cui quel foco ardente meno
rende invida Giunon, quel che ne l'onde
del gran padre Ocean s'accese, e donde
Venere apparve pria nel suo bel seno;

Per ristorar sue fiamme entro al sereno
raggio divin, e di virtù feconde
l'alme inalzar là, ov' ogni ben s'asconde,
da questo basso e vil carcer terreno.

Sopra questa gentil Colonna hor prende
suo seggio, et quinci ogn'alma incende, et falle
d'alto sentir le sue faville sante.

Di che noi ben spender, ch'ella n'apprende
et qual novo Israel per miglior calle
ne scorge à contemplar l'eterno amante. *

～

(Adverse Fortune)

Now you have done all you can,
cruel Fortune, now you have deprived my life
of all happiness,
filling it with anguish, suffering and pain.

What more can you do to me, what more
than close my body in a small grave, my life spent?
Why are you not yet
moved to end my torment with my death.

Oh, if you were only kind to me, oh, goddess
I beseech you, you would be as beloved by me
as you are hated now.

Lucia Albani
Avogradro
(ca. 1534 –
before 1568) [17]

---

* Ottavio Sanmarco, ed., *Il tempio della divina Signora Donna Geronima Colonna d'Aragona* (Padua, 1568). Included in *Rime funerali*, p. 94.

But I know well that you oppose
everything I desire, and are always angered against me:
yet it pleases you that I live, and languish.

~

◆ L'Avversa Fortuna

◉ Track 49,
Reading 50

Or hai fatto l'estremo di tua possa
crudel Fortuna, or hai d'ogni contento
privata in tutto la mia vita e scossa,
colmandola d'affanni, doglia e stento

Che puoi più farmi, fuor ch'in poca fossa
chiuder il corpo mio di vita spento?
Per qual cagion ancor non ti sei mossa
a terminar con morte il mio tormento?

Oh! S'a me fossi sì benigna, o Diva,
che ciò da te impetrassi, tanto amata
da me saresti, quanto odiata or sei.

Ma io so ben che sempre a i desir miei
contraria fosti, e sempre ver me irata:
*però ti piace che languendo io viva.**

Lucia was lauded after her death by Torquato Tasso with a sonnet that begins and ends with her name (Lucia: *luce*, light; Albani: *alba*, dawn):

Oh chiara luce di celeste raggio
ch'un alma pura, e duo begli occhi illustri,
e tra rose vermiglie, e bei ligustri
scopri nel volto quasi un lieto Maggio
. . .

Ben mi dolgo, che sì grave, e tardo
ti lodo, e canto, o mia serena LUCE,
che sei del vero sole aurora et ALBA.

~

Oh heavenly rays of bright light
that shines forth from a pure soul and beautiful eyes,
and like a happy May-time reveals her face
among vermillion roses and lovely privets,

Well may I regret that so sadly and late
I sing your praises, oh my serene LIGHT,
truly the sun that lights the daybreak and the DAWN.†

---

* Jolanda di Blasi, ed., *Antologia della poesia Italiana* (Parma, 1954).
† Tasso is thought to have written this some years after Lucia died; thus his regret praising her "sadly and late." For references here and bibliography on Lucia, see Arnaldo Foresti, ed. *Rime di Lucia Albani* (Bergamo, 1903).

~

• To the Divine Lady Geronima Colonna d'Aragona

A pure, sublime feeling moves within my heart
at the lofty thought that now guides me to where
the beautiful, gentle Sebeto waters the land and divides;
there the sky is most serene.

I look wonderingly at the strange, celestial forms
designed by the stars,
and I wish that I could paint them,
but my mind draws back at such a great task.

Let others more gifted lead us
in our homage to that divine beauty, that noble Colonna;
my humble intellect is not equal to it.

In the lovely, soft light that surrounds her
she appears to be more goddess than woman;
she overcomes every pen just as she dazzles every eye.

~

• Alla Divina Signora Donna Geronima Colonna d'Aragona

D'un chiaro eccelso oggetto entro al cor move
l'alto pensier, c'hor pur mi guida in parte
ch'l bello humil Sebeto irriga, e parte.
La ne ha più fortunato il ciel ch'altrove:

Ivi forme celeste altere, e nove,
ch'in un soggetto ogni stella comparte,
ammiro, e ben vorrei ritrarre in carte,
ma l'ingegno paventa a si gran prove.

Ch'al bel divin, che l'altrui mente induce
a riverìe quell' una alta Colonna
il mio basso intelletto non s'agguaglia

e quel vago, e gentil, che di fuor luce
ond'ella intanto anzi appare dea che donna;
vince ogni stil, si come ogni occhio abbaglia.*

Emilia Brembata [18]
◉ Track 50,
Reading 51

◉ Track 50,
Reading 51

---

* Sanmarco, *Il tempio*, p. 5.

NOTES

1   Bortolo Belotti, *Una sacrilega faida bergamasca nel cinquecento* (Bergamo, 1937).

2   "A glory to her feminine sex . . .": "Gloria del sesso feminile, pregio delle Dame di Bergamo," from Donato Calvi, *Effemeride sagro e profano* (Milan, 1677), 3 vols., vol. 1, p. 248. Giovanni Battista Licinio, ed., *Rime funerali di diversi illustri ingegni in morte della molto ill. Sig. Isotta Brembata Grumella* (Bergamo, 1587), p. 86. Two of Isotta's poems are included in the collection. A good bibliography on Isotta is found in P. L. F. Barnaba Vaerini, ed., *Gli scrittori di Bergamo* (Bergamo, 1788), vol. I, pp. 162–163. We wish to thank Mario Testa of Bergamo, who is writing a multivolume work on Bergamo and kindly allowed us to consult his research, offered with several glasses of grappa.

3   The iconography of the portraits was discovered by Ciro Caversazzi and published in his article "Una dama bergamasqua di quattrocent'anni fa riconosciuta in un ritratto del Lotto," *Dedalo 3* (February 1913): 574–576. Isotta's mother is identified as Daria Suardi by Francesca Bosco in "La luna accanto al sole: I ritratti di Lucina e Leonino Bremabati," *La Rivista di Bergamo* XLIII (May–June 1992): 14–16. However, Isotta married Gian Girolamo Grumelli in whose family inventory, held at the Archivio Vescovile (Episcopal Archives) in Bergamo (tome 63, folio 1), her mother's name is given as Roata.

4   We wish to thank Professor Leo Hoar, Fordham University, for his translation from the Spanish.

5   Girolamo Ruscelli, *Le Imprese Illustri con esposizioni et discorsi* (Venice, 1566).

6   For discussions of portraits of Isotta Brembate, see Mina Gregori, *Giovan Battista Moroni, tutte le opere: Estratto dai pittori bergamaschi* (Bergamo, 1979), entries 30 and 31.

7   Silvana Milese, *Moroni e il primo cinquecento bergamasco* (Bergamo, 1991), p. 50.

8   We wish to thank Count Antonio Moroni for inviting us to see the Brembate portrait as well as other paintings in the Moroni palazzo in Bergamo. My thanks go also to Patrick A. Heelan, S.J., professor of philosophy at Georgetown University, who has a special interest in the philosophy of visual perception; he solved the problem raised by the identical collars by pointing out that the head and collar were mirror images.

9   Gregori, *Giovan Battista Moroni*, p. 237, points out that the canvas shows obvious indications of having been enlarged. However, there is no record of *when* it was enlarged, and no record of anyone ever having seen the painting smaller in size. When Charles Eastlake saw it in the middle of the nineteenth century it was obviously already in its present size, inasmuch as Eastlake considered it a pendant to the Grumelli work. The portrait must have been actually painted on the enlarged canvas. Gregori, p. 232.

10   Gregori, *Giovan Battista Moroni*, entry 46.

11   We wish to express our warm thanks to Dr. Maria Teresa Agnesod for her great kindness in giving us a copy of her dissertation on Falletti, "Eleonora de La Ravoire Falletti poetessa casalese del XVI secolo" (University of Turin, 1979). Falletti was a poet of distinction in the Cinquecento. Twenty-one of her sonnets were included in Ludovico Domenichi's collection *Rime diverse d'alcune nobilissime et virtuosissime donne* (Lucca, 1559), and more than thirty others were included in various other anthologies. Her birth and death dates are unknown; she flourished ca. 1550–1565. The poem quoted here appeared originally in the Domenichi volume; we have printed it from Dr. Agnesod's dissertation. See also note 15.

12   See John Hale, *The Civilization of Europe in the Renaissance* (London, 1994), p. 136, "After Cateau-Cambrésis . . . a preoccupation with international peace-making passed from the hands of the politicians into the minds of intellectuals," and p. 141, "after Cateau-Cambrésis peace was seen to flourish for a few years throughout Europe." Bergamo, however, remained subject to Venice.

13   Milesi, *Moroni e il primo cinquecento bergamasco*, p. 11. The full account of the events related here is given in Belotti, *Una sacrilega faida.*

14   Episcopal Archives, Bergamo, vol. 78, *Testimenti e donazioni.*

15   The year of Eleonora de la Ravoire's birth is not known. She married Giovan Giorgio Falletti in 1552 and lived with him in the family castle of Melazzo, a small community in the Piedmont. An accomplished poet and much-admired intellectual, she is the principal interlocutor in *La Leonora,* a

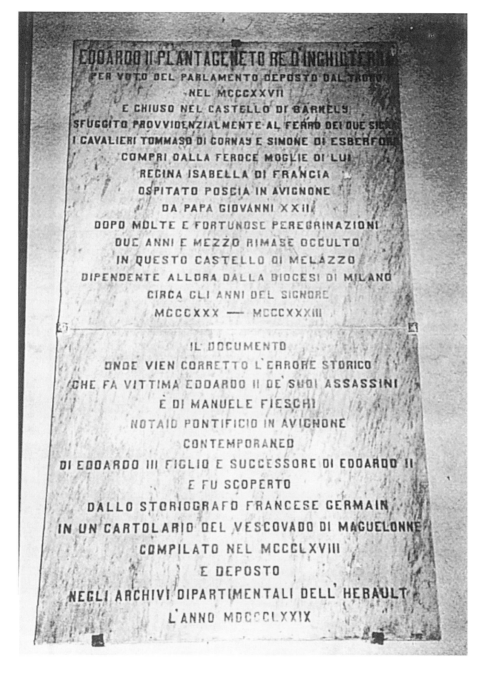

9.9.
Wall inscription,
Castle at
Melazzo.
Photo, G.
Colombardo.

dialogue on beauty by Giuseppe Betussi, reprinted in Giuseppe Zonta, *Trattati d'amore nel cinquecento* (Bari, 1912), pp. 306–364. Eleanora's castle at Melazzo is the location of an intriguing story about King Edward II of England, in which it is claimed that he was hidden there during 1330–1333. Although he is said to have been killed in 1327 in Berkeley castle, where he was held as a prisoner, according to this story he actually escaped to Italy. In the castle of Melazzo there is a stone encased in a wall inscribed in Italian that, translated, reads, "Edward II Plantagenet, King of England by vote of Parliament deposed from the throne in 1327 imprisoned in the castle at Berkeley fortunately escaped from the two assassins . . . sent by Queen Isabella of France, welcomed in Avignon by Pope Giovanni XXII after . . . wandering for two and a half years was hidden in this castle at Melazzo. . . . The document that corrects the historical error . . . was written by Manuele Fieschi, pontifical notary in Avignon contemporary with Edward III . . . and was discovered by a French historian, Germain, among episcopal letters in the archives of Maguelone compiled in 1368 and was deposited in the departmental archives of Herault in 1879." Fieschi, bishop of Vercelli (1343–1348), is said to have written the letter to Edward III. Not far from Melazzo, at the Abbey of St. Alberto, there is an empty tomb with an inscription that reads, "First tomb of Edward II King of England. . . ." This account, with bibliography, is given in *Melazzo nella storia* (Melazzo, 1995).

   16   We discovered this and twenty-two other poems by various writers in a previously unrecorded pamphlet in the Biblioteca Civica in Bergamo. It was privately printed in Perugia in 1572 by Valente Panizza under the title of *Le suntuosissime esequie celebrate nella magnifica città di Bergamo in morte dello illustrissimo Signor Astorre Baglione*. In his introduction to this publication addressed to Baglione's widow, Ginevra Salviati, Panizza describes in detail the indeed "sumptuous" funeral service of the hero, who was captured and beheaded by the Turks at the Battle of Famagosta. He mentions the large number of laudatory messages, including many poems, that one saw "all around." This must mean that they were posted in public places (notice of a funeral is still publicly posted by family and friends in some Italian towns) because he says furthermore that many were stolen. Isotta Brembate had been able to retrieve some of them, he writes, and had asked him to send them to the widow, which he did in the form of this pamphlet. Strangely, Pietro L. Ferri, in the catalogue of his collection of books written by women (about fourteen hundred), published in Padua in 1842, lists under Isotta's name "Lettera e rime" and says that the letter and verses were collected by Isotta Brembate under the title of *Elegie, sonetti, ed epitaffi di diversi spiriti di Lombardia, composti nelle esequie del Signor Estore Baglioni, celebrate in Bergamo* and printed by Cristoforo Draconi in Cremona in 1572. A computer search of all the libraries in Italy and the United States has failed to find any mention of this booklet. The poem appears publicly here for the first time.

   17   Lucia Albani, born in Bergamo, daughter of Gio. Girolamo Albani, later Cardinal, and Laura Longhi, was married in 1550 to Faustino Avogadro di Girolamo, scion of a patrician family of Brescia. She began writing poetry when she was a teenager, and a collection of her early poems was brought out in 1903. Lucia was known for her beauty as well as her poetry, which appeared in various anthologies in her lifetime.

   18   Emilia was a cousin of Isotta, famous for her oratory. A short biographical notice is found in Gianmaria Mazzuchelli, *Gli scrittori d'Italia* (Brescia, 1760), p. 2044.

CHAPTER TEN

TARQUINIA MOLZA
(1542 – 1617)

 *THE ONE AND ONLY*

t was literally true: Tarquinia Molza, born in Modena on 1 November 1542, was the one and only woman that had ever been granted honorary Roman citizenship. On 8 December 1600 the Senate and the People of Rome issued a decree that "although the Senate has never accepted women into the ranks of citizenship . . . [it is resolved that] Tarquinia Molza of Modena be numbered in the ranks of its most noble citizens with the title *l'Unica*, never before bestowed on anyone, in recognition of her singular virtues and merits." The document issued in connection with this event describes in detail the intellectual, literary, and musical gifts that made Tarquinia "unique" among her contemporaries, not neglecting to mention that she had "put aside the insignificant feminine arts of the needle, and housekeeping, not out of arrogance but because of the grandeur of her spirit, in favor of the arts and sciences, which she pursued with tireless tenacity." [1]

Tarquinia's mother, Isabella Colombi, had indeed tried to train her eldest of six daughters to the "insignificant feminine arts," but her father, Camillo, noticed with apparent delight that she constantly stole away from those duties in order to read secretly one or another book that she kept hidden under her clothes. He gladly acceded to her plea when she begged to be educated along with her brothers and other male relatives by Don Giovanni Politiano, whom he retained in his household, and he took great pleasure in the extraordinary intelligence she showed in her ability to learn; she surpassed them all in learning Greek, Latin, and Hebrew, and in mastering the philosophy of Plato and Aristotle. [2] However, both Camillo and Politiano died when Tarquinia was sixteen years old, and without a teacher and protector of her intellectual interests, she had to give up her studies. For the next few years she occupied herself as her mother wished, doing "woman's work." She seemingly had no option for, even if she married, her husband would normally expect her to fulfill the domestic responsibilities of their household. So she put off marriage, and unconventionally let her younger sisters marry before her, giving up the larger dowry that would have been hers if she had married first. Then she met Paolo Porrini, in whom she must have perceived a man who would allow her the intellectual freedom she needed. She married him in 1560.

One would like to know much more about Porrini, the man Tarquinia married at the then late age of eighteen. From indirect evidence, it can be inferred that Porrini had exceptional qualities that attracted Tarquinia and won her love. A few years after their marriage it happened that an elderly teacher, Lazaro Labandino, opened a school next to her house, and Tarquinia went back to school "with her husband's permission." This in itself, in a sixteenth-century husband anywhere in the world, was

enough to reveal Porrini as exceptional, as was the continued support, encouragement, and pleasure he took in his wife's achievements throughout their life.[3] From
that time on she devoted herself to learning and, if one can accept even by half what
her contemporaries said of her, she cultivated an encyclopedic knowledge of the hu-
manities and sciences. As Torquato Tasso remarked, "[Signora] you have read everything and you remember everything."[4] Foremost among the scholars with whom she
studied was Francesco Patrizi, a philosopher-humanist who held a professorial chair
first at the university in Ferrara, later invited by the pope to the university in Rome.
Tarquinia herself became a broad-ranging humanist, deeply familiar with the philosophy and poetry of the ancients, able to quote in discussions with friends appos-
ite passages from Plato (whose *Crito* and *Charmides* she translated), Aristotle, and the
Stoics as well as from the roster of Latin writers such as Cicero, Lucretius, Catullus,
Virgil, Horace, Tibullus, and Ovid. She studied mathematics and, doubtless aware of
the revolutionary work of Copernicus, published in 1543, wrenching the earth from
its central position in the universe, Tarquinia turned her face upward, contemplating
the cosmos. We have from Torquato Tasso a beautiful image of Tarquinia, looking
heavenward.

> *Tarquinia, were you gazing at*
> *the beautiful turning of the heavens,*
> *I would like to be the sky;*
> *then you might direct*
> *your sparkling gaze*
> *straight into my eyes*
> *so that I might delight*
> *in the infinite beauty of their scintillating lights.*[5] (p. 330)

Francesco Patrizi's *L'amorosa filosofia* is the most extensive source of information
about Tarquinia. This is a series of four dialogues written in 1577, modeled on Plato's
Symposium, in which Patrizi substitutes praise of Tarquinia for praise of love as the
subject of the first dialogue. Like the *Symposium, L'Amorosa Filosofia* presents a cast of
characters that comprises a group of male friends who are dining together. Patrizi
wittily copies Plato's fiction that the dialogue is narrated by one man who repeats to
the others what one of the guests at a previous dinner told him the other guests said
about the subject of their praise. "Tarquinia" as a character is also listed as present in
the first dialogue heading, although she does not speak. Each man describes at length
the various talents "Tarquinia" has received from each of the nine muses with the final speaker observing that "our divine muse combines the qualities of all the muses
so perfectly that one more perfect cannot even be imagined." Here Patrizi is recalling
Socrates in the *Symposium* who pretends to chide the others who have spoken in
praise of love: "I see that the intention was to attribute to Love every species of greatness and glory, whether really belonging to him or not." Given the close parallel of
Patrizi's dialogue with Plato's, it is clear that "Tarquinia" has been made the embodiment of Love with all its splendid attributes, with the added presumably jesting infer-
ence, which his listeners would have understood, "whether belonging to [her] or
not," and also represents Diotima, who enlightens Socrates on the subject of love,

with himself playing himself with the name "Patritio," in the role of Socrates. "The philosophy of this new Diotima was drawn not only from Plato, Xenophon, Plotinus and other great writers," "Patritio" says, "but beyond them she conceived in her own mind a new philosophy, born like Minerva from the head of Zeus."[6]

In the following two dialogues Tarquinia expounds her theory to Patrizi, who while engaged in discussion with her, found himself dazzled as he looked into her eyes. "What are you staring at as if you were lost in thought?" she asks him. "It is not my fault," he explains, "it's my school that is to blame." "What school is that?" she asks. "Platonist," he answers, explaining that adherents of the Platonic doctrine are obliged to love the good and the beautiful. Thus the subject of love is introduced, and "Tarquinia" is given the opportunity to expound her theory of love, "the amorous philosophy," which is a kind of pun, since *L'amorosa filosofia* could also mean "the loving philosophy," referring to the Platonic doctrine, the philosophy concerned with love.

"Tarquinia" claims that all love is really self-love. Her idea derives from Aristotle's conception of the love of benevolence, willing good to another: all good feelings originate with one's own will so that the love one feels for another is a satisfaction of one's own will to make oneself happy. This is contrary to the Platonic conception of love as the perfect communion of two souls. One by one she takes up the Aristotelian categories of good will, charity (in the Augustinian sense, the love of God), friendship, affection, and so on, and she argues that these are forms of "love" and are inspired by the desire or need to satisfy oneself. Patrizi presents himself as astounded by the originality of her idea and is persuaded point by point, in Socratic fashion, that what she says is true. However, in the fourth dialogue we find "Patritio" telling "Tarquinia" that he has told her husband, "Paolo," about her marvelous analysis of love, but that, at hearing it, "Paolo" had burst into laughter. Flustered and "blushing fiery red," Patritio had asked why Paolo was laughing at him. "'How not laugh,' Paolo said, 'when you believe such nonsense.' "But is it nonsense? . . ." "'It most certainly is,'" Paolo replied, proceeding to counterpose examples of love that cannot be construed as self-love: husbands and wives who grieve painfully for their dead spouses; women in India who throw themselves onto the funeral pyre of their husbands; Artemisia who shut herself up in the mausoleum she had built for her husband.

"Patritio" is now very confused. Which of the two is right? He had lost a night's sleep, he tells "Tarquinia," after listening to "Paolo's" confutation of her theory. Why did Paolo have to laugh at him?

"Oh, this is not the first time you have made even me laugh at your wavering so that anyone can pull you this way and that," "Tarquinia" tells him.

"What do you want me to do, my lady . . . you explain your point so well that it seems absolutely correct but then someone else persuades me to the contrary."

"Your attitude will always make you the butt of anyone who wants to make fun of you," she answered. [7]

It must be remembered that the dialogue is a work of fiction, and its speakers are inventions of the author, who is mirroring real people and who is, of course, the only "speaker." Patrizi has set up a philosophical discussion between "Tarquinia," an Aristotelian, and "Patritio," a Platonist (with Skeptic tendencies that keep him "wavering") and with the intervention of "Paolo" whose examples of self-sacrificing love derive from Aristotle's idea of virtue. He professes himself to be the most confused man in the world, mocking himself as a philosopher who considers all argu-   ments, and finds himself firmly planted with his feet in thin air. The heading of the fourth dialogue, "Resolution of the issues arising from the preceding dialogue," promised, it would seem, a possible synthesis of Plato and Aristotle that would bring the confused philosopher down to earth. Unfortunately, *L'amorosa filosofia* was never finished.[8]

The dialogue's tone make one suspect that Patrizi was perhaps mocking the deluge of dialogues on love that had appeared in the course of the century and furthermore was amusing himself in creating an academic exercise. The complicated presentation of the dialogue-within-dialogue is characteristic of the sixteenth century's taste for games, puzzles, and the artificial. Nevertheless, the characters all had their real counterparts in life, and we cannot doubt what Patrizi tells us about Tarquinia's extraordinary gifts and the wide esteem in which she was held, which culminated in the honor awarded her by the Senate of Rome as "Unique." One can compile from various sources a long list of male admirers who addressed her in Greek, Latin, and Italian verses that compare her with every woman in history known for her beauty, brilliance of mind, chastity, moral courage, benevolence, and spiritual radiance. That Patrizi was far from alone in his esteem for Tarquinia is evident in an oration given in the Accademy of Lucca on the subject of "The Excellence of Women," which included Tarquinia among those praised:

> Who does not know, or has not at least heard of the great and broad culture of Signora Tarquinia Molza of Modena? In singing and playing the lute she is almost as far superior to other women as those most perfect women already spoken of are to men; but in erudition, and in the knowledge of the three languages, Greek, Latin and the vernacular, she equals, not to exaggerate, the most accomplished Men of our time, writing beautifully in those languages, both in prose and verse, as one sees every day in her various compositions." [9]

Tarquinia was not only intellectually brilliant. She was gifted with an extraordinarily beautiful singing voice. According to one Livio Celiano,

> *There could not be a heart so hard*
> *that would not soften hearing your sweet singing;*
> *a thousand souls, dear Molza,*
> *light up at the sound*
> *that comes from your throat.*
> *Your womanly excellence*
> *and ingenious poems are gifts from Athena.*[10] (p. 330)

Patrizi, surely in love with the woman he praised as beyond compare in two literary works, might well have been the unidentified author of another sonnet about her singing.

> *The daughters of Achelous sang*
> *so sweetly to satisfy his greedy lust*

that the sailors, overcome by that amazing sound
fell asleep and were destroyed.

But whoever listens to TARQUINIA
with her divine, unique voice,
has only happy thoughts
and feels inspired, joyous, and fulfilled.

I do not know, Fallopia, if you were transfixed, as I was,
if, immersed in heavenly music,
you felt a sacred fire set you aflame:

There radiates such splendor from those beautiful eyes
that seeing and listening,
I found myself at once on earth and in Paradise.[11] (p. 330)

With Patrizi's help, it is not difficult to imagine the married life of Tarquinia and Paolo. They had their arguments, Patrizi does not tell us about what, but we have glimpsed a difference in opinion between them in Patrizi's account of Tarquinia's theory of love, and discussions of all kinds were a feature of their apparently unconventional relationship and freestyle living. Their home was a constant meeting place for the intellectuals of Modena and distinguished visitors from elsewhere, drawn there by the gifts of the hostess. Young and old, beautiful or not, rich and poor, noble or common, soldiers, musicians, writers, laymen, clergy, all fell in love with Tarquinia who charmed them with her wit even while refusing their amorous advances. She maintained a spotless reputation—she did not even flirt, Patrizi writes, like "French women"—and when Paolo died in 1578 she deeply mourned the man who had been her firm support, who had performed the part of *cantus firmus* while she thrilled their friends with her *cantus figuratus*. She determined never to remarry and took as her emblem the representation of a fallen oak tree from which a vine hangs helplessly; across the top are the words *non sufficit alter* (none other can suffice) (figure 10.1). Her poem explains her meaning:

I shall live alone from now on
like a vine in the field,
for Fortune, who steals our lives,
has taken from me my indispensable support;
nor will I ever lean on another,
in high places or low,
for in the terrible tempest
none other can suffice. (p. 331)

Tarquinia was thirty-seven years old when Paolo died. Years earlier she had allowed her hair, once "golden" according to Patrizi, to darken; she gave up using makeup and dressed in a reserved style (figure 10.2). But despite what seems to have been an ascetic style of life, she was always lively, jesting, and irresistibly attractive to the cir-

10.1.
Impresa of
Tarquinia Moza.
Photo, Countess
Giovanna Molza
da Gazzolo.

cle of men and women who frequented her home during her marriage as well as after Paolo's death to enjoy the pleasure of her brilliant conversation. She accepted the men as friends although at least some would have preferred to be lovers. One such, Geminiano Patini, seems to have been unable to accept the constraints of mere friendship after Paolo died, and was sent packing when he tried to overstep the role of advisor in her legal problem with her brothers-in-law who contested Paolo's will in which he left his estate to his wife as usufructuary.

Nevertheless, while we may believe in her virtuous reserve, there is no doubt that her adoring philosopher overly protests Tarquinia's chastity. She did fall in love while married to the still-living Paolo. In the spring of 1576 Modena had a highly distinguished visitor, a man who already at the age of thirty-one had won wide acclaim for his poetry. Torquato Tasso, as a courtier in the service of Alfonso II d'Este, Duke of Ferrara and Modena, had completed his masterpiece, *Gerusalemme Liberata* (Jerusalem Delivered), in 1575, and his highly influential pastoral poem, *Aminta,* in 1573. His psychologically disturbed personality often brought him into conflicts with those around him, and in 1576 his friend Ferrante Tassoni, governor of Modena, hoping to help him find relief from the intrigues of the d'Este court which he was convinced were directed against him, invited him to visit (figure 10.3). Tasso was embraced by the circle of intellectuals of Modena and its reigning queen of Modenese cultural life, Tarquinia Molza. Although previous writers have thought that Tasso and Tarquinia met for the first time when he went to Modena in 1576, it is evident that their acquaintance dates a few years earlier because Tasso's poem "Were you gazing at" (see p. 312), addressed to her, was set to music by Pietro Vinci and published in his *Fourth Book of Madrigals* in 1573. When Vinci had heard her sing some of his madrigals he "raised his hands to thank heaven and he ran to her, saying, "Oh, my little daughter, I thank God and you for giving me this consolation before I die to hear my music sung as I never would have or could have expected."[12]

Although the poet was drawn to her as a woman of exceptional gifts and marveled at her beautiful voice and musicianship, he did not fall in love with her on this visit to Modena. She did with him, however, as we discover in his sonnet to her from which we infer that she accused him of being cold; the poem also gives us a vivid picture of her style of singing.

> *Glowing with the light of transcendent passion*
> *are your eyes that sweetly turn this way and that;*
> *and the air becomes a flame as with every breath*
> *you create angelic harmonies.*
>
> *And fire are the flowing tears*
> *that you shed, and fire also are your sighs*
> *as your enticing glance falls on one and another of those*
> *whom you charm with your artful song.*
>
> *I alone, in the midst of those sparkling trills*
> *that excite your listeners, am not warmed,*
> *nor is my ardor aroused.*
>
> *Nor am I cold and hard as marble,*
> *but my heart consumed in another flame*
> *is now but ashes, and it can no longer burn.* (p. 331)

Tasso left Modena for Ferrara in April 1576 but returned there at the end of the year, and this time he was apparently more responsive to Tarquinia's allure. Whether or not they became actual lovers, the relationship was passionate on her part, as is clear from two poems a desperately unhappy Tarquinia wrote, the first when he was preparing to leave in March 1577, the second when he was actually gone.[13]

> *You then, Oh my soul,*
> *wish to leave me*
> *deprived of you, who are my life?*
> *Oh cruel murderer,*
> *with such a harsh destiny*
> *you leave me to die!*

10.2.
F. Zucchi.
Portrait of
Tarquinia Molza.
n.d. Pietro
Lancellotti,
Delle poesie
Volgari e Latine
di Francesco
Maria Molza.
(1750), vol. 2.

TARQUINIA MOLSA UNICA
PUDICITIÆ, EXEMPLAR, MUSAR, OCELLUS,
ET SCIENTIARUM DELICIÆ

At least let my anguish kill me
before the moment when you go
so that for pity's sake, perhaps as I die,
I will see a tear fall on your breast. (p. 331)

In the second she wrote,

> *After the bitter parting, I was left*
> *in great grief and infinite pain;*
> *now I am consumed with such fierce passion*
> *that I long more for death than for life,*

> *And if I do not find help for my despairing heart,*
> *my soul will surely depart;*
> *alas, crying ceaselessly I beg Love*
> *to kill me or help me.*

> *There is but one remedy I can imagine for my suffering,*
> *for the intense sorrow and anguish*
> *that I feel constantly in my afflicted soul:*

> *That heaven might let me die before you,*
> *to put an end to the severe, heavy load of torment*
> *that I carry because of you.* (pp. 331–32)

10.3.
Luigi Manzini.
Tasso Welcomed
at Modena.
Stage curtain.
ca. 1565–1575.
Photo, Countess
Giovanna Molza
da Gazzolo.

Tarquinia sent this poem to her close friend and advisor Giorgio Fallopia, who had loved her for many years but was apparently resigned not to press his love beyond the limits she imposed on her friends.[14] He replied with a sonnet in which he sympathized with her anguish, saying that a man who would leave her must be blind, deaf, and heartless and assuring her that he would never act like that if only he were the man she loved.

> *Oh why do you not feel such desire*
> *and love for me who has spent so many years*
> *loving you, which I do not regret.* (p. 332)

Although Tasso did not return to Modena, they did meet again in 1583 when he visited Marfisa d'Este, a cousin of the duke. As a consequence of his increasingly erratic and sometimes violent behavior, Alfonso had been confined to a hospital in 1579 and was a virtual prisoner for seven years. Marfisa was able to secure a brief release for him and invited him to stay with her at her villa in Medelana. Tarquinia and her friend Ginevra Marzi, also a Modenese, were visiting at the same time, and it was his conversation with the three women that Tasso memorialized in his dialogue *La Molza ovvero l'amore*. Here Tasso is asked by his interlocutors to discourse on the nature of love, and it is interesting that Tarquinia in participating in the dialogue does not mention her definition of love as self-interest, but agrees with Tasso that love is a kind of order whose members are all the virtues.[15]

Joanne Marie Riley notes that "Tarquinia wrote no romantic poetry that we can unequivocally assume to be directed to a man," and she further remarks that "three intensely emotional poems are explicitly addressed to women." One of these can be omitted from consideration because it was written in praise of her friend, Countess Angela Beccaria, as part of a poetic "garland" at a cultural gathering at the home of the countess.[16] But two others are passionate love poems to a woman.

> *Were there tears on your rosy cheeks*
> *my lady, the day I saw you,*
> *like pearls shining on rubies,*
> *and I sobbed*
> *with the passion you aroused*
> *and the feelings you inspired?*
> *When between the tears a laugh broke out,*
> *we, as the saying goes, felt*
> *water and fire at the same time;*
> *but we immersed ourselves in fire*
> *and burned ourselves with water,*
> *for the lover is tossed between*
> *flames and waves.*
> *Nor can mortal power defend itself*
> *when fire drowns and water sets aflame.* (p. 332)

In another, despairing because her love is unrequited, she wrote,

My Lady, if love does not keep me
far enough away from you,
let him bring wood and tinder
to increase the pain.

I hoped for help from you,
but if you are indifferent,
who will look at me lovingly,
where will I find the joy of living?

Cruel, powerful destiny,
you have given me a harsh fate,
you have taken away everything dear to me
and you wrap me in sorrow.

But who will protect me
against destiny, if I am afraid
of you? And deprived of love,
how can I go on living? (pp. 332 – 33)

Both of these poems were set to music, the first by Ascanio Trombetti (1583) and by Giovanni Palestrina (1585), the second by Trombetti (1583), and were sung by women who customarily sang love laments as if they were men serenading their lady-loves. These verses were chosen by the composers possibly as a compliment to Tarquinia Molza and surely for the emotional content that made them suitable for performance in the context of courtly love. But they were not written for that purpose, and, given the content and tenor of Tarquinia's writing, we do not believe they can be interpreted simply as poems in the Petrarchist manner, in which the female writer assumes the male voice in imitation of her model.

Let us look at another poem that seems deliberately ambiguous, not specifically addressed to a woman or a man.

Oh how many times my thoughts return
to that happy day and place
where love sweetly inflamed my heart
with its invisible fire,

When I saw combined in one human form
the radiance and beauty
the charm and candor
that I have seen only when I gaze up at the heavens.

My mind full of amazement
and my heart full of wonder,
I stared at those beautiful eyes, that beautiful face,

OPPOSITE
10.4.
Benvenuto Tisi
da Garofalo.
*Ceiling of the
Hall of the
Costabiliana.*
Museo
Archeologico di
Spina at Ferrara.
Photo, anon.

And, marveling, such a delight
was born in my heart that my sole desire
was to dream about uniting myself with that dear object. (p. 333)

The ambiguity is not apparent in English, which is the reason we have translated the last words of the poem, "unirmi al caro oggetto," with clumsy literalness: those words may be rendered "marrying the one dear to me." If marriage is meant, the object of her love was a man; but the phrase can also be translated, "unite myself with the one I love," or "tie myself to my beloved," or even "being close to my dear one," which makes the sex of the beloved unspecific. The evasion strikes us as deliberate. However, such phrases as "the radiance and beauty," "those beautiful eyes, that beautiful face," while possibly describing a man seem more typically attributed to a woman.

There is furthermore a sharply revealing passage in *L'amorosa filosofia* in which we learn from one of the interlocutors that at least ten painters had tried to make portraits of Tarquinia but had been unable to do so because they found that they could not convey a certain indescribable quality in her temperament. "What temperament?" the interlocutor is asked. "They say that Tarquinia's beauty is a seamless combination of the female and male in which both are mixed and merged so that one cannot discern one from the other, and each aspect appears ineffable and incomprehensible."[17]

Elsewhere describing her peerless virtues, Patrizi has one of the speakers compare her with other women of whom he avows "none have the quick repartee . . . or can mimic as she can anyone she wants to imitate or impersonate. Nor is there another as accommodating, as graceful, and so to say as masculine in figure so that she is not only skillful in dancing in a womanly style but can run like a man, jump, play ball, and joust."[18] Patrizi mentions that among the admiring crowd that surrounded Tarquinia, "there were not a few women," a comment that in itself would seem unremarkable were it not for the poems and the other clues that reveal her probably bisexual nature.

In the 1580s, Tarquinia's erudition, her poetry, but especially her voice and knowledge of music brought about her close and dramatic association with the House of d'Este. The court of the dukes of Ferrara had been known since the beginning of the century for its exceptional patronage of the arts, and under Alfonso II d'Este music and poetry flourished more brilliantly than ever in a court that had reached new heights of splendid, extravagant living (figures 10.4 and 10.5).[19] As Annibale Romei observed, "The Duke liveth with so great magnificence, that his highnes court seemeth rather a kingly and Royall Pallace, then the court of a great Duke: for it is not onely throughout replenished with the noble Lordes and valiant Knights, but further, is a receptacle for the most learned and gentle spirits, as likewise for men that in every profession are most excellent."[20] Musical concerts were held almost daily, sometimes "Great Concerts" *(concerti maggiori),* with more than fifty vocalists and instrumentalists participating in connection with important festivities "where the nobility danced in the German and Italian manner," and there were also small chamber concerts called "private concerts" *(musica secreta),* to which Alfonso invited very special guests.[21] These were the performances of a group of women singers (with the occasional participation of men[22]) which became known as the Concerto delle Donne. An earlier group, including the famous Bendidio sisters, Lucrezia and Isabella, with four

or five other vocalists, flourished during 1571–72, but their concerts ended with the death of the duke's second wife, who had sponsored their performances.

The concerts were revived in 1576 when Alfonso's sister Lucrezia returned to Ferrara after a failed marriage with Francesco Maria II, Duke of Urbino, but it was the second group, flourishing in the eighties, that won international acclaim. In 1579 Alfonso had married his third wife, Margherita Gonzaga, the sixteen-year-old daughter of Guglielmo Gonzaga, Duke of Mantua. She was passionately fond of music, and brought to Ferrara in her entourage the singers Laura Peperara, already well known, and Livia d'Arco, young and not yet fully accomplished. The third member of the group that was gradually brought together to form the core of the Concerto delle Donne was Anna Guarini, native of Ferrara, daughter of G. B. Guarini, chief poet of Alfonso's court, and niece of Lucrezia and Isabella Bendidio, the important singers in the first group of the previous decade. The women sang and accompanied themselves with musical instruments, Laura the harp, Livia the viola da gamba, and Anna the lute. Their concertmaster was the celebrated composer and organist Luzzasco Luzzaschi, who was the director of music at the Ferrara court from 1561 until his death in 1592. Tarquinia Molza became a permanent member of the group in 1583, when she was invited to become lady-in-waiting to the young Duchess Margherita, a position in which she enjoyed the luxurious, glamorous life of the court in company with a number of noble women. She participated not only as a singer but also as the supervisor and trainer of the others, and it was with her entry that the Concerto delle Donne began its most glorious years. Among the many poets who praised them was one whose clever, anonymous lyric, set to music by Paolo Virchi (1584), was characteristic of the sixteenth-century taste for puns on names, as we have seen. Because puns cannot easily be translated we will give it here in its original Italian, with our translation following.[23]

> *Se GU'A RINAscer LAURA e prenda L'ARCO*
> *amor soave e dolce*
> *ch'ogni cor duro MOLCE*[24]
> *e son nel mio dir parco,*
> *ma non havrà però di valor tanto*
> *quanto il celeste canto*
> *di queste, che coi vaghi e lieti accenti*
> *far gir' i monti e fan fermare i venti.*

> *Let the laurel be reborn and let him take up his bow*
> *that sweet and tender Cupid*
> *who softens every hard heart,*
> *but without exaggeration I can say*
> *they will not be as potent*
> *as the heavenly singing*
> *of these women who with charming and resonant voices*
> *make mountains move and stop the winds from blowing.*

Although Tarquinia did not formally become a member of the court until 1583, she sang at Ferrara and participated in the training of the singers even earlier. She had

10.5.
Interior of Italian Kitchen. **Cristoforo Messiburgo. From Emilio Faccioli, ed.,** *L'arte della Cucina in Italia* **(1987).**

sought the help of the duke in resolving litigation with her brothers-in-law over her husband's will, and she would have been at the court often in the early years of the 1580s. During a state trip to Modena in 1568, Alfonso had heard her sing with such pleasure that she had to repeat several times a song on a sonnet by Petrarch[25] and it seems probable that he had invited her to join in the musical performances at court during the years 1780–83. Because she was known not only for her beautiful voice but also as an exceptionally knowledgeable musician, it would have seemed advantageous to Alfonso to bring her into the Ferrara music circle to help train the singers. For the following six years she supervised the Concerto delle Donne, which under her leadership achieved the peerless reputation they won throughout Europe. She would indeed have been there longer, had it not been for her headstrong, independent character, which rebelled against authority over her personal life into which, not surprisingly, there now entered a man.

Giaches de Wert, a major sixteenth-century composer whose reputation—and music—is only now beginning to be revived, was the director of music at the court of

Mantua under Duke Guglielmo Gonzaga, a post he had held since 1565.[26] In the early 1580s he had reason to visit Ferrara in connection with lawsuits that had arisen from a scandalous affair: he had aroused the bitter jealousy of others of the musicians at court, including Agostino Bonvicino. Unsuccessful attempts had been made to drive him out of Mantua, and Bonvicino seduced Wert's wife as part of the plot. When the seduction was discovered, Wert informed the duke. Guglielmo banished Bonvicino from the court, and Wert sent his wife to her home in Novellara. There she became involved in a treacherous conspiracy against the counts of Novellara. Discovered, her possessions were confiscated (which brought about the lawsuits) and she was sent to prison, where she died in 1583.[27] Thus the widow Tarquinia, forty-one years old, met the widower Giaches de Wert, forty-eight years old, shortly after she became a lady-in-waiting to Duchess Marguerita with a yearly stipend of 160 *scudi* plus lodging for herself and family members.[28]

Highly gifted herself, Tarquinia was inevitably attracted to talented people such as Wert, whom Palestrina and others had described as "a great virtuoso."[29] Wert, for his part, had never known such an extraordinary woman. Drawn together by their mutual love of music and poetry (figure 10.6), they soon became lovers: by the fall of 1584 Wert was spending so much time in Ferrara that Guglielmo wrote to Alfonso, after Wert's absence of three months, requesting him to send his music director back to Mantua, which he did. Within a few weeks, Wert was back in Ferrara, where he spent the Carnival season.[30] Tarquinia began to pay attention to her person, dressing herself more attractively, grooming her hair carefully, and using perfume when she heard he was coming to Ferrara. They began to exchange love letters when they were apart, and when he was in Ferrara he was often in her apartments. The duchess noticed the change in her lady-in-waiting and guessed the reason, having seen Tarquinia and Wert acting and speaking familiarly with each other. She spoke to Tarquinia about her unsuitable behavior,[31] but, accustomed to the personal freedom she had always had in her marriage and in love with Wert, she did not heed the warning. She was happy in her role of supervising the Concerto delle Donne, of inspiring Wert to write innovative music,[32] and, doubtless, in feeling young again. But in October 1589 the ax fell.

Duke Alfonso confronted Tarquinia with what he had discovered in the intimate letters she had received from Wert, which he had had intercepted when he heard about the affair. The most serious aspect of her transgression, according to the duke, was the fact that Giaches was a poor Fleming of inconsequential family who had been brought to Italy as a nine-year-old choirboy in the service of the d'Este family[33] and had furthermore been married to a woman who died in prison. Some hint in the intercepted letters suggested they were contemplating marriage, a liaison that Alfonso considered would have been disgraceful; "she should be ashamed of herself for sustaining a love that so degraded her family and herself."[34]

Tarquinia denied the love affair, insisting that she and Wert were merely friends and claiming that she and Wert were being defamed by Vittorio Orfino, a musician and singer and a longtime friend of Tarquinia's who had given her a few lessons when she began her study of music.[35] He was ambitious to be recognized as a composer, and at Tarquinia's suggestion he composed a book of sacred music that he dedicated to the young duchess. According to Tarquinia, Orfino was jealous of her admiration and affection for Wert, and he lied to the duke about the nature of her relationship

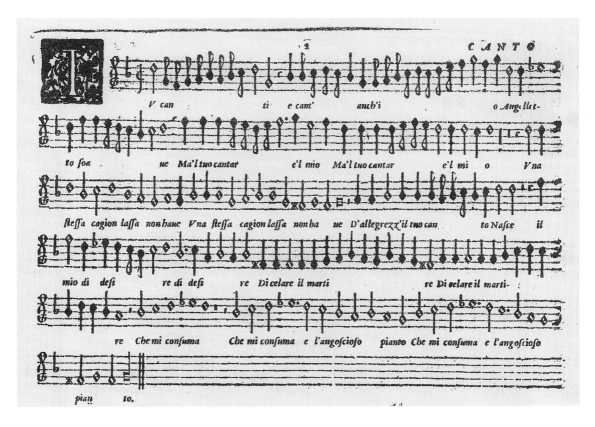

10.6.
Giaches de
Wert. *The Tenth
Book of Madrigals
for Five Voices.*
Verses by
Tarquinia Molza.
Civico Museo
Bibliografico
Musicale
(G. B. Martini),
Bologna.

with a man whom she loved only as a valued friend.[36] The duke, however, who had read the intercepted letters, knew the truth, and in the end she had to beg forgiveness of the duke and duchess. Nevertheless, Alfonso banished her from his court, allowing her, in view of her repentance, and out of respect for her family—she was the granddaughter of Francesco Maria Molza—to claim publicly that she had left of her own accord for reasons of health, but insisting that she break her relationship with Wert completely, with no contact even in writing. An observer attached to Alfonso's court wrote to a friend detailing the events, with the comment, "So Signora Tarquinia has been dismissed from the court by S[ignor]. A[lfonso]. while Vittorio remains here at the service of his patron and I am feeling very sorry for the Signora."[37] It would appear that this observer shared Tarquinia's view that Orfino was responsible for Tarquinia's unhappy departure from Ferrara.

Alfonso wrote to his governor in Modena to watch Tarquinia carefully and to intercept any letters that might pass between her and her lover. The malevolence with which he pursued the affair, and particularly the continued surveillance that he demanded even after her return to Modena, makes us suspect that the duke had himself been her secret lover, had arranged her position as his wife's lady-in-waiting to have her accessible, and became jealous when he discovered that her real affections lay elsewhere. That Tarquinia was exceptionally meaningful to him is perfectly clear, for in 1584 he arranged a tournament in which he jousted wearing her colors, very often a sign of love, and it was she who bestowed on him with her own hands the winner's prize. The event is recorded in a sonnet by Tasso, who was allowed his freedom occasionally from his confinement at the hospital, at the behest of some of his friends such as Marfisa d'Este and Tarquinia.

> *My lady, justly so esteemed that for you*
> *the great Alfonso girds his glorious sword to joust*
> *and feathers his helmet with your colors*
> *as he tilts with his knights.*
>
> *He could not display his colorful Arms*
> *to more beautiful eyes, nor are there more beautiful hands*
> *than yours which he will take with the prize,*
> *and hold in the dance.*
>
> *Nor can he receive elsewhere*
> *greater glory, for you know how to weave*
> *garlands and crowns not of silver and gold,*
>
> *But to celebrate honor with noble verse*
> *that brings unmatched immortal fame*
> *with the triumphant laurel.* (pp. 333 – 34)

Tarquinia remained in Modena for the rest of her life. As far as is known, the duke was successful in bringing about a complete break between her and her lover. Six years after their affair was forced to end, Wert died. Tarquinia became actively engaged in the sophisticated musical culture of the city and no doubt continued reading and writing, although we have no poems that can be dated to the last years of her life. Indeed, her reputation leaves no doubt that she wrote far more than the few poems that have survived; unfortunately, she never tried to collect her work in a volume for publication because, perfectionist that she was, she did not consider her poems worthy of comparison with those of Tasso, Guarini, and other prominent poets among her contemporaries.[38] In her will she left her manuscript writings together with her library to the city of Modena, but they have been dispersed and most of them lost.

Tarquinia died on 8 August 1617. She was buried in the Molza family vault in the cathedral of Modena, where her tomb is marked with the inscription,

> *Una Scientiarum*
> *ac Tarquiniae Molsae*
> *vita, idem occasus,*
> *commune sepulcrum.*
> *Obiit die VIII Augusti*
> *MDCXVII*
> *ETATIS SUAE ANN. LXXIV*

(The Life of the Sciences and of Tarquinia Molza went down to a common grave. Died 8 August 1617 at the age of seventy four.[39])

As we have noted, many artists attempted to portray Tarquinia. One supposed portrait, a terracotta bust apparently, crumbled during a bombing in World War II, and there is no photograph of it. A small portrait on ivory, artist unknown, was stolen from Countess Giovanna Molza in 1973; judging from the photograph she has of this work, which shows a very beautiful, quite feminine-looking young woman, we do not see it as fitting the written descriptions we have. Other pictures claimed by Countess Molza to represent her ancestor are also unsatisfactory.[40] The most plausibly authentic image is the engraving reproduced in *Delle poesie vulgari e latino di Francesco Maria Molza* (figure 10.2). This engraving may have been drawn from the image documented in a poem in Vandelli on a sculpture by Tarquinia's contemporary, Leone Leoni (called Aretino), in which the poet, Giuliano Goselino writes,

> *You may create a living figure in marble or metal*
> *with your marvelous sculptural Art,*
> *but, Leon, more noble is your art in creating*
> *the image of the soul,*

> *For whoever may see it will fall in love*
> *and describe her in verse;*
> *the beauty of your new creation raises you to heights*
> *above all others.*

> *I can see you already in the celestial realm*
> *where you shine with greater splendor than*
> *the other Leon, adorned with countless stars:*

> *But though the sky sparkles with beautiful stars*
> *one can breathe no more beautiful name than TARQUINIA*
> *for there is no greater star in the starry skies.* [41] (p. 334)

POEMS IN THE ORIGINAL ITALIAN

Torquato Tasso
◉ Track 51,
Reading 52

Tarquinia, se rimiri
i bei celesti giri
il cielo esser vorrei
perchè ne gli occhi miei
fisso tu rivolgessi
le tue doci faville,
io vagheggiar potessi
mille bellezze tue con luci mille. * (p. 312)

⁓

Livio Celiano
(Don Angelo Gril-
lo)

Non è cor duro tanto,
che non si spetri ai dolce vostro canto;
ed al suon che traete
da le sonore corde,
Molza gentil,
mill'anime accendete;
e sono i femminili pregi vostri
le dott'art d'Atene, e i colti inchiostri. † (p. 314)

⁓

Anonymous (Pa-
trizi?)
◉ Track 53

Le figlie insieme d'Acheloo cantaro
si dolcemente per empir le voglie
sue ingorde, e far de'naviganti spoglie
dal sonno presi, e da qual suono avaro.

Ma TARQUINIA con suo divino e raro
concento sola i pensier vaghi accoglie
da qualunque l'ascolta, e par che involglie
a tenersi vie più gradito e caro.

Non so, Falloppia, se da voi diviso
foste, com'io; e d'un beato ardore
se ardeste all'armonia celeste intento:

Da cui begli occhi uscia tanto spendore,
che mirando e ascoltando in un momento
esser m'accorsi e in terra, e in Paradiso. ‡ (pp. 314 – 15)

⁓

---

* Carlo Malmusi, *Memorie della Regia Accademia di Scienze, Lettere ed Arti in Modena* (Modena, 1862), p. 178.
† Domenico Vandelli, *Opusculi inediti di Tarquinia Molza* (Bergamo, 1750), p. 92.
‡ Durante / Martellotti (as in note 25), p. 42.

    Qual vite al campo sola
viver ormai disegno;
poichè 'l primo sostengno
mi tolse chi le cose umane invola.
Nè sia ch'io più m'appoggi
ad altro o in piani, o in poggi;
che da procella vasta
*serbarmi altri non basta.** (p. 315)

Tarquinia Molza

    Facelle son d'immortal luce ardenti
gli occhi che volgi in sì soavi giri,
e fiamma è l'aura che tu movi e spiri
a formar chiari angelici concenti;

    E foco sono le lacrime cadenti
che talor versi e foco i tuoi sospiri,
e quanti tu col dolce sguardo miri
e quanti rendi al dolce suono intenti.

    Sol io, fra i vivi raggi e fra le note
onde avvampa ciascun, nulla mi scaldo,
nè trova onde nutrirsi in me l'ardore:

    Nè già son io gelido marmo e saldo,
ma consumato in altro incendio il core,
or ch'è cenere tutto, arder non puote. † (p. 317)

Torquato Tasso
◉ Track 53,
Reading 54

    Voi pur, Anima mia,
lasciar quì mi volete
priva di voi, che la mia vita sete.
    O crudel omicida
con quanto dura sorte
mi conducete a morte?
Almeno il duol m'uccida
innanzi a voi ne l'ora del partire:
che forse al mio morire
una lagrima almeno
vedrò per la pietà bagnarvi il seno. ‡ (pp. 317, 319)

Tarquinia Molza

    Dopo l'aspra partita in gran dolore
lassa restai, e con pena infinita
mi vo struggendo in così fiero ardore
che più la morte bramo,che la vita:

◉ Track 54,
Reading 55

---

* Vandelli, *Opusculi inediti*, p. 81.   † Francesco Flora, ed., *Torquato Tasso Poesie* (Milan, 1934), p. 765.   ‡ Vandelli, *Opusculi inediti*, p. 81.

E s'io non ho soccorso al miser core,
L'alma farà da me certo partita;
Ahimè ch'ognor piangendo prego Amore
o che m'uccida, o che me porga aita!

Un sol rimedio trova al mio martire,
a l'intensa mia doglia, a tanti affanni,
ch'a l'afflitt'alma a tutte l'ore sento,

Che 'l ciel mi faccia innanzi a voi morire
per dar fin sempre ai gravi tristi danni,
che per voi porto, ed al mio gran tormento. (p. 319)

~

Giorgio Faloppia

Deh perchè in voi non muove un tal desire
amor verso di me, che il tempo, e gli anni
tutto in amarvi spendo, e non men pento † (p. 320)

~

Tarquinia Molza

Eran le vostre lagrime nel viso,
Donna, quel dì a vederle
qual in vermiglio vel candide perle
ed io gridava agli occhi
con l'ardor che farete
se con l'umor m'ardete?
Quando fra 'l pianto lampeggiando un riso
noi, dissero, in un loco
abbiamo l'acqua e 'l foco;
ma col foco immergiamo
e con acqua abbruciamo,
perch' abbagli l'amante, e si confonda
fra le fiamme e fra l'onda,
nè fia forza mortal che si difenda
ove il foco sommerga, e l'acqua incenda. ‡ (p. 320)

~

Donna, se da voi lunge
amor non mi disgiunge,
anzi, perché il duol cresca
vi porta legna ed esca.

Da voi sperava aìta,
ma se fate partita

---

* Vandelli, *Opusculi inediti*, p. 83.
† Vandelli, *Opusculi inediti*, p. 83.
‡ Giovanna Molza di Gazzolo, *Alfonso II D'Este Duca di Ferrara e Torquato Tasso nella vita di Tarquinia Molza*, p. 22 (added pages).

dov'avrò gli occhi e 'l core,
la vita e lo splendore?

Destin crudele e forte
m'a posto in dura sorte,
d'ogni mio mi spoglia,
e mi veste in doglia.

Dunque chi m'assicura
dal destin, s'ho paura
di voi? E d'amor privo
come rimarrò viva? * (p. 321) [42]

O quante volte mi ritorna a mente
quel dì felice e 'l loco
ove Amor dolcemente
il petto m'arse d'invisibil foco.

⦿ Track 55,
Reading 56

Alhor vidi raccolto in human velo
tanta luce e beltade,
leggiadria e honestade
quanta già vidi e contemplai nel cielo.

E piena di stupore
la mente e 'l core d'horrore
più volte gli occhi e 'l bel viso mirai.

Poi dalla maraviglia un tal diletto
mi nacque al cor, ch'altro più non bramai
che contemplando unirmi al caro oggetto. † (pp. 321 – 22)

Donna ben degna, che per voi si cinga
la gloriosa spada, e corra in giostra
il grande Alfonso; e s'altri a prova giostra,
e de' vostri color le piume ei tinga;

Torquato Tasso

Non sia, ch'a più begli occhi adorni e pinga
l'Arme dove i pensieri accenna e mostra:
nè da più bella man, cher da la vostra
prenda bel dono, e 'n ballo indi la stringa.

---

* Molza, *Alfonso II d'Este*, pp. 22–23 (added pages).
† Francesco Patrizi, *L'amorosa filosofia* (Florence, 1963), p. 64.

Nè ricevere altronde egli potrebbe
gloria maggiore, perchè ghirlande e fregi
sapete ordir non sol d'argento, o d'oro;

Ma celebrar con dotto stile e pregi;
sicchè per altro mai tanto non crebbe
fama immortale di trionfale alloro. * (p. 328)

~

Giuliano Goselini
◉ Track 57,
Reading 56

Far, che 'n marmi, e 'n metalli un corpo viva,
ben è del tuo scarpel mirabil arte;
ma de l'alma, Leon, più nobil parte
l'immagine formar parlando viva,

Si ch'altamente uom s'innamori, e scriva
di lei per forma, e la dipenga in carte;
questa dal vulgo in tutto ti diparte
nuova eccellenzia, ove null'altro arriva.

Onde già nel celeste alto soggiorno
giunto ti miro, e vincer di splendore
l'altro Leon di tante stelle adorno

Di TARQUINIA il bel nome, e 'l chiaro onore;
cosperso il Ciel de i più lumi intorno;
ne le labbra portando Astro maggiore. † (p. 329)

---

* Vandelli, *Opusculi inediti*, p. 90.
† Vandelli, *Opusculi inediti*, p. 91.

APPENDIX

The following two poems by Tarquinia are among others of hers that were set to music, the first by three composers: by Pietro Vinci, published in *Il terzo libro de madrigali* (*New Vogel*, #2918; 1571) and in *Il secondo libro de madrigali* (*New Vogel*, #2919; 1579); by MarcAntonio Pordenon, in *Il quarto libro de madrigali* (*New Vogel* #2239; 1573); and by Paolo Isnardi, in *Il primo libro de madrigali* (*New Vogel* #1354; 1589). The second poem was set by two composers: Leonardo Primavera in *Il quarto libro de madrigali* (*New Vogel* #2272; 1573) and by Regolo Vecoli in *Il secondo libro de madrigali* (*New Vogel* #2843; 1586).

> *In the gladsome season of Spring*
> *I will see myrtle and laurel,*
> *leafless from the icy winter,*
> *blossom forth happily, and roses and violets in flower.*
> *Before a new love could warm my heart, my sun, for another,*
> *My soul would have to melt away from you.*

> *Ne la dolce stagione di primavera*
> *senza foglie vedrò mirti e allori*
> *di vern'al ghiaccio i fior*
> *sorger lieti e fiorir rose e viole.*
> *Pria che da voi mio sole*
> *scioglia quest'alma o che per altro oggetto*
> *novo foco d'amor mi scaldi il petto.*

> *The light that gives light to you,*
> *my tired eyes,*
> *gives day to others, dark night to us,*
> *and thus I sing,*
> *"So it goes with those who put so much faith in it."*

> *La luce occhi miei lassi*
> *che dava luc'a voi,*
> *fa giorno ad altri, oscura notte a noi,*
> *ond'io sovente canto:*
> *"Così va ch'altrui pon fede tanto."*

NOTES

1   The entire document is quoted in Italian, translated from the original Latin, with a facsimile illustration, in Giovanna Molza di Gazzolo, *Alfonso II D'Este Duca di Ferrara e Torquato Tasso nella vita di Tarquinia Molza* (Modena, 1972), pp. 57–61. Countess Molza is a descendant of Tarquinia's eminent grandfather, Francesco Maria Molza, one of the most esteemed poets of the first half of the sixteenth century.

2   Francesco Patrizi, *L'amorosa filosofia*, ed. John Charles Nelson (Florence, 1963), pp. 18–19. Patrizi, who was well acquainted with Molza as her instructor in philosophy and literature, wrote this dialogue, in which she is the principal figure, in 1577. All details of her life in the present account of Molza are drawn from Patrizi unless otherwise noted.

3   Domenico Vandelli, *Opusculi inediti di Tarquinia Molza* (Bergamo, 1750), includes an elegiac verse by Giulio Morigi dedicated to Tarquinia "whose husband was completely devoted to her glory" (p. 36).

4   Torquato Tasso, "La Molza ovvero L'Amore," in *Torquato Tasso, Prose*, ed. Ettore Mazzali (Milan, 1959), p. 205.

5   This madrigal was set to music by Pietro Vinci, *Il quarto libro de Madrigali* (1573).

6   Plato, "Symposium," *Dialogues of Plato*, ed. J. D. Kaplan (New York, 1950), p. 201; Patrizi, *L'amorosa filosofia*, p. 65.

7   Patrizi, *L'amorosa filosofia*, pp. 134–135 passim.

8   Nelson suggests (p. xv) that the work was unfinished because Patrizi left Modena in 1577 to attend the Court of Ferrara and then received a chair in Platonic philosophy at the University of Ferrara. In 1581 he published his *Discussiones peripateticae*, in which he summarized the praises of Tarquinia that were given at great length in the first dialogue of *L'amorosa filosofia*. Or perhaps he could not work out the "Resolution"?

9   "Chi è non sappia per fama almeno l'altissimo, e generalissimo valore in Modena della Signora Tarquinia Molza? Ella nel cantare, e nel sonare è tanto all'altre superiore, quanto voi perfettissime Donne avanzate di perfezione gli uomini, e già si è mostrato: ma nelle dottrine, e nella cognizione delle tre Lingue Greca, Latina, Volgare, per non dir troppo, pareggia tutti i più esercitati Uomini de'tempi nostri, nelle quali tre lingue ella scrive e prose e versi maravigliosamente, comme tutto dì si vede per diversi componimenti." Vandelli, *Opusculi inediti*, p. 27.

10   This poem was put to music in a madrigal by Pietro Petracci, quoted in Vandelli, *Opusculi inediti*, p. 26. Other encomiastic verses by distinguished scholars and poets in Latin, Greek and Italian are included in this volume (see pp. 26–38, 84–93).

11   In addition to the unfinished and unpublished *L'amorosa filosofia*, another of Patrizi's works, *Discussiones peripateticae* (1581), is also about Tarquinia, repeating much of what he wrote in the earlier book. Achelous was a river god in Greek mythology noted for his seductions of goddesses and women. His daughters were the sirens who lived on an island in the Mediterranean; they sang so sweetly that sailors on ships drawing near the island forgot their homelands, became deprived of their wills, and wasted away on the sirens' island. For Giorgio Fallopia, see note 14.

12   The first writer to examine the relationship between Tasso and Tarquinia was Carlo Malmusi. First given as a talk in 1862, the material was published in *Memorie della Regia Accademia di Scienze, Lettere ed Arti in Modena* (Modena, 1862), pp. 167–187. See also Tasso's portrait, figure 9.2.

13   Malmusi, pp. 180–181.

14   The son or nephew of Gabriele Fallopio, the anatomist who discovered the tubes leading from the uterus to the ovaries, the Fallopian tubes.

15   See Mazzali, ed., *Torquato Tasso, Prose*, pp. 201–215.

16   Joanne Marie Riley, "The Influence of Women on Secular Music in Sixteenth Century Italy" (M.A. thesis, Wesleyan University, 1980), p. 99, n. 10. The poem is found in *La ghirlanda della Contessa Angela Bianca Beccaria* (Genoa, 1595); Tarquinia's poem is included in the second day of recitations: "Angela came down to us from the heavens / wafted on the delightful perfume of roses; / let not your charms / nor your overflowing garland / be hidden; Love sends them/from the third circle of the celestial garden; / they even flower / on your cheeks, on your lovely lips/to make an eter-

nal spring for us." The third circle, from Dante's *Paradiso*, is the sphere of Venus.

17   Patrizi, *L'amorosa filosofia*, p. 6.

18   Patrizi, *L'amorosa filosofia*, p. 14.

19   The castles and palaces of the d'Este family in the city of Ferrara and the extensive duchy are described in detail in Angelo Solerti, *Ferrara e la corte Estense nella seconda metà del secolo decimosesto* (Città di Castello, 1891), pp. xi–xvi. The main castle and the Palazzo Schifanoia still stand, but all else has been destroyed.

20   Annibale Romei, *The Courtiers Academie* (New York, 1969), a translation of Romei's *I Discorsi, gentiluomo ferrarese divisi in cinque giornate* (Venice, 1585). We have not changed any of the spelling in the English translation. See also Solerti, *Ferrara e la corte Estense*, pp. xlvi–lv, for the court life of the duke, the duchess and the courtiers, largely spent in amusements that included tennis matches, jousts, birding, boar hunting, boating, card games, performances of juggling, sleight of hand, and clownery in addition to musical concerts. Traveling companies of theatrical performers such as the Gelosi, the most famous of them, presented plays annually, and sometimes more often. The star of the Gelosi was Isabella Andreini (1562–1604), "the first distinguished actress of the European theatre, the first woman to break once for all the age-old tradition of a womanless and one-sided stage and to win for herself and her fellow actresses a position of dignity and respect in the theatre of the western world." Rosamond Gilder, "Isabella Andreini: The First Actress of Europe," *Theatre Arts Monthly* 14 (1930): 145. For a detailed and fascinating description of an ambassadorial banquet in a ducal court, including foods prepared and served and the splendid accoutrements, see in Emilio Faccioli, ed., *L'arte della cucina* (Turin, 1957), the chapter on Cristoforo Messisburgo, the majordomo of Alfonso I d'Este.

21   Anthony Newcomb, *The Madrigal at Ferrara, 1579–1597* (Princeton, 1980), p. 12.

22   One of the most famous of the male participants in the concerts was Giulio Cesare Brancaccio (1515–1586), known equally for his military achievements. See Carol MacClintock, *Giaches de Wert (1535–1595), Life and Works* (New York, 1966), p. 22, n. 14.

23   Paolo Virchi, *Il primo libro di madrigali à cinque voci* (1584).

24   Molce, i.e., Molza.

25   Elio Durante and Anna Martellotti, *Cronistoria del concerto delle dame principalissime di Margherita Gonzaga d'Este* (Florence, 1989), p. 42. The sonnet by Petrarch is number 164, "Hor che 'l cielo e la terra."

26   MacClintock, *Giaches de Wert*, p. 30.

27   MacClintock, *Giaches de Wert*, pp. 34–35, 41 (n. 95), 44.

28   Riley, "Influence of Women," pp. 19–20.

29   MacClintock, *Giaches de Wert*, p. 9.

30   Iain Fenlon, *Music and Patronage in 16th Century Mantua* (Cambridge, 1980), p. 137.

31   Riley, "Influence of Women," pp. 26–27.

32   Alfred Einstein, *The Italian Madrigal* (Princeton, 1949), vol. II, p. 831.

33   MacClintock, *Giaches de Wert*, pp. 20–21.

34   Riley, "Influence of Women," p. 27.

35   Patrizi, *L'amorosa filosofia*, p. 37.

36   Durante and Martellotti, *Cronistoria*, pp. 49–50.

37   Durante and Martellotti, *Cronistoria*, pp. 49–50.

38   Vandelli, *Opusculi inediti*, p. 17.

39   Tarquinia's tomb was moved at an unknown date from the wall between the baptistery and the door of the sacristy in the chapel of St. Geminiano. It is now in the wall of the left entrance of the chapel.

40   Molza di Gazzolo, *Alfonso II D'Este*, front matter, cover art, figure 1, and other illustrations.

41   "The other Leon": Leonardo da Vinci.

42   The original text of this poem has been questioned. Durante / Martellotti substitute the masculine endings *primo* and *vivo* for the feminine endings *prima* and *viva*, an alteration that we believe cannot be defended because Molza was writing of herself. They also change the text of lines 14–15, putting the question mark at the end of line 14 and changing *voi* to *vo*, which also does not seem well justified.

11.1.
Anon.
Portrait of
Veronica Franca.
1569-1575.
Manuscript
Collection,
Biblioteca
Nazionale
Marciana,
Venice.
Photo,
Biblioteca.

CHAPTER ELEVEN

VERONICA FRANCA
(1546–1591)

 ## *THE UNHAPPY COURTESAN*

enedetto Croce's assessment that "Veronica Franco[1] . . . unlike Tullia, felt no need to weave a veil of illusion, perfectly content and serene in the profession she embraced,"[2] continues a long tradition of romanticizing the Venetian courtesan *onesta*,[3] and has been shared by a number of writers who, it is true, can point to passages in her poems in which she writes of her skill in making love, giving the impression that she enjoyed it.

> *Lying alongside of you, tenderly*
> *I would have you taste*
> *the delights of love that I know so well.*
> *   And I could give you such pleasure*
> *that you would find yourself satisfied*
> *and even more completely in love.*
> *   I become so tender, so charming*
> *when I find myself in bed with a man*
> *who makes me feel loved and appreciated*
> *   That my pleasuring exceeds all former delights,*
> *and however tight had seemed the knot of love*
> *it becomes tighter still.*[4] (p. 369)

Expert in the ways of making love she doubtless was, and we believe this passage in her second *capitolo*[5] was meant to advertise her skill as a professional in giving pleasure to others, and not to express any personal pleasure in the erotic game she played for her livelihood. Reading through Veronica's oeuvre of twenty-five *capitoli*, fifty letters, and sixteen sonnets that have survived because they were published, we are struck by the anger and demand for respect that they frequently express. We may realize that she was far more like Tullia d'Aragona than Croce thought when we remember how unveiled Tullia was in telling Sperone Speroni and the other men in his *Dialogo di Amore* about the life of a courtesan: "If you knew the servility, the vileness, the depths and inconstancy of such a life, you would blame anyone . . . who said it was a good one and excused it. And anyone who helps a young girl, foolish enough to be pushed into such a life, to get out of it is saving her from misery."[6] Indeed, we may well believe that Veronica had read Sperone's *Dialogo* and had Tullia in mind when we read her long letter to a friend who was intent on making her daughter a courtesan.[7]

She had begged this woman many times to give up this plan for her daughter, she reminds her in this letter, and she is writing now, she says, hoping still to dissuade her:

I want to show you the hidden precipice toward which you are heading, shouting as loud as I can, so that there is time to avoid it.[8]

She makes it clear that her concern was not only for the daughter but also for the mother, her friend, who would be equally ruined, becoming her courtesan daughter's procuress. According to Venetian law, anyone (including mothers) involved in the corruption of young girls would be severely punished, exhibited on a platform in the plaza of St. Mark's for his or her crime and exiled from the city for two years.[9] Veronica had previously offered to help her friend by paying whatever it cost for the girl to be accepted into the Casa delle Zitelle (Home for Spinsters), a charitable institution for poor unmarried women, and to help the mother as well.

> Now I am writing you once more to beg you again not to destroy with one single blow your own soul and honorable reputation together with your daughter's. . . . You speak of luck but I tell you there is nothing worse than giving yourself up to fortune that can more easily bring woe than benefit. Sensible people . . .

and here we have an important key to understanding how Veronica went about managing her life,

> sensible people, in order to avoid being deceived, build on what they have inside them, and what they can make of themselves. (figure 11.1)

Even at best, Veronica writes, life is miserable, and it is horrible and contrary to reason to give your mind and body to a slavery that disgusts you even to think of it:

> To make yourself a prey to so many men at the risk of being swindled, robbed, killed, to have one man take away from you everything you've acquired from all the others for so many years, along with how many other dangers of injury and horrible contagious diseases. To eat with another's mouth, to sleep with another's eyes, to move according to another's will, obviously sailing headlong toward the shipwreck of everything you possess, as well as your life. . . . Consider the consequences, look at what happens to the countless women in this profession . . . your daughter herself will abandon you when she realizes how you have exploited and ruined her. (p. 369)

It is interesting, however, that Veronica did not abandon her own mother, who was responsible for making her a courtesan like herself. When she made her first will in 1564 she provided for her mother as long as she lived.[10] Throughout her life Veronica was concerned with the welfare of young girls who, lacking a dowry, were vulnerable and susceptible to the temptation of turning to prostitution as a means of livelihood. In 1577 she sent a petition to the Venetian government suggesting the foundation of a shelter for young married women or single women with children, who were ineligible for the Casa delle Zitelle. The Casa del Soccorso was indeed founded in the 1570s, and although there is no evidence that Veronica was involved in it, her petition might well have been the catalyst for its establishment.[11]

So much for the "content and serene" courtesan. We can hardly escape the impression that Veronica was writing not only for the women of her own time, but also for those in time to come, and we must wonder if indeed the letter had a real addressee. It is as if she hoped she could reach into the centuries ahead and thus make her warning, and herself, remembered. If such had been her intention, her letter was both a failure—certainly it never stopped any woman from becoming a prostitute— and a brilliant success. Had Veronica written nothing else, this letter would deservedly give her an honorable place in the social and literary history of women, exposing as it does the helplessness of women of her time and of all times without financial resources sufficient to allow them freedom to choose how to live. Its passion is as moving as any of her best poems, and the desperate fury behind the words suggests that it was written later than the collection of *capitoli,* which were composed before November 1575, the date when she wrote the volume's dedication to the Duke of Mantua, and not much before she brought out her collected letters in 1580, when she had already passed her frightening thirtieth birthday and was facing the despair of youth and beauty lost. Had she ever been happy as a courtesan? Not often. As Margaret Rosenthal remarks, "Venetian courtesans rose neither with ease nor without considerable difficulties through the ranks of Venetian society."[12]

Veronica was born in 1546, daughter of Francesco Francho and Paula Fracassa, as identified in her will of 1564. The family belonged to the rank of *cittadini originari* (Venetian citizens by birth) and was in modern terms middle-class. Nothing is known of Francesco, but in the famous directory of "the most reputable courtesans of Venice," the *Catalogo di tutte le principal et più honorate cortigiane di Venezia,* published in 1565, Paula was listed as a *pieza,* the person to whom the client paid the courtesan's fee, in Veronica's case said to be a very modest two *scudi.*[13]

As with most courtesans, Veronica's life as a purveyor of sexual pleasure evidently began quite early. By the age of eighteen she had already been married and separated from her husband; we learn from the will she drew up in 1564 that, in case of her death, she asks her mother to retrieve her dowry from Paolo Panizza, and that she was pregnant with her first child, whose father, she thought, was "probably" Jacomo Baballi, although she could not be sure. She requests that Baballi, one of the wealthiest merchants in Venice,[14] administer the care and financial interests of the boy or girl that was soon to be born, and as a token of her love bequeaths to him her diamond.

It is possible that Veronica really loved Baballi and not his wealth. She seems to have fallen sincerely in love with some of the men with whom she made love, to judge from the anguished *capitoli* she addressed at various times to one or another of them. But perhaps her first great passion was for a man who probably never was a sexual partner. Very young when she first saw him, she was in an instant overwhelmed by the handsome face and eloquent speech of the man who stood at the altar of the church she attended on that unforgettable day.

> *When from your eyes and beautiful face*
> *Love thrust his blazing torch at me,*
> > *intent on wounding me in countless ways,*
> *he then heightened with the power of your eloquence*
> *the raging fire within me.*

> *Your appealing habit and winning presence,*
> *your unique grace and manners*
> *and the lucid clarity of your excellent values*
>   *were the bright sun that dazzled my eyes*
> *and set me afire from afar,*
> *even beyond the realm of Phoebus . . .*

Unfortunately for Veronica, the man was a priest:

> *How often watching and listening to you*
> *as I sat among the others in church*
> *I was rewarded with your glance.*
>   *And even though I did not show my love*
> *I always found you kind,*
> *perhaps aimlessly, or perhaps there was some reason,*
>   *for now in one way, now in another,*
> *you turned your modest and pious face*
> *compassionately toward me as you preached.*
>   *And while you spoke of heaven's sovereign goodness*
> *you looked at me intently,*
> *your hands now extended, now joined together.*
>   *And there were other, similar things you did*
> *that led me to hope you had noticed*
> *my repressed and pious love . . .*

He had noticed, certainly, as she suspected. They became friends, and he did fall in love with her. But apparently faithful to his vows of celibacy, the priest and Veronica had to keep their relationship platonic, although it became clear that he wished he were free to share his life with her. Knowing that he loved her made her suffer all the more.

> *Thus my pain sharply deepened*
> *because we were unable to enjoy life joyfully and*
> *happily together as we both wished . . .*

He resolved what must have been a harsh dilemma for him by going abroad as a missionary, perhaps as one of the early Jesuits who followed Francis Xavier to India.

> *You went away to foreign lands*
> *and I remained here, victim of that fire*
> *that made my days sad and dark without you.* (pp. 369 – 70)

Miserable, enduring the pain of lost love, she suffered deeply for some time. But gradually she was able to turn her need for him to some good account, and doing so, she found the cure that helped to bring her back to "a healthy mind." She does not say what this cure was, but it seems likely that the deep hurt she felt drove her to turn to the one "cure" that now and for the rest of her life made disappointment bearable: writing.

In Veronica's will of 1564 Jacomo Baballi became custodian of the as yet unborn child, presumably his, and administrator of her estate for the child's benefit. Six years later, however, she made a second will, in which it appears that Baballi is no longer her lover, inasmuch as she refers to him only as having returned to her some money from her dowry that her brother had given him and a string of pearls that he had probably given her. By this time she had born a second child, and both children, boys she named Achiletto and Enea, she entrusts to Zuan (Giovanni) Battista Bernardo as their guard-ian, although she names the still living Andrea Tron, a Venetian patrician, as the father of the second boy. Baballi is out of the picture although he, too, was still alive. Curiously, it is another man, Lodovico Ramberti, who actually made himself respon-sible for Achiletto. Ramberti is named in Veronica's will only as one of the executors, and yet he himself had made a will in 1570 leaving property to Achiletto, the use and revenues of which he was to share with Veronica until he reached the age of twenty-five, when he would assume complete control of it. There is no mention of Enea. Ramberti's relationship with Veronica, loving and protective according to his will, en-dured over several years: three years after this will, he wrote a letter to his friend, Zuane Bragadin, dated 7 January 1573, phrased as if it were a will. Here Ramberti refers to his age, although still sound in mind and body, and to his "delicious" friend, Veronica Franco (*sic*) to whom he leaves his featherbed, which she must never use, sell, or pawn (possibly as a reminder to her of the pleasure they shared in it). This "will" was found among papers in the Biblioteca Civico Correr catalogued under mis-cellaneous items that Rosenthal translates as "academic exercises, translations, dis-courses and other instructive and pleasing things," which led her to believe that this document was meant to be amusing.[15] However, this cannot be considered an amus-ing document. In a codicil, Ramberti stipulates that a tombstone be constructed with the following epitaph, in Italian, not Latin, so that everyone can understand it, and with the letters *V* and *F* beneath it to record that the verse was written by "the very learned Madonna Veronica Franca":

> *Reader, I am not really buried here*
> *although you see my name written on this stone*
> *because my body was disposed of*
> *by a pitchfork as is the custom here;*
> *I wanted to put back together, whole,*
> *the quartered parts of my brother's body.*
> *This tomb is here for your convenience,*
> *If you have anything good to say about me, say it here.* (p. 370)

The epitaph refers to the events surrounding the dreadful sentence pronounced against Ramberti's brother thirty years earlier for a murder of which he was indeed guilty; he was to be drawn and quartered in the Piazza San Marco, where public exe-cutions were regularly held. To save his brother from this agonizing death, Ramberti managed to smuggle poison to him in prison, so that he died before the quartering. Because Ramberti's deed was prompted by brotherly devotion, Ramberti was not punished as severely as he might have been, but he nevertheless suffered banishment from Venice for four years. In the will of 1573, he requested that his body be quartered in order to replace the four parts of his brother's body, which he had "illegally, with his own hands, removed from those prongs."[16] As we reconstruct what happened, the brother's body was quartered after death, impaled on the prongs of a pitchfork, and thrown into a grave. Ramberti retrieved the body parts, reburied them in a grave marked with his own name, and ordered his own quartered body to be substituted as an act of love for his brother.[16] This was a bitter memory, and this part of the "will" proves that there was no intention to be amusing. He wished, he wrote in the will, to allay his conscience.[17] The gruesome punishment, often inflicted for high crimes, reminds us of the dark side of Renaissance Italy's most famous liberal city.

What is always taken to be the high point of Veronica's professional life occurred in 1574, when the French King Henry III visited Venice. He had become king of Poland in 1572 and was living there when on the death of his brother Charles IX, son of Henry II and Catherine de'Medici, he was called to ascend the French throne. On his way home to be crowned in Paris, he went by way of Venice to spend a few days in the glamorous city, sometime French ally against the British. Henry's reception in Venice was stupendous, with ten days of ceaseless entertainments and banquets from morning to night in his honor, and the visit was thoroughly documented hour by hour, one festivity after another.[18] There were some hours, nevertheless, that seem to have eluded contemporary chroniclers. According to Veronica, the twenty-three-year-old king spent one evening with her.

Our knowledge of the unscheduled visit comes from Veronica herself, recorded in a letter and two sonnets directed to the king.

> *To the Most Unconquerable and Most Christian King Henry III of France and of Poland*
>
> To the immense favor that Your Majesty deigned to show me, coming to my modest home and taking away with you my portrait in exchange for the vivid image that your heroic virtue and divine courage have left in my heart—an exchange beyond fortune and happiness for me—I am incapable of making equal return neither in thought or desire, for what can I create worthy of the supreme nobility of your heavenly soul and your blessed destiny? Nor can I in any manner of thanks express my gratitude for the infinite value of the beneficent and gracious offers you made me with regard to the book that I am dedicating to you, which offer testifies more to your grandeur and serene, royal splendor than to any accomplishment of mine. Nonetheless, just as the entire wide world can be drawn on the small space of a narrow sheet of paper, so I have in these few verses which I respectfully send to Your Majesty, made a sketch, however cramped and awkward, of my gratitude and of my immense desire to celebrate, beyond any hope of success, the countless and superhuman gifts that are sheltered happily within your breast. And with devoted and most particular affection, I bow down to embrace your sacred knees.
>
> Your Majesty's most humble and devoted servant,
>
> *Veronica Franca* (pp. 370 – 71)

From this letter it appears that Veronica intended to dedicate a book of hers to him, and that he not only approved her doing so but had also promised to help her with it in some way. The book was most likely the *Terze rime* that she brought out the following year, and we must wonder what happened that caused her in the event to dedicate the book to Guglielmo Gonzaga, Duke of Mantua and Monferrato, instead of to Henry III. We will return to this question later.

The first of the two sonnets to Henry center on the king's secret visit, disguised, as was Jupiter's custom when he visited one of his mortal lovers:

> *As occasionally Jupiter graciously descends*
> *from heaven to our humble abodes*
> *he takes on human form so that*
> *earthly eyes are not blinded by his radiant presence.*
>
> *So without royal pomp that shines and dazzles*
> *to my modest home came Henry,*
> *elected by destiny to rule a realm*
> *greater than one can comprehend.*
>
> *Even though he came incognito, his brilliance*
> *stamped its divine essence on my heart*
> *and overwhelmed my vitality.*
>
> *Certain of my deep feeling for him*
> *he took my enameled portrait*
> *when he left, with evident pleasure.* (p. 371)

Her second sonnet continues the subject of her portrait:

> *King by superior merit and perfection,*
> *take what this hand offers you,*
> *this carved and painted likeness*
> *in which my face and spirit are caught.*
>
> *And if this humble and imperfect model*
> *does not please your blessed eyes,*
> *think of the cause, not the effect.**
> *A small spark can light a great fire.*
>
> *Thus as your immortal, god-given courage*
> *in war and peace, proved again and again,*
> *fills my soul with vast amazement,*
>
> *See expressed and resolute in my face*
> *the desire of a woman who has striven*
> *to exalt you above all others.* (pp. 371 – 72)

---

* In other words, "Think of me, the original, when you look at the image."

As it happened, one of the young men in a group assigned to look after Henry's needs and desires during his Venetian sojourn was Andrea Tron, the father of Veronica's son Enea. It may have been Tron who brought Henry to Veronica, certainly a great favor inasmuch as knowledge of the royal visit could not have been kept perfectly secret, and Veronica's desirability would be much enhanced, for who would not want to make love with a woman who had made love with a king?

It was not until six years later that Veronica herself wrote about this extraordinary event. In the collection of her letters published in 1580, she included a letter to the king and the two sonnets.[19] It is possible, of course, that she was enjoined to secrecy and could not include her letter and sonnets to Henry in 1575 when she published her *Terze Rime*. But although the delay in making public what could have been a particularly advantageous event in her life as a courtesan is thus understandable, we find it curious that there has never been found any reference to it in any of the documents of the well-known people of Venice that fill the city's archives. In several of her letters she makes references that appear to relate to a celebratory collection of verses in honor of Henry in such a way as to suggest that she is assembling them, but although such a book of poems in praise of Henry's visit to Venice was in fact published in 1574 under the title of *Compositioni volgari e latine fatte da diversi nella venuta in Venetia di Henrico III Re di Francia e di Polonia* (Compositions in vernacular [Italian] and Latin written by various authors on the visit in Venice of Henry III, King of France and Poland), her name appears neither as editor nor contributor. Was it excluded because there were objections to a courtesan's participating in a book praising a king? The portrait she mentions remains undiscovered, but, surprisingly, there may be a copy of it, a possibility we will discuss farther along. We have to wonder if the great visit really occurred, but, despite the lack of corroborating evidence, it seems likely that it did. We can well imagine that the young king would have wanted to include what was for many male tourists and commercial travelers to Venice the highlight of their visit to Venice, a few hours with one of the city's prime attractions, the beautiful courtesan. And, if so, why not Veronica, one of the most beautiful and accomplished? Perhaps eventually some confirming document will be found; one wants to believe that there really was this brilliant moment in her otherwise mostly sad life.

Veronica, through no fault of her own, was in the wrong profession. She was happiest in the company of men with whom she was engaged in conversation about literature and art; and as a skillful rather than poetic writer (although occasionally her verse does achieve creative power), with good judgment and taking pleasure in giving advice, she would have made an excellent professor of literature or dean of students had such professions been available to a woman. To a would-be young suitor who had evidently threatened to run away from her and join some army if he could not win her love, she wrote,

> You had better stay here and try to control your feverish fantasies, but
> if you must don spurs, do not put on those that thrust you wildly out of
> your own country into a vain, wandering exile, but rather those that lead
> you to acquire virtue and act in accordance with your merit. In this way
> one can truly enjoy deserved leisure among his fellow citizens, and in the

presence of his beloved lady, try to surpass his peers in the theatre of public competition by acquiring merit greater than theirs, aspiring to rewards worthy of virtuous service. You know quite well that among all that hope to insinuate themselves into my love the most dear to me are those who are engaged in the practice of the disciplines and the liberal arts, of which, although a woman of little learning compared with my inclinations and interests, I am so fond, and it is such a delight for me to converse with knowledgeable people in order to learn from them, that, if only I were lucky enough, I would spend my entire life, all my time, happily in the company of accomplished men. . . . (p. 372; figure 11.1)

Veronica promises him that if he studies and works at his writing she might come to care for him.

She was, indeed, a kind of courtesan-in-residence for the men who frequented the salon of Domenico Venier (1517–1582), member of one of the most powerful of Venetian families and the man who for many years was the central figure among Venetian intellectuals; invalided by a crippling disease at the age of thirty-two (said to have been gout) he made his palazzo the gathering place of prominent men who congregated there informally to discuss the literary issues of the day. Among these was Marco Venier (1530–1602), with whom Veronica had a particularly close—and intriguing—relationship. Marco was not primarily a writer; he held various important political positions in Venice and was a figure of substantial influence in the affairs of the city. His importance in Veronica's life, both sexual and literary (and very possibly political), is underlined by the fact that she opened her volume of *Terze rime* not with one of her own *capitoli* but one of his, his authorship identified in the heading, "From the Magnificent Mr. Marco Venier to Signora Veronica Franca," the only poem in the collection that bears the name of the writer.

Marco Venier's name appears in two copies of Veronica's *Terze rime*. We know of only three copies of the book that have survived, and Marco's name is omitted in the third copy. Were there more printed? The book is dedicated to Guglielmo Gonzaga, Duke of Mantua, but there is no record of it, or indeed, any mention of Veronica, in the Gonzaga archives. When Michel Montaigne visited Venice in 1580 she sent him a copy of her recently published *Letters,* but not her book. Did she not have one to send him? Was it because of the plague that broke out in Venice late in 1575 and curtailed so much of Venetian life in all aspects, personal and commercial, that she apparently published the book herself, since it carries no publisher's name? The *capitoli* do not seem to be arranged in any evident order except for those that are paired as statements and responses by their rhyme endings: the original copies do not carry the headings, "To" or "From," as they do in modern editions. An engraved portrait of Veronica was planned as a frontispiece for her *Terze rime;* it was not included, however, and now exists as a detached sheet in the Biblioteca Nazionale Marciana in Venice. Why was it dropped? In short, Veronica's *Terze rime* raises many questions that cannot be answered with the available information. For this reason, we have elected to construct the following narrative in accordance with what seems plausible in light of what she herself has written in the *capitoli* and her letters. Furthermore, we have assumed that other *capitoli* now attributed to "author unknown" were written by

Marco Venier, as Giovanni degli Agostini and Emmanuele Cicogna believed.[20] Marco's opening poem begins,

> *If I love you as much as my own life*
> *cruel lady, why do you not offer me*
> *relief from the torment of such love?*
> *   And if in vain I beg for grace and sympathy*
> *why do you not at least put an end*
> *to the pain I suffer for love of you?*

We recognize, with this opening, that we are in familiar Petrarchist territory: the lover reproaching his lady for her unwillingness to surrender. He goes on at length (181 lines) with the usual variations on the theme of his suffering,

> *Oh if you could know my ardent yearning,*
> *to serve you alone night and day,*
> *calling and longing for you constantly,*

her coldness,

> *But how is it possible that in such soft flesh*
> *and the lovely whiteness of your breast*
> *there could be enclosed such a hard and pitiless heart?*

her beauty,

> *Oh, beauty beyond all others*
> *before which the soul gladly bows down*
> *and feels as if in paradise, here on earth!*

her talent, inspired directly from Apollo,

> *Take up your pen and paper, then,*
> *and write charming, graceful verses*
> *that carry away the prize from the greatest poets.* (pp. 372 – 73)

Turning from his conventionally ardent sentiments, we are all the more surprised by Veronica's answer, so candid, so level-headed, so dispassionate that we feel shocked, as if suddenly faced with a steady stream of cold air.

> *If I could be certain of your love*
> *judging from your words and your face*
> *which often hide a different feeling,*
> *   If the thoughts concealed in the mind*
> *were revealed in such a way*
> *that others were not often taken in by deceit,*

> *I would shake off this fear for which,*
> *although it serves to protect me,*
> *I would be derided as simple-minded and foolish . . .*

People are deluded by hope, she writes, and she must not allow herself to be fooled by words and charm. She wants proof that he really loves her, and she demands that he prove his love with "deeds." What kind of deeds she is requiring is not stated, but she makes it perfectly clear that she is not asking for money or anything of tangible value.

> *I do not want you to believe, with this reply,*
> *that I am avaricious*
> *for that vice is not hidden in my heart.*
> *But I want you to understand*
> *that in loving I try to be cautious, if not chaste,*
> *in expressing my desires.*

If she is satisfied that a man loves her, she "returns his principal with interest," but anyone who tries to fool her will find he himself is a fool. That understood, what she wants, she repeats, is to see him prove his love with deeds instead of words.

> *You know well what is most dear to me:*
> *follow then what I have already told you*
> *and you will be my one and only lover.*
> *My heart is in love with talent*
> *and you who possess so many gifts*
> *that the greatest knowledge abides in you,*
> *do not deny me your effort so that*
> *in this way I may see you eager to win*
> *the right to love me:*
> *. . .*
> *This will cost you little effort*
> *because with your ability, any undertaking,*
> *no matter how difficult, is easy for you.*

We may hazard a guess that the deed she was requesting had something to do with helping her get her *Terze rime* published.

Not ingenuously, she mixes scorn with promise. It would not be easy for him to make her fall in love with him,

> *to tell the truth, you want to fly*
> *without wings and instantly reach the heights,*

but if he gives her what she wants, of great value to her though without cost to him, his reward would be such that his most soaring hopes would be satisfied.

> *Phoebus, who serves the goddess of love*
> *and as a sweet reward receives from her*
> *blessing that is worth more than being a god,*
>   *comes from her to reveal to me*
> *those ways that Venus practices with him*
> *when she holds him in her tender embrace;*
>   *so that I, thus instructed, know how*
> *to behave in bed so well*
> *that I surpass the art of Apollo*
>   *and my singing and writing are forgotten*
> *by one who experiences me in this way,*
> *which Venus teaches to her followers.*

Despite the erotic imagery, her tone is one of negotiation rather than affection.

> *Let me see those works*
> *that I request, for then*
> *you will enjoy my caresses to the full;*
>   *and I will enjoy yours*
> *in the way of mutual love*
> *which gives pure delight.*

Her lover could hardly have been happy, even with such promises, when he came at last to the cool end of her reply.

> *My strong desire is to have good reason to love you:*
> *do whatever you wish,*
> *for whatever happens is up to you.* (pp. 373 – 74)

For some reason Veronica came to believe, mistakenly, that Marco Venier was the author of some scurrilous verses about her that someone sent her. Beginning with a pun on her name, *Ver* (truly) *unica* (unique), her attacker writes,

> *Veronica, truly unique whore,*
> *franca, i.e. cunning, clever, crafty, cheating,*
> *and scrawny, scrounging, screwing and swindling*
> *between the Castle, the Ghetto and the Customs,*
>
> *Woman-monster in human flesh,*
> *putty, plaster, leather, and board,*
> *loathsome phantom, scabby ogre.* (p. 374)

It would take countless poets to detail all her defects, he says, which are like those of the women who end up "on the bridges and in the hospitals," referring to the "Lament of the Ferrarese Courtesan."

If you do not learn what I am teaching you,
Arrogant courtesan,
Ponte Sisto and the hospital await you. [21]

Deeply hurt and believing that Marco Venier had written the vilifying verses, Veronica addressed a *capitolo* to him in which she challenges him to a verbal duel.

No more words: to action, to the field, to arms,
for I am resolved to die, if I must,
to free myself from such savage attacks.
    I do not know if this should be called a challenge,
since I am the one responding to provocation:
but why do we have to come to fighting over words?
    If you wish, I will say you have challenged me;
or else, I challenged you; I'll go either way,
and I am agreeable to any occasion.
    The field and arms are your choice
and I'll take what you have rejected;
in fact, let both choices be yours.
    Soon you will realize
how ungrateful and faithless you were
and how wrongfully you have betrayed me.

A few lines further along we are suddenly mystified to find her writing, in this poem addressed to Marco Venier,

Do you wish to meet for our duel
in that secret inn, insidious and cruel witness
of my bitterly remembered caresses?

that their meetings were clandestine. Why did they meet in secret, we must wonder, and why, then, did she publish the poem, exposing their secret? Is this why Marco's name was omitted from the book after the first two copies were printed? More than that, with the exposure she introduces a sudden change in the meaning of the duel she proposes, which she now casts in erotic language:

Here stands my bed
where I welcomed you to my breast, where you can still see
how our bodies were pressed to each other.
    . . .
    This very place,
once the beloved nest of my joy
where now I am alone, living in torment and anguish.
    Choose this place for our field of battle,
so that the cries of your treachery against me,
cruel, faithless one, may be spent within these walls.

> *Come here, and skillful as you are,*
> *carry your sharp weapon in your bold hand*
> *ready to injure me.*
> *Whatever weapon you bring me*
> *I will gladly accept*
> *the stronger and sharper it is.*
> *Let your armor be stripped from your breast*
> *so that nude and undefended*
> *the courage within it may be revealed.*
> *Let no one intervene in this struggle*
> *so that it is limited to the two of us, alone,*
> *without seconds, behind closed doors.*

However, eager for revenge though she is, she sees a possibility other than fighting to assuage the pain of the injury she has suffered: Suppose one is asked to pardon an affront; is it not proper and virtuous to do so?

> *What if you offered me peace?*
> *Suppose we threw down our weapons*
> *and you indicated the possibility of a love match in bed?*
> *. . .*
> *Perhaps I would even follow you to bed*
> *and lying there, striving with you*
> *I would not yield an inch to you.*
> *To pay back your contemptible attack*
> *I would fall upon you, and in our fierce struggle*
> *you would become heated, defending yourself.* (pp. 374 – 75)

Their combat, she assures him, would end climactically as at the end they would both collapse with the same final blow.

One can imagine Marco Venier's initial astonishment as he read this *capitolo* from a woman he loved, accusing him of insulting her, and challenging him to a "duel." He probably realized immediately that there was some mistake. He wrote her assuring her that he was not the guilty author of "Truly unique whore," and offered to be her second in the duel against her real attacker, if she should discover who he was. She was overjoyed to know that she had mistaken her enemy.

> Rumor . . . gave me to believe that you were the author of that satire.
> . . . Since, although I may not be talented myself, I certainly admire those
> who are gifted, indeed such as yourself for whom I have always felt affec-
> tion and respect, I was amazed that in exchange for my devotion I was re-
> paid with such defamatory libel, and I did not even entirely believe that
> you wrote it, given its faults and errors, unworthy of one of your in-
> tellect. Undecided what to believe, I wrote the Capitolo as an amusing
> pastime. . . .

She was delighted that he had offered to second her in the eventual duel with the guilty man, "if he ever comes to light," and in preparation (here we discern the wit that must have charmed her lovers) she suggests she would like some further training in the art of dueling.

> I beg your lordship as a master in dueling to teach me some secret stroke, or rather, to take up your sword, not one with a sharp edge but rather one for play, and engage me in a realistic battle, provoking me to reply with whatever proposal you wish in whatever language you prefer, and I will be much obliged to you and will do my best to reply with promptness equal to my delight and profit in reading what you send me. (pp. 375 – 76)

Marco thus took up her challenge, although not completely in the spirit of jesting.

> *No more war, but peace: and may the hatred and anger*
> *and whatever discord has come between us*
> *be turned to twice as much love.*
> . . .
>   *I regret that conflict arose between us,*
> *but if disdain may create greater love*
> *I am glad this disdain arose,*
>   *and even though reason may tell me to resent*
> *and take revenge for the injury*
> *that you always wanted to inflict on me*
>   *I prefer with the arms of friendship*
> *to fight this battle so well that in the end,*
> *unvanquished, I will be acknowledged the victor.*
>   *True love does not reject this,*
> *indeed it is with these and no other weapons*
> *that a generous spirit enters the fray.*
>   *Oh if you were willing thus to stand against me,*
> *if you wished to test with what strength you have*
> *whether you might possibly overcome me,*
>   *I would feel like Jove himself;*
> *but perhaps my hope is too bold*
> *wanting to fly without wings.*

Loving her as he does, he writes, her anger against him has pained him unbearably, but he nevertheless still longs to serve her—and now it is Marco who alludes to the need to keep their relationship secret: he behaves and governs himself as necessity requires, he tells her, he would like to explain himself to her but

> *I know there would be gossip about it so*
> *I devise ways to serve you in silence.*

I do not know but perhaps someone
disliked our being together so that
he spread his poison over our happiness.
. . .

But here I am, preparing for the duel,
armed with my pain and suffering
and protected by my innocence.
. . .

I know only too well that against me
you are well armed, and I
do not even cover my naked breast against your blows.
. . .

So strike, again and again, with one hand then the other
for your target is not far away
and your blows can hardly miss.
. . .

I give you all power over me . . .
and I grant you in good faith carte blanche
so that you have complete dominion over my heart.
In sum, I wish for more than I can hope for,
nor do I know if you made your invitation
to torment me, or perhaps sincerely.

I shall wait for you to let me know. (pp. 376 – 77)

We must imagine how the "duel" between Veronica and Marco Venier ended, for we hear no more of it. The insulting verse still had to be dealt with, and she soon discovered her real enemy, Marco's cousin Maffio Venier, a self-righteous moralizer who died at an early age of syphilis. In addition to his verse "Veronica, truly unique whore" he wrote others elaborating on the venality of her character and commenting explicitly on the practices of her profession in bald, obscene language, using both Venetian dialect and Italian. She thus set out to defend herself as she had done, mistakenly, against Marco, and she chose again the imagery of a duel, but the language of her challenge to Maffio is entirely different from that of her *capitolo* to Marco. Here her challenge is unmistakably to a verbal duel, with no playful suggestion of sexual confrontation and reconciliation, and in writing her dignified answer to Maffio she incidentally created her most important contribution to the history of women in literature. Not since Laura Terracina have we heard a woman's voice speaking forcefully in praise of women; because Terracina's *Commentary on the First Stanzas of All the Cantos of "Orlando Furioso"* was published in Venice by Giolito in 1549 and reprinted four times before 1561, it is impossible to imagine that Veronica had not read it, as surely as she had read *Orlando Furioso*.

It is not the deed of a brave knight
(if, kind sir, you allow me now
to state the truth),

> *it is not seemly of one*
> *who has noble virtue in his heartand who pursues honor*
> *to strike with insidious and hidden weapons*
> *a totally unarmed, unsuspecting woman*
> *wounding her mortally with fierce blows.*
> *Even less than to others would one expect*
> *a man to act thus to woman,*
> *created by nature to give the greatest delight to men.*

He had come upon her without warning, defenseless, she continues, and had injured her so severely she thought she would die. But she survived, and now, having dried her tears and quelled her pain, she was ready, she assures her opponent, to fight back. Although only a woman, she has learned how to use weapons, and found that she and therefore all women can be as agile as men.

> *When we women are armed and trained,*
> *we can give a good account of ourselves,*
> *and prove that our hands and feet and hearts are like yours.*
> *And though we are soft and delicate,*
> *there are also men who are delicate yet strong;*
> *and some men, coarse and crude, are far from brave.*
> *Women have not yet realized this;*
> *for if they had ever made up their minds to do so,*
> *they would have been able to fight you to the death.*
> *And to show you that I speak the truth,*
> *I want to be the first, among so many women,*
> *to set an example for them to follow.*
> *I turn against you, cruel toward all of us,*
> *with whatever weapon you choose,*
> *with the hope of knocking you down, and determined to do so.*
> *And I take up the defense of all women*
> *against you who attack them*
> *for indeed I am not the only one with reason to complain.*
> *. . .*
> *So now take up the weapon you have chosen,*
> *for constrained as I am by the scorn in my soul*
> *I can not suffer further delay.*(pp. 377 – 78)

Veronica assures him that she can meet him on equal terms whether he wants to "duel" in Venetian dialect, or Tuscan, or any other; she is comfortable in all of them. There is no record of a response from Maffio.

Marco Venier found Veronica "lacking in compassion." She charmed him with her wit, her talent—she sang and played for him on occasion—and gave him the pleasure he sought, but she withheld herself. Nevertheless, when he complained of her emotional detachment, accusing her of being cold, perfectly in control of her emotions, she answered with deeply touching honesty that he was mistaken.

> *I wish it were as you say*
> *that I live free and exempt from Love,*
> *not caught in his net or pierced by his darts,*

but, she tells him, she too had been struck by the weapons of that god against whom no one on earth, in heaven, or hell can stand, and just as she refuses the pleadings of this disappointed lover, so does the man with whom she is desperately in love refuse hers. Love was a mismatcher who mischievously makes us scorn those who love us and love those who scorn us.

> *Perhaps Love even laughs at our common complaints*
> *and to make the world weep even more*
> *mismatches and disjoins the desires of each.*

If only it could be otherwise, she sighs,

> *If one might love as one desired,*
> *without meeting opposed desires,*
> *the pleasure of love would be unequaled.* (p. 378)

And so Veronica had fallen in love with a man who had exactly those gifts that she found irresistible, a handsome face and eloquent speech, a man whose feeling for her was ambiguous. He flirted with her, made love with her, swore that he loved her, but she was never satisfied in her heart that his loving talk was sincere and the uncertainty in the relationship brought her all the miseries of anxious longing and jealousy and stormy, humiliating scenes. She went through the streets of Venice at night to his home where she touched the walls and stared up at the bedroom balconies and knocked on the forbiddingly closed doors until finally a watchman came, awakened by the barking dogs. He told her to go away, for the master was not at home. In *capitolo* XX, Veronica imagines the man she loves in another woman's bed, delighting another woman, perhaps both of them laughing at her pain. One day she came upon him unexpectedly as he was reading something in his notebook, and she caught something furtive in his movement as he began to put the book in his pocket. She accused him of having written something he want to hide from her, he denied it, and, enraged with jealousy, she tore the book from his pocket and found indeed what she suspected, verses he was writing to another woman. She fled and for a while refused to speak with him, but, compelled by her love, she sent him some verses and begged him to come to her (*cap.* XVII). The affair continued, but then suddenly he decided to go away "for the holidays" and left Veronica more distraught than ever, as she confessed to her friend and protector, Domenico Venier:

> *Sir, I have not come to see you for may days*
> *as I should have, to pay my respects,*
> *for which I will perhaps be criticized by some.*
> *But if a fair judgment is to be determined*

first my reasons must be heard
either in writing or in person.
. . .
    I know, unfortunately, that our group
usually makes unsympathetic judgments about everything,
without first having heard the explanation. . . .
    Well, this is my excuse, the love
that I feel for an extraordinary man
  has overwhelmed my life and taken my heart from me.
. . .
    Now my unjust fate has brought it about
that I surrender myself as a victim of his love,
cutting short the hours of my life;
    and he, cruel man, turning away from me
when I most yearn for his company,
has left our country.
    With no concern for my misery,
he has gone elsewhere to spend the holidays,
and worse yet, he left six days early. (pp. 378 – 79)

She was in no condition to visit him, she goes on, wretched as she was, boring to others and annoying to herself, unable to make good conversation. How could she go to his meetings attended by famous, distinguished men, to participate in their learned discourse, when she was unable to utter a word? Would he extend her apology to the others, and persuade them to forgive her until she is able to come and excuse herself in person?

Her resistant lover returned after the holidays, but the relationship was as problematic as it was passionate and made neither Veronica nor her lover happy when they were not making love. The pleading continued. She did not want to go over the same arguments,

    but I wish I could move you with my pleading
and tearful sighs, to feel some compassion for
my sad and suffering condition.
. . .
    Ease the steep, topless mountain of agony
that I suffer for love of you
and that in fact I am willing to suffer. (p. 379)

He suggested that she go away for a while, and to please him she left Venice to spend some time in the country. Whatever peace the separation might have afforded him, Veronica felt as wretched as ever, and as she had done before, languishing over the loss of her reverend lover, she turned to writing to make her anguish less un- bearable. Her fierce emotions enabled her to create one of her most vividly felt *capitoli*, in part a lament over the separation, in part a panegyric to the city that she loved.

Everything that offers renewal and joy
in this countryside and along the lovely shore
brings me anxiety and grievous sorrow.
*   The sunny valleys, the air filled with the scent*
of grass and trees, the birds, the cool springs
that flow from crystal-pure streams,
*   the shady woods, the cultivated hillside,*
so delightful and, gently rising,
easier to climb as one continues upward,
*   and all the things that industrious hands*
have artfully created here of the gifts of heaven and earth
are for me steep mountains and foreign deserts.

She wandered over the fields, the hills, and valleys, seeing in the trees and rocks the figure of her lover, and longing not only for him but for Venice.

*   In my memory there is constantly the thought*
of my beautiful homeland from which I fled
to escape the hatred of that man;
*   that serene and tranquil Adria*
beyond comparison with any other place
adorned with the delights of paradise on earth:
*   the sea turns to admire the beauty*
of those golden, sculptured palaces
that seem to rise on the water.
*   Here father Ocean brings*
the riches of the world, and the smiling sky
favors her above any other city.
. . .
*   Everything on earth*
that is useful and necessary for human life
is brought here from all over the world.
. . .
*   Distant from peaceful valleys and shadowy woods,*
quiet and tranquil, the palaces of Adria
appear rich and elegant.
. . .
*   Venus, surrounded by other gods*
descends from heaven to this beautiful shore
in company with the illustrious Graces.
. . .
*   The celebrated and magnificent adornments,*
the unsurpassable splendors of my native land
make me hate these woods and this countryside.
*   To Adria then I return, with devoted thoughts*
and weeping, expressly to prove

that I now discern my error.
> *But if one who repents diminishes her fault*
I do repent of having left you,
oh my lovely nest, and I deeply regret it,
> *and since my great risk does not lessen*
with distance, it is best that I die
of the great pain that I suffer for love,
> *rather than adding to my sorrow this one as well,*
of keeping such distance from those things most dear to me
by staying away so long.
> *So at last I have resolved to return,*
and if fate does not stand against me,
even though an hour feels like a century
> *in a few short hours I hope to be there.* (pp. 379 – 80)

Whatever happiness reunion with her lover brought her, it could not last; she was in thrall to the handsome man who from moment to moment was transformed in her thoughts from a virtuous, noble, and kind gentleman to a slippery eel with a wicked heart, and back again (*cap.* 20:158–159). It was perhaps in an effort to find some relief that she left Venice, this time on her own initiative, to visit her lover Count Marcantonio della Torre, canon of Verona and lord of the villa of Fumane. In the longest of her *capitoli* (565 lines) she recorded the memory of her sojourn at this famous, still extant villa. Traveling over rocky, rough roads, she recounts, she reached the villa, where she was splendidly welcomed.

> *I arrived at last at my fervently desired destination*
> *and I will never be able to describe*
> *the great cordiality with which I was received*
> . . .
> > *nor the splendid furnishings, and the staff*
> *of well-trained servants*
> *ready to serve their lord at every moment;*
> > *awaiting him in an orderly way,*
> *dressed alike, but of various ages and complexion,*
> *they do his bidding.*
> > *This, along with everything else, is an impressive sight,*
> *to see yourself surrounded*
> *by a double row of pleasant people in fine uniforms.*
> *Thus . . . Fumane, unique and beloved*
> . . .
> > *At such a charming sight, I cast off*
> *all the heavy and torpid thoughts*
> *that I brought with me when I left Adria.*

What impressed Veronica even more as the days went on was the way art and nature conjoined to make this villa an earthly paradise.

> *Here heaven sends its favors from above*
> *nor does the earth not do its part*
> *to compete in adorning this place.*
> *All the beauties gathered here*
> *contribute to creating a unified completeness*
> *that surpasses the human imagination in all the arts.*
> *And yet, this beautiful place also reminds us*
> *of the great heights achieved by art*
> *in creating beautiful things.*

There were gently sloping hills to climb, broad meadows and valleys in which to wander, accompanied by Flora and Pomona, the goddesses of spring and summer, and woods of pine and cypress where she could imagine seeing Apollo in pursuit of Daphne. A stream wound through the estate, providing water for the fountains and for the gardens designed and tended by the gardener, for

> *Art does not surrender the prize to nature*
> *in creating this garden, embellished with*
> *rare trees and an ever green mantle;*
> *above it, somewhat raised,*
> *there is a beautiful palace, in style like the Sun god's*
> *of which the poet sang.**
> . . .
> *The building for itself as well as for its decorations*
> *is worth an infinite treasure*
> *and it has no equal in richness and beauty.*

The furnishings offered unsurpassable luxuries and the walls carried frescoes illustrating scenes from Greek mythology, and portraits of the popes and saints, making this "divine residence" a virtual paradise.[22]

> *How powerful is our human genius*
> *that can make painted things seem to live*
> *by means of color and form.*
> . . .
> *The spiritual, natural beauty here*
> *invites the eyes outside the palace*
> *to see how rich is nature in this place,*
> *but then, within, art reveals such skill*
> *that it equals and surpasses nature*
> *so that the eye is totally intent just to look.*

And all of this was the domain of her host, Count Marcantonio della Torre, on

---

* This line refers to Ovid's description of the palace of Apollo in *Metamorphoses*; see Mary M. Innes, ed., *The Metamorphoses of Ovid* (Baltimore, 1962), p. 54.

whom Apollo himself, she wrote, bestowed those qualities she so profoundly valued, both intellect and eloquence.

It was hard to leave, remembering it was "bittersweet," and the memory would remain forever vivid:

> *I have that beautiful spot always in my mind's eye*
> *and although far away in fact*
> *I feel that I am still there.* (pp. 380 – 81)

Her stay at Fumane may have helped Veronica to recover from her desperate obsession with the lover who had caused her so much anguish, and to reconsider the devotion offered by others to whom she had been cool, for we find her writing, possibly to Marco Venier, possibly to Domenico,

> *Sir, your achievements, your fine values*
> *and your eloquence had such power*
> *that you have freed from the hand of another my heart*
> *   which soon I hope to see*
> *held in your kind breast*
> *to reign therein and do your every bidding.*
> *   What I most loved I now most scorn*
> *no longer caring for ephemeral, fragile beauty*
> *and regret that once it gave me pleasure.*
> *   Alas for me, who loved a mortal shadow*
> *that I should have hated, and loved you instead,*
> *gifted with infinite, immortal virtue!*
> . . .
> *Once I followed my senses, now reason leads me.* (pp. 381 – 82)

He answered,

> *Reason and love oppose each other*
> *and one who thinks he can predict anything about love*
> *is lacking in feeling and deprived of reason.*
> *   All the more thus must one appreciate*
> *your message in which you have chosen*
> *to hold virtue in high esteem,*
> *   and though indeed I lack that virtue*
> *I deeply desire, like you, to possess it,*
> *so much so that I expect a reward for my good will.*
> *   And if I am worried about my inner motives,*
> *I hope at the same time that despite my few merits,*
> *I may be chosen at least as a lesser evil.*
> . . .
> *   I know that a courageous soul,*
> *when she finds a man that abhors falsehood and follows truth,*

> goes to him with delight,
>   and the more if in that sincere heart
> she finds faithfulness and deep affection,
>   as in mine, which some day I hope to show you,
>   if powerlessness does not frustrate my desires. (p. 382)

Although a certain edge of humor colors this response, suggesting Marco as its author, the last line points to Domenico, whose illness must have to some extent inhibited his relationships.

Was the handsome "slippery eel" from whom she sadly learned that virtue is more important than beauty still on the scene? We cannot know. Certain it is that she had no hold on him, and eventually he left her. In any case, on her return to Venice Veronica perforce took up her accustomed, very busy life as a mother, a courtesan, and an intellectual. Her children had been ill with smallpox, she wrote Domenico Venier, and although now they were better, she hardly had time to breathe because of her other countless obligations, and she felt as if she were fighting a hydra whose heads multiplied every time she cut one off (Letter 39). She entertained the various men on whom she was dependent,[23] she constantly wrote poems and letters, she invited friends to her home to dine and to perform music for them, she kept up her relationship with Domenico Venier, attending his salon to participate in the ongoing literary discussions there, and led a fully active literary life. When Estore Martinengo, brother of her lover Francesco, was killed in 1575 fighting against the Turks at Corfu,[24] Veronica, probably in response to a request of Francesco, undertook to compile an anthology of sonnets in honor of Estore. She wrote to Domenico asking him to contribute some poems and to help her recruit other writers to contribute. The anthology was published without a date or publisher's name, but it was probably brought out not long after Estore's death. Veronica contributed nine sonnets to the collection, of which we present one as typical, praising not only Estore but also Francesco.

> Oh, Lord, for the mercy and comfort
> of this sad and grieving family,
> give back to slain Estol, brother of the great Francesco,
> the years of his valiant life.
>
> Let his glory never before seen
> equaled in this world
> be preserved by You on earth
> and his soul in heaven.
>
> He who still lives and breathes,
> for his courage in arms and superb kindness,
> will forever live, after death, eternally,
>
> May he be always happy among us,
> where the whole world honors
> and admires your greatness, Oh Venice, alma mater. (pp. 382 – 83)

In 1576 Veronica went to Rome, probably to escape the plague that broke out late in 1575.[25] When she returned to Venice she found, as did many others, that her home had been looted and that she had been robbed of jewelry, silverware, and other objects of value. The city had been devastated, perhaps as many as forty thousand people had died from the disease, and ordinary life had come to a standstill.

Gradually both Venice and Veronica recovered, although neither ever again enjoyed the splendid luxuries of past years. Nevertheless, Veronica was still living comfortably in 1580 with a tutor for her son and valuable objects in her household, when the tutor and the objects came close to destroying her. The terrible affair began when she suffered a robbery in May 1580 and accused the tutor, Redolfo Vannitelli,[26] and her maid, Bortola, of having been involved in the theft. Vannitelli countered by bringing charges against Veronica of practicing witchcraft to the Inquisition's tribunal in Venice. When she was called to appear before the tribunal on 8 October 1580, she knew that although the Venetian Inquisition had not executed or severely tortured persons accused of witchcraft, the possible punishments were horrendous: she was facing possible whipping in Piazza San Marco or other forms of public humiliation, and possible exile from Venice for many years.[27] None of the anguish she had felt because of unrequited love could have equaled the terror she must have felt, a lone woman, facing without defense the tribunal of four men who had the power to bring her life to total ruin. That she could have endured two dreadful days of questioning and maintained sufficient strength to defend herself is commands infinite admiration.

She answered the questions put to her and described in detail the "magic" water ritual that was supposed to reveal the guilty person or persons whose identities were being sought by showing their reflections in the water. Yes, Vannitelli, Bortola, and some of her neighbors had prevailed upon her to let the ritual take place in her home, but the children who were brought in to recite the magic verses and tell who or what they saw in the water gave varying answers; nothing was discovered, and Veronica sent the children away over the objections of the others who said she was insane because she did not believe in the ritual. Quite cleverly, she told the judges that she had participated in this ritual when she was a child and at that time believed in it although now, of course, she did not: for telling the truth once the devil lies one hundred times. The confession must have made her appear ingenuous and certainly helped her defense. She denied having invoked demons, having eaten meat on Friday except when she was ill or pregnant (she had had four more children, all of whom died) and needed special nourishment. She was called to appear again the following week, when she pleaded guilty to having sinned, and the case against her was ended with no penalty exacted. It seems likely that her old friend and lover, Marco Venier, now one of the most powerful men in Venice, was influential behind the scene in saving her from even a light punishment.

The thefts during her absence in the years of the plague and the new robberies of 1580 left Veronica impoverished, with a very small income from various properties that brought her a little rent. In her mid-thirties, she doubtless lost some of her wealthy clientele, and she may have had to give up her courtesan status in order to live; she moved to a section in Venice near the church of San Samuele frequented by poor prostitutes.[28] In 1582 Domenico Venier died, bringing to an end the literary salon that had been the center of her intellectual life; the writers with whom she had mingled went their separate ways, and we have the impression that she more or less dropped out of sight, although she continued to write: on 30 October 1591 Muzio Manfredi wrote Veronica from Nancy thanking her for the sonnet she had sent him in praise of his controversial tragedy, *Semiramis,* adding, "and I wish you health and strength enough to give the finishing touches to your epic poem," not knowing that she had died three months earlier.[29] Although he was living in France, he was in touch with fellow writers in the Italian literary community and thus would have known of her death if anyone had informed him; the fact that he did not know indicates that no one wrote him that the once famous poet-courtesan had died. No letters, no poems have been discovered in which her death was noticed. Only the official in charge of death records in Venice entered the event in his register: "1591, 22 luglio. La Sig.ra Veronica Franco d'anni 45 da febre già giorni 20. S. Moisè" (1591, 22 July. Madam Veronica Franco, forty-five years old, [died] of fever on 20 [July]. [Buried in the church of] S[aint] Moisè). Her small estate presumably went to her two sons; what must have been an enormous mass of unpublished writing, including the almost finished epic, was evidently thrown away.

Several portraits of women have been thought to represent Veronica Franca. In a pamphlet of 1826 under the title of *Alcuni ritratti di donne illustri delle provincie veneziane* (Portraits of illustrious women of the province of Venice) Bartolomeo Gamba published an engraving purporting to be Veronica (figure 11.2).[30] Gamba did not give the sources for the twelve portraits in his booklet, but because some can be authenticated from known portraits, this gives credibility, in Croce's view, to all of them. The woman is presented in the height of fashion, her hair curled into two tall horns, richly dressed in an elaborate gown, with a high collar, deep décolleté, and a single strand of pearls. A regal crown and a part of a laurel crown are visible on the left side of her head, which is turned toward her right, the laurel covering a bit of her forehead. The hair style and décolleté , however, are in the fashion of the later 1580s, as we will see in the authentic engraving of Modesta Pozzo / Modesta Fonte, drawn in 1589 (figure 12.1), years in which an impoverished Veronica could not reasonably be portrayed dressed so fashionably. Furthermore, the regal crown looks as if it has comically slipped down from the top of her head, and the laurel crown, broken, no longer encircles her head. We believe this portrait was intended as a malicious satire against Veronica, actually not drawn from life, for she obviously would not have lent herself to such a ridiculous portrayal of herself as a pretentious and absurd failed poet.

A painting of a young woman in the Worcester (Massachusetts) Art Museum is possibly a copy of the portrait of Veronica known to have been painted by Jacopo Tintoretto since a letter to him about it is included in Veronica's volume of *Lettere* (plate VIII). The portrait was so true to nature, she wrote him (Letter 21), that she was not certain whether she was looking at a painting or an illusion of the devil to fool her into thinking she was so beautiful. The whereabouts of this portrait is now unknown; the Worcester Art Museum picture is catalogued as "Portrait of a Lady (Veronica Franco?)," attributed to a "Follower of Tintoretto." The sitter is shown with a single strand of pearls and her left breast bare to the nipple, which suggests that she may have been a courtesan. The face resembles the woman portrayed in a watercolor drawing in an album in the Beinecke Library at Yale University that is labeled Veronica Franca and is certainly acceptable as an authentic likeness (figure 11.3). In the

Veronica Franco

11.2.
Anon.
*Portrait of
Veronica Franca.*
ca. 1589. Museo
Civico, Padua.
Photo, Museum.

Prado Museum *Catálogo de las pinturas,* curator Wenceslao Ramirez de Villaurrutia attributed *A Woman With Bared Breasts* (figure 11.4) to Tintoretto and speculated that it might represent Veronica Franco; following his lead, both Rosenthal and Lawner believe there is a resemblance between the Prado picture (now downgraded to "School of Tintoretto") and the Worcester portrait. We find the differences too great to accept the identity; given the generic type of Venetian blonde with the fashionable off-the-forehead, high-rising hairdo, an authentic painting by Tintoretto of a round-faced

woman in the Prado titled *Flora,* with a sprig of laurel tucked into her bosom, could easily be seen as Veronica Franca wearing her single strand of pearls and earrings like many models, probably courtesans, who posed in various stages of undress for Titian, Tintoretto, Veronese, and other artists. (See, for example, Tintoretto, *Flora* [Prado]; Veronese, *Leda and the Swan* [Dresden, Staatliche Kunstsammlung].)

The one completely documented portrait of Veronica known today is the engraved image on the sheet possibly intended as the frontispiece for her *Terze rime* (figure 11.1). It was first described by Giovanni degli Agostini in his history of Venetian writers as an "engraving on copper, in quarto," the same size as the pages of the *Terze*

rime. "Around [the portrait] can be read VERONICA FRANCA ANN xxiii MDLXXVI. . . . Above the portrait is an emblem showing a flaming torch with the motto AGITA-TA CRESCIT and below it there is a heart on the shield of which there is a band with four stars and at the bottom three little mountains." He attributes the engraving to Giacomo Franco (1550–1620), possibly a relative of Veronica.[31] In this bust-length portrayal Veronica claims to be twenty-three years old, which dates it to 1569, but, because the sheet matches the page size of her *Terze rime*, this tends to support the

11.4
School of Jacopo Tintoretto.
Woman with Bared Breast.
n.d. Museo del Prado, Madrid. Photo, Museum.

theory that the portrait was done specifically for use as the frontispiece for her book, thus dating it to 1575, at which time she was twenty-nine, and that she shaved off seven years from her public age. However, there is another possibility, going back to the visit of Henry III: we wonder if this could be an engraving after the small enamel portrait of herself that she gave the king of France in 1574. In that case, she may actually have been twenty-three years old when the portrait was executed some years before she gave it to the king, and years before she decided to have the image incorporated into the elaborate design of Manneristic architecture (which Agostini does not mention) for the frontispiece of her book.

We see Veronica in a seven-eighth view facing toward her left, her eyes shifted toward her right, looking out coolly, noncommittally toward the viewer. Above is the emblem with the Latin motto; below is the medallion designed with the four stars and three mountains, her family shield, set in the center of a wreath of laurel. She announces in her motto, "When it is moved it rises higher," by which we take her to mean that as the torch (her mind) is moved, her imagination (the flame) rises to greater heights; that is, her inspiration is fired by her learning. This is Veronica the poet and intellectual.

POEMS AND LETTERS IN THE ORIGINAL ITALIAN

Dolcemente congiunta al vostro fianco,*
le delizie d'amor farò gustarvi,
quand' egli è ben appresso al lato manco;
 e 'n ciò potrei tal diletto recarvi,
che chiamar vi potreste per contento,
e d'avantaggio appresso innamorarvi.
 Così dolce e gustevole divento,
quando mi trovo con persona in letto,
da cui amata e gradita mi sento,
 che quel mio piacer vince ogni diletto
sì che quel, che strettissimo parea,
nodo de l'altrui amor divien più stretto. . . . † (p. 339)

⊚ Track 57,
Reading 58

mostrandovi di lontano un grandissimo precipizio nascosto e cridando ad alta voce, perchè, prima che 'l sopravegniate, vi rimanga spazio da poterlo schivare. . . . Or finalmente non ho voluto mancar di farvi queste righe, essortandovi di nuovo ad avvertir al caso vostro, a non uccider in un medesimo colpo l'anima e l'onor vostro insieme con quello della vostra figlia . . . mi potreste dir che questo sia giuoco di fortuna, prima vi rispondo che non si può far peggio in questa vita che darsi in arbitrio della sorte, che può così facilmente e più esser ministra del male come del bene; ma chi ha buon senno, per non trovarsi finalmente ingannato, fabrica le sue speranze sul fondamento di quel ch'è in lui e che può esser fatto da lui. . . . Darsi in preda di tanti, con rischio d'esser dispogliata, d'esser rubbata, d'esser uccisa, ch'un solo un dì ti toglia quanto con molti in molto tempo hai acquistato, con tant'altri pericoli d'ingiurie e d'infermità contagiose e spaventose; mangiar con l'altrui bocca, dormir con gli occhi altrui, muoversi secondo l'altrui desiderio, correndo in manifesto naufragio sempre della facoltà e della vita. . . . Considerate al fin delle cose; e se volete pur osservar gli essempi, guardate quel che sia incontrato e che tuttodí incontra alle moltitudine delle donne in quest' essercizio. . . . Nè trascorrerà forse molto tempo che vostra figliola medesima, avvedutasi della grandissima offesa da voi fattale, vi fuggirà. ‡ (pp. 339 – 40)

quando da' be' vostr'occhi e dal bel volto
contra me spinse Amor la face ardente:
 ed a piagarmi in mille guise vòlto,
dal fiume ancor de la vostra eloquenza
il foco del mio incendio avea raccolto.
 L'abito vago e la gentil presenza,

---

* All of Veronica's poems are *capitoli* or *sonetti* from Abdelkader Salza, ed., *Gaspara Stampa—Veronica Franca* (Bari, 1913), except where noted. We follow Salza's numbering in roman numerals.   † II:148–159.

‡ Extracted from Stefano Bianchi, ed., *Veronica Franca, Lettere* (Salerno, 1998), letter 22, pp. 71, 73–74, 75.

la grazia e le maniere al mondo sole,
e de le virtù chiare l'eccellenza,
fur ne la vista mia lucido sole,
che m'abbagliar e m'arser di lontano,
sì ch'a tal segno andar Febo non suole.

    Di molta gente nel comun concorso
quante volte vi vidi e v'ascoltai,
e dal bel vostro sguardo ebbi soccorso!
    E se ben il mio amor non vi mostrai,
o che 'l faceste a caso, o per qual sia
altra cagion, benigno vi trovai:
    per ch'ora in una ed ora in altra via
di devoto parlar, con atto umano,
volgeste a me la fronte umile e pia;
    e nel contar il ben del ciel sovrano
v'affisaste a guardarmi, e mi stendeste,
or larghe or giunte, l'una e l'altra mano;
    ed altre cose simili faceste,
ond'io tolsi a sperar che del mio amore
cautamente pietoso v'accorgeste.
. . .
    Quinci s'accrebbe forte il mio dolore
di non poter al gusto d'ambo noi
goder la vita in gioia ed in dolzore.
. . .
    Voi ve n'andaste a popoli stranieri,
ed io rimasi in preda di quel foco,
*che senza voi miei dí fea tristi e neri.** (pp. 341 – 42)

"Epitaph for Lodovico Ramberti"

Lettor, no son qua minga sopello,
seben ti vedi il mio nome in sta piera,
perchè 'l corpo fu destribuio
per le forche ordinarie de sta tera
chè a sto modo ho volesto dar in drio
i quarti de mio frael che za ghe giera.
St'arca xe qua per to commodità
sti me vol dir del ben, dimelo qua.† (p. 343)

All'Invittissimo e cristianissimo re Enrico III di Francia e di Polonia
All'altissimo favor che la Vostra Maestà s'è degnata di farmi, venendo all'umile abitazione mia, di portarne seco il mio ritratto, in cambio di quella viva imagine che

---

* XIX:17–27, 58–60, 91–108.   † See Salza, *Epitaph*, p. 385.

nel mezo del mio cuore Ella ha lasciato delle sue virtù eroiche e del suo divino valore—cambio per me troppo aventuroso e felice—io non sono bastevole di corrispondere, nè pur col pensiero, nè col desiderio: imperochè qual cosa può nascer da me che sia degna della suprema altezza dell'animo suo celeste e della sua beata fortuna? Nè posso con alcuna maniera di ringraziamento supplire in parte all'infinito merito delle sue benigne e graziose offerte fattemi nel proposito del libro ch'io sono per dedicarle convenienti alla sua grandezza ed al suo serenissimo splendor regale più che ad alcuna mia qualità. E nondimeno, sì come nel breve spazio d'alcuna angustissima carta soglia talvolta disegnarsi tutto il mondo intiero, ho fatto in questi pochi versi, che riverentemente mando alla Vostra Maestà, il disegno, benchè ristretto e rozo, della mia gratitudine e della mia immensa ed ardentissima volontà di celebrar sopra il termine d'ogni mondana speranza le innumerabili e sopraumane doti che dentro del suo generoso petto albergano felicmente. E con devoto e singulare affetto reverentemente m'inchino ad abbracciarle le sacre ginocchia.

Umilissima e devotissima serva della Maestà Vostra,
Veronica Franca * (p. 344)

~

Come talor dal ciel sotto umil tetto
Giove tra noi qua giù benigno scende,
e perchè occhio terren dall'alt'oggetto
non resti vinto, umana forma prende;

Così venne al mio povero ricetto
senza pompa real ch'abbaglia e splende,
dal fato Enrico a tal dominio eletto,
ch'un sol mondo nol cape e nol comprende.

Benchè sì sconosciuto, anch'al mio core
tal raggio impresse del divin suo merto,
che 'n me s'estinse il natural vigore.

Di ch'ei di tant'affetto non incerto,
l'imagin mia di smalt' e di colore
prese al partir con grat' animo aperto. † (p. 345)

~

Prendi, re per virtù sommo e perfetto,
quel che la mano a porgerti si stende:
questo scolpito e colorato aspetto,
in cui 'l mio vivo e natural s'intende.

E, s'a essempio sì basso e sì imperfetto
la tua vista beata non s'attende,
risguarda a la cagion, non a l'effetto.
Poca favilla ancor gran fiamma accende.

● Track 58,
Reading 59

---

* Extracted from Bianchi, *Lettere*, pp. 30–31   † Salza, *Sonetti*, p. 353.

E come 'l tuo immortal divin valore,
in armi e in pace a mille prove esperto
m'empio l'alma di nobile stupore,

Così 'l desio, di donna in cor sofferto,
d'alzarti sopra 'l ciel dal mondo fore,
*mira in quel mio sembiante espresso e certo.** (p. 345)

Più tosto fermatevi ed ordinatevi nella vostra fantasia troppa vaga e troppo ansiosa; e s'avete da adoperar sprone, adoperate non quello che furiosamente vi precipiti fuori della patria vostra in peregrinoso e vano essilio, ma più tosto quello che v'inviti all'acquisto della virtù ed all' adoperar secondo il vero valor. Nel che si riesce grandemente nel godimento dell'ozio onesto nella sua patria, tra i suoi cittadini ed alla presenza della sua donna amata, tentando di superar gli altri suoi uguali nel teatro della publica concorrenza per acquistarsi merito sopra di loro, aspirando a degno premio della sua virtuosa servitù.

Voi sapete benissimo che tra tutti coloro che pretendono di poter insinuarsi nel mio amore a me sono estremamente cari quei che s'affatican nell' essercizio delle discipline e dell'arti ingenue, delle quali (se ben donna di poco sapere, rispetto massimamente all'mia inclinazione ed al mio desiderio) io sono tanto vaga, e con tanto mio diletto converso con coloro che sanno, per aver occasione ancora d'imparare, che, se la mia fortuna il comportasse, io farei tutta la mia vita e spenderei tutto 'l mio tempo dolcemente nell'accademie degli uomini virtuosi.† (pp. 346 – 47)

Marco Venier
◉ Track 59,
Reading 60

S'io v'amo al par de la mia propria vita,
donna, crudel, e voi perchè non date
in tanto amor al mio tormento aita?

E se invano mercé chieggio e pietate,
perch'almen con la morte quelle pene
ch'io soffro per amarvi, non troncate?
. . .

Oh, se vedeste in me l'ardente brama,
c'ho di servir voi sola a tutte l'ore,
con quel pensier ch'ognor vi chiede e brama.
. . .

Ma com'esser può mai che, dentro al lato
molle, il bianco gentil vostro bel petto
chiuda sí duro cor e sí spietato?
. . .

O beltà d'ogni essempio altro divisa,
di cui l'anima in farsi umil soggetta,
stando lieta, qua giù s'imparadisa!
. . .

---

* Salza, *Sonetti*, p. 354.   † Extracted from Bianchi, *Lettere*, pp. 59–60.

La penna e 'l foglio in man prendete intanto,
e scrivete soavi e grate rime,
*ch'ai poeti maggior tolgono il vanto.** (p. 348)

~

S'esser del vostro amor potessi certa
per quel che mostran le parole e 'l volto,
che spesso tengon varia alma coperta;
    se quel che tien la mente in sé raccolto
mostrasson le vestigie esterne in guisa
ch'altri non fosse spesso in frode còlto,
    quella téma da me fora divisa,
di cui quando perciò m'assicurassi,
semplice e sciocca, ne sarei derisa:
. . .

    Ben per quanto or da me vi si risponde,
avara non vorrei che mi stimaste,
ché tal vizio nel sen non mi s'asconde;
    ma piaceríami che di me pensaste
che ne l'amar le mie voglie cortesi
si studian d'esser caute, se non caste:
. . .

    Voi ben sapete quel che m'è più caro:
seguite in ciò come io v'ho detto ancora,
ché mi sarete amante unico e raro.
qDe le virtuti il mio cor s'innamora.
E voi che possedete di lor tanto,
ch'ogni più bel saver con voi dimora
qnon mi negate l'opra vostra intanto,
chè con tal mezzo vi vegga bramoso
d'acquistar meco d'amador il vanto:
. . .

    A voi poca fatica sarà questa,
perch'al vostro valor ciascuna impresa,
per difficil che sia, facil vi resta,
. . .

ma, per contarvi il ver, volar senz'ale
vorreste, e in un momento andar troppo alto:
  . . .

    Febo, che serve a l'amorosa dea,
e in dolce guiderdon da lei ottiene
quel che via più che l'esser dio il bea,
    a rivelar nel mio pensier ne viene
quei modi che con lui Venere adopra,
mentre in soavi abbracciamenti il tiene;

Veronica Franca
◉ Track 60,
Reading 61

---

* I:1–6, 43–45, 13–15, 61–63, 76–78.

ond'io instrutta a questi so dar opra
sì ben nel letto, che d'Apollo a l'arte
questa ne va d'assai spazio di sopra,
   e 'l mio cantar e 'l mio scriver in carte
s'oblía da chi mi prova in quella guisa,
ch'a'suoi seguaci Venere comparte.

. . .

   Fate che sian da me di lei vedute
quell'opre ch'io desío, chè poi saranno
le mie dolcezze a pien da voi godute;
   e le vostre da me si goderanno
per quello ch'un amor mutuo comporte,
dove i diletti senza noia s'hanno.
   Aver cagione d'amarvi io bramo forte
prendete quel partito che vi piace
*poi che in vostro voler tutta è la sorte.** (pp. 348 – 50)

Maffio Venier

   Veronica, ver unica puttana,
franca, "idest" furba, fina, fiappa e frola,
e muffa e magra e marza e pì mariola,
che si' tra Castel, Ghetto e la Doàna

   Donna reduta mostro in carne umana,
stucco, zesso, carton, curàme, e tòla,
fantasma lodesana, orca varuola.

Anonymous

   E se non imparate la recetta
Ch'io v'insegno, superbe cortegiane
Ponte Sisto e il spedal presto v'aspetta.† (p. 350)

Veronica Franca

   Non più parole: ai fatti, in campo, a l'armi,
ch'io voglio, risoluta di morire,
da sí grave molestia liberarmi.
   Non so se 'l mio "cartel" si debba dire,
in quanto do risposta provocata:
ma perchè in rissa de' nomi venire?
   Se vuoi, da te mi chiamo disfidata,
e se non, ti disfido; o in ogni via
la prendo, ed ogni occasion m'è grata.
   Il campo o l'armi elegger a te stia,
ch'io prenderò quel che tu lascerai;
anzi pur ambo nel tuo arbitrio sia,
   Tosto son certa che t'accorgerai

---

* II:1–9, 82–87, 103–111, 115–117, 131–132, 160–171, 181–189.
† Rosenthal, *The Honest Courtesan*, p. 188.

quanto ingrato e di fede mancatore
fosti, e quanto tradito a torto m'hai.
. . .

Vuoi per campo il segreto albergo, quello
che de l'amare mie dolcezze tante
mi fu ministro insidioso e fello?
Or mi si para il mio letto davante,
ov'in grembo t'accolsi, e ch'ancor l'orme
serba dei corpi in sen l'un l'altro stante.
. . .

Ma pur questo medesimo soggiorno,
che fu de le mie gioie amato nido,
dov'or sola in tormento e 'n duol soggiorno,
per campo eleggi, accioch'altrove il grido
non giunga, ma qui teco resti spento,
del tuo inganno ver'me, crudele infido;
qui vieni, e pien di pessimo talento,
accomodato al tristo officio porta
ferro acuto e da man ch'abbia ardimento.
Quell'arme, che da te mi sarà pòrta,
prenderò volontier, ma più, se molto
tagli, e da offender sia ben salda e corta.
Dal petto ignudo ogni arnese sia tolto,
al fin ch'ei, disarmato a le ferite,
possa 'l valor mostrar dentro a sé accolto.
Altri non s'impedisca in questa lite,
ma da noi soli due, ad uscio chiuso,
rimosso ogni padrin, sia diffinita.
. . .

Ma se da te mi sia la pace offerta?
Se la via prendi, l'armi poste in terra,
a le risse d'amor del letto aperta?
. . .

Forse nel letto ancor ti seguirei,
e quivi, teco guerreggiando stesa,
in alcun modo non ti cederei:
per soverchiar la tua sí indegna offesa
ti verrei sopra, e nel contrasto ardita,
scaldandoti ancor tu ne la difesa.* (pp. 351 – 52)

La fama che nel riportar delle cose non si obliga tanto al vero quanto al verisimile, con alcune ragioni probabili m'avea dato da credere che quella satira fusse fattura di Vostra Signoria…se non sono virtuosa in me stessa, sono almanco amatrice della virtú nelle persone che ne sono adornate, sí com'è Vostra Signoria, a cui, per questo

---

* XIII:1–15, 31–36, 40–57, 70–72, 79–84.

rispetto, ho sempre portato affezzione e riverenza. E per questo mi son forte mara-
vigliata che'l cambio della mia devozione mi fosse retributo con tai libelli infamatori,
ed anco non ho voluto compiutamente credere che quella fosse sua fattura, avendo
risguardato all'imperfezzione dell'opera, piena d'errori e per altra causa non degno
parto del nobile intelletto suo. Pur nondimeno son stata dubiosa per diversi riscontri
avutime . . . m'è occorso per mio passatempo di scriver il capitolo. . . prego Vostra Signoria, sí come perfetto maestro, a insegnarmi alcun segreto colpo; anzi pur tolga la
spada in mano, non quella tagliente di filo ma quella da giuoco, e m'adopri seco in cosí
virtuosa rissa, provocandomi alla risposta con quelle proposte che le piacerà di man-
darmi in quella lingua che le sarà di più destro uso, ed io gliene terrò obligo e m'esser-
citerò nel risponder con tanta prontezza con quanto diletto e frutto leggerò le cose da
lei mandatemi.* (pp. 352 – 53)

~

Marco Venier

> Non più guerra, ma pace: e gli odi, l'ire,
> e quanto fu di disparer tra noi,
> si venga in amor doppio a convertire.
> . . .
> Che nascesse tra noi rissa, mi spiace;
> ma se lo sdegno in amor s'augumenta,
> che tra noi si sdegnassimo, mi piace:
> e se pur ragion vuol ch'io mi risenta
> e vendicata sia l'ingiuria mia,
> de la qual foste ognor ministra intenta,
> voglio con l'armi de la cortesia
> invincibil durar tanto a la pugna,
> che conosciuto alfin vincitor sia.
> Né questo da l'amor grande repugna,
> anzi con queste e non mai con altre armi
> ogni spirto magnanimo s'oppugna.
> O se voleste incontra armata starmi,
> se voleste tentar, con forza tale
> se possibil vi sia di superarmi,
> fora 'l mio stato a quel di Giove eguale;
> forse troppo è la speranza ardita,
> che studia di volar non avendo ale.
> . . .
> ma perché so che romor ne sarebbe,
> col silenzio m'ingegno d'obedirvi.
> Non so, ma forse ch'a taluno increbbe
> del viver nostro insieme; che 'l suo tòsco,
> nel nostro dolce a spargerlo, pronto ebbe.
> . . .
> Ecco che nel duello mi preparo,
> con l'armi del mio mal, de le mie pene

---

* Bianchi, *Lettere*, letter 17, pp. 111–112, 113.

de l'innocenza mia sotto 'l riparo.

. . .

   Pur troppo armata, e so ben ch'io non erro,
contra me sète; ed io del seno ignudo
l'adito ai vostri colpi ancor non serro.

. . .

   Ripetete pur via di mano in mano,
mentre dal segno alcun colpo non erra,
e che l'oggetto avete non lontano:

. . .

   E vi mando per fede carta bianca,
ch'abbiate del mio cor dominio vero,
sí che veruna parte non vi manca.
   Del resto assai desío più, che non spero,
né so se in via di straziar m'abbiate
fatto l'invito, o se pur da dovero.
   *Aspetterò che voi me n'accertiate.** (pp. 353 – 54)

   D'ardito cavalier non è prodezza   Veronica Franca
(concedami che 'l vero a questa volta
io possa dir, la vostra gentilezza),
   da cavalier non è, ch'abbia raccolta
ne l'animo suo invitto alta virtute
e che a l'onor la mente abbia rivolta,
   con armi insidiose e non vedute,
a chi più disarmato men sospetta
dar gravi colpi di mortal ferute.
   Men ch'agli altri ciò far poi se gli aspetta
contra le donne, da natura fatte
per l'uso che più d'altro a l'uom diletta:

. . .

   Quando armate ed esperte ancor siam noi,   ◉ Track 61,
render buon conto a ciascun uom potemo,   Reading 62
ché mani e piedi e core avem qual voi;
   e se ben molli e delicate semo,
ancor tal uom, ch'è delicato, è forte;
e tal, ruvido ed aspro, è d'ardir scemo.
   Di ciò non se ne son le donne accorte;
che se si risolvessero di farlo,
con voi pugnar porian fino a la morte.
   E per farvi veder che 'l vero parlo
tra tante donne incominciar voglio io,
porgendo essempio a lor di seguitarlo.

---

* XIV:1–3, 10–27, 62–66, 76–78, 91–93, 130–132, 145–151.

A voi, che contra tutte sète rio,
con qual'armi volete in man mi volgo,
con speme d'atterrarvi e con desio;
    e le donne a difender tutte tolgo
contra di voi, che di lor sète schivo
sí ch'a ragion io sola non mi dolgo.
. . .
    Prendete pur de l'armi omai eletta
ch'io non posso soffrir lunga dimora
*da lo sdegno de l'anima costretta.** (p. 354 – 55)

⌣

    Ben vorrei fosse, come dite voi,
ch'io vivessi d'Amor libera e franca,
non còlta al laccio o punta ai dardi suoi;
. . .
    Fors'anco Amor del comun pianto ride,
e per far lagrimar più sempre il mondo,
l'altrui desir discompagna e divide;
. . .
    chè s'uom potesse a suo diletto amare,
senza trovar contrarie voglie opposte,
l'amoroso piacer non avría pare. † (p. 356)

⌣

    Signor, ha molti giorni ch'io non fui
(come doveva) a farvi riverenza:
di che biasmata son forse d'altrui;
    ma se da far se n'ha giusta sentenza,
le mie ragioni ascoltar pria si dènno
da me scritte, o formate a la presenza
. . .
    Io so pur troppo che da la brigata
far mal giudizio de le cose s'usa,
senza aver la ragion prima ascoltata.
. . .
    benché quest'è mia scusa, che l'amore
ch'io porto ad uom gentile a maraviglia
mi confonde la vita e toglie il core.
. . .
    Permesso alfin ha la mia iniqua sorte
che 'n preda del suo amor m'abbandonassi,
di che fien l'ore del mio viver corte;
    ed ei, crudel, da me volgendo i passi,
quando più bramo la sua compagnia,

---

* XVI:1–12, 64–81, 109–111.   † VIII:1–3, 76–78, 82–84.

fuor de la nostra comun patria vassi:
senza curar de la miseria mia,
a far l'instanti ferie altrove è gito
ma d'avantaggio andò sei giorni pria. * (p. 356 – 57)

    ⌣

ma del mio stato ingiurioso e tristo
cerco indurvi a pietà con le preghiere,
e di sospir col largo pianto misto.

. . .

Scemate il grave innaccessibil monte
di quei ch'amando voi sostengo affanni
con voglie in tutti i casi a soffrir pronte. . . † (p. 357)

    ⌣

Tutto quel che ristoro e gioia apporte,
per questi campi e per le piagge amene,
reca a me affanno e duol gravoso e forte.
L'apriche valli, d'aura e d'odor piene,
l'erbe, i rami, gli augei, le fresche fonti,
ch'escon da cristalline e pure vene,
l'ombrose selve, e i coltivati monti,
che da salir son dilettosi e piani,
e più facili quant'uom più su monti,
e tutto quel che con industri mani
qui l'arte e la natura e 'l ciel opraro,
sono per me deserti alpestri e strani.

. . .

chè sempre avanti a la memoria stassi
quanto, per fuggir l'odio di colui,
da la patria gentil mi dilungassi;
da quell'Adria tranquilla e vaga, a cui
di ciò che in terra un paradio adorni
non si pareggi alcun diletto altrui:
da quei d'intagli e marmo aurei soggiorni,
sopra de l'acque edificati in guisa
ch'a tal mirar beltà queto il mar torni;

. . .

Quivi tributo il padre Ocean dàlle
d'ogni ricco tesoro, e 'l cielo amico
ciascun'altra a lei pon dopo le spalle:

. . .

Quanto per l'universo si comparte
d'utile e necessario a l'uman vitto,
da tutto l'universo si diparte;

---

* XV:1–6, 16–18, 28–30, 34–42.   † XX:112–114, 139–141.

. . .

    Altro che valli amene e colli ombrosi
sembrano d'Adria placida e tranquilla
i palagi ricchissimi e pomposi.

. . .

    Venere in cerchio ancor degli altri dèi
scende dal ciel su questa bella riva,
con l'alme Grazie in compagnia di lei.

. . .

    E de la patria mia celebre e magna
gli alti ornamenti e lo splendor superno,
qui 'l bosco odiar mi fanno e la campagna:
    ad Adria col pensier devoto interno
ritorno e, lagrimando, espressamente
a prova del martir l'error mio scerno.
    Ma se 'l suo fallo scema che si pente,
esser da te partita mi pentisco,
o mio bel nido, e me ne sto dolente;
    e da poi che non cessa il mio gran risco
per lontanza, il meglio è ch'io mi mora
del gran dolor che per amar soffrisco,
    senz'a miei danni aggiunger questo ancora,
di far da le mie cose a me più care
per tanto spazio sí lunga dimora.
    Perch'alfin mi risolvo di tornare,
e se non m'è contraria a pien la sorte,
se ben un'ora un secolo mi pare,
    *spero tornare in spazio d'ore corte.** (pp. 358 – 59)

⊙ Track 62,
Reading 63

    Alfin pur giunsi a la bramata stanza,
né potrei giamai dir sí com'io fossi
raccolta con gratissima sembianza.

. . .

    né con più vago e splendido apparato
di vasi, e di famiglia bene instrutta,
che pronta al signor serve d'ogni lato,
    e intorno a lui con ordine ridutta,
di varia età, di vario pelo mista,
vestita a un modo, corrisponde tutta.
    Questa tra l'altre è ancor nobile vista,
veder d'intorno a sé ben divisata
d'onesta gente vaga e doppia lista.
    Dunque . . . Fumane, unica, amata

. . .

---

* XXII:13–24, 151–159, 166–168, 178–180, 187–189, 193–195, 217–235.

A sí dolce spettacolo rimossi
tutti i miei e torbidi pensieri
che venner meco, allor che d'Adria mossi.

. . .

Quivi 'l ciel manda il suo favor di sopra,   ◉ Track 62,
né men la terra in adornar tal parte   Reading 64
con gli altri, a gara, elementi s'adopra
Vince l'imaginar d'ogni umana arte
la disposizion di tutto 'l bene,
ch'unito quivi intorno si comparte:
e pur di quell'altezza, ove perviene
l'eccellenza de l'arte in cose belle,
vestigie espresse il bel luogo ritiene.

. . .

Non cede l'arte a la natura il vanto   ◉ Track 62,
ne l'artificio del giardin, ornato   Reading 65
d'alberi cólti e di sempre verde manto;
sovra 'l qual porge, alquanto rilevato,
d'architettura un bel palagio tale,
qual fu di quel del Sol già poetato:
infinito tesor ben questo vale
per l'edificio proprio, e gli ornamenti,
che 'n ricchezza e in beltà non hanno eguale.

. . .

Quanto è possente il nostro umano ingegno,   ◉ Track 62,
che vive fa parer le cose finte   Reading 66
per forza di colori e di disegno!

. . .

La bellezza del sito, alma, natía,
gli occhi fuor del palazzo a veder piega
quanto ivi ricca la natura sia;
ma poi di dentro tal lavor dispiega
l'arte, che la natura agguaglia e passa,
ch'ivi l'occhio, a mirar vòlto, s'impiega;

. . .

sempre davanti gli occhi ho 'l bel soggiorno,
da cui lontan col corpo, con la mente,
senza da me partirlo unqua, soggiorno.* (pp. 359 – 61)

⁓

Signor, la virtù vostra e 'l gran valore
e 'l'eloquenzia fu di tal potere,
che d'altrui man m'ha liberato il core;

---

* XXV:532–534, 544–553, 535–537, 49–57, 127–135, 178–180, 268–273, 19–21.

il qual di breve spero ancor vedere
collocato entro 'l vostro gentil petto,
e regnar quivi, e far vostro volere.

    Quel ch'amai più, più mi torna in dispetto,
né stimo più beltà caduca e frale,
e mi pento che già n'ebbi diletto.

    Misera me, ch'amai ombra mortale,
ch'anzi doveva odiar, e voi amare,
pien di virtù infinita ed immortale!

. . .

    già seguí 'l senso, or la ragion mi mena. * (p. 361)

    Marco? Domenico?

        Venier

    Contrarti son tra lor ragion e amore,
e chi 'n amor aspetta antivedere,
di senso è privo e di ragion è fuore.

    Tanto più in prezzo è da doversi avere
vostro discorso, in cui avete eletto
voler in stima la virtù tenere;

    e bench'io di lei sia privo in effetto,
con voi di possederla il desio vale,
sí che del buon voler premio n'aspetto:

    e se 'timor de l'esser mio m'assale,
poi mi fa contra i merti miei sperare,
ché s'elegge per ben un minor male.

    Io non mi vanto per virtù d'andar
a segno che, l'amor vostro acquistando,
mi possa in tanto grado collocare;

    ma so ch'un alma valorosa, quando
trova uom ch 'l falso aborre e segue il vero,
a lui si va con diletto accostando:

    e tanto più se dentro a un cor sincero
d'alta fé trova affezzion ripiena,
come nel mio, ch'un dí mostrarvi spero,

    se 'l non poter le voglie non m'afrena. † (pp. 361– 62)

    Veronica Franca

    Del gran Francesco a la vita onorata
gli anni del suo fratello Estor morto
rendi, Signor, per grazia e per comforto
de la famiglia sua mesta e turbata:

    anzi in questo da te pur sia servata
del ciel la gloria in terra, ove mai scorto
non fu gran pregio da l'occaso a l'orto,
di quanto è di costui l'anima ornata.

---

* V: 1 – 12, V: 22.

Questi, che vive e spira, e vivrà ognora
per valor d'armi e somma cortesia
dopo la morte eternamente ancora.

Lungo secol tra noi felice stia,
dove la sua virtute il mondo onora,
e te difende, alma Vinezia mia. (p. 362)

---

* *Sonetti*, p. 357.

NOTES

1   Writers always give Veronica's last name as "Franco." As with Battiferra, however, we use the feminine form because she signed her letters and referred to herself as Franca; see Stefano Bianchi, ed., *Veronica Franco, Lettere* (Salerno, 1998), Letter 1, and Abdelkader Salza, ed., *Gaspara Stampa— Veronica Franco* (Bari, 1913), *capitolo* III, l. 1.

2   Benedetto Croce, *Poesia popolare e poesia d' arte* (Bari, 1933), p. 414.

3   For *cortigiane onesta*, see chapter 3, p. 71. Far from romanticizing courtesans, many writers attacked them as greedy and dishonest; see Arturo Graf, *Attraverso il cinquecento: Una cortigiana fra mille: Veronica Franco* (Turin, 1888), pp. 217–351; see also Marcella Diberti-Leigh, *Veronica Franco: Donna, poetessa e cortigiana del Rinascimento* (Ivrea, 1988), for a study of Franca's *Terze rime* and *Lettere*; and Margaret F. Rosenthal, *The Honest Courtesan: Veronica Franco, Citizen and Writer in Sixteenth-Century Venice* (Chicago, 1992), pp. 2–3, for a realistic perspective on Veronica Franca and courtesans in general. We are indebted to Dr. Rosenthal's very fine and scrupulously researched book, which brings together countless aspects of Venetian culture that bear on the life and work of Veronica Franca. We prefer to translate *"onesta"* as "virtuous."

4   Salza, ed., *Gaspara Stampa*; see the Poems and Letters in the Original Italian section for Salza's numbering of the poems. We are responsible for the translations. The original volume of Franca's book, *Terze rime di Veronica Franca al Serenissimo—Signor Duca di Mantua et di Monferrato,* carries no publisher or date, although the year of publication, 1575, is known from the dedication to the duke, which is signed "Di Venezia a' 15 Novembre MDLXXV." Although we worked from one of the few known copies of this book in the Pietro Leopoldo Ferri collection of books by women writers in the Civic Library of Padua, *Biblioteca femminile italiana* (Padua, 1842), for the convenience of the reader we cite the easily accessible and entirely reliable Salza publication of her *capitoli* and sonnets. See also Ann Rosalind Jones and Margaret F. Rosenthal, eds., *Poems and Selected Letters* (Chicago, 1998), a dual-language edition (English-Italian) where all twenty-five of Franca's *capitoli* are translated; the letters are in English only.

5   A *capitolo* is a verse form composed of triplet lines, called *terze rime,* in which the rhyme endings follow the pattern ABA, BCB, CDC, DED, etc. A *capitolo* has no set number of lines and lends itself well to a flowing expression such as narrative, as used by Dante in *The Divine Comedy,* or speech, as used by Veronica Franca.

6   See chapter 3, p. 76.

7   Veronica may also have read the poem "Il Vanto e il Lamento della Cortegiana Ferrarese," which we cite in chapter 3, note 1. See also Lynne Lawner, *Lives of the Courtesans* (New York, 1987), pp. 10, 12.

8   We have translated extractions from Franca's letters from Benedetto Croce, *Veronica Franco: Lettere dall'unica edizione del MDLXXX con proemio e nota iconografica* (Naples, 1949). More easily accessible for the reader, however, who may want to read the entire collection of letters is Bianchi (see note 1).

9   Rosenthal, *Honest Courtesan,* p. 130.

10   This will and another made by Veronica Franca in 1570 are conserved in the Archivio di Stato in Venice. We have drawn on the transcriptions of both wills in Rosenthal, *Honest Courtesan,* pp. 111–115.

11   Rosenthal, *Honest Courtesan,* p. 131.

12   Rosenthal, *Honest Courtesan,* pp. 2–3.

13   Some courtesans charged more than forty *scudi*. Graf, *Attraverso il cinquecento,* pp. 251–252. The fee of two *scudi* was almost certainly a misprint, common enough in those early days of printing.

14   Rosenthal, *Honest Courtesan,* p. 293, n. 46.

15   The handwriting on this document in the collection of Biblioteca Civica Correr, numbered 275, is difficult to read in some places. Rosenthal, *Honest Courtesan,* p. 296, n. 54, misread *piera* (pear) for *pietra* (stone), which led her to write that the grave site was marked with a pile of pears, instead of a pile of stones. She believed, therefore, that this document was meant as a joke.

16   Salza, ed., *Gaspara Stampa,* p. 385. Biblioteca Civica Correr, #275. We interpret the Italian

phrase in this document, *quattro forche da man,* as "pitchfork."

17   Our interpretation of this "will" differs from that of Rosenthal, who sees it as "satirical. . . perhaps composed extemporaneously in the company of friends" (*Honest Courtesan,* p. 296, note 54). See above, note 15.

18   See Pierre de Nolhac and Angelo Solerti, *Il viaggio in Italia di Enrico III Re di Francia e le feste a Venezia, Ferrara, Mantova e Torino* (Turin, 1890), which contains contemporary accounts of the visit.

19   *Lettere familiari a diversi della S. Veronica Franca all'Illustriss. Et Reverendiss. Monsig. Luigi d'Este Cardinale,* letters I and II. No publisher or date is given, but the date of 1580 can be assigned on the basis of the dedicatory letter to the cardinal, dated 2 August 1580. Also in Bianchi, *Veronica Franco, Lettere,* pp. 30 – 32.

20   Giovanni degli Agostini, *Notizie istorico-critiche intorno le vite e le opere degli scrittori veneziani;* Emmanuele Antonio Cicogna, *Delle iscrizioni veneziane* are cited by Salza, *Gaspara Stampa,* pp. 381–382, in his documentation concerning the three copies of *Terze Rime.* See also L. P. Ferri, *Biblioteca femminile Italiana,* p. 172 concerning the three copies.

21   For "Lament" see note 7 above, Graf, Apendix A, pp. 358–361; for the lines quoted, see p. 360, lines 55–57. According to Graf (p. 355, note 1), the author is unknown.

22   The frescoes are almost completely lost. On Fumane see Arturo Sandrini, *Villa della Torre a Fumane* (Verona, 1993), especially the chapter by Gian Paolo Marchi, "Marcantonio della Torre e Veronica Franco," pp. 197–219; Veronica's *capitolo* in praise of Fumane is included in an appendix.

23   According to Matteo Bandello (1485–1561), Venetian courtesans assigned certain nights of the week to dine and sleep with each of their several lovers. "During the day she is free to entertain whomever she wishes. . . . Once in a while a wealthy foreigner insists on having one of her nights. . . . In this case it is her duty to request permission from the lover whose evening that would ordinarily be and to arrange to see him during the day instead. Each lover pays a monthly salary and their agreement includes the provision that the courtesan is allowed to have foreigners as overnight guests" (quoted in Lynne Lawner, *Lives of the Courtesans,* p. 9). Although Veronica may have entered into some such arrangements, we believe she was far too independent and discriminating to have ordered her life in this way.

24   Graf, *Attraverso il cinquecento,* p. 328.

25   From Veronica's dedication of the *Terze Rime* to the Duke of Mantua (see note 4), we assume she went to Rome sometime after November 1575, possibly when the plague broke out near the end of the year. During the spring and summer of 1576 she was still there and may have remained until the beginning of 1577, when the plague had begun to wane: see Rosenthal, *Honest Courtesan,* p. 277, note 107.

26   The given name is variously spelled; we follow Rosenthal in giving it as Redolfo.

27   Rosenthal, *Honest Courtesan,* p. 158.

28   Rosenthal, *Honest Courtesan,* p. 86.

29   Graf, *Attraverso il cinquecento,* p. 327.

30   Bartolomeo Gamba, *Ritratti di donne illustri* (Venice, 1826).

31   Giovanni degli Agostini, *Notizie istorico-critiche intorno la vita e le opere degli scrittori venetiani* (Venice, 1752–54), vol. II, p. 616. For an extended commentary on the problem of portraits of Veronica Franca, see the appendix to Croce, *Veronica Franco.*

12.1. Anon.
Portrait of
Modesta da Pozzo
(Moderata
Fonte). ca.1589.
Museo Civico,
Padua. Photo,
Museum.

MODESTA À PVTEO VENETA
POES.ᴵ HVMAÑQ. LITTER. STVDIOS.ᴬ

CHAPTER TWELVE

Moderata Fonte/ Modesta da Pozzo

(1555–1592)

 *Worthy Women*[1]

oderata Fonte wore her chosen name as Risamante, the heroine of her epic poem *Floridoro*, wore her shield; she concealed herself behind it while she thrust her words/sword at her adversary.[2] The daughter of Marietta di Mazzi and Girolamo da Pozzo, a wealthy Venetian *cittadino*,[3] she was named Modesta when she was christened in the Church of Saint Samuel on the feast day of Saint Modestus (June 15). The name Modesta da Pozzo did not suit the image that she had of herself as she grew up; she was ambitious to achieve fame and an immortal name as a writer, and modesty (Modesta) inappropriately suggested shyness or timidity, while a well *(pozzo)* was silent. So she changed "modesty" to "moderate" (the moral virtue of being able to choose a moderate position between extremes), and transformed the quiet well to a singing fountain *(fonte)* whose gently streaming, steady voice poured forth the "clear, fresh, sweet waters."[4] She was thus a metaphor of herself, and metaphor remained through her tragically short life the vehicle of her creative thought.

The only contemporary account we have of Moderata's life, published as a preface to her most important book, *The Worth of Women* (*Il merito delle donne*), was written by her life-long friend and uncle-in-law, Giovanni Niccolò Doglioni (1548–1629), a Venetian civil servant and a man of literary taste and accomplishments. This account, which he wrote in 1593, must be followed in some detail, for it reveals some of those factors that rooted her perceptions of women in society and produced her one book, for which alone she deserves fame.[5] Girolamo and Marietta died in 1556, Doglioni relates, leaving Modesta and her three-year-old brother Leonardo heirs to their considerable estate. They were taken to live at first with their grandparents, Prospero Saraceni, a well-to-do lawyer, and his wife, Cecilia di Mazzi, until Modesta was placed in a convent where she learned to read and write and to recite verses. According to the biographer, it became evident that even as a young child she had an extraordinary memory and quick wit: a priest visiting the convent, a portly man, was astonished hearing her talk and recite and "could not resist telling her that she seemed to be a spirit without a body," to which she spiritedly replied that "he seemed to her like a body without a spirit."[6]

When Modesta was nine years old she returned to live with her grandparents and her young aunt Saracena, Prospero's daughter. She had no further formal schooling, but she managed to educate herself by begging her brother to repeat each day what he had learned in school, and by reading. Grandfather Prospero, recognizing her unusual abilities, gave her books and encouraged her to read and to write verses, which she did incessantly. About her early writing Doglioni recounts another engaging anecdote: Modesta was traveling with her family to their country estate and took with her the basket in which she carefully kept all her writing. As they crossed over the swift-flowing Piave River in their open carriage, bouncing and rolling as high-sprung carriages did, the precious basket fell into the river and was swept away. The child was devastated and inconsolable for quite some time, but she eventually set herself to rewrite the lost work and succeeded in doing so because of her extraordinary memory. Modesta apparently also had a talent for drawing figures from life, played the harpsichord and the lute, sang well, and excelled in embroidering, able to design whatever motif was suggested to her.

Doglioni married Prospero's daughter, Saracena Saraceni, and because she and Modesta had been raised like sisters and were dear friends, he took Modesta to live with them. Fully aware of her gift for writing, he not only encouraged her, as Prospero had done, but also undertook to see that her writing was published. Her first appearance in print occurred in 1581, when she wrote a work for performance, *Le Feste*, performed at one of the annual *rappresentationi* before "Their most Serene Highnesses, the Princes of Venice." In the form of a debate set to music, a Stoic and an Epicurean philosopher discuss the nature of the supreme good.[7] In the same year was also published her chivalric epic *Tredici canti del Floridoro* (Thirteen Cantos of Floridoro). It is in this work that we first find the early mature Moderata Fonte immersed in the woman problem. She begins canto IV,

> *Women of every age have been endowed by Nature*
> *with great judgment and spirit*
> *nor are they less apt in revealing with attentive study*
> *the same wisdom and courage with which men are born,*
> *and since our bodies*
> *are made of the same substance,*
> *we eat the same food, speak the same way,*
> *what difference can there be in courage and intelligence?*

> *It has always been seen (and there was always*
> *some woman with the desire)*
> *that more than one of them has been successful in warfare*
> *and taken away the rewards and applause from many men,*
> *and thus in literature and in every*
> *undertaking common to men*
> *women have succeeded and do so now,*
> *so men have no right to be envious.*

> *And even though there are not many*
> *in the ranks of the worthy and famous*
> *this is because they have not aspired*
> *to acts of heroism and virtue.*
> *Gold that is hidden in the mine*

is no less gold because it is buried,
and when it is taken out of the ground and used
to fashion something, it is as precious as all gold.

   If a father set his daughter, at birth,
to some task equal to that of his son,
whether he put her to learn something of the liberal arts,
or in a military squadron with her brother,
she would not be inferior to him
in carrying out whatever the task may be;
but she is raised to do other things
and is not deemed worthy of education. (p. 405)

A quick glance at Canto 37 of Ariosto's *Orlando Furioso*, quoted in chapter 6, is enough to recognize not only the source of Moderata's stanzas quoted here but also to remind us of Veronica Franca's *capitolo* addressed to Maffio Venier (chapter 11). It is likely that both Moderata and Veronica had read Laura Terracina's *Commentary*.

Floridoro tells the story of Risamante, one of twin daughters of the King of Armenia, who when a baby was stolen from the palace by a sorcerer, Celidante, who knew she was destined for greatness. He hid her on a rock in the middle of the Mediterranean (the localities mentioned in the poem are on its north or south coast) until she was seventeen years old, at which time he told her who she was. Risamante returned to her home and found that her twin sister, Biondaura, had inherited the throne because their father believed that Risamante was dead. Biondaura was unwilling to acknowledge her sister and share the throne. Thus begins the "quest" that drives the story: Risamante must travel here and there, meeting one adventure after another in her effort to find help in order to gain her rightful place, sharing the rule of Armenia with her sister. The twins are reverse images of each other, Risamante daring, actively engaged in achieving her goals, "like an armed warrior," Biondaura, "soft and delicate." In light of *The Worth of Women*, where we shall see that Moderata sets up a self-reflecting, two-sided but unequal argument in which the active side of Moderata's nature is stronger than the passive, it seems we may read *Floridoro* as emotionally and psychologically autobiographical. We may also see Biondaura as Moderata's brother, Leonardo, who tried to usurp her right to their shared inheritance.

Floridoro follows the conventions of the genre, with the protagonist involved in many heroic adventures, threatened by natural and supernatural evils, protected by sorcerers and magic objects, and overcoming all obstacles. Where Moderata breaks with convention is in her choice of protagonist, for Floridoro, hero though he is, is not the main character; this role is given to Risamante, who first appears suddenly on the scene (fully armed, rather like Athena) as an unknown cavalier to challenge the giant who has already defeated the greatest knights from many different nations in a series of combats over the king's daughter, Celsidea. After fierce fighting Risamante slays the giant and, full of praises, the king requests that the stranger remove "his" helmet, whereupon it is discovered that the victor is a beautiful woman.[8] Moderata is careful to make her heroine not an Amazon but an ideally beautiful woman:

She removed her helmet and revealed
gleaming, golden blond hair
and starry eyes so shining
as to make the jealous sun sink into the sea;
lilies and roses would be envious of
her fresh, rosy cheeks;
her hand, now holding no weapon,
seemed to be whiter than snow (pp. 405 – 6)

After this revelation, the Queen and Celsidea lead Risamante into a room where she can take off her armor and be dressed as a woman for the festivities in her honor, so all could see "she was as beautiful as a woman / as she was brave as a mounted warrior" (II, 38–39).

While the woman-hero retains her femininity, Floridoro is far from the ideal of a manly hero, as Valerie Finucci points out. He is an adolescent not only in age—he is sixteen years old—but also psychologically.[9] He is described as effeminate, looking like a lovely, lustrous young girl (V, 46). Dressed in white (inevitably calling up the association of virginal purity) he takes the false name Biancador (*bianca*, white) when he enters the tourney in disguise. The other male characters in the poem with one exception are weak and incompetent, and it seems evident, again in light of *The Worth of Women,* that this characterization of the male personages was deliberate, not the result of any ineptitude on the part of the author for drawing a male character. She was intent on forcing her readers to become aware, by changing the genders of the active and passive characters, that the reading to which they were accustomed reflected the different socially prescribed roles for which men and women were differently trained, roles that required men to be active and women to be passive. *Floridoro* is meant to raise consciousness by thwarting the reader's conventional expectations.

Fonte did not finish her epic. Doglioni relates that she wrote the poem while living in his house, but adds, "not the published one but another."[10] It is not possible to know exactly what he meant, but perhaps the cantos to which he refers were intended to be the last part of the poem that was published. Writers have supposed several reasons for its incompletion, principally that her marriage in 1582 interrupted her writing, which seems plausible.

It was Doglioni's responsibility, acting as her guardian, to find a suitable husband for Moderata, which he did—but not, curiously, until she was twenty-seven years old, much older than the usual age for Venetian upper-class women to marry. Why the delay we can only speculate. Virginia Cox considers that the delay had something to do with a lawsuit against Leonardo, her brother, in connection with his attempt to deprive her of her inheritance, bequeathed to her as her dowry.[11] We believe that she had made up her mind never to marry, and that perhaps the man who changed her mind, Filippo Zorzi, was the lawyer who helped her win her case against her brother—and won her as well. In *Floridoro* she writes that there are few lawyers who are willing to defend orphans who are cheated of their inheritance,

But among the few are some unlike others
whom I praise to the skies,

those that faithfully and with friendly zeal
try to help me, so abused am I;
I shall never stop glorifying to heaven
the immense courtesy and service on my behalf
which with the deepest sincerity
I will acknowledge with words and deeds. (p. 406)

In any case, she was an independent-spirited woman, and it was probably well known that she had strong convictions about gender relationships. It cannot have been easy for Doglioni to find a man of suitable class and wealth that she was willing to marry, on one hand, and who on the other hand was also willing to marry *her*. The man Doglioni chose, or more likely she found for herself, was indeed suitable. He came from an old *cittadino* family and was well educated. From Moderata's point of view, the fact that she was three years older than Filippo Zorzi might have seemed to her a possible advantage, for, as Cox points out, this could have the effect of making the relationship more equal than was usual in marriage. Nevertheless, her marriage in 1583 took its toll. The literarily productive years that culminated with the publication of the two works already mentioned plus one other, *La Passione di Christo descritta in ottava rime da Moderata Fonte* (1582) gave way to biologically productive years: her first child, Pietro, was born in 1583; the second, Cicilia, in 1585; the third was born in 1587; and she died giving birth to her fourth child in 1592; the two last did not survive childhood.

These dates are revealing. She published nothing after she married until 1592, when she published *La Resurrezione di Gesù Christo Nostro Signor.* She finished her dialogue, *The Worth of Women,* the day before her death. Because she had had difficulty with her 1585 pregnancy and had made her will that year, she probably feared the following pregnancies and completed what she must have felt was her most precious "legacy" when she realized that the fourth birth was very near. The first three pregnancies were two years apart, then there is a period of four years before she became pregnant again. This suggests that she began to write again after the birth of the third child, and perhaps planned to have no more children. She seems to have written *The Worth of Women* over a period of a few years: discussing the arts, when one of the characters in the dialogue, Adriana, asks, "who is there alive today who is worthy to be called an extraordinary and celebrated painter?" another, Lucrezia, answers, "I've heard mention of Signor Giacomo Tintoretto, and of a marvelously talented daughter of his," and Adriana adds, "Signor Paolo Veronese has created miracles as a painter, as I've seen with my own eyes" (p. 160)*. Marietta, daughter of Tintoretto, died in 1590, Veronese in 1588.

Because *The Worth of Women* was published posthumously, we must wonder with Beatrice Collina about whether her text was altered for publication, and if so, by whom and by how much.[12] It appeared eight years after her death, and a few years after the death of her husband (in her dedication of her mother's book to Livia Feltria della Rovere, Duchessa of Urbino, Cicilia d'I Zorzi writes that she and her

---

* All quotations in this chapter are translated from Chemello (see note 1); numbers following quotations refer to page numbers in Chemello.

brother Pietro are the only ones left of her mother's family, "all the others having died, including my father"[13]). Although Collina believes the title was "certainly" chosen by Moderata,[14] there is more certainly reason for doubt: the title leads one to believe the book is mostly about the virtues of women, whereas in fact there is far more space devoted to the vices of men. The publication was overseen by Doglioni, who edited it and might well have made some revisions. His decision to see it published after so many years almost certainly was made because of the publication of a number of books attacking women that appeared in the last years of the century, particularly Giuseppe Passi's *I donneschi difetti,* published in 1595 and again in 1599, and Onofrio Filarco's *Vera narratione delle operationi delle donne*[15]; a hint of this is found in the text when one of the characters guesses, in response to another who wonders what men would say if they heard what the women were saying about them, "Oh, they would probably write some scornful book about women in reply" (p. 71) This could well have been added by Doglioni, who might also have chosen the title himself to contrast it with the contemporary misogynist titles and texts published in the years after Moderata's death. Whatever Doglioni's role, it is likely that Moderata finished the work, as he relates, "the very day before she died,"[16] and there is overwhelming pathos in imagining the fervor, the passion, the wholly devoted determination with which she wrote her perfectly controlled and cool dialogue, racing with possible death.

It is particularly interesting to realize that the strongest and most sustained single attack in the Cinquecento on the male-shaped society was raised by a woman who personally had had uncommonly favorable experiences with the men in her life. Her grandfather had encouraged her from the time she was a child; her guardian, Doglioni, continued that encouragement and supported her work by arranging for its publication. She seems to have had a good marriage: her husband gave her control of a portion of her dowry when they married because of his love for her, according to a document of 1583, and in 1585, when she made her will, her affection for him is evident in that she not only made him the principal beneficiary of her estate but included bequests to members of his family while omitting any legacy to her brother.[17]

In *The Worth of Women,* in which all seven of the women who participate in the dialogue together represent the author, Corinna/Moderata praises Moderata's husband, Filippo Zorzi, thinly disguised under the name Filippo Giorgi; "he is my lawyer and fiscal advocate for the prestigious Office of Water Administration, and his diligence, loyalty, and efficiency are well recognized by our much respected Senate. And it is certainly true that, even if he is not yet famous because of his age (he is quite young), he is known for his honesty, skill, and integrity and he is so solicitous and tireless in his cases that he is held in great esteem by his colleagues" (p. 138).

Although Corinna/Moderata speaks forcefully in attacking husbands in general, "When people say that we must be subject to men, it should be understood in the same sense that we are subject to natural disasters, illness, and all the other accidents of this life: it does not mean subjection in the sense of obedience, having to serve them out of fear, but of helping them out of Christian charity, since they have been given to us as a spiritual trial" (p. 26), she also describes what she considers the basis of an ideal marriage, which may allude to her own. "It is friendship that . . . is the basis of marriage that preserves the individual in the species" (p. 80). Here and elsewhere in

the book it does not appear that women enjoy the sexual relationship with their husbands, but endure it for the sake of having children. "It is very shameful," Leonora
says, "when we . . . deign to consort intimately with those who are less worthy than
ourselves, especially outside the necessity of marriage, which, since it is demanded of
us, we can hardly avoid; but even though we must, this lowers men's respect for us"
(p. 54). Doglioni only indirectly gives us a picture of Moderata's marriage when he
writes that "she was so capable in managing the household that her husband paid
hardly any attention to it and confessed many times that he had no idea what it meant
to take care of the children, or the house, since she took everything out of his hands,
and did everything herself, efficiently and diligently."[18] We get the impression of a har-
monious, mutually agreeable relationship, Zorzi providing financial resources and
Moderata providing care of their children and household; clearly this was not a marriage in which the husband dominated. *The Worth of Women*, then, is not the angry
outpouring of an abused, injured woman, but the honest attempt of an intelligent
woman to record her observations of a society that was unjust, and sometimes abusive, to women. Moderata keeps the tone light; the women often laugh, as if exhila-
rated by their freedom to utter their accusations against men out loud, they laugh
sometimes hearing exaggerations, but beneath the bantering lie the very real grievances that Moderata intends to expose.

Thus fathers, brothers, sons, husbands, and lovers are accused in *The Worth of
Women* of every fault, failing, vice, and sin known to humankind. Moderata's dialogue
is like a trial, with three prosecutors, three defenders, and a judge,[19] a structure that
was probably suggested to her by her husband's profession. It must be said, however,
that it was not exactly a fair trial: the "judge" (whom they elected queen for the day)
was Adriana, grateful for her good luck to have been twice widowed; for the "prosecution" there were Leonora, a young widow whose husband had been a miser ("Remarry? I'd rather drown") (p. 21), Cornelia, married to a man who browbeat her
("Women who are married, or martyred [to be more accurate], have infinite sources
of misery") (p. 33) and Corinna, a poet who is determined to remain single and thus
free of family obligations that made an intellectual or artistic life difficult if not impossible for a woman:

> *Free is the heart in my breast*
> *I serve no one, nor do I belong to anyone but myself.*
> *I nourish myself with modesty and chastity*
> *virtue exalts me and chastity adorns me.*
>
> *My soul yields only to God, to whom I turn,*
> *although now I am enveloped in my mortal veil,*
> *and disdains the world and its evil perfidy*
> *that fools and scorns the simple-minded.*
>
> *I esteem not at all,*
> *if they are mine by luck,*
> *rewards for the purity of my mind and my desires.*

Thus in my green years as in the mature ones to come,
since I will not be distracted by the falsity of men,
I hope for fame and glory in life, and death. [20] (p. 406)

These, then, were all women who had had plenty of time and reason to formulate their ideas about their relationship to the men in their lives.

For the "defense" there were Helena, young and newly married ("It's possible that they're not all bad" (p. 17), Virginia, Adriana's daughter, young but not yet married ("if [men] did not love us why do they spend so much time and energy day and night courting various women?) (p. 60), and Lucrezia, a married woman who considers the unmarried Corinna's situation ideal—"Oh happy Corinna," she exclaims, "What other woman in the world can be compared with yours? Not one! Not a widow for she cannot boast [of being free] since earlier she went through a bit of suffering, not a wife, for she is still suffering, not a young girl awaiting marriage, for she has suffering ahead of her . . . you, by rejecting all contact with those false, false men, you are free to devote yourself to those glorious pursuits that will win you immortality" (p. 18). These were not exactly strong voices on the side of the defense.

Moderata's dialogue begins with a tribute to her city, Venice, which, she emphasizes, is not only isolated from the mainland by the Adriatic sea, but also surrounded by walls and guarded by fortresses. The city is dependent on commerce with the rest of the world by means of ships that bring her the necessities and luxuries of Venetian life, for she herself produces nothing. She is ahead of every city in the world, both ancient and modern, Moderata continues; the pomp and grandeur of the city is inestimable, her riches, the sumptuousness of the buildings, the splendor of the clothes people wear, their free way of life, their affability is beyond imagining. She is both loved and feared. Just as the members and arteries of our bodies are connected to our hearts, so the cities and all parts of the world are connected to Venice. The city is home to an immense diversity of peoples who despite differences in blood and customs live in perfect peace and equality with each other. The finest talents in all the arts mingle here, virtue rules, vice is extirpated. The men are courageous, wise, and courteous while the women are beautiful, intelligent, and chaste. The city is blessed by God's greatest gifts and by the Doge, who is unequalled in goodness, prudence, and justice. This city, Moderata tells her readers, unlike any other is a new and marvelous work of God, and her paradisiacal description reminds us that Venice is not only *La Serenissima*, born in the sea like the goddess Venus, but an urbanized Garden of Eden.

The Worth of Women is indeed set in a garden, which, although in Venice, is closed off from the city, a private precinct belonging to Leonora, who has recently inherited the house and property from an aunt. Thus the author invents the need for Leonora to describe the garden in detail for the six women friends who are visiting it for the first time; these are the women who with herself will participate in the dialogue. She leads them from the house into this outdoor stage where there were "rows of little bright green shrubs in all kinds of shapes—some in the form of pyramids, others like mushrooms or melons or some other shape, surrounded by various kinds of trees—laurel, chestnut, box tree, pomegranate—intermingled and carefully clipped so that they were all of the same size. There were . . . beautiful urns that held lemon trees and many kinds of flowers, and tiny myrtle shrubs, and beds of fresh herbs, cut into triangles, ovals, squares, and other cunning inventions" (p. 19).[21]

The garden with its geometrized plants and flowers is thus nature carefully designed by art as Venice is the artifact of the Great Designer. The city, the garden, indeed the book itself are simulations of living phenomena (nature) as they are reflected and reordered by art, and as such they constitute metaphors of the just society created by the all-embracing virtue of women, the supreme virtue born of art, the unity of order and beauty.[22] As Moderata develops her metaphorical text it becomes evident that the society that has developed *outside* the garden, *outside* of Venice, is one that had grown throughout the ages without design, simply according to the passions and vices of men.

Leonora leads her friends further into the garden, which has at its center a beautiful fountain surrounded by six statues representing women from whose breasts flowed "clear, fresh, sweet waters." Each figure wears a garland of laurel on her head and holds a slender olive branch in her left hand, with a scroll wrapped around it, and in her right hand each one carries an emblem whose meaning is expressed in the incised words on the scroll. One held an ermine over her shoulder which she held away from her breast to keep it dry; the words on her scroll were

> *Prima morte, che macchia al corpo mio*

> *Let me die before suffering any stain*

The next one carried in her right hand a phoenix, and in her left hand she displayed the message,

> *Sola vivomi ogn'or, muoio e rinasco*

> *Alone I live for all time, I die and am reborn*

The third carried a sun, and her scroll read,

> *Solo, porgo a me stesso e ad altri luce*

> *I illuminate myself and enlighten others*

The next one held a lantern, in whose flame one could see a butterfly burned. Her emblem read,

> *Vinta da bella vista, io stessa m'ardo*

> *Overcome by the vision of beauty, I set myself afire.*

The fifth had as her emblem a peach, with a leaf from a peach tree, tongue-shaped, with the words,

Troppo diverso è dalla lingua il core

All too different is the tongue from the heart

The sixth carried a crocodile, and the words of her scroll read,

Io l'uomo uccido e poi lo piango morto

First I kill then cry over the dead (p. 20)

Her guests ask Leonora to explain the meaning of the figures and their devices, which she does, explaining first that the aunt from whom she had inherited the house was unmarried by preference and on receiving a handsome inheritance from her father had had the garden designed and the fountain built as an expression of her own ideas about how she wanted to live—alone—and of her views about men—not favorable. Then she begins her exegesis of the figures. The one holding the ermine represents Chastity; the next one with the phoenix represents Solitude, a solitary (legendary) bird that showed how her aunt enjoyed living alone and that she was reborn in the fame of her good works; next is Liberty with the sun as her device, which itself independent and unique gives light to the whole universe, illustrating that her aunt, independent and solitary shone like the sun with her many meritorious and honored qualities and that she shared the treasures of her mind with every virtuous person whom she came to know—which perhaps she would not have been able to do governed by the rule and authority of a husband. The figure with the lantern in whose flame a butterfly is consumed is meant to signify naivete, and it refers to young girls caught by deceitful men to whom they are attracted and who are then destroyed by their own innocence; the peach together with the peach tree leaf stands for the deceitfulness of men because the fruit is heart-shaped, a symbol of love, but the leaf is shaped like a tongue that speaks falsely; last is the crocodile, symbol of men's hypocrisy (p. 22–23).

The fountain therefore balances three virtues to which women should aspire: chastity, everlasting fame (the reward of solitude), and liberty, with three faults against which women must be warned: naivete, deceit, and hypocrisy. It hardly has to be said that Moderata is herself the art/life-giving fountain and that the scrolls are her book: At the end of Lucrezia's speech she tells Corinna, "You with your wonderful intellect should certainly write a book on this subject, teaching young girls who have not yet leaned to recognize the good from the bad what their best interests are, for in this way you would win double glory, serving both God and the world." Answering her, Corinna tips her shield aside for a moment and reveals Moderata Fonte: "It certainly would be a good idea," Corinna/Moderata replies, "and I must thank you for suggesting it; perhaps one of these days I just might do it" (p. 18).

As we have said, Moderata is indeed all seven of the participants in the discussion, arguing for and against men. At the end of the second day, it is Leonora/Moderata who invents the speech she wishes she could really make in public, to persuade men to give up their tyrannical ways with women, and Cornelia sighs, "Oh, how many women would have felt encouraged if you had, as much by the warnings that you've given them to be careful not to make mistakes as for persuading those men who fail in their obligations to mend their ways and behave as they should" (p. 182). Early in the first day and here again at the end of the second Moderata reveals her purpose and her hopes in writing this book. Throughout, the metaphor functions on two levels: the social, which through *The Worth of Women* exposes the unjust society, and the personal, by which Moderata herself by virtue of her art—her book—will bring order and beauty to society. The book is both a vision and a critique.

The dialogue, as we have seen in previous chapters, was a literary form of choice among many intellectuals in the Cinquecento. Like other cultural phenomena of the Renaissance, it was closely linked to the development of academies, and it lent itself to the invention of highly realistic conversations of the kind that actually took place both in the academies and in private settings. However, although *The Worth of Women* may be categorized as a dialogue, it differs from other works in this genre in three significant ways. It is tightly structured to balance the discussion in the garden with three speakers on each side and a moderator at the center like justice weighing the scales; the speakers are all women; and each opposing side represents the author, just as in *Floridoro* Risamante and Biondaura each represented Moderata's opposing sides.[23]

As in *Floridoro*, the end is also inconclusive; in *The Worth of Women* the speakers agree that the subject is inexhaustible, but accusers and defenders have drawn their positions closer to each other. Queen Adriana, who has lent some weight to the accusers here and there ("those miserable gossips," she says of men who lie about their amorous conquests, "I've known more than a few! How many innocent women have been victimized by their slander!") (p. 51), now assures her daughter that there are some men who are less arrogant than others, and if women act lovingly, "they can be made to be reasonable. If you answer back they get angrier than ever" "But," her worried daughter asks, "suppose he turns out to be the jealous type?" "A jealous man," Leonora interposes, "is never going to change." "He will change," Adriana insists, "if you act as I've told you." The alternative to marriage is not appealing. "Just imagine what your life would be if I don't marry you off. You'll have to stay home every day and dress soberly, not like you do now, because that's how girls who don't want to marry have to live." And Lucrezia adds, "even though men have all the faults that we've been talking about, life being as it is these days, it's still better to let them govern us, and have their company. . . . We poor women are subjected every day to all kinds of abuses, cheated out of our money, our honor, our very lives; so it's better to have at least one man as a friend, to defend us from the others. . . . And if by chance, as sometimes happens, one has a good husband . . . then one can not imagine how happy a woman can be, united with such a man inseparably until death" (p. 172). And even Leonora, who has been so uncompromising, when she gets the last word is willing to reconsider her decision never to marry again (p. 183).

The conversation among the women takes place over two days. The tone is often jocular, with the women described as laughing over one remark or another, and they take up the subject rather in the spirit of a game, with the intention of amusing themselves.[24] The first day is given over entirely to the comparison of men and women, with much more attention given to men's faults, with examples from everyday life experience, than to women's virtues, either asserted or exemplified with the famous women of history and legend: warrior heroines like Camilla, who led the Volscians to war against Aeneas (Virgil, *Aeneid,* Book 12); Penthesilea, the Amazon queen who was killed in combat with Achilles; Zenobia, warrior queen of Palmyra, who fought against the Romans; "and other warlike women about whom those histories even though written by men have not been able to remain silent" (Chemello edition, p. 62); literary figures such as Carmenta, who was said to have adapted the Greek alphabet to Latin; Sappho, the greatest woman poet of antiquity; and Corinna, the Greek lyric poet who beat Pindar five times in musical contests; and women celebrated for their chastity and self-sacrifice. The men are accused of arrogance, bullying, cruelty, deceitfulness, envy of women's merits, falsity toward each other, gambling, hatred of women, injustice, jealousy, lust, miserliness, neglect, odious habits, profligacy with their wives' dowries, rashness of judgment, selfishness, tyranny, unreasonableness, viciousness, wantonness, and zealotry. As Corinna tells Virginia, "it's easy to see that men are full of flaws, whereas women embrace all the virtues. . . . It is obvious that in women, instead of anger there is gentleness and prudence, where they are greedy women are generous, instead of arrogant women are compliant, where men are self-indulgent women are self-restrained, women offer peace in place of discord, love instead of hate and in fact every moral and intellectual virtue can be found more in women than in men" (p. 61). When Helena demurs, "Oh, please, don't deny that we women too fall into error," Cornelia defends the sinners, "the origin and true cause of so much evil are the men who trapped, tempted, importuned, and incited these women . . . who despite their miserable lives have more dignity than those men because at least they aren't the ones who pay. . . . There is no doubt that when a virgin loses her honor it can only be because of a man who has shamelessly flattered and tempted her and overcome her naivete and little by little has taken away from her all of her feminine dignity and power and then abandons her so that without resources, she becomes a prostitute" (pp. 51–52).

Moderata's "defenders" balance the "prosecutors" as best they can. When Cornelia asks rhetorically, "How many fathers are there who never provide for their daughters while they are alive, and when they die leave everything or the bulk of their estate to their sons," Helena replies "I couldn't say that. My father gave me his loving consideration and provided very well for me to marry well." "One is not many," Cornelia observes. "And the lucky daughters whose fathers either provide for their dowries, or who share in the estate with their brothers, are kept in the house like slaves by those brothers, their rights taken away from them...and so they grow old at home under their brothers' rule, serving their relatives and spending their lives buried alive." Lucretia rose for the defense. "You are mistaken, Cornelia, about there being no loving brothers. I can testify to that because when my father died he left me very little but my brothers used part of their own inheritance to find a husband for me." Cornelia was ready again. "Are you not aware that God on occasion reveals miracles?" (pp. 28–29).

Sons are no better. "How many miserable mothers there are who besides carrying their sons in their bellies for nine months and giving birth to them with great anguish and danger, nourish them, wean them, care for them lovingly, and if unfortunately they lose their husbands, they sweat and slave for them . . . and then when these sons have reached the age when they should support their mothers as a reward for her toil, they abandon them and give no heed to their needs . . . and if the mothers have any money, these sons will spend it all . . . there are even those who cruelly beat their mothers." But Queen Adriana had had a son who was "an angel of goodness." It was her great misfortune that he died. The prosecution was unimpressed. "He might have turned out worse than other men," Cornelia consoled her (p. 30).

Husbands were no better. They drove women to infidelity by keeping them on such a tight leash they could hardly breath. Jealous husbands made life so unpleasant that they, too, were responsible for wives becoming unfaithful. Some husbands neglected their wives "and make fools of themselves over some shameless woman (for inevitably you do find a few such amid so many women) . . . such men inflict a thousand hardships on their wives, even stripping them of their most treasured things to give them to prostitutes, besides which, they often make mistresses of their servants and fill the house with bastards" (p. 34). Some men are just as obsessed with gambling as they are with women. Such had been Queen Adriana's luck with her second husband, thankfully dead. Lucretia's husband was so foul-mouthed that she had no peace except when he was out of the house. Cornelia's husband was a reckless spendthrift (pp. 34–37).

Worst of all were lovers. Young lovers were unstable, foolish, proud, insolent, and indiscreet. "But can't we trust more mature men?" Helena asks Cornelia hopefully, "at least when they appear to love faithfully?" "They are even worse," Cornelia assures her, because they are more expert at deceiving." In that case, Virginia wanted to know, "Do you want us to love old men, since we shouldn't have anything to do with youths, still less men in their best years?" "Old men are just as tricky as middle-aged men," Cornelia answered, "even worse, because they lack the zest they once had and have passed the age when they feel real joy . . . they are jealous and suspicious, lazy and incompetent, and furthermore they are stingy" (pp. 41–42).

However, mindful of avoiding extremes, Moderata has Cornelia consider the few men who, she admits, can truly love. Such men "behave virtuously and never give cause for scandal. True love makes the arrogant become humble, the ignorant learned, the cowardly brave, the wrathful gentle, fools clever, and lunatics rational. In sum, love can change a man's nature, make a bad man good and a good man better; that's why it is compared with fire in which gold is refined, just as in the flame of true love, a man can be purified, refined, and perfected" (p. 45).

The context of the argument on the first day is society—the unruly society that men, whom women distrust, have made; in this context they are uncomfortable. On the second day, the context is the nurturing nature that God, whom they trust, has designed; in this context women are at home, familiar with the earth and sky, the animals, vegetables, and minerals over which God has given them dominion, equally with men. This is an orderly world, as Moderata sees it, paying tribute to Doglioni, "who is knowledgeable on many subjects and who has written many books." She recites her sonnet in praise of his book *L'Anno* (The Year):

> *Like an embroidery of pearls on cloth of gold*
> *or masses of flowers on a green field*
> *such is the image that your lofty thoughts*
> *create with your felicitous pen.*

> *To think that a mortal can explain and discern*
> *every celestial and earthly force,*
> *every boundary, state, motion, surface, and depth,*
> *time, the elements, the heavens, nature, and art.*
>
> *With a wave of his hand the great Architect*
> *gave spirit and form to this immense mass*
> *whose various aspects you interpret.*
>
> *Now, for your great work he encircles your head*
> *with a wreath of stars, and inspires your mind,*
> *transforming the small universe you are into himself.* (pp. 406 – 7)

While the metaphor of art versus nature, order versus disorder, is expressed on the first day mainly through the women's accusations against men, with *The Worth of Women* exposing the social jungle, on the second day the metaphorical frame is widened by means of the extended discussion of natural phenomena. The talk proceeds in an orderly but broadly discursive way from observations about outer space (the sun and moon, the stars), through the atmosphere (clouds, rain, birds), to the seas (fish, whales), rivers, springs, and earth (animals, vegetation, stone), providing incidentally for the modern reader a fascinating survey of popular knowledge and belief in Moderata's time. "The sun concludes its daily course in twenty-four hours," Corinna confidently tells her friends (p. 81), and "we are all made up of four elements, which generate in us the four principal substances or dispositions, that is, phlegm comes from air, blood from water, anger from fire and depression from earth, each of which opposes the others" (p. 128). Each phenomenon provides a metaphor for the relationship between men and women. When the second day's discussion begins with Lucrezia's question, Why do women love men even knowing how unworthy they are? Corinna explains that women by nature are kind and moreover women are often under the influence of the stars. "But couldn't these celestial influences dispose men to love us?," Virginia asks. "They could if the material were disposed to receive the impression," Corinna answers (p. 76). The stars also influence friendship, she says, and "the friendship and harmony of the elements maintains the health of our bodies, makes the air fine and clear, calms the seas, brings peace so that cities may be built all over the world, makes kingdoms expand, and cheers all creatures" (p. 80). Discord, on the other hand, brings disaster. "When there is discord among men, we have war," Cornelia observes.

"True," Corinna agrees, "then provinces and families are exterminated, states are conquered and people destroyed. When there is discord in the air we have thunder and lightning, storms at sea and earthquakes on land" (pp. 80–81). It is tacitly understood that God has reasons for creating discord that go beyond what the human can know.

Leonora becomes impatient with this talk about natural phenomena. "Excuse me please, but you are all out of bounds. We're supposed to be talking against men . . . now if you want to speak about something unstable, what better subject than men? Do you want to talk about discord? And if you want to talk about things that fly in the air, you don't have to look further for a subject than men's brains which are just like birds' who fly around here and there, talking about this and that, and don't know where they're going" (p. 83).

The talk about nature continues, however, with a rollicking series of metaphors to which even ancient Latin grammar is forced to yield: In Latin, Corinna points out, "the agreements are wrong, and with them the relative never agrees with the antecedent. . . . They have the passive of the first verb, but not the active, which is ours because we love and they are loved . . . for genders they have the masculine and the indefinite, for the cases theirs are the accusative because they are always accusing us, the dative because they sometimes beat us, the ablative because they take themselves and all our possessions away from us. On the contrary, we have the nominative for speaking with dignity to them, the genitive because we are all theirs, and the vocative for calling to them always with love" (pp. 139 – 40).

Soon we realize that Moderata has led us here into an extended joke and that she has a thinly veiled purpose in developing this conversation in addition to letting Corinna/Moderata display her erudition. Wittily and humorously she reveals that the talk about nature mocks men, who would laugh at them for talking about subjects that men consider are only proper for men to discuss, believing that women should confine themselves to talk about clothes and fashion, but since this comment immediately follows the women's discussion of fashion and hairdo, she is also mocking women. Elena believes that blond hair (which demanded constant care) made a woman look feminine and noble, and appear more beautiful.[25] "But what about those curls, those horns that men criticize? I don't like this style myself," Adriana admits. "I believe," Corinna replies, that it is not only acceptable but just as pleasing as any other style . . . and when done with moderation it lends charm to the face." Corinna's comment is highly interesting because in the portrait of Moderata Fonte published as the frontispiece to her book she is indeed wearing her hair with those "horns" (figure 12.1).

The conversation meanders, with "scientific" information about birds, fish, animals, agricultural products, and precious metals becoming embedded in double meanings. When Corinna exclaims at the great number of species of animals there are in the world and Cornelia supposes that there are many more wild animals than domestic, Leonora doubts this. "There are more domestic ones than you think, but they aren't always recognized. . . . How many lions, how many tigers, how many bears are there that aren't counted—just as cruel and terrible, I can tell you" (p. 104). Balsamic ointment keeps the face youthfully fresh, preserves dead bodies from putrefying, Corinna tells her friends, and can cure everything except the subject under discussion. "We've talked about the stars, the air, birds, water, fish, different kinds of animals, herbs, plants but we haven't yet found anything that can change the attitude of these men so that they will respect us and love us truly as we deserve" (p. 128). "If only men could be moved by words," Leonora sighs, "I would force myself to give them an oration, praising them and offering them all our affection, if I thought it would be worthwhile." The idea was immensely appealing, and the women coax her to go ahead and speak. "I don't know where to begin. . ." "Say the worse you can," Cornelia urges, and the women settle back to hear her appeal for reason, for decency, for respect, for love, hardly able to hold back their delighted laughter (pp. 131–32).

Although the conversation is unremittingly critical of men in general, *The Worth of Women,* true to its author's moderating sense of fairness, finds some men beside her husband and uncle worthy of praise. Those, we are not surprised to find, are mostly the Venetians who are responsible for the glory of Venice, starting with the head of state, the Doge. "What can we say about the divine excellence of our most serene Prince?"[26] asks Corinna. Virginia agrees. "How beautiful it is to see him in procession going to some ceremony accompanied by all the pomp and magnificence of the foreign ambassadors, our dignified senators, and most noble secretaries." "It's as if one is watching the most precious jewels and greatest treasures of our country passing by." Corinna adds, "These are the men who govern and sustain her and who, after God, provide her with every necessity. These are the men of strength, judgment, wisdom, knowledge, intellect, piety, and the true fear of God by which the well-being of our great republic is maintained. These men although they are the lords, nevertheless act like loving fathers who study, tire themselves out, engage themselves constantly for the benefit of all . . . they administer justice . . . they oversee the upkeep of the lagoons, the fortresses, and public buildings and everything necessary for the benefit of the city. And besides, they protect, and love, and respect all the inhabitants of the city" (pp. 141–42).

Earlier the group had paid tribute to a number of beautiful and intelligent women of Venice whom they knew, and Corinna observed, "If one wanted to name one by one all the beautiful and virtuous women in this city one would have to know them all by name, a task that would have no end; there are so many that they could provide subjects for no matter how many poets there were, there would not be enough" (p. 153). The talk then turns to poetry and poets for a moment, unexpectedly revealing Corinna's own unconscious male bias. "Truly," Adriana says, "there's no better or more beautiful subject than women for poets to write about," and Lucrezia laments that there are no more "rare and marvelous talents in our modern world." "Pardon me, you are mistaken," Corinna protests, "there are some who equal or even surpass those of the past." "You must know some poets, Lucrezia, since you enjoy and write poetry yourself." "I've heard of many," Corinna answers, "but I know only a few, personally" (p. 154). She then goes on to name eight contemporary men poets, all but one from Venice. Can we believe that Corinna / Moderata was unaware of Vittoria Colonna, Laura Terracina, Isabella di Morra, Tullia d'Aragona, Gaspara Stampa, and Veronica Franca, all of whose poetry was published in Venice? Their poems were available, and surely an intellectual woman interested in poetry must have come across at least some of their books. Although Veronica Franca was a courtesan and the two women could not have known each other, Franca, as we have seen, was well known among the city's literati and enjoyed the friendship of Domenico Venier, one of the eight men that Moderata names, and whom she characterizes as the leader of the intellectuals who will be remembered eternally. She must have known of Franca, and the other women poets, but she did not take the opportunity to mention them and evidently did not consider them worth mentioning. Only men could be worthy poets, Moderata?

And so the day comes to an end, the women having amused and satisfied themselves airing their grievances against the other half of humanity, but not before Corinna, in a long poem of thirty-six octaves, explains the mythical source of the problem, reinforces her plea to women to resist love for their own protection and peace of mind, and once more returns to her hope that she will achieve immortal fame.

Love, her poem begins, had bested all the heavenly gods with his skill and now, arrogant, he was sure he would be equally triumphant on earth. So he swooped down and began shooting his darts on earth, never missing a target. Soon all the world was in love, and Love ruled the universe. The other gods were neglected, their sacrificial altars cold. Juno, the wife of Jupiter, became furious with jealousy and vowed revenge. She enlisted the help of Pride and Avarice, also enraged because Love had exiled them from the world. Avarice managed to trick Love into falling asleep, and while he slept she took his quiver of arrows from him. Juno and Pride then joined her, took the arrows and blunted them against a mountain of diamonds that Juno created on the spot, tied a veil around his eyes and returned the blunted arrows. When Love awoke he did not realize that his arrows were no longer sharp, for he could not see, and the arrows hardly made a dent in his targets. That is why there is no longer true love in the world; Love shoots his blunted arrows in vain, and blinded cannot see that he has lost his power.

> *And since neither virtue nor kindness*
> *can cure the injuries Love has suffered*
> *nor can your charm and natural beauty*
> *create in men's breasts anything but deceit,*
> *you must gird and harden your hearts*
> *so that you are never again tricked by their falseness,*
> *for the force of true love has been overpowered*
> *and only the name of Love remains.*

> *So scorn their faithless promises,*
> *avoid the error that you will repent,*
> *that will bring you nothing but scorn and injury,*
> *do not let mercy into your heart.*
> *Instead, turn your high aspirations*
> *to study and to achieve noble works,*
> *crown yourself with a shining, eternal name*
> *and shame every arrogant and greedy heart.* (p. 407)

As the sun began to set, the women rose and walked through the garden, Corinna and Virginia singing a madrigal.

> *Just as the stars adorn the sky*
> *so do women adorn the world*
> *with whatever is beautiful and delightful.*
> *And just as life has no value*
> *to one who has no heart and soul*
> *so it is with men without women*
> *whom they need as helpmates;*
> *for Woman is man's heart, his soul, and his life.* (p. 407)

They moved along the orderly paths, enjoying the quiet and cool of the early evening, past the artfully arranged, well-cared-for beds of flowers and plants, past the fountain, which joined their singing as the water streamed from the breasts of the statues and fell gently into the basin. They said their farewells, Moderata wrote as she came to the end of *The Worth of Women,* and the next day she gave birth to a baby girl, and died.

POEMS IN THE ORIGINAL ITALIAN

Le Donne in ogni età fur da Natura
di gran giudicio e d'animo dotate
né me' atte a mostrar con studio e cura
senno, e valor degli huomini son nate
e perchè, se comune è la figura,
se non son le sostanze variate,
s'hanno simile un cibo, e un parlar denno
diferente haver poi l'ardire, e'l senno?

Sempre s'è visto, e vede (pur ch'alcuna
donna v'habbia voluto il pensier porre)
ne la militia riuscir più d'una
e'l pregio, e'l grido à molti huomini torre
e così ne le lettere, e in ciascuna
impresa, che l'huom pratica e discorre,
le Donne sì buon frutto han fatto, e fanno
che gli huomini à invidiar punto non hanno.

E benchè di sì degno, e sì famoso
grado di lor non sia numero molto,
gli è perchè ad atto heroico, e virtuoso
non hanno il cor per più rispetti volto.
L'oro che stà ne le minere ascoso
non manca d'esser or, benchè sepolto,
e quando è tratto, e se ne fà lavoro
e così ricco, e bel come l'altro oro.

Se quando nasce una figliuola al padre
la ponesse col figlio à un'opra eguale
non saria ne le imprese alte, e leggiadre
al frate inferior nè disuguale;
o la ponesse in fra l'armate squadre
seco, ò à imparar qualche arte liberale;
ma perchè in altri affar viene allevata,
per l'education poco è stimata.* (pp. 388 – 89)

~

Si tolse l'elmo, e discoprì le bionde
chiome de l'or più terse, e luminose;
e due stelle apparir tanto gioconde,
che per invidia il Sol nel Mar s'ascose;

Moderata Fonte
◉ Track 63,
Reading 66

---

* *Floridoro*, canto IV:1–4.

movean le guancie fresche, e rubiconde
invidia à i gigli, e à le purpuree rose;
la man, che disarmata anco tenea,
*la neve di candor vincer parea.** (p. 390)

⁓

Ma frà quei pochi hò da lodar il cielo
ben io di tai che non di questi sono,
i quai cercan con fede e amico zelo
di solevarmi, ove sì oppressa sono;
di cui mai cessarò di alzar al Cielo
l'immensa cortesia, l'officio buono
riconoscendo le grate opre sole
a mio poter con fatti, e con parole. † (pp. 390 – 91)

⁓

● Track 64,
Reading 67

Libero cor nel mio petto soggiorna,
non servo alcun, nè d'altri son che mia,
pascomi di modestia, e cortesia,
virtù m'esalta, e castità m'adorna.

Quest'alma a Dio sol cede, e a lui ritorna,
benchè nel velo uman s'avvolga, e stia;
e sprezza il mondo, e sua perfidia ria,
che le semplici menti inganna, e scorna.

Bellezza, gioventù, piaceri, e pompe,
nulla stimo, se non ch'a i pensier puri,
son trofeo, per mia voglia, e non per sorte.

Così negli anni verdi, e nei maturi,
poichè fallacia d'uom non m'interrompe,
fama e gloria n'attendo in vita, e in morte. ‡ (pp. 393 – 94)

⁓

Qual ricamo di perle in or cosparte
o di fior copia in verde campo ameno
tal figura il tuo stil, felice a pieno
alta materia in gloriose carte.

Gran saper, ch'uon mortal spiega e comparte
ogni poter celeste, ogni terreno,
termine, stato, moto, sito, e seno,
tempo, elementi, ciel, natura, ed arte.

---

* Canto II:26.   † Canto III:4.
‡ Chemello, pp. 18–19.

Sì con un cenno sol l'alto Architetto
a sì gran mole diè spirito e forma
qual tu rassumi in variato aspetto.

Or per tant'opra, ei mentre al tuo crin forma
fregio di stelle, e inspira il tuo intelletto,
te picciol mondo in se stesso trasforma.* (pp. 399 – 400)

~

E poi che nè virtù nè gentilezza
può del misero Amor scontare i danni
nè vostra grazia e natural bellezza
può crear n'lor petti altro, che inganni;
cingete il vostro cor d'aspra durezza
sì, che lor falsità mai non v'inganni,
che son del vero amor le forze dome,
e sol riman d'Amor nel mondo il nome.

Per non far dunque error, sì ch'a pentire
non ve ne abbiate poi con danno e scorno
sdegnate il loro instabile servire,
nè la pietà con voi faccia soggiorno.
E rivolgendo il vostro alto desire
a miglior opre ed a più bei studi intorno,
ornatevi d'un nome eterno e chiaro
a onta d'ogni cuor superbo e avaro. † (p. 403)

~

S'ornano il ciel le stelle,
ornan le donne il mondo,
con quanto è in lui di bello e di giocondo.
E come alcun mortale
viver senz'alma e senza cor non vale,
tal non pon senza d'elle
gli uomini aver per sè medesmi aita;
che è la donna de l'uom cor, alma e vita. ‡ (p. 403)

◉ Track 65,
Reading 68

---

* Chemello, *Merito*, p. 84.   † Chemello, pp. 173–181.

‡ Chemello, p. 183.

NOTES

1   Our subtitle for this chapter refers to Moderata Fonte's book *Il merito delle donne*, which Virginia Cox renders in her copiously edited translation as *The Worth of Women* (Chicago, 1997). The original Italian text, published in Venice in 1600, has been edited by Adriana Chemello, *Il merito delle donne* (Venice, 1988). We have made our translations from the Chemello edition of Moderata's text; for the preface we have used G. N. Doglioni's "Vita della Sig.ra Modesta Pozzo D'I Zorzi, Nominata Moderata Fonte," the preface to *Il merito delle donne* (Venice, 1600), included in both Chemello and Cox.

2   *I Tredici canti del Floridoro* (The Thirteen Cantos of Floridoro) (Venice, 1581).

3   The term *cittadino* signified an elite status in Venice, but below the patrician class. See Cox, *The Worth of Women*, pp. 31–32.

4   The reasons for Moderata's choice for her name are our own conjecture. For "Clear, fresh, sweet waters," see Petrarch's poems CXXVI: 1.

5   Doglioni, "Vita della Sig.ra Modesta Pozzo."

6   Doglioni, "Vita della Sig.ra Modesta Pozzo," p. 3.

7   Cox, *The Worth of Women*, p. 36, n. 17.

8   Ariosto's Bradamante, in *Orlando Furioso*, is probably the source for Moderata's conception.

9   Valeria Finucci, "La scrittura epico-cavalleresca al femminile: Moderata Fonte e *Tredici Canti del Floridoro*," *Annali d'Italianistica* 12 (1994): 215–233.

10   Doglioni, "Vita della Sig.ra Modesta Pozzo," p. 4.

11   Cox, *The Worth of Women*, p. 37, n. 19.

12   Beatrice Collina, "Moderata Fonte e *Il merito delle donne*," *Annali d'Italianistica* 7 (1989): 150.

13   The second boy, Girolamo, died 1597, her husband in 1598, both of endemic fever.

14   Collina, "Moderata Fonte," p. 150.

15   Filarco is cited by Andrea Chemello, "La Donna, Il Modello, L'Immaginario: Moderata Fonte e Lucrezia Marinella," in G. Zancan, ed., *Nel cerchio della luna* (Venice, 1983), p. 102, n. 12.

16   Doglioni, "Vita della Sig.ra Modesta Pozzo," p. 5.

17   Cox, *The Worth of Women*, p. 37, n. 19.

18   Doglioni, "Vita della Sig.ra Modesta Pozzo," pp. 5–6.

19   Adriana Chemello, "Gioco e Dissimulazione in Moderata Fonte," preface to her edition of *Il merito delle donne*, p. xxxix, also sees the discussion as a kind of tribunal, but is not concerned with developing this image. I wish to acknowledge my fundamental admiration for her article, although we are not in agreement on all points of interpretation.

20   A number of Moderata's poems are introduced in *Il merito delle donne*, all of them evidently written earlier; "Free is the heart in my breast" was probably written before her marriage.

21   Moderata is probably describing an actual garden; see John Dixon Hunt, *The Italian Garden* (Cambridge, 1996), especially the chapter by Margherita Azzi Visentini, "The Gardens of Villas in the Veneto from the Fifteenth to the Eighteenth Centuries" (pp. 93–126).

22   There are countless definitions of art: we accept with reservations the Aristotelian-grounded notion of art as an orderly creation that combines a relationship of parts that forms a whole susceptible to reason, with an inexplicable but perceptible aura, susceptible to intuition; even in modernist art, in which "wholeness" is often difficult to perceive, it can be felt.

23   A number of sixteenth-century dialogues are published in Giuseppe Zonta, *Trattati d'amore* (Bari, 1912), including *Il Raverta* by Giuseppe Betussi, *Il Ragionamento* by Francesco Sansovino, *Dialogo* by Tullia d'Aragona, *Specchio d'amore* by Bartolomeo Gottifredi, and *La Leonora* by Giuseppe Betussi. Other important dialogues include Pietro Bembo's *Gli Asolani*, Baldesar Castiglione's *The Book of the Courtier*, Leoni Ebreo's *Dialogues on Love,* and Sperone Speroni's *Dialogo d'amore*. Many of the ideas expressed by one or another of the characters in *The Worth of Women* can be found among these dialogues, not necessarily because Moderata had read them but because they had become the common currency of conversation.

24   See Chemello, "Gioco e dissimulazione in Moderata Fonte." From her point of view the entire book is conceived as a game of paradoxical simulating and dissimulating. It should be noted that

whatever there is of amusement and sport in Moderata's book, a ploy is adopted to make her very serious message acceptable to both men and women readers.

25   Bleaching their hair was an ordeal for Venetian women. They sat in the hot sun on the roofs of their homes, sometimes in little cabins built for the purpose, wearing a wide-brimmed but crownless hat, so that they could lay out their tresses on the brim while they kept applying the bleach.

26   Pasqual Cicogna was Doge of Venice from 1585 to 1595.

ADDITIONAL BIBLIOGRAPHY

Works consulted in addition to those cited in the chapter notes. For authors and editors cited in the chapter notes, see the names listed with an asterisk in the index.

Abrantès, Laura. *Les femmes celebrées de tous les pays.* 3 vols. Paris, 1839.

Allen, Beverly, Muriel Kittel, and Leala Jewell. *The Defiant Muse: Italian Feminist Poems from the Middle Ages to the Present.* New York, 1986.

Andrews, Marion. *The Most Illustrious Ladies of the Italian Renaissance.* London, 1911.

Arslan, Antonio, Adriana Chemello, and Gilberto Pizzamiglio, eds. *Le stanze ritrovate: Antologia di scrittrici venete dal quattrocento al novecento.* Mirano-Venice, 1994.

Atanagi, Dionigi, ed. *Rime di diversi nobilissimi ed eccellentissimi autori in morte della Signora Irene delle signori di Spilimbergo.* Venice, 1561.

Baldacci, Luigi, ed. *Lirici del cinquecento.* Milan, 1975.

Bandini Buti, Maria, ed. *Enciclopedia biografica e bibliografica italiana: poetesse e scrittrici,* series VI. 2 vols. Rome, 1940.

Bartsch, Adam von. *The Illustrated Bartsch,* ed. Mark Zucker. New York, 1978.

Belvigliere, Carlo. *Tavole sincrome e genealogiche.* Florence, 1875.

Bembo, Pietro. *Prose della volgare lingua.* Turin, 1931.

———. *Prose e poesie.* C. Dionisotti, ed. Turin, 1960.

Berenson, Bernard. *I pittori italiani del Rinascimento.* Florence, 1957.

Bertelli, Sergio, Franco Cardini, and Elvira Zorzi. *The Courts of the Italian Renaissance.* Oxford, 1986.

Bezold, Friedrich von. *Stato e società nell'età della contrariforma.* Venice, 1929.

Bonora, Ettore. *Critica e letteratura nel cinquecento.* Turin, 1964.

Buck, Claire, ed. *The Bloomsbury Guide to Women's Literature.* New York, 1992.

Bulifon, Antonio. *Rime di cinquante illustri poetesse di nuovo date in luce di A. Bulifon.* Naples, 1695.

Burckhardt, Jacob. *The Civilization of the Renaissance in Italy.* New York, 1929 [1958].

Burke, Peter. *The Italian Renaissance: Culture and Society in Italy.* Oxford, 1987.

Cannon, Mary Agnes. *The Education of Women During the Renaissance.* Washington, D.C., 1916.

Casagrande di Villa Viera, Rita. *Le cortigiane venicene nel cinquecento.* Milan, 1968.

Castiglione, Baldassare. *Il libro del cortigiano.* Venice, 1964.

Cesnola, Alessandro Palma di. *Catologo di manoscritti italiani esistenti nel Museo Britannico di Londra.* Turin, 1890.

Chemello, Adriana. "Donna di palazzo, moglie, cortigiana: I ruoli e funzioni sociali della donna in alcuni trattati del cinquecento." In A. Prosperi, ed., *La corte e il 'Cortigiano.'* Rome, 1980.

Contini, Gianfranco. *Letteratura del quattrocento.* Florence, 1976.

Cox, Virginia. *The Renaissance Dialogue: Literary Dialogue in Its Social and Political Contexts, Castiglione to Galileo.* New York, 1992.

Crawford, Francis M. *Southern Italy, Sicily, and the Rulers of the South.* New York, 1905.

Crescimbeni, Giovan Maria. *Istoria della Volgar Poesia.* 5 vols. Venice, 1702–1711.

Crane, Thomas F. *Italian Social Customs of the Sixteenth Century.* New Haven, 1920.

Cropper, Elizabeth. *The Beauty of Women.* Chicago, 1986.

Dionisotti, C. *La letteratura italiana nell'età del concilio di Trento.* Milan, 1938.

Dizionario biografico degli italiani. Rome, 1960–.

Donadoni, Eugrenio. *Breve storia della letteratura italiana dalle origini ai nostri giorni.* Milan, 1938.

Donno, Elizabeth Story. *Three Renaissance Pastorals: Tasso, Guarini, Daniel.* Binghamton, N.Y., 1993.

Einstein, Alfred. *The Italian Madrigal.* Princeton, 1971.

Eisenstein, Elizabeth L. *The Printing Press as an Agent of Change.* New York, 1979.

Enciclopedia dello spettacolo. Rome, 1975.

Enciclopedia biografica et bibliografica. Milan, 1940–1948.

Facchini, Guido Angelo. *La storia di Ferrara illustrata nei fatti e nei luoghi.* Ferrara, 1933.

Faccioli, Emilio, ed. *L'arte della cucina in Italia.* Turin, 1987.

Fachini, Genévra C. *Prospetto biografico delle donne italiane rinomate in letteratura.* Venice, 1824.

Ferri, Pietro Leopoldo. *Biblioteca femminile italiana.* Padua, 1842.

Ferrighi, Mario. *Aldo Manuzio*. Milan, 1925.

Ferroni, Giulio. "Il Sistema Poetico Cinquecentesco e il Petrarchismo." In *Poesia italiana del cinquecento*. Milan, 1978.

Fiske, George C. "Lucilius and Horace." *Atti Accademica USA* 7 (1920): 25–63.

Forster, Leonard. *The Icy Fire: Five Studies in European Petrarchism*. Cambridge, 1969.

Franco, Giacomo. *Habiti delle donne venetiane*. Venice, 1610.

Fubini, Mario. *Lirici del cinquecento*. Turin, 1968.

Gardner, Edmund G. *Dukes and Poets in Ferrara: A Study in the Poetry, Religion and Politics of the Fifteenth and Early Sixteenth Century*. New York, 1904.

————. *Italy: A Companion to Italian Studies*. London, 1934.

Gelli, Jacopo. *Diviesi, motti, impresia di famiglie e personaggi italiani*. Milan, 1916.

Geymonat, Ludovico. *Storia del pensiero filosofico e scientifico,* vol. 2. Milan, 1970.

Goldscheider, Ludwig. *Unknown Renaissance Portraits: Medals of Famous Men and Women of the XV and XVI Centuries*. London, 1952.

Gottheim, E. *Stato e società nell'età della contrariforma*. 2d. ed. Venice, 1923.

Hackenbruch, Yvonne. *Renaissance Jewelry*. London 1979.

Hunt, William. *History of England*. London 1883.

Jacobs, Frederika H. *Defining the Renaissance Virtuosa: Women Artists and the Language of Art History and Criticism*. New York, 1997.

King, Margaret L. *Women of the Renaissance*. Chicago, 1991.

————, and Albert Rabil Jr. *Her Immaculate Hand*. Binghamton, N.Y., 1983.

Labalme, Patricia. *Beyond Their Sex: Learned Women of the Renaissance*. New York, 1984.

Lawner, Lynn. *Lives of the Courtesans*. New York, 1987.

Leone, Ebreo. *Dialoghi d'amore*. Bari, 1929.

Levi-Pisetzsky, Rosita. *Storia del costume in Italia*. 3 vols. Milan, 1966.

Linscott, Robert N., ed. *Complete Poems and Selected Letters of Michelangelo*. Princeton, 1980.

Litta, Pompeo. *Famiglie celebri italiane*. Milan, 1819–1883.

Manfredi, Mutio. *Del Signor Mutio Manfredi il Vinto Academico Confuso*. Bologna, 1575.

Mazzuchelli, Gian Maria. *Gli scrittori d'Italia*. Brescia, 1753–63.

Migiel, Marilyn, and Juliana Schiesari. *Refiguring Women's Perspectives on Gender and the Italian Renaissance*. New York, 1991.

Mitchell, Bonner. *A Year of Pageantry in Late Renaissance Ferrara*. Binghamton, 1990.

Molmenti, Pietro. *La storia di Venice nella vita privata*. Trieste, 1973.

Newcomb, Anthony. *The Madrigal at Ferrara, 1579–1597*. Princeton, 1980.

Ozzola, Leandro. *Il vestiario italiano dal 1500 al 1550*. Rome, 1940.

Percivallo, Bernardo. *Rime e imprese*. Ferrara, 1588.

Pompeote, Arturo, ed. *Storia della letteratura italiana*. Turin, 1962.

Ponchiroli, Daniele, ed. *Lirici del cinquecento*. Turin, 1968.

Pozzi, Mario. *Trattati d'amore del cinquecento*. Bari, 1975.

Quadrio, Francesco Saverio. *Della storia e della ragion d'ogni poesia*. 7 vols. Milan, 1739–1752.

Répertoire International de l'histoire de l'Art.

Rodocanachi, E. *La femme italienne*. Paris, 1922

Romei, Annibale. *The Courtier's Academy*. Amsterdam, N.Y., 1969 [1598].

Rose, Mary Beth, ed. *Women in the Middle Ages and the Renaissance*. Syracuse, 1986.

Rosenthal, Margaret. *Women in Culture and Society*. Chicago and London, 1992.

Ruscelli, Girolamo. *Che la donna sia di gran lunga piu nobile e più degna dell' huomo*. Venice, 1552.

———. *Lettere di diversi autori eccellentissimi*. Venice, 1556.

———. *I fiori delle rime dei poeti illustri*. Venice, 1558.

Russo, Luigi. *Il petrarchismo italiano nel cinquecento*. Pisa, 1958.

Schiesari, Juliana. *The Gendering of Melancholia: Feminism, Psychoanalysis and the Symbolism of Loss in Renaissance Literature*. Ithaca, N.Y., 1992.

Schroeder, H. J. *Canons and Decrees of the Council of Trent*. St. Louis, 1941.

Settembrini, Luigi. *Lezioni di letteratura italiana*. Naples, 1866.

Speroni, Sperone. "Della dignità delle donne." In *Trattatisti del Cinquecento*, ed. Mario Pozzi. Milan, 1978.

Stortoni, Laura Anna, ed. *Women Poets of the Italian Renaissance*. New York, 1997.

Tacchi, Venturo. *Storia della religione in Italia alla metà del secolo XVI*. Florence, 1907.

Tasso, Torquato. *Discorso della virtù femminile donnesca*. Venice, 1582.

Toffanin, Giuseppe, ed. *Il cinquecento*. Milan, 1935 (*Storia Letteraria d'Italia*, vol. 9).

Tusiani, Giuseppe. *Italian Poets of the Renaissance*. New York, 1971.

Vecellio, Cesare. *Habiti antichi et moderni di tutto il mondo*. 2 vols. Venice, 1598.

Venturi, Adolfo. *Storia dell'arte italiana: la pittura del cinquecento*. Milan, 1926.

Villani, Carlo. *Stelle femminili: Dizionario biobibliografico*. 2 vols. Naples, 1915.

Weinberg, Bernard. *A History of Literary Criticism in the Italian Renaissance.* 2 vols. New York, 1961.

Whitfield, John H. *Petrarch and the Renascence.* New York, 1965.

Wilson, Katharina, ed. *Women Writers of the Renaissance and Reformation.* Athens, Ga., 1987.

Woodward, William H. *Studies in Education in the Age of the Renaissance, 1400–1600.* Cambridge, 1924.

Wright, A. D. *The Counter-Reformation: Catholic Europe and the Non-Christian World.* London, 1982.

Zeidberg, David S, and Fiorella Gioffredi Superbi, eds. *Aldus Manutius and Renaissance Culture: Essays in Memory of Franklin D. Murphy.* Venice and Florence, 1994.

INDEX

INDEX OF FIRST
LINES & CD TRACKS